Empir

Empire of Honour

The Art of Government in the Roman World

J. E. LENDON

OXFORD
UNIVERSITY PRESS

*This book has been printed digitally and produced in a standard specification
in order to ensure its continuing availability*

OXFORD
UNIVERSITY PRESS

Great Clarendon Street, Oxford OX2 6DP

Oxford University Press is a department of the University of Oxford.
It furthers the University's objective of excellence in research, scholarship,
and education by publishing worldwide in

Oxford New York

Auckland Cape Town Dar es Salaam Hong Kong Karachi
Kuala Lumpur Madrid Melbourne Mexico City Nairobi
New Delhi Shanghai Taipei Toronto
With offices in
Argentina Austria Brazil Chile Czech Republic France Greece
Guatemala Hungary Italy Japan South Korea Poland Portugal
Singapore Switzerland Thailand Turkey Ukraine Vietnam

Oxford is a registered trade mark of Oxford University Press
in the UK and in certain other countries

Published in the United States
by Oxford University Press Inc., New York

Oxford is a registered trade mark of Oxford University Press
in the UK and in certain other countries

Published in the United States
by Oxford University Press Inc., New York

ISBN 0-19-924763-3

Preface to the paperback edition

For thirty-seven years the hermit Nathaniel kept to his desert cell, and for thirty-seven years a hard-working demon schemed to tempt him out. Twice the demon nearly succeeded. Once he appeared in the semblance of a boy pleading for help lest he be eaten by hyenas. 'God will help you!' the anchorite shouted, from within. Another time, there appeared at Nathaniel's cell a visitation of no fewer than seven holy bishops. Having prayed with the hermit, the bishops made ready to leave. And so—by the demon's connivance—Nathaniel was presented with an excruciating choice. To pass the door of his cell was to fail in piety to God. But not to leave the cell was to fail in a fundamental social duty to men. For an inferior must do superiors the honour of escorting them on their way. And when Nathaniel did not come forth, the bishops' deacons reproached him for setting himself above their masters: 'this is a haughty thing you are doing, Father, not escorting the bishops.' But Nathaniel stayed within: 'I am dead to my lord bishops, and to the whole world.' And so Nathaniel—although not so dead to the world as to deny the bishops their honorific address—passed a supreme test of devotion (Palladius, *Historia Lausiaca* 16).

Continuing to chance upon stories like this, stories that testify to the power of the forces identified in *Empire of Honour*, has been one of the pleasures of the several years since the book first appeared. So too has been reading which confirms that Rome was perfectly unexceptional among pre-industrial states in harnessing such forces to the service of government. Nor can the author complain that his joy has been much soured by the book's reception. Not everyone will like a book with an argument: depending on how bold the argument is, there will be scattered cries of 'Wrong!' or 'We knew it all before!' The good fortune of *Empire of Honour* is that its several critics were fairly evenly divided between those who found the argument preposterous and those who found it so obviously true that it did not need saying. The author is delighted, therefore, to refer the former to the reviews of the latter, and the latter to the former.

Nevertheless, if the author were to write *Empire of Honour* again, he would do two things differently: the reviews recommend a change in tone, and the perspective of years a slight change in trajectory.

The book, first, would express in harsh shouts—rather than in subtle wafting colours—the way it conceives the relative importance of honour, force, patronage, and other factors in undergirding the Roman imperial regime. It was a mistake to allow readers—loyally following what they took to be the author's implicit logic—license to conjure for themselves the illusion of an argument that honour was the empire's single most important buttress. In fact, to assign exact relative strength to the struts of a regime is fruitless: we cannot begin to do so even for the modern states in which we live. The best we can do, rather, is to distinguish a list of props without which the regime would not have been possible. If we think away the Roman army, could the Roman empire stand? No. If we think away the Roman law, could the Roman empire stand? Yes. Distinguishing necessary causes from second-rank causes, *Empire of Honour* argues that the culture of honour belongs in the company of the necessary, but does not attempt to claim for it pride of place among them.

A new *Empire of Honour* would strive also to place rulership by honour in the context of its Greek history. The mechanisms of ruling by honour described in *Empire of Honour* mature in the Hellenistic centuries, grow in Classical Greece, and are visible *in ovo* in Xenophon's *Cyropaedia*, a work—among other things—of political theory. Xenophon's analysis of honour as a method of ruling is more extended and profound than that of any later author. The regime of honour depicted in *Empire of Honour* hangs like a crystal, unchanging and without a past. Critics have grunted at the lack of change over time within the centuries of the Roman empire: the author would defend that, because he sees little evidence of change. But tracing the roots of the system back to Classical Greece would deepen our understanding of how Greek and Roman honour worked in the Roman period.

J.E.L.

Charlottesville, Virginia
March 2001

ACKNOWLEDGEMENTS

BLINKERED, heel-dragging, mulish obstinacy—the natural state of all authors, but especially of young authors, and of this author in particular—makes giving them advice at best ungratifying and often positively disagreeable. My gratitude to those I thank here is therefore as much for their courageous honesty as for their generous erudition. Ramsay MacMullen, who directed the Yale dissertation of which this book is a distant descendant, has long mastered the difficult balancing act of being both a close friend and a frank critic. Elizabeth Meyer's ideas, suggestions, and corrections have always directed my thinking along new and profitable lines. Gordon Williams and Richard Garner cheerfully read the manuscript several times and the book has profited enormously from their attention. I had no legitimate claim upon the time of Richard Saller, R. F. Tannenbaum, or Kenneth Harl, but from kindness and collegiality they, too, read the manuscript and offered signal improvements. John Drinkwater and David Potter, the perceptive readers for the Press, cast off their judicial robes and laboured happily along with the rest, providing deep counsels. Errors that remain are not only my own, but have probably been maintained against better advice to the contrary.

To my friends D. A. Cohen and J. Freeman I am grateful for illuminating conversations about honour. Editorial duties I have ruthlessly levied upon my family and friends (especially D. and M. Lendon, J. Campbell, and R. Berkhofer III), and this editorial mantle has been ably inherited by Julian Ward, copy-editor for the Press. Hilary O'Shea and Liz Alsop at the Press have been ceaselessly cheerful, helpful, and tolerant. Both financial support and relief from teaching have been provided by the John M. Olin Foundation and my generous employer, the Massachusetts Institute of Technology. I am also grateful to the Corcoran Department of History of the University of Virginia, which gave a visiting scholar a hospitable home where much of the book was written.

A project of this scope enforces a highly selective citation of modern scholarship, and this must inevitably fall short of paying off in full the author's intellectual debts. Similarly, while translations are my own unless signalled otherwise, they cannot fail in many cases to echo the work of selfless generations of previous translators. To those I may have slighted I offer my grateful acknowledgements here.

J.E.L.

Cambridge, Massachusetts
September 1996

CONTENTS

ABBREVIATIONS

Standard abbreviations (sometimes expanded) are used for ancient authors and works cited in the notes. See especially the list of abbreviations in the *Oxford Classical Dictionary* (3rd. edn.). I have used the following abbreviations for modern journals, reference books, collections of inscriptions (of which I have tried to cite accessible publications), papyri, and some *variorum* assemblages of ancient material.

AE	*L'Année épigraphique*
AJP	*American Journal of Philology*
ANRW	*Aufstieg und Niedergang der römischen Welt*
BCH	*Bulletin de correspondance hellénique*
BICS	*Bulletin of the Institute of Classical Studies of the University of London*
CE	*Carmina Latina Epigraphica*
CGL	G. Goetz (ed.), *Corpus Glossariorum Latinorum*, 7 vols. (Leipzig, 1873–1901)
CIL	*Corpus Inscriptionum Latinarum*
CPL	R. Cavenaile (ed.), *Corpus Papyrorum Latinarum* (Wiesbaden, 1958)
CSEL	*Corpus Scriptorum Ecclesiasticorum Latinorum*
EJ	V. Ehrenberg and A. H. M. Jones (eds.), *Documents Illustrating the Reigns of Augustus and Tiberius*, 2nd edn. (Oxford, 1976)
FGH	F. Jacoby (ed.), *Die Fragmente der griechischen Historiker* (Leiden, 1923–58)
Gk. Const.	J. H. Oliver (ed.), *Greek Constitutions of the Early Roman Emperors from Inscriptions and Papyri* (Philadelphia, 1989)
GRBS	*Greek, Roman, and Byzantine Studies*
HSCP	*Harvard Studies in Classical Philology*
IG	*Inscriptiones Graecae*
IGR	R. Cagnat *et al.* (eds.), *Inscriptiones Graecae ad Res Romanas Pertinentes*, 3 vols. (Paris, 1906–27)

IK Eph.	*Die Inschriften von Ephesos* in the series Inschriften griechischer Städte aus Kleinasien
IK Smyrna	*Die Inschriften von Smyrna* in the series Inschriften griechischer Städte aus Kleinasien
I.L.Alg.	S. Gsell *et al.* (eds.), *Inscriptions latines de l'Algérie*, 2 vols. (Paris, 1922–57)
ILCV	*Inscriptiones Latinae Christianae Veteres*
ILS	H. Dessau (ed.), *Inscriptiones Latinae Selectae*, 3 vols. (Berlin, 1892–1916)
IRT	J. M. Reynolds and J. B. Ward-Perkins (eds.), *The Inscriptions of Roman Tripolitania* (Rome, 1952)
JHS	*Journal of Hellenic Studies*
JRS	*Journal of Roman Studies*
LSJ	H. G. Liddell, R. Scott, and H. S. Jones, *A Greek–English Lexicon*, 9th edn. (Oxford, 1940)
MAAR	*Memoirs of the American Academy in Rome*
MAMA	*Monumenta Asiae Minoris Antiqua*
McC. & W.	M. McCrum and A. G. Woodhead (eds.), *Select Documents of the Principates of the Flavian Emperors* (Cambridge, 1961)
OGIS	W. Dittenberger (ed.), *Orientis Graeci Inscriptiones Selectae*, 2 vols. (1903–5)
OLD	P. G. W. Glare (ed.), *Oxford Latin Dictionary* (Oxford, 1982)
PBSR	*Papers of the British School at Rome*
PCPS	*Proceedings of the Cambridge Philological Society*
PG	*Patrologia Graeca*
PGM	K. Preisendanz *et al.* (eds.), *Papyri Graecae Magicae: Die griechischen Zauberpapyri*, 2 vols. (Stuttgart, 1973–4)
PL	*Patrologia Latina*
PLRE i	Jones, A. H. M. *et al.*, *Prosopography of the Later Roman Empire*, i (Cambridge, 1971)
P.Oxy.	*The Oxyrhynchus Papyri*
RDGE	R. K. Sherk (ed.), *Roman Documents from the Greek East* (Baltimore, 1969)
RE	*Paulys Realencyclopädie der classischen Altertumswissenschaft*
RIB	*The Roman Inscriptions of Britain*
SEG	*Supplementum Epigraphicum Graecum*

Sel. Pap.	A. S. Hunt *et al.* (eds.), *Select Papyri* (London and Cambridge, Mass., 1932–42)
Small. *Gaius*	E. M. Smallwood (ed.), *Documents Illustrating the Principates of Gaius, Claudius, and Nero* (Cambridge, 1967)
Small. *Nerva*	E. M. Smallwood (ed.), *Documents Illustrating the Principates of Nerva, Trajan, and Hadrian* (Cambridge, 1966)
TAM	*Tituli Asiae Minoris*
TAPA	*Transactions and Proceedings of the American Philological Association*
TLL	*Thesaurus Linguae Latinae*
ZPE	*Zeitschrift für Papyrologie und Epigraphik*

1

Introduction

O N what was to be the last day of his life, the emperor Nero awoke to find that the palace sentries had abandoned their posts. His friends did not respond to his summons. He rushed around to their rooms with a handful of servants, and pounded on the doors. If they were within, they did not answer. Returning to his own chamber he found that his very bodyguards had slipped away, taking with them the bedclothes and his box of poison. To the empty halls of his vast palace he cried, 'Have I neither friend nor foe?' Here was an emperor who no longer commanded obedience, an emperor at last bereft of his power. And the last hours of Vitellius were eerily similar: he wandered an empty palace, tried locked doors, and shuddered at vacant rooms until he was finally discovered and dragged away to his death.[1]

Yet only a few hours, a few days, earlier, thousands upon thousands of people had stood prepared to do the emperor's bidding: some formally in the imperial service, but the vast majority not; some at Rome, but most scattered far and wide across the empire. A few perhaps were personally acquainted with the emperor, but most had never set eyes upon him. It is, as a consequence, easier for a modern observer to understand why Nero and Vitellius were finally deserted than to explain why they were ever obeyed at all. To us the emperor seems a terribly lonely figure. How to armour him again in the obedience which fell away *in extremis*?

This book is a contribution to the solution of that mystery—an attempt to advance our understanding of how power worked under the empire, to illuminate how the emperor got his officials and subjects to do what he wanted, how officials procured the obedience of subjects, and how subjects and officials could bend other officials, and even the emperor, to their will. It is a study of the nature, and some of the historical consequences, of the system of thought and emotion we call honour.

---

[1] Nero, Suet. *Nero* 47. 3; Dio 63. 27. 3. Vitellius, Tac. *Hist.* 3. 84; Suet. *Vit.* 16. Cf. Didius Julianus, Herod. 2. 12. 7; *HA Did. Jul.* 8. 6; and this vision of the abandoned emperor was resonant, Orig. *Cels.* 8. 68.

It is, therefore, a study of government, but not a study of government institutions: it is an investigation of a slow-changing facet of human motivation, an investigation carried on with an eye to fears, desires, and beliefs expressed across the empire—common to the Greek East and the Latin West, to the capital and the provinces. The focus, moreover, is not on what changed over time, but on methods of rulership that can be shown to have worked consistently over the four centuries from the founding of the Empire to the barbarian sack of the city of Rome.

It is best, at the outset, not to overstate the responsibilities and abilities of Roman government. Its aims were limited: the gathering of taxes, the fielding of an army, and the maintenance of civil peace—that is, the prevention of civil war and major riot.[2] Justice also was administered, at least to those whose wealth, influence, or misdeeds secured them a place on the governors' overloaded court schedule.[3] The Roman government did not undertake to provide food, housing, mass education, or any of the manifold social services taken for granted from modern governments, the supply of grain, water, and amusements to a few great cities notwithstanding. It is, then, unsurprising that the Roman government did not bulk very large in the consciousness of a majority of its subjects, who had, from week to week and month to month, few, if any, dealings with it at all.[4] But even the achievement of the modest aims of Roman government is astonishing. The Roman authorities kept peace and collected taxes from a population of some fifty to sixty million souls, a bafflingly diverse throng speaking many different languages, and living their lives in infinitely varied ways: the emperor's subjects ranged from the magnificent nobles of Rome to savage tribesmen lurking half-unseen in hill and wood, from the superb grandees of the great cities of Asia Minor to the Berber on the slopes of the Atlas mountains, the Bedouin wandering the wastes of Arabia Felix, and the fellah of Egypt, solemnly convicted of cannibalism by Juvenal.[5] Over this vast and scattered multitude, the Romans

[2] Millar (1977: esp. 6), emphasizing Roman government's passive, reactive quality; Garnsey and Saller (1987), 20. For ancient analyses of imperial concerns, see Dio 52. 14–40; Pliny, *Paneg. passim.*

[3] Pressure on the governor's court docket, judged by petitions received in Egypt, Hopkins (1991), n. 9. And the administration of Egypt (of old deemed an exceptional case) was not essentially different from other provinces, see Lewis (1970) and (1984); Bowman and Rathbone (1992); Rathbone (1993).

[4] Lack of contact with government: the *locus classicus* (if perhaps somewhat exaggerated) is Syn. *Ep.* 148 (Garzya); see also D. Chr. 7; and, for 2nd-cent. Galilee, Goodman (1983), 141, 151. But the workings of Roman justice did make a considerable impression on provincials, Lieberman (1944–5).

[5] Juv. 15. 13, 79–83.

presided with a tiny civil administration. At its largest extent, in the fourth century, the imperial government had somewhat over thirty thousand functionaries, roughly one for every two thousand subjects. And in the earlier centuries, when the empire was at the height of its power and glory, it employed only a fraction of that number.[6] By contrast, the Federal Government of the United States, a country under-governed by European standards, employs more than three million civilians, one for every eighty inhabitants; and the governments of the fifty states employ four and a half million more.

Yet this relatively small number of officials was able to keep enough peace and extract enough tax to maintain an army of more than three hundred and fifty thousand men under the high empire, with the weapons, transport, roads, and fortifications required for the defence of an imperial frontier thousands of miles in length.[7] In the fourth century, the paper strength of the army was larger.[8] And while the military payroll was surely the imperial government's single greatest expense, there was money available for vast building projects which still inspire awe, and for the feeding and entertainment of the masses at Rome and, later, at Constantinople.[9] How were the Roman authorities able to accomplish this? Necessarily by a combination of means and ways. Conventional views—quite right as far as they go—have stressed the crude application of force (or its insidious threat), reliance on the willing compliance of the subject to authority he acknowledged as legitimate, and the subtle workings of patronage.

The disproportion between the size of the army and the civil administration naturally leads to a suspicion that the army was expected both to defend and to govern the empire—that ruling depended on the direct action of the soldiers upon the civilian population, that Roman government depended largely on force and its handmaiden, fear. The army, the

---

[6] Fourth cent., A. H. M. Jones (1964), 1057 n. 44. The size of the administration in earlier centuries is harder to estimate: Eck (1980: 16) counts some 10,000 in the provinces under Trajan, mostly seconded soldiers (see n. 11 below); independently R. F. Tannenbaum (private communication) estimates a total of some 10,000–12,000 including Rome and Italy, but excluding the central and local administration of Egypt. Hopkins (1980: 121) observes that 12th-cent. China, with a population roughly equal to that of the Roman empire, had twenty-five times as many élite officials in the provinces.

[7] Army size, MacMullen (1984a).

[8] But the paper strength bore more relation to payroll than to fighting strength: MacMullen (1980); (1988), 173–4; Liebeschuetz (1990), 40–1; cf. esp. Kennedy and Riley's (1990: 19–20, 45, 131) observations on the small sizes of forts that late-antique units occupied.

[9] Budget, Duncan-Jones (1994), 33–46.

ultimate prop of imperial power, was called upon to put down the occasional great rebellions against imperial authority. Moreover, its appallingly brutal campaigns, however rare, did create a terrifying impression out of proportion to their number: the Roman destruction of Jerusalem and its temple is still vividly remembered, as any visitor to the Wailing Wall today realizes. Soldiers were also involved in the day-to-day business of government, police work, and the collection of taxes.[10] The imperial legate governing a province had a military staff and guard, and, in a border province, the latter could be substantial.[11] And where banditry and sedition were endemic, as in Judaea, the army might strive for centuries to bring them under control.[12] The great cities of the empire—Rome, Carthage, and Alexandria—had substantial garrisons to maintain civil order, as did other towns with quarrelsome reputations, like Jerusalem; much of the army on the eastern frontier seems to have been billeted near cities, and perhaps this became a more general practice all over the empire in the fourth century.[13] Even where only a modest force was available, the Roman authorities stretched it as much as they could by inspiring terror: the governor progressed through his province dealing with malefactors in a way that locals would remember, by having them crucified, or burnt alive, or fed to wild beasts. And the provincials did remember: the prospect of coming to such ends inspired nightmares in Greeks.[14]

Fear is a very economical way of ruling: a great deal of fear can be produced with very little force. Necessarily, for force had its limits. As King Agrippa said, in Josephus' *Jewish War*, 'What of the five hundred cities of Asia, do they not bow down before a single governor and his consular

[10] Army involvement in ruling the Eastern provinces, Isaac (1990), 56–218, 269–91; and esp. for police functions, Hirschfeld (1891); Lopuszanski (1951); Alston (1995), 79–96.

[11] Austin and Rankov (1995: 151–2) estimate a military staff of 100–150 for the legate of a province with one legion; proconsuls had smaller, largely civilian staffs (pp. 154–5). Add also a governor's guard of some hundreds in military provinces, Speidel (1978a), 13–14. Whether provinces without major legionary armies had garrisons is uncertain. Literary evidence (esp. Jos. *BJ* 2. 365–87) would imply that garrisons were exiguous or non-existent: yet inscriptions recording auxiliary cohorts and *alae* keep turning up, although it can rarely be known if the units were stationed in the province, summoned for an emergency, or just passing through. It may be safest to assume, with Speidel (1983a: 12), for Asia Minor, that the *inermes provinciae* (the term is Tacitus', *Hist.* 1. 11) were each garrisoned with at least an auxiliary cohort or *ala* (*c.*500 men).

[12] Judaea, Isaac (1990), 77–97; elsewhere, Nippel (1995), 101–2.

[13] Rome, Nippel (1995), 90–8; Carthage, Le Bohec (1989), 21; Alexandria, Lesquier (1918), 388–93; the East, Isaac (1990), 123–31, 139, 157, 269–82; on Jerusalem, ibid. 279–80, 428; 4th cent., MacMullen (1988), 209–17.

[14] Horrors of governor's justice, publicity, MacMullen (1986a); nightmares, Artem. 2. 52–4.

fasces without need of a garrison?'[15] Over the whole of the empire in its prime, as Aristides remarked in a telling comparison to the Spartan and Athenian hegemonies centuries before, 'the cities are free of garrisons; cohorts and wings of cavalry suffice as the guard of whole provinces, and few of these are quartered among the cities of each race . . . they are scattered in the country: many provinces do not know where their garrison is.'[16] He was putting the best face on Roman government's weakness: the imperial authorities lacked the strength to patrol the hinterland. So travellers went armed and guarded outside the cities of the Roman world, and still people vanished, even people with retinues.[17] The business of government, if done with soldiers, had to be done with a handful: a freedman procurator in Bithynia, charged with the collection of taxes, had to make do with four troopers.[18] The emperor was stingy with his armies, unwilling that soldiers should be detached to help with the business of government in the interior. When the prefect of the Pontic shore, an important equestrian official, complained to the emperor that his military escort of thirteen was insufficient, his request for more men was refused on the grounds that, in the emperor's words, 'all care must be taken that soldiers not be called away from the standards'.[19] If, in the fourth century, there were more soldiers near centres of population, there still were astonishing gaps: hardly any soldiers were available to keep the peace in either Rome or Antioch, and it was by no means certain that soldiers in other cities would co-operate with the civil authorities. Indeed, they might well work at cross purposes to them.[20]

Nor could the imperial authorities rely upon police to fill in where soldiers were unavailable or unwilling. There was no imperial civilian police force—no police force worth the name at all outside a few great cities. Under the high empire, what passed for a secret service—army supply sergeants who came to serve as couriers and had subtler duties as well—

---

[15] Jos. *BJ* 2. 366; cf. Herod. 7. 8. 5. Perhaps not strictly true, see n. 11 above.

[16] Aristid. 26. 67 (Behr).

[17] Shaw (1984*a*), 9–12; the law expected travellers to go armed, *Dig.* 48. 6. 1 (Marcianus); and there was trouble even in towns because of the distance of the *auxilia praesidis*, Apul. *Met.* 2. 18.

[18] Pliny, *Ep.* 10. 27–8.

[19] Ibid. 10. 22 (for number see 10. 21); cf. 10. 20, 10. 78; and note the suggestion that if all foreign foes were conquered, the army could be abolished, *HA Prob.* 20. 3–6—so its domestic duties did not come instantly to mind.

[20] Rome, A. H. M. Jones (1964), 693; Antioch, Liebeschuetz (1972), 116–26; despite the fact that there seem to have been plenty of soldiers in the area, Isaac (1990), 272–6. Non-co-operation of army in the 4th cent., MacMullen (1988), 159–93, and esp. Lib. *Or.* 47.

was no more than eight hundred strong.[21] Late-antique government offers a mysterious bureau, that of the 'Doers of Things' (*agentes in rebus*), which may have served as a secret service, but which was only slightly over a thousand strong.[22] By contrast the government of the former German Democratic Republic (East Germany) employed nearly a hundred thousand secret policemen, lavishly equipped with modern means of surveillance, and relied upon three hundred thousand informers, to watch over a compact population of only seventeen million.[23]

The force at the emperor's disposal seems less unequal to the task of ruling upon the recognition that the empire's territory was, for the most part, divided among her cities. The day-to-day business of government— collecting taxes, providing drafts for the army, and keeping the peace— was invested in those cities, and was the responsibility of the local notables who presided over them.[24] The power to collect rents (the basis of the delectable manner of life of most of those notables) presupposed the power to collect the emperor's taxes.[25] 'As many town councillors, so many tyrants', observed Salvian, bluntly.[26] Thus, instead of needing to coerce many millions, all the emperor needed was the force to coerce some thousands; these, in turn, could compel the rest. Yet it was precisely those local strongmen, with their castle-like houses and their swarms of well-armed slaves and club-wielding tenants, whose force could dwarf that which the Roman official had at his disposal. When official and local

---

[21] *Frumentarii*, Clauss (1973), 82–113. A strength of 800 is the high estimate of Austin and Rankov (1995), 152. Sinnigen (1961: 67), estimates a more modest 200.

[22] *Agentes in rebus*, Blum (1969); Giardina (1977); the bureau had an authorized strength of 1,174 in AD 430 (*CTh* 6. 27. 23). Against the *agentes* being secret policemen at all, Liebeschuetz (1970).

[23] Kramer (1992), 43, 52.

[24] On the general responsibilities of cities and their notables to the imperial government see, briefly, Garnsey and Saller (1987), 32; Lepelley (1979–81), i. 207. For collecting imperial taxes, see esp. A. H. M. Jones (1974), 165 n. 83; Liebeschuetz (1972), 161–6; in general on tax collection under the principate, Neesen (1980), Brunt (1981). Furnishing military recruits, Brunt (1974a), 113–14; keeping the peace, Hopwood (1983) and (1989). Also transport services, Mitchell (1976); and the custody of prisoners, Millar (1984), 130.

[25] Power of the local notables over their inferiors: Aug. *Ep.* 58 takes it for granted that a great proprietor has the religious faith of his tenants in his gift; see also MacMullen (1974), 6–12, 34–7 (including the brutal extraction of taxes); (1988), 84–6; also, with emphasis on tax collection, Brown (1992), 26–7; and see esp. for force, Apul. *Met.* 9. 35–8. For the power of landlords over tenants, Foxhall (1990); creditors over debtors, Philostr. *VS* 2. 1 (549): the family of Herodes Atticus held debts going back generations (cf. Antonio Savorgnan in 16th-cent. Friuli, Muir (1993), 122–3).

[26] Salv. *Gub. Dei* 5. 18. 27.

strength clashed, local strength often won. In the empire the power to collect taxes might well presuppose, also, the power to resist taxes.[27]

In fact, the imperial authorities and the local élites did not often come to blows; at least in the first two centuries AD, their relations were cosy. 'There is no need of garrisons holding acropolises, but the most important and powerful people in each place guard their countries for you,' as Aristides observed to the Romans.[28] One of the roles imperial force played in the ruling of the empire was that of supporting the power of local notables over their social inferiors. And this was a service for which, in turn, the locally eminent returned the loyalty necessary to drive Roman government.[29] Yet too often, in practice, when the power of local notables was threatened—as when the mob came to burn down Dio Chrysostom's house, and was deterred only by its strong location—the imperial authorities were nowhere in sight. During a grain riot, it was said, Apollonius of Tyana found a local magistrate clinging to a statue of the emperor as the populace merrily lit a fire to burn him alive: surely if any live Roman official had been available to protect him he would have clung instead to him.[30] The day-to-day invisibility of Roman government in the provinces could make it as impotent in defending the local authorities as it was in getting its own way by force.

It is certainly true, then, that the Roman empire could not be ruled without force and the fear that force inspired, but the modest provision of force available makes it unlikely that it was the sole operative principle of Roman imperial government. Moreover, the realization of the importance of force and fear to imperial power just pushes the question back a step. For it still remains to explain how the imperial authorities, and especially the emperor, commanded the obedience of the agents of force, the soldiers. This may be in part beyond the scope of historical enquiry to answer: everywhere and in all eras, regardless of cultural peculiarities and barring exceptional circumstances, soldiers seem to obey, and armies seem to work. For the most part civilians too, in all societies, obey the authorities established over them. 'We charge you yield—in Queen

---

[27] Local armed power, MacMullen (1988), 72–3 (including castle-like houses, cf. Hopwood (1986)); notice too the wide availability of weapons in the Roman world, Brunt (1975a); and local bigwigs' co-operation with bandits, Shaw (1984a), 38. For local strength bettering official strength, MacMullen (1988), 94–6, and esp. Cic. 2 *Verr.* 1. 67–70, 1. 85, 4. 95; Herod. 7. 4. 3–6; Tac. *Hist.* 2. 16; Sym. *Rel.* 31; also, the rich assumed to be able to resist taxes, Amm. Marc. 16. 5. 15 (on which see Matthews (1989), 89).

[28] Aristid. 26. 64 (Behr; trans. Behr); cf. Jos. *BJ* 2. 569–71.

[29] Ste Croix (1981), 307–17.

[30] D. Chr. 46. 12–13 and Philostr. *VA* 1. 15; cf. Philostr. *VS* 1. 23 (526).

Victoria's name,' sing the policemen, and the pirates (*of Penzance*) reply, 'We yield at once, with humble mien, because, with all our faults, we love our Queen.' At some level obedience may be bred in the bone; or perhaps it is an essential quality of men living in society, a disposition that a previous century would have rooted in the social contract. Whatever its origins, moreover, obedience would have become habit and then tradition as the imperial centuries wore on. The Greeks and Romans were fiercely conservative peoples, and there was plenty of time for conservatism to assert itself: Augustus himself outlived most of those who remembered the free Republic, and from Actium to the Gothic sack of Rome were thirty generations of men. Yet beyond pointing to such universal tendencies to obedience, it is useful to identify specific sources of authority that men obey uncompelled, sources of authority that they obey because they have been brought up to deem them legitimate.

Legitimate authority can, for example, be vested in the idea of a nation, and the mantle of that authority can rest on the shoulders of men whose commands are obeyed by virtue of its citizens' patriotism. Some of the power of the Roman emperor may have been rooted here. Yet the ability of the empire of the Romans to inspire such devotion may have been more limited than that of modern Germany, say, or Serbia. 'You have made a city from what was once the world', said a poet, for contemporaries conceived of the Roman empire less as a nation and more as a city with vast possessions.[31] Although in the Roman world loyalty to one's home city, or tribe, or creed, was often intense, it cannot be known whether a loyalty to a distant Rome (despite suggestions that it might be encouraged) could ever have been more than a pallid affection among the millions who had never seen the city, even if they were, at law, its citizens.[32] Those resolute parochial loyalties might, however, offer a powerful bulwark to a government that could somehow draw strength from them.

Authority can also be vested in the law, and imperial subjects brought up to obey the law and respect legal claims to their obedience. The hypnotic majesty of Roman jurisprudence inclined the learned of generations past to ground the empire in the rule of law, and so to devote themselves to minute examination of the legal nature of the power of

---

[31] Rutil. Nam. *de Redit.* 66; cf. Athen. 1. 20b–c.

[32] On local loyalty, see pp. 88–89 below. Provincials' loyalty to Rome discussed, urged, Dio 52. 19. 6, Aristid. 26. 59–64 (Behr) with Oliver (1953), 926–9. For lack of patriotism for empire, refs. gathered by Paschoud (1967: 13 n. 17), detecting an increasing devotion to Rome among Latin intellectuals after Adrianople; but the rest of society cheerfully gave comfort to the enemy, E. A. Thompson (1980).

governors, and exactly what legal powers—proconsular *imperium*, tribunician authority, and so on—the emperors enjoyed. Authority grounded in law and constitutional tradition is a real part of imperial power; yet visions of a law-based empire tended to exaggerate it.[33] From day to day, among the vast mass of peoples in the empire—even among aristocrats and the emperor's servants themselves—little attention was paid to constitutional niceties. Indeed, the perennial legal ignorance of officials and subjects, remarked upon by Justinian, was equalled only by their lack of interest in technicalities: the centurion, nailing a bandit to a cross, never gave a thought to whether his struggling victim was to pant out the last hours of his life by virtue of the proconsul's *imperium* or his *ius gladii*.[34] 'For a king, the laws are no protection against betrayal', said an orator to Trajan with refreshing frankness. No conspirator against the emperor ever slept less well at night because the emperor technically had tribunician sacrosanctity: it was visions of glowering German bodyguards that woke him with a start.[35]

Authority can, furthermore, be vested in a man: could the Roman emperor have ruled as some medieval kings did, by a magical or supernatural authority? Certainly Vespasian and Hadrian were each twice credited with having miraculously cured the sick, and Vespasian with awareness of the political potential of such acts. Perhaps some part of imperial power lies here.[36] Yet compared to other miracle-working monarchs, the Roman emperors were distinctly unmagical. Only a handful of imperial miracles are attested before the fourth century, even though miracles were exactly the kind of detail that ancient writers would have reported, judging by their attention to omens and portents. By contrast,

[33] Honoré (1978: 35 n. 373) collects ancient statements grounding the empire in arms and the law. For an effective attack on law-based views of the empire, Ste Croix (1981), 383–91; cf. (by a Romanist) Kunkel (1973), 48–55; and Millar (1977), 616–17.

[34] Justinian, *C. Tanta* 17. For officials' ignorance of the law, and their seeming lack of concern to provide themselves with assistants who were learned in it, see Brunt (1975*b*), 132–6. Indicative is Men. Rhet. 415. 24–416. 26: one is to praise a governor for experience in the law (415. 26–7) but this is only one of nineteen headings under which he is to be praised. For ignorance of the law on the part of Tacitus and Cassius Dio, both of whom had official careers, R. S. Rogers (1933).

[35] D. Chr. 3. 88; fear of bodyguards, Jos. *AJ* 19. 6; Herod. 4. 13. 3–6.

[36] Vespasian, see p. 110 below; Hadrian, *HA Hadr.* 25. 1–4 (reported with some suspicion). Other imperial wonders (usually, like Vespasian's healing, depicted as indicating the favour of the divine rather than emperors working miracles in their own right), *HA Marcus* 24. 4 with Dio 71(72L). 8 (on which see Jobst (1978)); Herod. 1. 7. 5; Dio 74(75L). 7. 6–8 with Herod. 3. 3. 7–8 (see Rubin (1980), 117–20); *HA Aur.* 25. 3–6; Zos. 1. 67. 1–2 with Zon. 12. 29; and they become more common under 4th cent. Christian emperors, MacMullen (1968), especially as described in 5th-cent. works, Brown (1992), 134.

the healing touch of the medieval kings of Britain and France was frequently remarked upon, and came to be systematically applied to scrofula on a regular basis. Louis VI touched the sick every day, and as late as the 1680s, Charles II was applying his marvellous touch to the King's Evil more than eight thousand times a year.[37] In comparison, Roman emperors of the empire in its prime seem to partake of little more than the ambient magic of a superstitious world. Hadrian was a devoted sorcerer, but his magical knowledge was gained like that of any other inhabitant of the empire, by paying an Egyptian wizard, and his magical power in the conventional way, by sacrifice: some reported that he had even slain Antinous as a blood offering.[38]

Yet temples were built to the Roman emperor by the hundred, and their altars smoked with sacrifices. Could it be said that the emperor ruled by divine authority—as a god, or demi-god, on earth? It would not do to underrate the political significance of the imperial cult; nor to overrate it. For the emperors, especially the principate's architects Augustus and Tiberius, were reluctant to be worshipped; even the third-century Greek historian Cassius Dio, fixing the empire of his day with a gimlet eye, urged the emperor to forbid temples to be built to him. Emperors could accept or refuse cult as they saw fit, so perhaps religious devotion to the emperor was not an indispensable source of imperial power. An understanding of the imperial cult is central to an understanding of Roman government, but it may be as much part of the question as part of the answer.[39]

Perhaps the emperor ruled by a manufactured charisma—perhaps he appeared as superhuman, and thus worthy of obedience, by means of a cult of personality crafted by propaganda.[40] Certainly what survives of imperial pronouncements—chiefly the legends on coins—lays stress on the supreme moral virtues of the emperor, as well as his victories, and

[37] On the King's Touch, Bloch (1924) (Louis VI, p. 94); Barlow (1980); Charles II, Thomas (1971), 193; for magic of early medieval kings, J. M. Wallace-Hadrill (1971), 8–20.

[38] Hadrian and the magician, *PGM* 4. 2447–55; and Antinous, Dio 69. 11. 2–3. For nonwondrous nature of emperor, note also the lack of ex-voto dedications, Fishwick (1990*a*).

[39] For the imperial view of cult and that of Cassius Dio, pp. 168–172 below; on the cult in general, pp. 160–172 below. Against a crass understanding of the imperial cult as *Herrschaftslegitimation*, Price (1984*a*: 240–8), who also discusses the strategies Greeks used to distinguish 'divine honours' for the emperors from their worship of the Olympian gods (pp. 146–56, 207–20); Veyne (1990), 308.

[40] For surveys of forms of publicity available to emperors, J. B. Campbell (1984), 142–55; Potter (1994), 110–30.

sometimes the coins claim also that he is the chosen of the gods.[41] The omens and portents that litter imperial history may be the spoor of lost attempts to attribute to the emperor—or rebellious, would-be emperors—divine sanction.[42] Imperial ceremonial was awe-inspiring; imperial art and architecture, too, sounded the ponderous themes of victory, conquest, and might.[43] Yet the efficacy of such methods—if they are viewed as the self-conscious practising of a cynical few upon a passive multitude—is hard to gauge. The late twentieth century has seen the fall of regimes which had for decades employed all possible contemporary media (newspapers, radio, television) to mould public perceptions of the leader, without fully convincing the people; although most of the emperor's subjects were much more naïve, the techniques at the emperor's disposal were much feebler, and much less systematically applied. It is by no means certain, indeed, that the emperors purposed the creation of mass loyalty with their various forms of publicity. But the emperor's intention is less interesting than his subjects' reactions. Paul Zanker has shown how imperial subjects came actively and willingly to participate in the ideology that Augustus' art and architecture expressed, adopting its themes and motifs for their own use.[44] A similar voluntary process of imitation and adaptation can be traced in provincial use of that most potent and ubiquitous imperial symbol, the sculpted image of the emperor.[45] So it may be profitable, later, to consider ways in which loyalty to the emperor might be useful to his subjects; and rather than investigating merely the imposition of imperial dogma on the ruled, to study also the connivance of the ruled with the rulers in the exaltation of the monarch.

The preceding interpretations of the working of Roman government arise from modern experience or comparison to other societies; the explanation of Roman government in Roman terms begins with the thesis of von Premerstein. Noticing the large role played in Roman writings by the rhetoric of favours given and owed, he argued that imperial power actually rested upon patronage. The emperor was the patron, the benefactor, of his every subject. The subjects, in turn, paid him back for his

---

[41] Imperial virtues, Charlesworth (1937); A. Wallace-Hadrill (1981a); victory, Gagé (1933); McCormick (1986: 11–46), discussing also the related festivities, esp. the triumph. Chosen of the gods, Fears (1977), 189–315; divine election stressed especially by Christian emperors, MacCormack (1981).

[42] Rubin (1980); Bowersock (1987); Potter (1994), 161–73; also miracles, see n. 36 above.

[43] Ceremonial, Alföldi (1970 (1934–5)); and esp. for the great public ceremony of *adventus*, MacCormack (1981), 17–61.

[44] Zanker (1988). [45] Zanker (1983); Smith (1987).

benefactions with their loyalty; this was the basis of his power. Thus, the empire was a single enormous spider's web of reciprocal favours. As the younger Seneca put it: 'An emperor is kept safe by benefaction: he has no need for guards—weapons he keeps for decoration.'[46]

Although scholars have successfully criticized some of the details of von Premerstein's thesis, its basis has gained wide acceptance. Given the size of the empire the emperor could not possibly have been everyone's direct patron, as von Premerstein more or less assumed. Nor need he have been. The emperor did favours for leading aristocrats and generals, who repaid him with loyalty. These men had clients of their own, who looked to them for boons; and these clients might thereby be put, albeit indirectly, at the emperor's disposal, thus creating a great spider's web made up of smaller spiders' webs. And where the emperor seemed to have a hundred servants, suddenly he had thousands. 'It is the web of favors given or owed that enables an imperial administration of only a few hundred really to rule an empire,' as MacMullen puts it.[47] A neat, elegant, and, as far as it goes, convincing thesis; helpful too because it offers insight not only into how the great could command the small, but into how the comparatively small could influence the great, how consent could be widened by placing government at the service of the subject.

Yet there are puzzles. How exactly do boons produce loyalty? For the loyalty that follows benefaction is more than a canny appraisal of the likelihood of getting more boons in future (although that certainly plays its role). In AD 360, Julian, having assumed the purple and revolted against Constantius, administered an oath of loyalty to his followers. Surrounded by Julian's enraged soldiery, and facing the greatest likelihood of death, the praetorian prefect, Constantius' appointment, refused to swear, 'because he was bound to Constantius by many and frequent benefactions'.[48] The prefect is driven by something he valued more than his life. What? Von Premerstein imagined that the force of the patron–client relationship lay in mighty oaths sworn by the client, but this aspect of his argument has been battered to pieces, for oaths of clientage are a myth.[49] Part of the psychological basis of patronage as a method of rulership remains obscure.

---

[46] Sen. *Clem.* 1. 13. 5; cf. Dio 53. 4. 1. Von Premerstein (1937), 13–116; and in practice, Syme (1939), 349–86.

[47] MacMullen (1988), 121; see also 111–12; cf. e.g. Garnsey and Saller (1987), 148–50; A. Wallace-Hadrill (1989), 79–84. For a detailed criticism of aspects of von Premerstein, Rouland (1979), 348–400, 500–9.

[48] Amm. Marc. 21. 5. 11.   [49] Oaths, Herrmann (1968), esp. 93.

Consideration of some conspiracies against the emperor, moreover, points to the limits of patronage as an explanation for the working of Roman government. The man who stabbed Caligula, many of the men who formed the ill-fated Pisonian conspiracy against Nero, and the men who arranged and carried out the murder of Caracalla suffered no lack of benefactions from the emperors they plotted against; indeed, Caligula's killer had frequent occasion to thank him for boons, one of the Pisonian conspirators was a consul designate while others were familiars of the emperor, and Caracalla's nemesis, Macrinus, was praetorian prefect. Rather, when the historians deduce conspirators' motives, they often insist that such men conspired against the emperors because, to put it somewhat quaintly, the emperors had offended against their honour. Caligula had mocked Cassius Chaerea, and had publicly accused him of effeminacy. Caracalla had treated Macrinus similarly, and had baited the centurion who actually slew him with his base birth and cowardice. Nero had composed a saucy poem about the senator Afranius Quintianus, and had denied Lucan what the poet felt was his rightful share of fame. Indeed, as Tacitus tells it, the one man the Pisonian conspirators approached precisely because they believed that Nero's failure to requite him for his services might have turned him against the emperor, promptly informed Nero of what was going on. He was Volusius Proculus, a naval captain at Misenum who had assisted in the murder of Nero's mother, Agrippina.[50] So the empire was more than a colossal back-scratching scheme; in the eyes of some observers the principate evidently depended not only on a well-directed stream of boons, but also on careful regard for the honour of those around the emperor.

Looking at Roman Imperial Government

Force, authority, and patronage cannot, therefore, complete the reconstruction of imperial power. There are still aspects that need explaining: the workings of honour and pride, the underpinnings of loyalty and gratitude for benefactions. Nor, I think, are these incidental oddities: a glance at how inhabitants of the empire perceived those who ruled them reveals the centrality of this constellation of thoughts and feelings to an

---

[50] Cassius Chaerea, conspirator against Caligula, Suet. *Gaius* 56. 2; Jos. *AJ* 19. 21, 29–32; Dio 59. 29. 2; cf. Sen. *Const.* 18. 3. The Pisonian conspirators, Tac. *Ann.* 15. 48–51; Suet. *Vit. Luc.*; Dio 62. 29. 4; Tac. *Hist.* 1. 20 reports that Nero had given HS 220,000,000 to his friends. Macrinus conspires against Caracalla, Herod. 4. 12. 1–2, 4. 13. 1–2, 5. 1. 3. See also, Commodus, Herod. 1. 8. 4; Pertinax, *HA Pert.* 10. 9; and cf. *Tyr. Trig.* 8. 6–7.

understanding of Roman government. To understand Roman government, it is helpful to try to get a glimpse of government through Roman
eyes. If a Roman official appears to attract more attention as a dignitary
than as a functionary, if the most clearly perceived hierarchy of which he
is a part is social and not administrative, and if he seems to be interested
more in being honoured than in being dutiful, an explanation of Roman
government must account for these perceptions.

First, how was the top, the emperor, viewed by the bottom—the lowest social stratum whose opinions can be canvassed—peasants in the
provinces, far away from Rome? 'There are among us', wrote Synesius of
Cyrene about the rustics of North Africa, 'those who think that
Agamemnon, son of Atreus—he who went to Troy—still rules, a man
exceedingly good and true, whose name was handed down to us as royal
from childhood.'[51] At the most extreme remove, therefore, two aspects
appeared important to the subject: the name and the personality of the
emperor, even if drawn from fable.

Another depiction stressing the same aspects, again from an observer
far from the centre and not of high status, is the vision of the emperor fig-
ured as Revelation's beast from the sea:

And I stood upon the sand of the sea, and saw a beast rise up out of the sea, having seven heads and ten horns, and upon his horns ten crowns, and upon his
heads the name of blasphemy. And the beast which I saw was like unto a leopard,
and his feet were as the feet of a bear, and his mouth as the mouth of a lion: and
the dragon gave him his power, and his seat, and great authority. And I saw one
of his heads as it were wounded to death; and his deadly wound was healed. And
all the world wondered after the beast. And they worshipped the dragon which
gave power unto the beast: and they worshipped the beast, saying, who is like
unto the beast? Who is able to make war with him? And there was given to him a
mouth speaking great things and blasphemies; and power was given unto him to
continue forty and two months. And he opened his mouth in blasphemy against
God, to blaspheme his name, and his tabernacle, and them that dwell in
heaven. . . . Here is wisdom. Let him that hath understanding count the number
of the beast: for it is the number of a man; and his number is six hundred three-
score and six.[52]

Here the emperor's name lies concealed by a code—so well concealed,
indeed, that the exact emperor meant is still hotly disputed—but
although the expression is metaphorical, the concerns were the same:

[51] Syn. *Ep.* 148 (Garzya).
[52] Rev. 13: 1–6, 18 (Authorized Version trans.). On this passage, see Price (1984a), 196–8.
We deduce John's low social origin from his corrupt Greek, S. Thompson (1985).

who and what is the emperor?[53] What is his nature? What are his (in this case horrible) characteristics and attributes? This description is no badly regurgitated civics lesson: the emperor at far remove was not seen as a collection of duties and powers, as the American president is depicted in the classroom to every American child.[54] He was, rather, an individual with personality.

Further up the social scale, the views of those more knowledgeable and closer to the emperor show more continuities with than differences from this most distant view. When the educated and sophisticated Philostratus imagined the advice given to the sage Apollonius of Tyana to prepare him for his trial before Domitian, it was the emperor's appearance—his beetling brow and puffy cheeks—as well as the grim tone of his voice which seemed worth relating. Indeed, in general it seems that it was the personal appearance of the emperor, and his quirks, that interested educated provincials.[55] It was his 'personhood' that attracted attention: this was the emphatic category.

Moreover, through panegyric modern readers can approach the imperial presence, and listen to how those actually addressing him describe him. Here too the emperor was perceived just as those further away perceived him, for panegyrics to an emperor assumed that his actions were the result of various attributes of personality—good attributes, obviously, of the reigning emperor, or bad ones in the case of an evil predecessor adduced for purposes of comparison. Thus, for example, his success in war was a result of his personal courage, his achievements in peace the result of self-control, justice, and wisdom.[56] In this view, an emperor was, as it were, a self-activating actor: his actions grew out of his

[53] Which emperor is concealed behind the number 666 is a notorious crux. The key is that Greek and Hebrew letters serve as numbers, giving rise to the magical practice of *gematria*, expression of words as the sum of the numerical values of their letters. The traditional view (recently well expressed in Collins (1976), 174–86; older discussions are collated in Böcher (1980), 84–7) favours the numerical value for the Hebrew 'Nero Caesar', which has the dual advantage of explaining the beast's death-wound (Rev. 13: 3—in legend, Nero does not die, but goes into hiding and returns) and the textual variant 616 (a slightly different spelling in the Hebrew).

[54] On the progress of American children, with age and education, from a person-based to a duty-based conception of the US president, Easton and Dennis (1969), 142–207.

[55] Apollonius, Philostr. *VA* 7. 28. Also D. Chr. 21. 6; Tac. *Hist.* 1. 7; *HA Macr.* 1. 4; MacMullen (1988), 114; and Potter (1990: 139) on the Sibylline Oracles. Cf. *PGM* 12. 279, 13. 251–3: when the emperor appears in magic spells, it is as an individual whose anger the mages seek magically to assuage.

[56] Men. Rhet. 372. 28–376. 23; cf. Pliny, *Paneg.* 25; [Aristid.] 35 (Behr), *passim; Pan. Lat.* 2(12). 25–9. On the genre of panegyric to emperors see MacCormack (1975); (1981); and Nixon (1983).

own character. The emperor was perceived not as the occupant of an abstract box, 'emperorship', into which the man fitted, and which prescribed his duties *qua* emperor; the emperor was not thought of as formulating policy as a function of his position; rather, he did what he did because of the kind of man he was.

Of course remarks made at court in the presence of the imperial bodyguards should not be taken too seriously: woe to the orator who strayed very far from what the emperor wanted to hear. But the way the panegyrists organized their thoughts is none the less significant. And historians, who had no cause to flatter and, indeed, often took a very dim view of the emperors they wrote about, viewed the emperors in exactly the same way. When as hardbitten an observer as Ammianus Marcellinus described the low taxes in the reign of the emperor Julian as testimony to his 'liberality', and high taxes in the reign of Valentinian as evidence of his 'avarice' (even though he was fully aware of the financial stringency under which Valentinian operated), he offers more than rhetorical commonplace: this was how well-educated, knowledgeable people preferred to think about their emperors.[57]

As the emperor, so the emperor's officials. Beginning again at the furthest and lowest point, with Synesius' peasants, we read, 'and the worthy rustics name a certain Odysseus as the emperor's friend, a bald man, but remarkable in dealing with affairs and at finding expedients in difficulties'.[58] Last to fade into obscurity was a name, an appearance, a personality, even if of the wrong individual. Closer in and higher up, in one of those rare contexts where there is no reason to suspect flattery, a distinguished Alexandrian described a Prefect of Egypt:

[He was] a man who at the start gave countless examples of gentlemanliness, for he was shrewd and persevering, quick to think and perform what he had deliberated, extremely apt at speaking and perceiving what was not said as well as what was. In a short time he became experienced at all Egyptian affairs, as complicated and intricate as they are, nay, understood with difficulty even by those who have put themselves to that labour from their youth. . . . And all matters concerned with accounting and the revenues he managed successfully, and if these deeds, as great and necessary as they were, did not display an example of a soul meet for a governor, he performed ones which showed a more glorious, nay, a kingly [or

---

[57] Amm. Marc. 25. 4. 15, 30. 8. 8, with Matthews (1989), 239–40. See also Philo, *Leg. Gaium* 86–91; Suet. *Tib.* 59. 1; *Claud.* 34–5; Herod. 7. 1. 2, 7. 3. 3; Dio 67. 1. 1, 73(74L). 5. 1–2; *HA Claud.* 1. 3; *Prob.* 18. 4; cf. MacMullen (1976), 30–1. Even the emperor himself takes this view: Julian, *Symp.* 308d–315d; *Ep.* 73 (Bidez); *Gk. Const.* 275.

[58] Syn. *Ep.* 148 (Garzya).

imperial] nature: he bore himself rather grandly, for pomp is most advantageous to a ruler, and judged important cases together with those in authority . . .[59]

The official's competence and success were attributed to his 'gentleman-liness', not his devotion to duty. His conduct as a judge showed not that he was a good official, but that he had a kingly soul. And when the author moved on to examine why the same Prefect of Egypt's administration decayed into a tyranny, he was not interested in how he ceased to perform his official functions, but in how he came to be a bad man.[60]

This view of officials as self-activating actors appears in a great many contexts in the historians, in the orators, in the astrologers—it was the *communis opinio* of the educated classes.[61] It was no different from the way the emperor thought of his officials. Trajan wrote to Pliny, governor of Bithynia, in some irritation at his subordinate's insistence on consulting him over trivial matters: 'I chose your wisdom', said he, 'so that you would exercise a moderating influence on the morals of your province.'[62] He didn't say, 'shut up and do your job.' He said, 'shut up and be yourself.'

Much more immediately visible to most inhabitants of the empire than the emperor or the governor were soldiers and tax-collectors. These were not viewed fondly: 'He goes into the city and a tax-collector meets him, then it is as though a bear had come upon him.' They were considered the most horrific menaces, the tax-collectors for extortion and dishonesty, the soldiers for murder, pillage, rape, any crime that monsters with swords in their hands could possibly commit against the unarmed.[63] Such men did not perform terrible misdeeds because they were appalling *ex officio*; rather, they were perceived as personally and morally appalling. 'I cannot serve in the army, I cannot do evil, I am a Christian,' cried a martyr objecting to his conscription, illustrating how inseparable, to this Roman mind at least, joining the army was from falling into moral vice.[64]

---

[59] Philo *Flacc.* 2–4, καλοκἀγαθία.   [60] Ibid. 8–103; cf. Amm. Marc. 29. 2. 22–3.

[61] See esp. Tac. *Agric.* 9, and also Pliny, *Ep.* 9. 5; Tac. *Hist.* 3. 49; Apul. *Apol.* 102; Herod. 1. 12. 3–4, 2. 8. 2; Firm. Mat. 3. 10. 1; *HA Trig. Tyr.* 6. 6–7; Musurillo (1972), 4. c. 1, 14. 2; Amm. Marc. 26. 8. 12, 27. 8. 10, 28. 1. 10; Eunap. *VS* 480; John Lyd. *Mag.* 3. 57–65 (6th cent.); and on a great many honorific inscriptions, e.g. *AE* 1931. 38. Cf. Saller (1982), 102–3.

[62] Pliny, *Ep.* 10. 117; cf. *AE* 1962. 183a.

[63] Quoted, *Bavli Sanhedrin* 98b, trans. Sperber (1978), 83. Menace of tax-collectors, Cic. *Off.* 1. 150; Luke 3: 12–13; Artem. 4. 57; D. Chr. 14. 14. Crimes of soldiers, Luke 3: 14; Petr. *Sat.* 82; Apul. *Met.* 9. 39; Goodman (1983), 143, and see MacMullen (1963), 85–9. More generally, a rabbi describes the retinue of a governor as bandits, Sperber (1978: 54), citing *Leviticus Rabba* 9. 8.

[64] Soldiers, quoted, Musurillo (1972), 17. 1; cf. Juv. 16 *passim*. Moral badness of tax-collectors, Luke 19: 2–10; Matt. 9: 9–13; 21: 31; Artem. 1. 23.

Thus the representatives of the Roman government, at several levels, were perceived as moral agents, and not as professional puppets jerked about by their official duties, pursuing policies emanating from their job descriptions. The Romans were not incapable of seeing their officials in other terms, but it was the perception of their rulers as people first that was most important to contemporaries. This realization poses a series of allied questions: how did these men seem to relate to one another in the context of government? To what extent were they seen as organized in hierarchies, and how were they ranked one against another?

A soldier shook down the peasants because he was a horrible man, but the same soldier obviously did not obey his centurion by virtue of his character—he did so by virtue of military discipline. 'I am a man under authority,' says the centurion in Matthew, 'and I have soldiers under me, and I say to one "go", and he goes, and to another "come", and he comes.'[65] Even at a great distance from the capital, in far Judaea, military discipline and military hierarchy were clearly understood: the power to command and the obligation to obey were seen to arise chiefly from the respective positions of individuals in the hierarchy, not from considerations of personality.[66] Here categories natural to us, and those natural to antiquity, are very close. But if we leave aside the army, and look for other official hierarchies, ancient perceptions rapidly blur. The Romans did not see their government as an abstraction.[67] To the emperor's subjects all their rulers together were 'the authorities' rather than 'the state'.[68] They did not automatically see the connection between government's parts. It was possible to hate the tax-collectors and soldiers, as nearly everyone did, without hating the emperor, or even the governor. Josephus described King Agrippa II patiently explaining to the Jews that they could not make war on the procurator Florus without making war against Nero as well, and that their refusal to pay tribute would be interpreted not as a blow against Florus, but against the emperor.[69] In the same part of the world, gleefully contemplating the ruin of the enemies of Israel, the rabbis listed (in transliteration) what would be destroyed—consuls, governors, centurions, Roman matrons—an apparent nonsense list, a jingle.[70]

[65] Matt. 8: 9; cf. Livy 8. 34. 7; Tac. *Hist.* 1. 83–4.

[66] Judaea, Goodman (1983), 144; Isaac (1990), 137–8.

[67] Kunkel (1973), 9. By contrast, US children develop a conception of 'government' quite early, Easton and Dennis (1969), 112–13.

[68] Rom. 13: 1, ἐξουσίαι; Musurillo (1972), 1. 10; Goodman (1983), 151.

[69] Jos. *BJ* 2. 402–5; cf. Goodman (1983: 166), citing *Sifre Num.* p. 102, 11. 14. 14–16, *Belhaalotekha* 103.

[70] Goodman (1983: 51), citing *Sifre Deut.* 317 p. 360.

At a distance, they see only the individuals, or the positions, not the relations between them.

Among the more knowledgeable, official hierarchies were perceived, although not entirely the ones we might expect. For example, ancient observers are prepared to tell us that an official received his authority from Caesar. 'I am judge over the Greeks,' a great magnate was imagined as saying to Epictetus. 'So you know how to judge? How come?' 'Caesar wrote me a codicil.'[71] The educated provincial public were not deeply impressed by fine distinctions between senatorial and imperial authority; rather, this public by and large perceived that the authority of Roman officials derived from the emperor by a very literal form of delegation. Said the apostle Paul to the governor of Judaea: 'I have not offended against the Law of the Jews, nor against the temple, nor against Caesar . . . I stand at the tribunal of Caesar, where it is necessary that I be judged . . . I appeal unto Caesar.' The governor, in this view, simply stood in for Caesar by sitting atop Caesar's judgement seat. He was an outlet for the emperor's power.[72] Later, this literalism would produce the perception that portraits of the emperor actually had to be present in court for judicial business to be done:

Consider how many governors there are in all the world. Since the emperor is not present at the side of them all, it is necessary for the image of the emperor to stand in courts of justice, in markets, in meeting-houses, and in theatres. The emperor's image must consequently be present in every place where the governor acts, in order that his acts have authority.[73]

This view has its parallel in his subjects' views of the emperor's coinage: a coin could not reliably circulate in the market-place without the emperor's head upon it.[74]

The origin of the authority of officials was, therefore, perceived by contemporaries: they could imagine a crude hierarchy based on delegation by the emperor. Some relations of obedience between persons in the emperor's service also attracted contemporaries' attention. Soldiers have already been seen to obey by virtue of military discipline and their position in a military hierarchy. Slaves and freedmen in the imperial service were thought to obey by virtue of their status. Thus in the emperor's

---

[71] Arr. *Epict.* 3. 7. 30; see also Small. *Nerva* 216; *Gk. Const.* 17.

[72] *Acts* 25: 8–11; see also 1 *Pet.* 2: 13–14; Philo, *Leg. Gaium* 230; Men. Rhet. 378. 10.

[73] Severian, *de Mund. Creat. Or.* 6. 5 (= *PG* 56. 489). Imperial portraits are clearly present in court from the 2nd cent., Apul. *Apol.* 85. For a convenient compendium of the power of the imperial image in society, see Price (1984*a*), esp. 170–206.

[74] Lendon (1990).

letter of appointment to a freedman functionary he describes the freed-man's duty as an *opera*, the technical term for the services owed to a patron by his freedman after manumission. Members of what is even today too often called the 'slave and freedman civil service' performed their duties not as civil servants (in our sense) who happened to be slaves or freedmen, but as slaves and freedmen whose duties happened to fall in what we would call the public realm. His slaves obeyed the emperor as their master, his freedmen obeyed the emperor as their patron.[75]

Between upper-class officials, however, relations of obedience were far more problematic. A good entrée into the thought-world of such men, and into their views of obedience to each other and the emperor, is a work of the satirist Lucian, who wrote to defend his acceptance of a post in the imperial government late in life. A defence was needed because some time earlier he had written an essay on how disgraceful it was for educated men to take up salaried posts in the houses of the rich. Now he defended himself against a hypothetical charge of hypocrisy, a charge based on the fact that 'in both cases there is pay and one obeys another'. To escape from this embarrassing conundrum required a good deal of puffing and blowing on Lucian's part, and readers are left with this fact: the relations between an official and his superior (either another official or the emperor) were very similar, in the mind of Lucian's presumed audience, to those between a magnate and his wretched hireling, a rela-tionship which he described, in turn, as not much different from that of master and slave.[76]

Far from surprising, then, is the audible quiet of the ancient sources on the subject of aristocrats' obedience. The stigma which slavery cast on such relations was of the most profound significance to Roman govern-ment. Although it was understood that a gentleman official had to obey his chief's orders, he might be insulted if another gentleman official pre-sumed actually to give him an order.[77] Thus even the emperor was extremely tactful, phrasing his directives to his grand officials as sugges-tions and advice.[78] Letters of appointment for his equestrian officials,

---

[75] *Opera, CIL* vi. 8619; and Dio 57. 8. 2 for the emperor and his slaves; see also Boulvert (1974), 10–109, 180–97, and Burton (1977), 165.

[76] Lucian, *Apol.* 11; cf. Hopkins (1983), 178–9. Lucian's previous essay was his *de Merc. Cond.* On these works, C. P. Jones (1986), 78–84.

[77] Duty to obey, Polyb. 6. 12. 2; Cic. *Leg.* 3. 7. 16; *ad Q. Fr.* 1. 1. 11; Jos. *AJ* 18. 89; *HA Verus* 4. 2. Danger of insult, Cic. *ad Fam.* 13. 26. 3.

[78] Pliny, *Ep.* 10 *passim*, for the correspondence of Pliny and Trajan. There are, of course, exceptions, Philo, *Leg. Gaium* 256; *Gk. Const.* 276. And late emperors were more brusque: see Eus. *Hist. Eccl.* 10. 5. 17 and some of the forged imperial letters in the later lives of the *HA*.

where, of all places, a modern reader expects some reference to obedience, avoided all mention of it.[79] And this antipathy to seeming to obey manifested itself in practical terms: the early and high empire simply avoided hierarchies of obedience as much as possible. Pliny (for example), when he governed Bithynia and Pontus, had no authority over the equestrian prefect of the Pontic shore.[80] Where there was an explicit hierarchy of obedience, there was groping for a metaphor to describe the relations of one official to another: a consul to his quaestor is like . . . perhaps a father.[81] In late antiquity, when the number of officials became larger and the administration was regularly more than one aristocrat deep, another metaphor was employed: now it was envisioned that the functionaries served in the army, because it was especially under military discipline that aristocrats could obey one another without loss of face.[82] These evasions are symptoms of more than the euphemistic concealment of an ugly reality; they were an attempt to ameliorate the acute discomfort that stark relations of obedience between one aristocrat and another inspired. This was a world where aristocrats, even privately, did not think of themselves primarily as the servants of others.

One key to understanding the hierarchy that Romans thought was most important among aristocratic officials lies in noting the significance of the Roman practice of granting the insignia of political offices—the robes and tokens, both on the municipal and imperial level—to persons who had not held those offices, for use either from day to day, or on special occasions.[83] This only makes sense when it is understood that offices were social distinctions, and that the hierarchy that was marked to contemporaries was not any official hierarchy, in our sense, but a social hierarchy—a hierarchy of prestige and standing—in which official rank was a vital criterion of ranking. When an aristocrat received his callers in the morning, the cry went up, 'first the praetor, second the tribune!'[84] Thus the scandal when Claudius' assistant Pallas, a freedman and therefore a person of low social status, was given the insignia of a praetor, because a praetor ranked much higher in society than any freedman should.[85] And another scandal, one which provoked extended debate in the senate

---

[79] *AE* 1962. 183a; *CPL* 238.
[80] Pliny, *Ep.* 10. 21, 22; see Sherwin-White (1966), 588.
[81] Pliny, *Ep.* 4. 15. 9; Cic. *ad Fam.* 13. 10. 1; also for quaestor and praetor, *Div. Caec.* 61.
[82] A. H. M. Jones (1964), 377–8, and esp. MacMullen (1963), 49–76. No stigma attached to obedience in war, see esp. Plut. *Fab. Max.* 24. 3, and see p. 248 below for obedience in the Roman army.
[83] Mommsen (1887–8), i. 455–67; Borzsák (1939).
[84] Juv. 1. 101, 'da praetori, da deinde tribuno'.   [85] Pliny, *Ep.* 8. 6.

about the conduct of youth, erupted when the glittering young Lucius Sulla failed to give up his seat at the games to an ex-praetor. Having been praetor, the aggrieved party had achieved a certain position in society, and was entitled to social deference.[86] Three centuries later, one of the central interests of surviving late-antique law, and late-antique observers, was still the social rank signified by the holding of various offices. Ammianus Marcellinus lauded the late emperor Constantius because 'under him no military officer was advanced to the station of *clarissimus* ["most glorious", the level of senators]. They were, as I recall, *perfectissimi* ["most perfect", a lower level].' Ammianus thus praised the emperor for having avoided Claudius' solecism with Pallas.[87]

Ancient perceptions of how officials were ranked were echoed by two unequally emphatic views of the subject's duty to officials. There was perceived, without question, a duty to obey the emperor, the governor, or a local official when he gave an order: 'Let every soul obey the governing authorities, for there is no authority except from God, and the authorities that exist are established by God,' as St Paul wrote to the Romans.[88] But when the Christians found a problem with this dictum—during persecution pagan sacrifice was required, thus making obedience impossible—their reaction is informative: men about to be martyred patiently explained to their judges, and Tertullian expounded in detail, the view that despite this disobedience Christians too could be loyal subjects as long as they 'honoured' the emperors.[89] And, in fact, even allowing for obvious self-interest when this subject is broached by Christians, the duty to 'honour' or respect officials, whether local, imperial, or the emperor himself, is vastly more prominent in ancient writings than the duty to

[86] Tac. *Ann.* 3. 31. Cf. Plut. *Quaest. Rom.* 283a; Aul. Gel. 2. 2; Lib. *Or.* 2. 7–9. Putting this outlook another way, Veyne (1990), 48; for more on this subject, Ch. 4 below.

[87] Amm. Marc. 21. 16. 2. Rank of offices, see *CTh* 6 *passim*; cf. John Lyd. *Mag.* (6th cent.). *passim*.

[88] Rom. 13: 1; for patristic discussions, Clark (1991). See also 1 *Pet.* 2: 13–14; cf. Justin Martyr, *Apol.* 1. 17. Duty of obedience to local officials, Plut. *Praec. Ger. Reip.* 816f; to Roman officials, Cic. *Leg.* 3. 3. 6; Plut. *Praec. Ger. Reip.* 814e; to the emperor, Tac. *Ann.* 6. 8; Pliny, *Paneg.* 9. 4; D. Chr. 3. 6; Dio 52. 15. 2; Eus. *Hist. Eccl.* 9. 1. 6–7 (by civic officials). But of six surviving inscriptional texts of loyalty oaths to the emperor (Herrmann (1968), 122–6, two are rather fragmentary), only one (*SEG* xviii. 578) specifies duties ὑπακούεσθαι πειθαρχήσειν, 'to be obedient and to obey one in authority'.

[89] Musurillo (1972), 1. 10, τιμὴν . . . ἀπονέμειν (note esp. the martyr's reinterpretation of Rom. 13: 1 from a question of obedience to a question of paying honour), 6. 9, 7. 6. Tertullian, *Apol.* esp. 33–6, a work intended for both Christian and pagan readers, Barnes (1971), 103–4, 109–10. Earlier, Rom. 13: 7, 1 *Pet.* 2: 17.

obey.[90] Cicero, when expounding the 'law of nature', placed duty to officials under the rubric of 'respect': 'The duty of respect', said he, 'requires us to reverence and cherish those outstanding because of age or wisdom, or office, or any other claim to prestige.'[91] The duty to obey could be viewed as a subset of the wider duty to honour one's rulers.

The marked perception, therefore, is not of subjects, officials, and emperor dealing with each other in terms of obedience. Rather, the subject paid 'honour' to his rulers as individuals deserving of it in themselves, and, in turn, the rulers are seen to relate to their subjects by 'honouring' them.[92] Subject and official were linked by a great network of honouring, and obedience was an aspect of that honouring. Moreover, it was very largely in terms of honour that relations between individuals in the government were described: 'Both military and civil officials looked up to the praetorian prefects with the ancient custom of reverence, as at the apex of all distinctions,' as Ammianus Marcellinus said.[93] And at the very centre of this network stood the Roman emperor, relentlessly honoured by the men and cities of his world, and busily honouring them in return, or augmenting the honours they had bestowed upon others. This focus on the business of honouring in no way set the relations of subject and official, or official and official, apart from relations within society at large. As Cicero revealed, there was nothing specifically governmental in honouring people: it was an everyday social function, the constant expectation of a man in any respect distinguished. In the eyes of contemporaries, just as officials' marked hierarchy was social, rather than specifically governmental, so was the way in which people interacted with their rulers, and the rulers with each other. Government was no separate mental category, sharply distinguished from civil society; it was something 'embedded' in society, to borrow a term from the anthropologists. When the objective was the governor's crucifixion of a Jewish trouble-

---

[90] Duty to honour local officials, Plut. *Praec. Ger. Reip.* 816a, 817b–c; imperial officials, D. Chr. 31. 105; Pliny, *Ep.* 1. 23. 2; *Dig.* 3. 1. 5 (Ulpian); the emperor, Lucian, *Apol.* 13; Nic. Dam. *FGH* 90 F 125; Philo, *Leg. Gaium* 140–54; Herod. 4. 2. 9; Men. Rhet. 368. 19. This is matched by a concern on the part of officials and the emperor that they be honoured, e.g. D. Chr. 1. 27; Dio 53. 6. 4. For much more on this subject, Chs. 3–4 below.

[91] Cic. *Inv.* 2. 66, 'observantiam, per quam aetate aut sapientia aut honore aut aliqua dignitate antecedentes reveremur et colimus'; cf. *Off.* 1. 149.

[92] For emperor honouring, Ch. 3 below; imperial officials, Ch. 4 below; local officials, Plut. *Praec. Ger. Reip.* 808b–c.

[93] Amm. Marc. 21. 16. 2, 'ut honorum omnium apicem, priscae reverentiae more, praefectos semper suspexere praetorio'. See pp. 177–80 below. Officials' duty to honour emperor, Suet. *Vesp.* 15; Dio 66(65L). 12. 1; Lib. *Or.* 18. 159.

maker, the crowd did not cry, 'Do your duty', or 'Do your job'; it cried, 'If you let him go, you are no friend of Caesar's.'[94]

The curious circumstances surrounding the conspiracies against Caligula, Nero, and Caracalla suggested the presence of sentiments of honour on the imperial stage. Now their significance seems corroborated: when a contemporary thought about his government, he first perceived individuals, acting by virtue of their individual character, ranked in relationship to each other chiefly in accord with their position in the greater social hierarchy, and relating to each other, and to the rest of society, through socially prosaic relations of 'honour'.

The purpose of this book is to investigate the ramifications of these perceptions; to describe and analyse the role relations of honour played in Roman imperial government. Chapter 2 offers evidence of honour working as a form of power in society at large. The following chapters consider how honour contributed to the power of the rulers over the ruled, and how it contributed to the power of the ruled over the rulers, on the level of the emperor (Chapter 3), of imperial officials (Chapter 4), and in the Roman army (Chapter 5). An understanding of power directed upwards is no less essential to an understanding of government: such power dictates the degree to which the rulers govern in the interest of the ruled, thus, in part, the consent the rulers can rely upon, and so how powerful government must be to succeed.

To be more precise, these chapters offer the testimony of authors who describe honour as working in these ways. For one of honour's main functions was to conceal sterner realities. It was a fanciful and grandiose icing on a predictably bitter cake. When a subject or official says honour or shame has moved him to action, it can never ultimately be known whether honour is a plaster fig-leaf concealing something less publicly acceptable. Old and reputable, honour was ready to hand as a face-saving way to describe the interaction of man and authority, to conceal greed and fear, to depict obedience in a world where slavery cast a stigma upon it. A rhetoric of concealment so elaborated invites investigation in its own right: permitting the efficient exercise of brute power under an unobjectionable veil, it allows proud men to obey without balking, orders to be

---

[94] John 19: 12. Non-governmental outlook of officials, Saller (1982), 96–108; MacMullen (1988), 59, 79, 205–8; Veyne (1990), 205–6.

given without inspiring hatred, sacks of gold to be accepted without shame by men who could not bear to be imagined other men's hirelings. First, then, honour is part of power because it acts as a cloak or a lubricant to other forms of power.

Yet perhaps honour had a deeper significance also, for not only do men describe themselves (suspiciously, we might think) as moved by honour, but other men may—many years, even centuries, later, with no reason to conceal realities—describe their predecessors in the same way. Tacitus can hardly be accused of trying to hide the bad motives of most of the people he depicts; his vice is meanness of spirit, not generosity. If the historical tradition depicts honour as an important part of ruling, then honour is more than a rhetoric: it is at least an ideology. If fooling is going on, the historians are fooling not only their contemporaries, and us, but themselves as well. So here relations of honour are studied also as the articulation of power of other types—as one of the ways Romans and Greeks represented power to themselves, as one of the ways they reconciled themselves to it, in order to make living under, and participating in, a cruel and often alien authority tolerable, even attractive. The psychological techniques by which subjects extorted from themselves consent to government are also an important aspect of empire.

I suspect, finally, that honour was useful as a rhetoric of concealment, and appealing as an ideology, not least because it did have a day-to-day practical function in society and government. A terrified or greedy man could say (and even convince himself) that he acted out of respect, yearning for honour, or fear of shame, because he knew plenty of people who had. A good screen, because a believable one. In the ancient world, honour was a form of power in its own right; it had its own independent wellspring in the soul, in the sense of pride, in that aggression for social ends anthropologists call the pecking order, and had broad significance for Roman imperial government. It could therefore be a real tool of rulership, mingled with fear (and, in part but not in whole, a consequence of fear), greed, and obedience to legitimate authority. It seems to me that the evidence is not inconsistent with honour playing a considerable role in the day-to-day business of government, not only because ancient authors portray the emperor using honour to secure the obedience of his great officials, other distinguished men, and the cities of his empire; not only because we are shown great officials using honour to gain the cooperation of the local notables in whose hands the actual governing of the empire largely lay; but finally because the Graeco-Roman system of honour underlay political gratitude—thus patronage—and was perceived to be important also to understanding the obedience and loyalty of the emperors' agents of force, Roman soldiers.

Historically, there is nothing at all peculiar about using honour to rule. Few Roman practices in this sphere would have been inexplicable to Louis XIV, honorific admission to whose royal person was regulated to a nicety from the moment he rose, one class of courtiers attending on him as he got out of bed, an inferior order being admitted only after he had put on his dressing-gown.[95] The granting of titles, medals, and orders of chivalry as an instrument of policy is a broad theme of European history. Living under a government of this sort, Montesquieu naturally concluded that while the operative principle of democracy was virtue, and that of despotism fear, the operative principle of monarchy was honour.[96] As late as 1790, Edmund Burke could stand on the edge of an old world in many ways similar to that of the Romans and look with horror upon the new, comparing old turmoils in France to the Revolution. In former days,

a conscious dignity, a noble pride, a generous sense of glory and emulation was not extinguished. On the contrary, it was kindled and inflamed . . . All the prizes of honour and virtue, all the rewards, all the distinctions remained. But your present confusion, like a palsy, has attacked the fountain of life itself. Every person in your country, in a situation to be actuated by a principle of honour, is disgraced and degraded, and can entertain no sensation of life except in a mortified and humiliated indignation.[97]

With a native understanding of how men could be driven by honour, Burke was far better equipped than we to understand Roman imperial rule. That a government making broad and systematic use of appeals to honour seems odd and alien to us, that the concept of honour itself seems impossibly distant and romantic, is a consequence of the particular outlook of the late twentieth century; a sign of our removal from the ancient rhythms of rulership and subjection, an indication that we have finally arrived in Burke's nightmare, among the sophisters, economists, and calculators. Historically, government by honour is usual; it is we who are strange.

Historically unexceptional too is the power that honour permitted inferiors to exert over superiors in the Roman world. 'L'honneur a ses lois et ses règles, et qu'il ne saurait plier.'[98] For those in power to be honourable in their own eyes, they must follow honour's laws, and frequently

---

[95] Saint-Simon (1983–8), v. 605.

[97] Burke (1955 (1790)), 55.

[96] Montesquieu, *Esprit des lois* iii. 7–8.

[98] Montesquieu, *Esprit des lois* iii. 8.

those laws—a code of chivalry, say—embody expectations about relations between high and low, even the honourless low, or create other vulnerabilities in the great which the small can exploit. I suspect that Roman imperial government, despite its autocratic structure, was more amenable to influence from below than has perhaps been realized, and that this power of the ruled over their rulers is to be understood not least in terms of honour.[99] The ability of local notables and cities to use influence grounded in honour to control the governors set over them (sometimes even the emperor), or at very least to protect themselves, is important for understanding their consent to and co-operation with Roman government. Honour softened the brittleness of an authoritarian regime and introduced an easy, flexible quality into government, helping to ensure that the empire was responsive and adaptable enough to rule its world for centuries. At the same time, the ability of increasingly honourable subjects to face down officials in late antiquity may play some role in explaining the troubles of that era.

The Use of Evidence

Whatever the ultimate importance of honour to Roman government, the road to understanding it is necessarily somewhat circuitous. Our own inherited concept of honour inhabits a misty, half-familiar, treacherous region, not yet alien enough for us to view it dispassionately as utterly exotic, nor now familiar enough for us to be sure we properly understand it and use it as a reliable basis for comparison. We live in honour's churchyard. Honour's bones are still with us, but the muscles that drove them and the tissues that joined them have rotted away. We speak casually of a person being honoured by the Queen, but entirely without the consequence once naturally assumed, that something fundamental about him changed, that he came thereby to possess more honour. The honour of the Greeks and Romans, moreover, is naturally far different from later Anglo-European honour. To approach the ancient evidence, only a very broad chronological and geographical focus, providing the fullest possible context, will permit us to understand the often puzzling information that survives. The foreignness of the territory demands that as little as possible should be taken for granted. The camera must be pulled back far enough to allow a comprehensible picture, even if some blurring results, even if the distance imposes a certain spurious sameness on the subjects.

---

[99] On such influence, Brown (1992), emphasizing common literary culture and religious authority.

A broad focus, furthermore, allows a certain compensation for the eccentric way the ancient testimony must be treated. The quality of the evidence, as conventionally estimated, is uniformly poor. Not only do a great proportion of the statements made about honour by contemporary subjects or officials labour under the suspicion of being insincere; statements made by non-contemporaries, say historians looking into the past, are *post hoc* attributions of (usually secret) motive, and are properly treated with the greatest scepticism. The only practical method is to use the data we have not as sure indications of motive in individual instances, but as clues to how observers expected things to work; that is, to treat *all* the evidence as a kind of fiction, but as fiction that gives the historian legitimate insights into norms and broader realities. So this is an investigation of political culture rather than political history; the aim is not to discover why individual events occurred, but (ideally) to discover how a whole political world worked by studying how a range of people expected it to work.

In consequence, a great deal of perfectly dreadful evidence is employed. Not only are attributions of private motive in good historians used, but also anecdotes from bad historians, like the late fourth-century forger of the *Historia Augusta*, whose later lives are largely invention; statements (like some in Herodian) contradicted by superior ancient authorities (like Cassius Dio); statements whose reliability is vitiated by an overwhelming suspicion of flattery (from imperial panegyrics and honorific inscriptions especially), a known enmity, or any other sort of bias; and, finally, material from avowed works of the imagination—all of these are used, for all of them, whatever their relation to fact, reveal how people expected things to work, and deducing a pattern of expectation is the goal.[100]

The test applied to such material can hardly be whether it is true, but rather whether it broadly represents common perceptions and common expectations, and whether one man's expectations, if they cannot be precisely paralleled (as often), can at least be fitted in, like the pieces of a jigsaw puzzle, with the contiguous expectations of others. If men make the same guesses, and tell the same lies, over several centuries and many miles, we can deduce something from those guesses and lies. So the net has been cast wide, and evidence from all over the empire, and from a great span of years, is marshalled, while the conventional distinctions between Greek East and Latin West, between first century AD and fourth, are not given their usual weight; indeed anecdotes from the middle and

---

[100] For the date of the *Historia Augusta*, Syme (1971), 16. Readers must, of course, apply the conventional filters for veracity to any ancient anecdotes they seek to export from the logic of this book.

late Republic and the sixth century AD are cited, sometimes in vertiginous proximity. This is not to imply that the outlooks of Cicero and Libanius were identical; far from it. But if first-century BC Rome and fourth-century AD Antioch seem to agree on how government worked and how government could be influenced, that is a singularly valuable datum.

Cicero and Libanius may share the same expectations, of course, because they had seen much the same things, or because they had read the same books. The expectation that unwise insults destroy monarchical governments, which we have seen manifested in the falls of emperors, is an old commonplace of ancient political thinking, attested in Aristotle and Polybius.[101] The danger is that the authors we rely upon for our descriptions of political reality are mechanically applying the shop-worn *topoi* of political philosophy learned in school to a world which operates on entirely different principles. But the historical actors were, for the most part, educated in the same assumptions as the authors. The creaky tale of Harmodius and Aristogeiton—the *locus classicus* for insult leading to a plot against tyranny—may well contaminate our literary descriptions of the murders of emperors, but probably no more than it contaminated the minds of those actually contemplating imperial assassinations. The old stories were part of the political as well as the literary culture, guiding lines of action as well as lines of text, and influencing bloody reality.

Yet as the particularities of time and place are ground away, as Tacitus is dispatched, blushing, to the dungeon usually reserved for the mendacious *Scriptor Historiae Augustae*, so broad a focus results in a considerable loss of nuance. There is always the danger, moreover, of reforming into a single false mosaic the tesserae of several real originals. This approach to evidence also produces an unusual volume of material, and that, together with the foreignness of honour, requires somewhat narrow concentration on the book's main theme. Depicted here is not the whole Roman world, but a selective one, dominated by the emotions of pride, envy, and shame. Other emotions—fear, greed, and civic patriotism especially—appear, but for the most part where they illuminate, are illuminated by, or seem visible behind the primary emotions under study; a properly encyclopaedic account would give them much greater prominence. Other emotions have been downplayed, the lights upon them dimmed, in order to allow our eyes to adjust to the gloom of a dark and puzzling area. Half-light and close attention may reveal something about the strange, cold genius of the Romans.

---

[101] Arist. *Pol.* 1311^{a-b} with Fisher (1992), 27–31; Polyb. 6. 7. 8–9.

2

Honour and Influence in the Roman World

No rich man am I, said the orator Dio Chrysostom to his townsmen. His father had relied upon his influence in managing the family's financial affairs, trusting to it to ensure that no one would controvert his claims; on his father's death Dio found it very difficult to reclaim money in other men's hands. Dio's admission transports his reader from a mental cosmos in which power depends largely on money to one where money depends as largely upon power, from New York to the Mafia's Sicily. In the Roman world personal influence could be mobilized for the cheap purchase of a farm, for the return of a loan, for a roof over a traveller's head far from home, for a post in the army, or even for the capture of a runaway, book-stealing slave; it pervaded the whole sphere of action. What a great man wanted, he frequently turned first to his influence to gain.[1]

Many of the forms of influence mobilized in the Roman world are perfectly familiar, or easily imagined: the favour done by employee for employer, debtor for creditor, tenant for landlord—economic power by other means—but also that of man without knife for man with knife, cousin for cousin, friend for friend, townsman for townsman, or by the pious for the churchman rattling the keys to heaven and hell. Yet the Romans cast across their world other, less familiar, webs of influence too, broad and powerful ones, of great historical significance—as vital to the working of Roman government as they were to the working of Roman society in general.

These less familiar forms of influence were strong because they were rooted in strong foundations: the Graeco-Roman sense of personal honour, of prestige, of dignity, of distinction—words that are used interchangeably here and which stand for a galaxy of partial synonyms, *gloria*,

---

[1] D. Chr. 46. 5, δύναμις. Farm, Pliny, *Ep.* 1. 24; debt, ibid. 6. 8; traveller, Basil, *Ep.* 31; army post, Pliny, *Ep.* 7. 22; slave, Cic. *ad. Fam* 13. 77. 3.

honos, dignitas, auctoritas, τιμή, δόξα, ἀξίωμα.[2] In this chapter the importance of honour to ancient upper-class people—an irreducible fact—must first be made explicable in modern terms, expressed as something with which we can sympathize. Secondly, the nature of the honour which aristocratic men and women sought will be scrutinized, for the complex make-up of that honour—created both by public opinion and the expressed opinions of individuals—explains its wide-ranging force in society. Next to be considered is how ancient aristocrats were moved, and moved each other, to action by virtue of their sense of honour, honour as a form of power. The ancient mind, moreover, did not confine honour to humans: honour was assigned to things and institutions as well, especially cities. Since Greeks and Romans lived in a world of cities, and Roman government in large part worked through those cities, the interaction of the honour of men and cities must be considered, especially the characteristic product of that interaction, the phenomenon of public benefaction. Finally, potential challenges to aristocratic conceptions of honour posed by philosophy, Christianity, and communities of honour other than the aristocracy will be surveyed. After the workings of those aspects of influence rooted in honour are understood, the workings of Roman government can be approached.

A system of beliefs, thoughts, and feelings is inherently difficult to describe, for there are few clear lines, no obvious beginnings and endings. An alien civilization's unconscious adherence to alien norms must be presented as conscious strategy where they would have seen none. Even imagining the constraints a system of honour exerted over ancient conduct in terms of social norms imposes a spurious formality on the flexible standards of behaviour that are themselves one of the battlegrounds of a politics of reputation. As we shall see, one of the benefits of being held in great honour was the ability to ignore, or even manipulate, the rules that bound others. An attempt to schematize perceptions so natural to ancient man that he needed no such explicit ordering is at once artificially tidy and incomplete, but perhaps adequate to offer an inkling of how men and entities to which honour was ascribed could exert power in their world.

ARISTOCRATIC HONOUR

The conceptions of honour held by aristocratic Greek- and Latin-speakers of the Roman empire evolved from the values of their distant

---

[2] For a discussion of these words, see Appendix.

ancestors. The mental world of the *Iliad*—which reflects, however dimly,
the outlook of the Greek dark ages or early archaic period—is one where it
is essential to be able to affirm 'that I am not forgotten for the honour that
should be my honour among the Achaeans'.[3] The values of Homeric
heroes bear striking similarities to those the anthropologist finds in the
modern Mediterranean, where the state is distant or weak, and where men
are thrown upon their own resources for the defence of their lives, property, and self-opinion—which is contingent upon the opinion others have
of them.[4] Thus the application of the insights of modern anthropology to
Homeric conceptions of honour, and honour as it existed in classical
Athens, has proved extremely fruitful.[5] The evidence for early Roman attitudes is much inferior to that for the Greeks. But if scattered indications
and lexical survivals be credited, and if the Romans' old stories—the rape
of Lucretia and the vendetta which arose from it, the murder of Verginia
to preserve her chastity—echo old values even if they are unsafe guides to
old events, primitive Romans too had a fierce and bloody sense of honour.
Whether it arose from social circumstances similar to those in old Greece,
or a common Indo-European heritage, cannot be known.[6]

The luxurious, sophisticated, cosmopolitan world of the well-to-do in
the Roman empire was profoundly different from Homer's Greece and
primitive Rome. But a vivid sense of honour remained. It was fundamentally the same sentiment which had moved Achilles that launched the ver-
bose contests of rhetoricians in second-century AD Smyrna. It was the same
emotion that elicited juristic *responsa* on what—in the Roman law—constituted an actionable insult that had driven out the Tarquins so many centuries before. A revolution of circumstances, of ways of life, of attitudes in
other areas had not uprooted the Greek or Roman sense of honour.

---

[3] *Il.* 23. 648–9, τιμή, τιμάω (trans. Lattimore). On Homeric honour see esp. Adkins
(1960); Lloyd-Jones (1990 (1987)), 254–9; van Wees (1992).

[4] For the substantial anthropological literature on honour in the modern Mediterranean
littoral see esp. the collections of papers by Peristiany (1966) (within which Pitt-Rivers
(1966) is fundamental), Gilmore (1987*a*), and J. Campbell's (1964) book. On the non-exis-
tence or weakness of the state, Black-Michaud (1975), 146–9.

[5] See esp. Walcot (1970); Cohen (1991), with an able defence of the legitimacy of such
comparisons (pp. 38–41), noting that historical continuity need not be assumed; Cairns
(1993); Cohen (1995). We will note some ethnographical parallels, but not rely on them:
while anthropologists concentrate on the experience of low-status persons, evidence from
Roman antiquity is confined largely to those of high status, and, as Pitt-Rivers (1966)
stresses, conceptions of honour can be very different at different levels of society.

[6] The Twelve Tables (451–450 BC) made slander a capital offence (Cic. *Rep.* 4. 12), perhaps
implying that it inspired blood vengeance. Lexical survival: not only the rich vocabulary of
honour (see Appendix), but also words like *ulciscor*, to take vengeance. Lucretia, Livy 1.
57–60; Verginia, Val. Max. 6. 1. 2; cf. Livy 3. 44–50.

The abiding psychological strength of honour derives at least in part from the universal human desire for the esteem of those around one. The middle-aged head, shaking sadly over the deaths of teenagers propelled into impossibly hazardous behaviour by 'peer pressure', can understand, even if it cannot approve, some of the force of honour in ancient society: the yearning for human solidarity, to be included, is an extremely powerful motivation. But so is the other side of that longing: one man's desire to exclude others, to distinguish himself, to excel, whether by having more money, a more beautiful mate, or supremacy at squash. Graeco-Roman honour drew its vigour from both impulses, from its ability to include and from its role in differentiating one man from another.

Artemidorus of Daldis' second-century AD work on the interpretation of dreams quite inadvertently demonstrates this second, exclusionary aspect of honour, by offering a remarkable treatment of the criteria for social ranking in the Greek provinces of the Roman empire. In his analysis, the meaning of dreams varies with the social status of the dreamer; thus, to dream one is sleeping on a heap of dung signifies to a poor man that he will become rich, but to a rich man that he will gain public office. Because his interpretations are differentiated by status, his books are a mine of data on attitudes towards status in the city.[7]

Artemidorus' universe, schematically represented, has four levels:

City magistrate and/or priest
The rich man
The poor man
The slave; the prisoner; the debtor

These divisions are basic to Artemidorus' thought, and are emphasized by inversions of the portent of omens: a dream that is auspicious to one status category will often bode ill for its neighbouring categories. Thus, for example, to dream that one is wearing a purple robe is good for rich men and slaves, and bad for poor men.[8] Each of these social levels has a characteristic ambition, whose fulfilment or frustration dreams regularly

[7] Dung, Artem. 3. 52; Artemidorus' mental world is that of the Greek city under the empire with its council (2. 37), magistrates, municipal priests and colleges of priests, athletes, and public benefactions (2. 30). The most illuminating recent discussion of this author, although with a quite different focus, is Winkler (1990), 23–44.

[8] Purple robe, Artem. 2. 3. Important *loci* for working out the basic social structure envisioned are: 1. 17, 2. 3, 9–10, 53, 68, 3. 47. Notable inversions: 1. 69, 2. 9, 20, 3. 14, 23, 39, 4. 15, 26. This is by no means a neat scheme. The poor are often assimilated to the fourth category, as the magistrates are to the rich. It is far from clear what happens to members of the fourth category when their problems are solved. Debtors, at least, may take their place again among the rich.

portend. For the lowest, it is liberation from a plight: freedom from slavery, fetters, or debt.[9] For the poor man, it is wealth, which advances him into the category of the rich man.[10] For the rich man, it is fame, honour, which he seeks, and which distinguishes him from the highest category, which is associated with more of that attribute.[11] Further, that same fame or honour—yet more of it—is viewed as the goal of magistrates and municipal priests (in practice, another type of magistrate).[12] According to Artemidorus, then, there is not one single criterion of social ranking through the whole of society; but it is arresting that honour, in his work, is the essential criterion for social ranking among the rich.[13]

A pecking order defined by honour was natural to ancient authors. A bishop might describe someone as 'a distinguished man, indeed, as the secular world esteems pre-eminence, extremely glorious'.[14] To Mark Antony's magnificent grandfather, compared by Cicero to his descendant, 'life itself, and good fortune, was to be equal to others in liberty, and first in honour'.[15] Honour was certainly not the only way in which ancient aristocrats reckoned themselves against one another. 'In birth and nobility and wealth he was easily the first man not only of his town, but indeed of the whole vicinity,' says Cicero of Sextus Roscius, his client's father. Yet ranking by honour was emphatic—aristocrats were inclined to think of it first—and tended to subsume other methods. For faced with the need to establish the ranking-order of men with a variety of claims to standing, the ancient mind tended to convert their claims into the common currency of honour. When Sextus Roscius appears again in Cicero's speech, his various attributes have been mentally cashed in for prestige: he is 'splendidus', distinguished.[16] Thus the competition for honour in society might subsume all other competitions, and become overwhelmingly important to its participants. If, therefore, Caesar believed that Pompey 'desired that no one be his equal in dignity', and if

[9] Artem. 2. 3, 14, 3. 13, and esp. slaves, 2. 9, 30, 61.

[10] Ibid. 1. 14, 17, 33, 76, 2. 10. [11] Ibid. 2. 3, τιμή and εὐδοξία; 2. 30, 3. 47.

[12] Ibid. 2. 9, 27, 3. 13, 4. 49.

[13] For this contrast of goals, money vs. glory, between low and high, cf. Cic. *Part. Orat.* 91–2; *Amic.* 34; Lib. *Ep.* 154; a snobbish topos, but the reality is not so clear, see pp. 96–103 below.

[14] Eus. *Hist. Eccl.* 8. 5. 1, τῶν οὐκ ἀσήμων τις, ἀλλὰ καὶ ἄγαν κατὰ τὰς ἐν τῷ βίῳ νενομισμένας ὑπεροχὰς ἐνδοξοτάτων.

[15] Cic. 1*Phil.* 34, 'principem dignitate'. For honour as criterion of social ranking see also, Cic. *Planc.* 32; *Mur.* 15; Suet. *Vesp.* 9. 2; Tac. *Ann.* 2. 33; D. Chr. 31. 74; Eus. *Hist. Eccl.* 2. 2. 4; Jer. *Ep.* 66. 7; *Dig.* 49. 15. 7. 1 (Proculus). Cf. Garnsey and Saller (1987: 118), '[a] Roman's status was based on the social estimation of his honour, the perception of those around him as to his prestige.'

[16] Cic. *Rosc. Am.* 15, 20; see also 2*Verr.* 3. 56.

it seemed to Cicero that Caesar and Pompey were 'pretty well equal in dignity', this was a likely recipe for civil war.[17] How little surprising, then, the sentiments of Pliny the Younger: 'Men differ in their views, but I deem that man happiest of all who enjoys the anticipation of good and abiding fame, and who, assured of posterity's judgement, lives now in possession of the glory that he will then have.'[18] To the historian, it was naturally the pursuit of renown that raised man above the animal.[19] And the orator took it for granted that honour stood at the root of human motivation and human institutions:

You will discover that, among most men at any rate, there is nothing else that calls them forth to scorn danger, endure labours, and forgo a life of pleasure and ease.... This certainly is clear: neither you nor anyone else, Greeks or barbarians, who are considered to have become great, advanced to glory or power, for any other reason than that you were fortunate enough to have ... men who lusted after honour ... And you could not get a single man out of a multitude to do what he deems a noble deed for himself alone, if no one else shall know of it.[20]

Honour, decked out with a luxuriant vocabulary (the ancients having as many words for what was important to them as fashion designers have for blue), occupied, as any reader of classical texts quickly realizes, a conspicuous place in the attention of antiquity. Aristocratic life often appears to us as a ceaseless, restless quest for distinction in the eyes of one's peers and of posterity.[21] From Achilles to Alcibiades to Alexander to Scipio Africanus to Trajan, and on to the end of empire, soldiers and generals made war for it, men of affairs intrigued for it, orators spoke for it, historians wrote for it, poets sang for it.[22] One rounded up one's friends to protect one's reputation—and reassured them that one would devote one's attention to the protection of theirs.[23] Failing them, one might apply to an Egyptian sorcerer, who, amidst his reeking beast carcasses,

[17] Quoted, Caes. *BC* 1. 4, 'neminem dignitate secum exaequari volebat', and Cic. *Lig.* 19, 'dignitas ... par'; cf. Flor. 2. 13. 14 and Wistrand (1978), 29–31. On rivalry for honour, see e.g. Sall. *Cat.* 7. 3–6; Tac. *Hist.* 3. 38; Plut. *de Se Ips. cit. Invid. Laud.* 546c; Philostr. *VS* 1. 8 (490–1).
[18] Pliny, *Ep.* 9. 3, 'fama ... gloria'.   [19] Sall. *Cat.* 1. 1–4, *gloria*; 2. 9; cf. Polyb. 6. 14.
[20] D. Chr. 31. 17, 20, φιλοτίμων, 22; cf. Cic. *Arch.* 28–9.
[21] Rampant desire for honour, see Wistrand (1978), 28–9; Dupont (1992), 8; Wiseman (1985) and esp. Cic. *Off.* 1. 65; *Arch.* 14; Knoche (1934), 114 n. 66; Lucian, *Pereg.* 38; J. Chr. *de Ian. Glor.* 4–14; at a very early age, Mart. 6. 38. Cicero wrote two books on *gloria*, now lost (*Off.* 2. 31).
[22] Soldiers, Sen. *Ben.* 6. 38. 3; men of affairs, Plut. *Praec. Ger. Reip.* 804c–d; for history, Sall. *Cat.* 3. 1–2; poetry, Tac. *Dial.* 5.
[23] Cic. *Mil.* 68; *ad Fam.* 12. 17. 3; Fronto *ad Am.* 2. 4 (van den Hout); Sid. *Ep.* 1. 10. 2, 9. 1. 3.

cast dreadful enchantments for honour. To the rhetorician, honour was patently more important than life itself.[24]

THE ELEMENTS OF ARISTOCRATIC HONOUR

In Seneca's words, honour is 'the favourable opinion of good men; for just as good reputation does not consist of one man's remarks, and bad of another's ill opinion, distinction is not simply a matter of pleasing a single individual.'[25] A man's honour was a public verdict on his qualities and standing, established publicly; and, among those who (in Cicero's words) 'are in such a position of life . . . that men will talk about us all the time', life was lived under the constant, withering gaze of opinion, everyone constantly reckoning up the honour of others.[26] The qualities deemed honourable will be the first subject here, followed by a description of the unceasing process of weighing that honour—for the court of prestige met many times a day, wherever men gathered, in the baths or where wine flowed.[27]

The elements that elicited the community recognition that was honour—that is, the qualities that would be perceived as honourable—included high birth in an illustrious home town, wealth (provided it came from reputable sources, and preferably in the form of landed estates), legal status (that of a senator or an equestrian, or at least a citizen, not that of a freedman or slave), a great house, a grand procession of slaves and clients on the street, expensive clothes.[28] And there were more

[24] Sorcerer, *PGM* 12. 271–2; 22a. 25. Rhetorician, Cic. 3*Phil.* 35.

[25] Sen. *Ep.* 102. 8, 'claritas autem ista bonorum virorum secunda opinio est. Nam quomodo fama non est unius sermo nec infamia unius mala existimatio, sic nec claritas uni bono placuisse'. The speaker, Seneca's imaginary interlocutor, is presenting common opinion (see also *Ep.* 102. 13).

[26] Cic. *ad Q. Fr.* 1. 1. 38; for the public nature of honour, see also Cic. *Off.* 2. 31–6, 44–5; *Tusc.* 3. 3–4; D. Chr. 66. 12; Aug. *Civ. Dei* 5. 12; Dupont (1992), 10–11. The classic anthropological definition of honour is that of Pitt-Rivers (1966: 21), 'honour is the value of a person in his own eyes, but also in the eyes of his society. It is his estimation of his own worth, his *claim* to pride, but it is also the acknowledgement of that claim, his excellence recognized by society, his *right* to pride.'

[27] Court of δόξα, D. Chr. 66. 18, and cf. Pliny, *Ep.* 4. 17. 8; Sid. *Ep.* 7. 14. 1.

[28] Birth: Juv. 8; Tac. *Ann.* 4. 44; Pliny, *Ep.* 10. 12; Philostr. *VS* 2. 14 (594); Men. Rhet. 435; Quass (1993), 44–74; on legitimacy, Plut. *de Lib. Educ.* 1a–b. Home town: D. Chr. 44. 9, 45. 6; Philostr. *VS* 1. 25 (532); Eunap. *VS* 498; *HA Aur.* 3. 2. Wealth: Pliny, *Ep.* 10. 4; Basil, *Hom. in Ill. Dict. Evang.* 3 (= *PG* 31. 265); and esp. Lucian, *Nigr.* 23. On good and bad sources of wealth, n. 38 below. Legal status: Cic. 2*Verr.* 1. 127; Suet. *Vesp.* 9. 2; Tac. *Ann.* 2. 33; on freedmen and slaves see pp. 96–108, 101 below. Conspicuous consumption and display in general: Tac. *Ann.* 3. 55; Philostr. *VS* 2. 21 (603); and see MacMullen (1988), 238 n. 9. Specifically for houses: Tac. *Ann.* 3. 55, and see A. Wallace-Hadrill (1994: esp. 4), citing Cic. *Off.* 1. 138–9. For

subtle qualities, all the signs of a proper upbringing and education and an aristocratic manner: the proper accent, words, posture, bearing—in short, elegance. Two aristocrats never needed to enquire of genealogies to realize that they were both gentlemen; all they needed was a glance.[29]

Among the upper classes, these characteristics enjoyed prestige only because aristocratic opinion accorded it. But who were these aristocrats? Within the general category of the rich, the possessors of property, a sub-group can be distinguished—call it the aristocracy, although neither Greek nor Latin had an exactly equivalent word, since 'us' and 'them' sufficed—a group defined by its shared values, and in particular by its members' esteem of the same qualities. The aristocracy was an opinion-community; it granted, and was defined by, honour. 'For prestige to exist, the agreement of many who are illustrious and outstanding [that is, have prestige themselves] is required,' as Seneca put it.[30] No quality was honourable in and of itself. Honour was mediated through the perceptions of others, and even a superfluity of worthy qualities was of no use unless these qualities were publicly known, and approved by other aristocrats. You have no standing in aristocratic society if, like Apuleius' rich provincial adversary in court, 'you are, through rusticity, an unknown'. To be an aristocrat, then, was essentially to be thought well of by other aristocrats. It was not an objective quality, it was membership in a co-opting club, and fundamentally it was membership in this club which distinguished, say, the unquestionably aristocratic Pliny the Younger from the enormously rich but (to aristocratic opinion) *déclassé* freedman, Trimalchio.[31]

late antiquity, Shaw (1987), 13–14. Clients: Tac. *Ann.* 3. 55; and esp. John Lyd. *Mag.* 1. 20 (6th cent. but describing practices long before his time); see A. Wallace-Hadrill (1989), 82–3. Retinue: MacMullen (1974), 107, and add *Comment. Pet.* 36; Plut. *Pomp.* 23. 3; Philostr. *VS* 1. 25 (532). Lucian (*Nigr.* 23) gleefully imagines the plight of aristocrats if all the toadies were to go on strike. Clothes: Philostr. *VS* 2. 5 (572); Amm. Marc. 14. 6. 9. One can deduce whole lists of honourable qualities by turning catalogues of deficiencies or vices on their heads; Val. Max. 2. 10. 8; Amm. Marc. 14. 6. 7–17, 28. 4. 6–21 (see Matthews (1989), 414–16). For regional variation in standards, pp. 43–5 below. Cf. an analysis of the make-up of aristocratic honour in 16th-cent. Spain, Caro Baroja (1966), 106; in Hobbes's world, *Leviathan* i. 10.

[29] Aristocratic demeanour: Cic. *Off.* 1. 130–1; Apul. *Met.* 1. 20, 23; Sid. *Ep.* 4. 9. 2; and see Brown (1988: 11–30) and Gleason (1995: 70–3) for the upbringing that produced these qualities. Apul. *Flor.* 9 contrasts the conduct of the town crier. On solecisms of speech to be expected from lower-class persons, MacMullen (1974), 107 n. 58.

[30] Sen. *Ep.* 102. 8, 'consentire in hoc plures insignes et spectabiles viri debent, ut claritas sit'. Cf. Cic. *Sest.* 137.

[31] Apul. *Apol.* 16; cf. Pliny, *Ep.* 6. 24, 7. 25. Simply becoming widely known was therefore vital. It was in this sense that having a famous enemy (Aul. Gel. 7. 11. 3 with Epstein (1987), 21; Tac. *Hist.* 2. 53), or being ceaselessly prosecuted (Pliny, *Ep.* 4. 9. 1–2, 22), might confer prestige upon one: fame, for good or ill, was the first step; cf. Pliny, *Ep.* 4. 12. On Trimalchio,

Slowly evolving custom laid down for aristocrats prestige value for various attributes and accomplishments, and aristocratic opinion enforced those values in aristocratic society by means of an honour sanction. Consider the prestige offered to literary accomplishment, whether in rhetoric (most prominently), or in poetry or philosophy.[32] High culture, 'which pertains to the greatest praise of the most brilliant men', as Cicero put it, and its practitioners came to be universally revered among aristocrats and would-be aristocrats.[33] Thus Trajan's utterance to the sophist and philosopher Dio Chrysostom, 'I don't understand a word you're saying, but I love you as myself.'[34] So closely were high culture and high status associated that a schoolmaster could pass himself off as a senator in late second-century Gaul, and when, in the fifth-century whirlwind of barbarian invasion, all other claims to honour had been turned topsy-turvy, literature could be deemed the defining quality of aristocracy.[35] To admire high culture was required of all gentlemen, and the least talented nabobs at Rome, even the emperors themselves, produced streams of turgid prose and excruciating poetry.[36] To do otherwise was to violate an aristocratic code, and to risk slighting asides of 'not our class, dear'.[37] For it was likewise crucial to one's honour not to trip over any of the many codes which regulated aristocratic conduct. The club had rules. A member must not work with his hands—indeed, best not to work for profit at all.[38] An aristocrat must not make a public display of himself—not sing in the street or dance in the forum.[39] Pompey was reviled for the licen-

D'Arms (1981), 97–120. The term 'aristocracy' is used with due respect for the warnings of Shaw (1984*b*), 455; it is not fully satisfactory, but it seems to connote the defining sense of solidarity, the 'we-feeling', better than alternatives like 'upper classes' or 'élite', terms which do not sufficiently exclude Trimalchio; cf. Mathisen (1993), 10–13.

[32] Literary pursuits, Cic. *Tusc.* 1. 4–6; *Off.* 2. 48–9; Juv. 10. 114; Pliny, *Ep.* 6. 6. 3; Fronto, *ad Am.* 1. 4 (van den Hout); Tac. *Ann.* 12. 28; *Dial.* 5–7; Suet. *Galba* 3. 3; Apul. *Flor.* 16; Men. Rhet. 425–6; Amm. Marc. 29. 1. 8; Neri (1981). Even a vociferous attack on, for example, poetry—Aper's remarks in Tacitus' *Dialogus*—does not deny that prestige can be derived from it (*Dial.* 5, cf. 10); Aper merely insists that this prestige is more fleeting than that derived from oratory (9).

[33] Cic. *Rep.* 3. 5, 'quod ad summam laudem clarorum virorum pertineret'.

[34] Philostr. *VS* 1. 7 (488).

[35] Schoolmaster, Dio 75(76L). 5. 1–3; 5th cent., Sid. *Ep.* 8. 2. 2, and see Mathisen (1993), 105–18. For an early modern élite defining itself in terms of culture, Amelang (1986), 102–215.

[36] Expectation, Brown (1992), 35–40; Kaster (1988); and see esp. [D. Chr.] 37. 27; Amm. Marc. 28. 4. 15. List of great aristocrats who wrote poetry, Pliny, *Ep.* 5. 3. 5. Emperors' literary efforts, below, Ch. 3 n. 57.   [37] e.g. Amm. Marc. 14. 6. 1.

[38] Work with hands, Dio 52. 25. 7; J. Chr. *de Ian. Glor.* 13; small-scale trade unacceptable, D'Arms (1981); Veyne (1990), 49–54 and esp. Cic. *Off.* 1. 150–1.

[39] MacMullen (1974), 112. Sing, Cic. *Off.* 1. 145; dance, Cic. *Off.* 3. 75, 93. Also bad: pulling faces, Plut. *de Vit. Pud.* 535a; appearing in shows, Juv. 8. 183–99; Dio 61(62L). 17. 3–5; Levick (1983).

tious practice of scratching his head with a single finger, Crassus for extravagant grief at the death of his pet lamprey.[40] By the 370s AD aristocrats' chewing in public had become such a scandal at Rome that the Prefect of the City forbade it, to the vast relief of Ammianus Marcellinus and, one assumes, all other right-minded residents.[41] Clearly taste is one of the most slippery aspects of any society—'The unwritten norm of a civilization resembles a melody more than what modern physicists and jurists call a law,' as a modern commentator on Japan observes—and it is very difficult to deduce what else Roman aristocrats would have approved of and what they would have found uncouth.[42] Suffice it to say that it would have been instantly obvious to them.[43] And an aristocrat could go through life constantly checking his behaviour by studying the faces of his peers: 'from a glance of the eyes, a raising or lowering of the brows, a groan, a laugh', he could regulate his conduct. His competitors were always watching him.[44]

Indeed, the greater a man's honour, the higher his position in society, the more people watched him, and the more he felt his actions hemmed in by his own rank. It was signally disgraceful—especially destructive of honour—for a *nobilis*, one of the highest born in Roman society, to waste his fortune, or to be morally vicious, because of the 'bright light' his ancestry held over him.[45] When a senatorial deputation sent to Germanicus fell among mutinous soldiers in the German camp the other envoys fled; but Munatius Plancus did not, for his greater dignity forbade such a course, and thus he was nearly killed.[46] To remind a man of the glory of his family and his need to act in accord with it was a usual way of pressing him on to action; the unwelcome requests of a distinguished man could be beaten off by sharply pointing out that they did not accord with his dignity.[47]

The opinion-community of the aristocracy granted honour to men for a great many attributes and accomplishments, military and civil, as well

---

[40] Pompey, Plut. *Praec. Ger. Reip.* 800e; Crassus, ibid. 811a.

[41] Amm. Marc. 28. 4. 4.

[42] Singer (1973), 92; see similar remarks in Cic. *Off.* 1. 145. There are even disapproved ways of killing one's self, Tac. *Ann.* 6. 49; *Hist.* 1. 72.

[43] See Petr. *Sat.* and Apul. *Apol.* (esp. 82) for men who are sneered at for failing to conduct themselves properly despite their pretensions.

[44] Glance, Cic. *Off.* 1. 146; cf. D. Chr. 66. 13.

[45] Tac. *Ann.* 6. 7; Sall. *Jug.* 85. 23; Juv. 2. 143–8; 8 *passim*; quoted, 8. 139. Cf. Cic. *Off.* 2. 44.

[46] Tac. *Ann.* 1. 39, *dignitas*; and see also Cic. *ad Att.* 16. 3. 4. Cf. Tac. *Hist.* 2. 32; Aul. Gel. 1. 6. 5; Cass. *Var.* 6. 11. 1.

[47] Act according to dignity, Tac. *Hist.* 3. 66; unwelcome requests, Plut. *de Vit. Pud.* 535b; and cf. Cic. *de Or.* 2. 286; *Mur.* 13.

as for popularity among the lower orders and for political and religious—
in late antiquity, including ecclesiastical—offices.[48] A brilliant speech in
court or in declamation, a profound knowledge of the Roman law, the
destruction of a political enemy, paying off a friend's debt, the proper
education of a young wife, or the possession of a remarkable ass: anything
praised by aristocrats conferred glory.[49] Consider Sallust's famous equa-
tion of the honour of Julius Caesar and Cato the Younger:

In greatness of spirit they were equal, and in glory as well (although in other
things they differed). Caesar was deemed great because of the favours he did and
his generosity, Cato because of the moral stringency of his life. The former
became brilliant through his kindness and clemency; his austerity gave the latter
dignity. Caesar gained glory by giving, assisting, and pardoning, Cato by never
giving a bribe. The one was a refuge for the wretched, the other a bane to the
wicked. The one was praised for his adaptability, the other for his firmness.
Caesar . . . longed for a new war, a great command, an army, where his virtue
could shine; Cato's devotion was to moderation, propriety, and especially to austerity. He competed not in riches with the rich nor in faction with the factious,
but with the hardworking in zeal, with the unpretentious in modesty, with the
guiltless in self-denial: he preferred to be good, rather than to seem it. Thus, the
less he sought glory, the more it panted after him.[50]

As the description of Cato indicates, moral excellence formed an important element of prestige. Thus Pliny observed that enforcement of the ban
on the taking of fees for legal work would result in 'less praise and
obscurer fame' for him, who had never taken them and who had derived

---

[48] Offices and performance in office (including military glory), see below, pp. 181–201;
ecclesiastical office, below, p. 95. Popularity among inferiors: Cic. *Off.* 2. 31; *Planc.* 21; an element in decline under the empire, according to Tac. *Ann.* 3. 55; but still there in Boeth.
Consol. 3. 2.

[49] Speeches: Pliny, *Ep.* 6. 29. 3; Philostr. *VS* 2. 8 (579); Cicero possesses a 'splendorem . . .
forensem', *ad Att.* 4. 1. 3; Sid. *Ep.* 8. 10. 3. Study of the law: Cic. *Off.* 2. 65; Tac. *Ann.* 3. 75; *Pan.
Lat.* 3(11). 20. 1; but see Cic. *Mur.* 25. Destruction of enemy, Epstein (1987), 22; debt, Philostr.
VS 2. 21 (603); education of wife, Pliny, *Ep.* 1. 16. 6; ass, Apul. *Met.* 10. 17.

[50] Quoted, Sall. *Cat.* 54, 'magnitudo animi par, item gloria, sed alia alii. Caesar beneficiis
ac munificentia magnus habebatur, integritate vitae Cato. Ille mansuetudine et misericor-
dia clarus factus, huic severitas dignitatem addiderat. Caesar dando, sublevando, ignos-
cundo, Cato nihil largiundo gloriam adeptus est. In altero miseris perfugium erat, in altero
malis pernicies. Illius facilitas, huius constantia laudabatur. . . . Caesar . . . sibi magnum
imperium, exercitum, bellum novom exoptabat, ubi virtus enitescere posset. At Catoni
studium modestiae, decoris, sed maxume severitatis erat. Non divitiis cum divite neque fac-
tione cum factioso, sed cum strenuo virtute, cum modesto pudore, cum innocente absti-
nentia certabat; esse quam videri bonus malebat; ita quo minus petebat gloriam, eo magis
illum sequebatur'. Cf. Tac. *Hist.* 2. 4–5; also for glory from giving, Mart. 12. 36; Juv. 5. 107–11.

social distinction from his moral restraint.[51] In neither Greek nor Latin are morality and prestige clearly distinct mental realms; if asked to put a name to their stratum of society, Greek aristocrats would probably call themselves 'the fair and good', Romans simply 'the good'.[52] It would be perverse to deny that ancient aristocrats felt the pangs of conscience, but the fact that moral reputation was numbered among the qualities for which aristocratic opinion conferred honour ensured that Graeco-Roman society was to a great degree a shame culture, that concern for reputation could be considered the main bulwark of morality, for 'to scorn fame is to scorn virtue'.[53] The ghastly thing about doing wrong was being found out: as Pliny said, 'How few have the same concern for honesty in secret as in public. Many stand in awe of bad reputation, few of conscience.'[54] The chief danger was that one would lose face. Of course fear of public shame was internalized to a large degree: shame assailed those even contemplating their undiscovered crimes. An ancient student of the habits of mind of his contemporaries does not see them paralysed by guilt, as a modern psychiatrist might, but instead diagnoses, and prescribes a course of treatment for, those afflicted with a surfeit of unreasonable shame.[55] Little surprise; in the Roman world one's moral reputation was an integral part of one's rank in society.

Of the moral virtues in which Greek aristocrats competed for honour, one, *sophrosyne*, the wisdom of self-restraint, deserves a closer look. Viewed comparatively, the remarkable quality of Graeco-Roman aristocratic honour under the empire is the rarity of personal violence over it: there was no day-to-day expectation of duels, vendettas, or blood-feuds,

---

[51] Pliny, *Ep.* 5. 13. 9, 'minor laus et obscurior fama'. The most useful source for the relations of morals and prestige is Val. Max. bks. 3–6 (with 2. 10. 8); also, for honour from good morals, Cic. *Planc.* 60; Sall. *Jug.* 1. 3; Plut. *Cato Min.* 1. 1, 16. 4. Dishonour from bad morals, Hor. *Sat.* 1. 2. 12, 57–61, 133; Juv. 8.

[52] Καλοὶ κἀγαθοί from καλός = beautiful, morally beautiful, honourable (LSJ) and ἀγαθός = good and well-born, gentle (LSJ). *Boni* from *bonus* = morally good and (in plural) men of substance and social standing (*OLD*), on which see Achard (1973); or they might call themselves *optimi*, 'the best'. Cf. *honestus* = title to respect, honour and moral rectitude, integrity (*OLD*).

[53] Quoted, Tac. *Ann.* 4. 38, 'contemptu famae contemni virtutes'; see also *Rhet. Her.* 4. 14; Sen. *Clem.* 1. 22. 1; Plut. *an Rect. Dict. Lat. Viv.* 1129a–b; *de Se Ips. cit. Invid. Laud.* 545e. But note Cairns's (1993: 27–47) reservations on the over-facile use of the shame culture/guilt culture dichotomy.

[54] Pliny, *Ep.* 3. 20. 8–9, 'eadem honestatis cura . . . multi famam, conscientiam pauci verentur'.

[55] Surfeit of shame, Plut. *de Vit. Pud. passim* and esp. 529a–e.

so often honour's terrible accompaniment.[56] It was not always thus, as the Homeric poems show; and nothing certain can be said about the reasons for the drift away from violence. But it is striking that the departure from violence over honour was accompanied by a shift in the meaning of *sophrosyne*. In Homer *sophrosyne* means 'shrewdness', but by classical times it had acquired a strong sense of 'self-control'.[57] Under the empire, *sophrosyne* was one of four cardinal virtues, and Greek aristocrats were trained in self-control almost from birth, tutored and tested in the impassive solemnity that was the badge of their rank.[58] Failure in self-control brought dishonour.[59] Under the empire, restraint was honourable and lashing out with a fist was shameful; thus the sense of honour and shame, which had once required violence, now perhaps contributed to preventing it. While Latin never found a fully adequate translation for *sophrosyne*, a life distinguished by the marmoreal quality of *gravitas*, which contributed to the honour of Roman aristocrats, hardly permitted brawling over slights.[60] It was among the inferior classes, deficient in self-control according to their betters, that insults led to blows.[61]

All qualities and accomplishments, estimable or disgraceful, were added together when honour was reckoned up and a final estimate was reached. 'He damaged his reputation under the emperor Nero,' said Pliny of the poet Silius Italicus, 'for it was believed he accused people willingly, but he conducted his friendship with Vitellius wisely and tactfully, brought back glory from his proconsulate of Asia, and removed the stain on his honour, which his previous activity had inflicted, by praiseworthy leisure'—here the rattle and jingle of the aristocratic honour cash-registers can be heard. It seems odd today that a verdict could be reached by adding and subtracting dissimilar activities. But for Romans, honour, although it arose from the recognition of various qualities, was a unitary attribute: Silius Italicus' poetry (his 'praiseworthy leisure') actually wiped

---

[56] Violence over honour usual, Pitt-Rivers (1966), 29; and not totally unknown in imperial Rome, see Cantarella (1991: 230–3) on the Augustan adultery law, which countenanced it under limited circumstances. Note also the violence—even lethal violence—to insolent social inferiors by great men's retainers, Aul. Gel. 10. 3. 5; Philostr. *VS* 2. 10 (587–8); but violence over honour was rare between aristocrats, except in the exceptional context of civil war, see p. 50 below.

[57] *Sophrosyne* and its evolution, North (1966).

[58] Brown (1988), 12; Gleason (1995), 71; cf. Plut. *de Lib. Educ.* 8c, 10b–e.

[59] See esp. Philostr. *VS* 2. 1 (556–7), the excessive grief of Herodes Atticus.

[60] Roman translations of *sophrosyne*, North (1966), 258–311. *Gravitas*, Hellegouarc'h (1963), 280; honourable, Cic. *Rosc. Com.* 7; Vel. Pat. 2. 86. 2; Pliny, *Paneg.* 46. 5.

[61] Sen. *Clem.* 1. 7. 3–4; but not, it seems, to a full-fledged culture of vendetta, which would surely be remarked upon even in our class-bound sources.

out the disgrace he incurred through his delation under Nero. The primary identification of an ancient aristocrat was *qua* aristocrat, not as—say—a lawyer or a littérateur (or indeed, later, as a bishop). One's *gloria* as a poet or soldier or son was part and parcel of one's general prestige in aristocratic eyes, and would be estimated as such by anyone who himself had a claim to be an aristocrat.[62]

Of course no two aristocrats, considering another man's honour, would necessarily arrive at exactly the same total. Men in public life inspired strong emotions: one wonders how many of their contemporaries would have accepted Sallust's neat equivalence between the honour of Cato and Caesar. Martial's high estimate of Silius Italicus is less reserved than Pliny's; it might well have been even if the magnificent Silius had not been in a position to do things for Martial.[63] Moreover, not all aristocrats everywhere in the Roman world—from Antioch to Gades—granted the same degree of honour to the same qualities and achievements. Quintilian reminds the panegyrist to adapt his praise to the character of his audience: don't laud a man's frugality at old Sybaris or his luxurious life at old Rome.[64] Some things were more valued in one place than another. Aristocrats of the Greek East could gain honour in athletic competition; adult Romans of rank, only disgrace.[65] Just as American signs of status—uncomfortable, smelly sailing shoes worn without socks—are hilarious to the English, so the slippers of office of a gymnasiarch of Alexandria might have caused the upturning of noses at Rome. But a man far from home ensured that he was properly received by providing himself with letters of introduction which laid out his claims to honour in terms comprehensible to the recipients, a genre of letters of which many survive. The aristocracy of the whole empire was not a single community of honour, but many overlapping communities as prepared to accept each others' standards of honour as they were, by and large, prepared to accept other's gods. A Roman aristocracy whose members had long held out against becoming doctors themselves was prepared to receive Galen with the honour that doctors received in the Greek East, where medicine was an honourable practice. Standards of what was honoured might vary, but the fundamental structure—the

---

[62] Quoted, Pliny, *Ep.* 3. 7. 3, 'laeserat famam suam . . . sed . . . ex proconsulatu Asiae gloriam reportaverat, maculam veteris industriae laudabili otio abluerat'. Cf. Tac. *Ann.* 3. 75, 4. 44, 14. 19; Plut. *Galba* 3. 1–2; *HA Max. et Balb.* 2. 7. For primary identification *qua* aristocrats, see Veyne (1990), 46–9. Bishops, see pp. 94–5 below.

[63] Mart. 7. 63, 8. 66.   [64] Quint. *Inst.* 3. 7. 23–4.

[65] On the aristocratic origins of Greek athletes under the empire, Robert (1934), 54–61; Pleket (1974), 72–9. Roman attitude, Tac. *Ann.* 14. 20.

understanding that honour was the appropriate response to esteemed qualities—was largely the same.[66]

The tolerance of others' standards was sharply bounded, and scarcely extended beyond the dominant cultures of Greek- and Latin-speakers. As powerful or honourable as he might be at home, an unhellenized Jewish notable or unromanized Celtic chief was excluded, *déclassé* by virtue of his non-participation in the ruling civilizations, a cultural, religious, or linguistic Trimalchio. The ever-shrinking class of grandees who lived in the empire but did not participate in Greek or Latin culture formed quite separate communities of honour, or perhaps had distinctive value systems where honour was not as central. But within the world of the Roman and Romanized, the Hellenic and the Hellenized, standards of honour converged over time; the long centuries of empire were a quiet solvent of aristocratic particularism. Responsible in part was the monolithic quality of ancient rhetorical education, which tended to ensure that all boys of upper-class upbringing commanded extremely similar cultural material over many miles and centuries.[67] The disparity of outlook we see best was that between Greek East and Latin West, but even here attitudes had converged to a great degree by Augustus' day, and continued to do so through the empire. A proper smattering of literature had certainly been no essential part of the Roman aristocratic persona in the second century BC. It became so as part of that great process of cultural adaption we call Hellenization. The size of the crowd at a great man's levee, his *salutatio*, so rigorously scrutinized at Rome as a sign of honour and influence, was not so valued in Greek-speaking lands; indeed, large retinues of slaves, clients, and hangers-on, so vital to one's estimation in Rome, could offend against propriety in the early imperial East. But by the early second century AD some Greeks had adopted retinues, and by the fourth century no man of position could bear to be seen on the streets of Antioch without at least a score of satellites.[68] By the mid-second century a variety of Latin descriptive terms had begun to harden into titles of honour, such as *vir clarissimus*, 'most glorious man', for senators, *vir egre-*

---

[66] Slippers, Musurillo (1954), 11. 64–5, an anti-imperial text, where the strangeness to Romans of his outfit is emphasized. For the reception of a letter emphasizing a traveller's status, Apul. *Met.* 1. 22. Roman reluctance to practise medicine, Pliny, *NH* 29. 17; Galen, Bowersock (1969), 59–69.

[67] Education, Marrou (1982 (1948)), 242–98; Kaster (1988), 11–96; producing minds like that of Aulus Gellius, see Holford-Strevens (1989).

[68] *Salutatio*, Tac. *Hist.* 2. 92; Dio 58. 5; retinue embarrassing, Plut. *Quaest. Conviv.* 615d; Lucian, *Nigr.* 13. Early 2nd cent., Philostr. *VS* 1. 25 (532); cf. *VS* 2. 10 (587); Antioch, Lib. *Or.* 33. 12.

grius, 'excellent man', for equestrians. The Greeks drafted words of their own into service as translations of these, using them initially with infuriating imprecision, but with greater accuracy as time went on: standards of honour were converging and Easterners were learning to appreciate fine Roman distinctions.[69] Finally, by the fourth century, in a synagogue at Tiberias in Galilee, one can read of a benefactor glorying (in Greek) in his membership of the household of 'most glorious' Jewish patriarchs.[70]

Although honour was a personal quality, its aura extended over household and connections by blood and marriage: a man's family was part and parcel of his social persona.[71] Its members' conduct reflected on him, his on them: 'if my son is taken in adultery, I blush.'[72] Thus Cicero was desperately concerned about his brother's performance as governor of Asia, for it impinged directly upon his own reputation, and he urged his brother to keep watch on his household as well, lest the misdeeds of its members bring the governor into disrepute.[73] Having refused to let Pompey marry a kinswoman of his, Cato was pleased to be free of the disgrace which would have seeped across the bonds of marriage when Pompey practised outrageous bribery in the consular elections of 61 BC.[74]

Women shared in the honour of their male relations by blood, and their male relations shared in theirs. Thus Cicero refers to

Caecilia . . . a lady of the greatest distinction, who, although she has a brilliant father, illustrious uncles, and a most distinguished brother, nevertheless, so remarkable is her virtue that, as much honour as she draws from their dignity, she, woman though she is, in turn confers upon them no less distinction from the praise bestowed upon her.[75]

---

[69] For the Latin titles, Ch. 4 n. 46. Greek usage, Stein (1912); Arjava (1991).

[70] Lifshitz (1973: 51), θρεπτὸς τῶν λαμπροτάτων πατριαρχηῶν; λαμπρότατος being the Greek translation of *clarissimus*. By 404 patriarchs were *viri spectabiles*, a higher rank, *CTh* 16. 8. 15.

[71] Saller (1994), 93–4. The reach of honour's nimbus is reflected in that fact that legally, *iniuria*, an actionable insult, extends 'in his . . . qui vel potestate nostrae vel affectui subiecti sint', *Dig.* 47. 10. 1. 3 (Ulpian).

[72] Quoted, Sen. *Ben.* 5. 19. 5; cf. Tac. *Ann.* 16. 17; Pliny, *Ep.* 5. 11; Plut. *Cato Min.* 39. 4; D. Chr. 44. 3; Fronto *ad Am.* 2. 7. 13 (van den Hout); *IGR* iii. 173. Cf. modern Greek shepherds, J. Campbell (1964), 40.

[73] Cic. *ad Q. Fr.* 1. 1. 43–4; household, 1. 1. 12–13, 17.　　[74] Plut. *Cato Min.* 30. 5.

[75] Cic. *Rosc. Am.* 147, 'spectatissima femina, quae cum patrem clarissimum, amplissimos patruos, ornatissimum fratrem haberet, tamen, cum esset mulier, virtute perfecit, ut, quanto honore ipsa ex illorum dignitate adficeretur, non minora illis ornamenta ex sua laude redderet'. And see esp. van Bremen (1996: 82–113) on the family context of female *philotimia* in Asia Minor.

Wives shared in the prestige of their husbands, husbands in the prestige of their wives.[76] The prestige of high birth—or the disgrace of low—came from the maternal line as well as the paternal.[77] Women could be participants in the rivalry for honour, and were well positioned to employ the patterns of influence dependent on honour, although the qualities perceived as honourable in women were different:

> Let her be beautiful, becoming, rich, and fertile;
> let her arrange her ancient ancestors about her porticoes;
> more chaste let her be than the Sabine woman
> with streaming hair, war's interrupter.[78]

Like men, women derived distinction from high birth and wealth, and, although they could not participate fully in political life or go to war themselves, they shared in the glory of their male relatives, for they 'number triumphs in their dowry'.[79] The prestige of high morals was available to them, as was the obloquy of low. Their moral standards were, however, different from those of men: important were chastity, faithfulness to the husband, care for the family and house.[80] Honour was conferred also by admirable actions, like participating in the prosecution of the man who had destroyed one's late husband, but was lost by base ones, like marrying a rich old man.[81]

A natural consequence of the ascription of honour by the aristocratic community, of aristocrats regulating their conduct by close attention to the opinion of those around them, was the ostentatious imitation of celebrated men. Since, as Cato the Censor is reported to have said to the Roman people, 'Your young men learn and are zealous for such things as gain your praise,' it made sense to act like, and be seen to act like, those

---

[76] Wives share in husbands' prestige, Apul. *Met.* 2. 3; Herod. 4. 2. 3; *HA Aelius* 5. 11; husbands in wives', Tac. *Ann.* 4. 39–40; *Agric.* 6; Plut. *Galba* 19. 2; Sid. *Ep.* 2. 8. 3; on both, van Bremen (1996), 114–41. The independence of Roman women's honour, and that men and women reflect honour on each other mutually, confounds the anthropologist's expectation, e.g. Gilmore (1987*b*: 90), of a strict one-way dependence of the honour of men upon the chastity of their women. But these are aristocratic women, and their honour may be different from that of their inferiors, Pitt-Rivers (1966: 62–73).

[77] Maternal line, Apul. *Met.* 1. 2; Suet. *Otho* 1. 2.

[78] Juv. 6. 162–4. Rivalry, Herod. 1. 8. 4; *IGR* iii. 116, φιλότιμον.

[79] Triumphs, Juv. 6. 168. Conspectus of the elements of women's honour, *ILS* 1259; Tac. *Ann.* 13. 45; Eus. *Hist. Eccl.* 8. 14. 15. Birth, Suet. *Titus* 4. 2; and see esp. *IGR* iii. 500, the vast genealogical inscription of Licinnia Flavilla. Proper retinue and clothes necessary, Pliny, *Ep.* 6. 32; cf. Apul. *Met.* 2. 2.

[80] Honourable female virtues, Robert (1965), 34–42; Sid. *Ep.* 2. 8. 3. Obloquy, Cic. *Rep.* 4. 6; Apul. *Met.* 9. 26.

[81] Prosecution, Pliny, *Ep.* 9. 13. 5; cf. 3. 16, 6. 24; *ILS* 8393 with Wistrand (1976). Old man, Pliny, *Ep.* 8. 18. 8–9.

whose behaviour had been praised in the past.[82] A young man would thus not only ensure that his conduct would be approved, but the imitation would be noticed, and he would be perceived to possess the prestigious qualities of the model. Thus by always being seen at 'the house of Publius Mucius, Publius Rutilius gained a reputation for incorruptibility and learning in the law', both honourable qualities.[83] Particularly approved was imitation of one's own ancestors: the antique inflexibility of a Cato the Younger—so vexing to his would-be political allies, but so honourable—was modelled upon that of his great-grandfather, Cato the Censor.[84] A contemporary, Cicero, saw in this urge-to-imitate one of the strongest forces controlling men's conduct in society. 'A few men—a handful—great in honour and glory can either corrupt or correct the morals of the city.'[85]

Judgement by Honour and Dishonour

Emphasis on Graeco-Roman honour as a quality conferred on an individual by the aristocratic community as a whole tends to conceal its physical realness, its visible quality to the Roman mind. When the great Gaius Marius was at the nadir of his fortunes, a slave was sent to murder him, but dropped his sword and fled—'blinded by the prestige of the man,' as Valerius Maximus has it.[86] Cicero also imagined prestige visibly to glow, to shine, to blind. He castigates the wretched Vatinius for having tried to destroy Lucius Domitius Ahenobarbus, 'whose dignity and splendour, I think, blinded your eyes'.[87] And one need not accept that these great men actually glowed in the dark to appreciate the consequences of this metaphor for describing honour: Roman honour was sharply reified. More than merely the insubstantial sum of public perception, honour was perceived as something with real existence. It could be conceived as the possession of—or adhering to, or essential to—an individual, much as we conceive merit as a quality that someone 'has', although upon reflection we realize that merit is no more than an assumption about other people's opinions. Moreover, unlike merit, honour was a

[82] Plut. *Cato Mai.* 8. 4.

[83] Quoted, Cic. *Off.* 2. 47. Imitation of men of prestige, urged, discussed, Cic. *Off.* 2. 46; *Sest.* 102; Plut. *Praec. Ger. Reip.* 805f–806a; Sid. *Ep.* 5. 11. 3. In practice, Plut. *Cato Mai.* 3. 4; Pliny, *Ep.* 6. 11, 7. 20, 8. 23. 2–3.

[84] Ancestors, Cic. *Mur.* 66; *Off.* 1. 78, 116; Tac. *Ann.* 14. 52; Pliny, *Ep.* 8. 13; how inculcated, ibid. 3. 3.

[85] Cic. *Leg.* 3. 30–2, quoted 3. 32, 'honore et gloria amplificati'.

[86] Val. Max. 2. 10. 6, *maiestas, claritas.*

[87] Cic *Vat.* 25, *dignitas, splendor*; cf. Sid. *Ep.* 1. 7. 4.

possession which its possessor could grant to another, although not losing his own thereby.

For while ancient authors describe honour being granted by the community of those with honour, they admit that the court of honour was neither impartial nor omniscient; its members were unbound by the juryman's oath, often ignorant, and apt to disregard witnesses and evidence.[88] In practice, therefore, honour came to exist also through one's being 'honoured'—publicly praised—by individuals who possessed it. To be praised by any given aristocrat added to one's own prestige in proportion to that aristocrat's prestige: 'My testimony can make no addition to your honour. For the old saying runs "to be praised by a praiséd man", and my humbleness cannot much help the brilliance of your reputation.' The author of these words, Symmachus, one of the most distinguished men of the fourth century, was being over-modest, but the principle is plain.[89] Such a remark only makes sense if Roman honour was not merely a quality attributed by the community, like fame, but could be attributed by one individual to another, and that attribution accepted by the community. When one man honoured another in the Roman world, he granted him a quantum of honour, which, provided that the bestower was sufficiently distinguished himself, the aristocratic community at large then accepted that the recipient possessed; a man's ability to mobilize aristocratic opinion in favour of another man was proportional to his own honour.

The practical consequence of this was that in the Roman world the good opinion of distinguished men was hoarded, as if stored up in coffers, in the form of laudatory letters. A letter of recommendation from Cicero conferred a distinction (*ornamentum*) on its recipient—it puffed him up, added to his honour.[90] A certain high military officer in the fourth century thought nothing of being asked for a letter by a lower official to increase the latter's distinction: in this case he should have thought again, for his flattering sentiments were erased and treasonable ones

---

[88] Court, n. 27 above.

[89] Sym. *Ep.* 9. 110, 'nihil tibi ex meo testimonio honoris accedere. Nam etsi laudari ab laudato viro vetus dictum est, nostri tamen mediocritas non multam famae tuae claritudinem iuvat'. See also Cic. *ad Fam.* 15. 4. 1, 11; 15. 6. 1; Fronto, *ad Am.* 1. 6 (van den Hout); Apul. *Flor.* 16; *Pan. Lat.* 3(11). 2. 5. Of course the views of great aristocrats on all subjects are widely known, Cic. *Rosc. Am.* 2–3; Sen. *Contr.* 5. 2.

[90] *Ornamentum* from letter: Cic. *ad Fam.* 13. 36, 49; see also Basil, *Ep.* 153; Lib. *Ep.* 1036. 3 with Liebeschuetz (1972), 196; Aug. *Ep.* 230; Sid. *Ep.* 9. 2. 1. There are Victorian parallels, Mayhew (1987 (1882)), 357–8.

inserted over his signature.[91] Letters from the exceedingly prestigious (emperors, consuls, governors, and the like) were collected, shown around, published, and even inscribed on yard after yard of stone. A letter in the writer's own hand (a great man would usually dictate) was even more honorific. The author of a letter need not be still alive: that Domitian once thought well of you was enough.[92]

Not only letters were valuable: a great man's laudatory remarks—or speeches—in public, his greetings on the street, prompt admission at his levee, his kisses, all such things were honours, closely watched by contemporaries, and added to the recipients' honour.[93] His visit bestowed prestige upon one, as did his invitations to visit and his presents.[94] To be known to be such a man's intimate, that was indeed worth boasting about, as it conferred an *ornamentum*, a quantum of honour, upon one, as did receiving favours from him, the tokens of his esteem. Favours and honours mingle and cling in the ancient mind: even the most ordinary acts of men towards one another might not be wholly devoid of honorific quality.[95] Above all, there were grandees' dinner parties, for here a compliment could be paid not only by invitation, but also by where a guest was seated (each place on the couches having a ranking value in relation to the others), what food and drink was given him, and the utensils and

---

[91] Amm. Marc. 15. 5. 3–4, 'commendaticias ab eo petierat litteras ad amicos, ut quasi familiaris eiusdem esset notissimus'.

[92] Collections of testimonials, D. Chr. 77/78. 26; Pliny, *Ep.* 10. 58 (Domitian); Basil, *Ep.* 112; *IGR* iv. 1756; and esp. *TAM* ii. 905. For letters of praise from emperors, see Ch. 3 nn. 128, 214; from Roman officials, Ch. 4 nn. 221, 235. Libanius publicizing others' letters to him, *Ep.* 1004; others his to them, Lib. *Ep.* 476–7; and see Julian, *Ep.* 40 (Bidez) for proudly showing around letters from emperors. Writers expect their letters to be shown around, Cic. *ad Fam.* 15. 21. 4; *ad Att.* 8. 9. 1–2; Liebeschuetz (1972), 22. Handwriting, Ambr. *Ep.* 1. 5, 47. 3.

[93] Remarks, Pliny, *Ep.* 4. 17. 7–9; speeches, Cic. *ad Fam.* 15. 4. 11–12; *ad Att.* 1. 16. 5; Pernot (1993), ii. 663; Aristid. 30 (Behr) is an example of such a speech, and rhetorical works describe how such speeches (as well as speeches of insult) should be given, Pernot (1993), i. 134–78, 481–90. Greeting, D. Chr. 51. 9; admission at levee, *salutatio*, Sen. *Ben.* 6. 33–4; Epict. *Ench.* 25. 1. Kissing, Lucian, *Nigr.* 21, and see MacMullen (1988), 239 n. 12.

[94] Visit, Apul. *Met.* 1. 23; Greg. Nys. *Ep.* 9. 3. Invitation, Plut. *Cato Min.* 3. 2. Presents, Fronto, *Add. Ep.* 5. 4 (van den Hout).

[95] Known intimacy, Cic. *ad Fam.* 3. 10. 9; *Rosc. Am.* 15–16; *Balb.* 63, 65; Pliny, *Ep.* 6. 18; Apul. *Flor.* 16. Favours, Cic. *ad Fam.* 13. 25; Basil, *Ep.* 112; and see Liebeschuetz (1972), 192, 196. Favours and honours indistinguishable, D. Chr. 31. 36–7 *et passim*; Herod. 2. 3. 6–7; Dio 59. 23. 2–4; Greg. Naz. *Ep.* 208. 5. Cf. van Wees (1992: 71): 'in Homeric society almost anything that involves any kind of deference to anyone's wishes or interests, can be described in terms of *honour* acknowledged and conferred, or denied and withheld.' For the mingling of favours and courtesies in 16th-cent. France, Neuschel (1989), 74–6.

plates he was given.[96] In general, as Cassius Dio put it, 'it is native to the human creature to rejoice in anything from a more powerful individual which makes them seem his equal in honour.'[97]

By the same token, the public blame of eminent aristocrats was alarming in the highest degree. Although Greek and Roman aristocrats did not fight duels or pursue blood-feuds, they acted vigorously to avenge insults and defend themselves against affront. The writings of the imperial jurists indicate a lively tradition of lawsuits over insult, and there was a special procedure, the *sponsio*, consecrated to legal battles over honour.[98] Sometimes things went beyond the courtroom: Sallust's Catiline insisted that it was exactly the protection of his honour against insult which moved him to plot against the Republic. Julius Caesar, in a work written in self-justification, represented the defence of his dignity as his chief reason for beginning a civil war. This was the most acceptable explanation he could give for his acts, and he could rely on the fact that powerful contemporary opinion would believe this motive to be perfectly reasonable.[99]

The great threat to honour was insult, *contumelia* or *iniuria* in Latin, *hybris* in Greek, which attacked it at two levels, reflecting the fundamental tension in honour's make-up.[100] First, honour could be damaged by the simple fact of the bad opinion of a prestigious aristocrat—justified or unjustified—whether publicized by nasty remarks, abusive speeches, the circulation of letters and pamphlets, or by acts of contempt: by failure to reply to a greeting in the street, by failure to admit a caller to the morning levee, by failure to invite a man to dinner, or if invited, by seating him in a low place.[101] Refusal to reply to a man's letters advertised to all the

---

[96] Juv. 5 *passim*; Arrian, *Epict.* 4. 6. 4; Epict. *Ench.* 24. 1, 25. 1; Plut. *Quaest. Conviv.* 619b–f; Pliny, *Ep.* 2. 6; Sid. *Ep.* 7. 12. 4; see MacMullen (1988), 64–5, and esp. D'Arms (1984), 334, 346–8 with refs.

[97] Dio 52. 32. 1, ἰσότιμοι. Cf. Basil, *Ep.* 104.

[98] Horror of bad opinion, Cic. *ad Q. Fr.* 1. 1. 43; Pliny, *Ep.* 2. 9. 1–2. Jurists, *Dig.* 47. 10 *passim*. *Sponsio*, Crook (1976).

[99] Catiline, Sall. *Cat.* 35. 3–4. Caesar, *BC* 1. 7 (cf. Pompey's plea at 1. 8), see Raaflaub (1974), 125–52; Wistrand (1978), 30–2; and Caesar could be considered easy-going, Suet. *Caes.* 73. Cicero disapproves of taking things to such extremes, *Off.* 1. 84, but note *Off.* 1.71: even those who do not seek glory are terrified of humiliation.

[100] *Hybris* in this sense, Fisher (1992).

[101] Insults of great men more damaging than those of others, Cic. 3*Phil.* 22; Dio 59. 26. 9. Conspectus of insults, *Dig.* 47. 10 (a rich catalogue); Sen. *Const.* 10. 2, *Ira* 2. 24. 1 (both in the context of a philosophical attack on sensitivity to such things, see pp. 90–92 below). And see esp. for remarks, Cic. *Balb.* 57–8; Sen. *Const.* 16. 4–17. 2; speeches, e.g. Cic. *Sul.* 2; *Sest.* 18–19; *Vat.*; *Pis.*; 13*Phil.*; and rhetoricians give instructions for speeches of insult, see n. 93 above; letters, Cic. *ad Att.* 11. 12. 1–2, 11. 13. 2; pamphlets, Cic. 2*Phil.* (see *ad Att.* 15. 13. 1); [Sall.] *in M. Tull. Cic.* Failure to reply in the street, Mart. 4. 83, 5 .51; to admit to *salutatio*, Mart. 9. 7; Lucian, *Nigr.* 22; to invite to dinner, Epict. *Ench.* 24. 1. Insulting seating at

world that you deemed him 'unworthy'.[102] Just as the good opinion of a conspicuous individual added to another's honour in proportion to the great man's prestige, so too did his bad opinion detract: his honour also allowed him to mobilize opinion against his enemies. Insult also damaged honour in a second way, by undermining an individual's claims to be perceived as honourable by the community, usually by representing him as morally vicious, or, say, as an insolvent debtor. Here the status or identity of the critic did not matter: the shouted abuse of the base, anonymous lampoons and verses, anonymous gossip, and anonymous slander all excited acute concern.[103] Insult also argued weakness, the inability to defend honour. Thus the need for punishment of the insolent, which exists 'when the dignity and distinction of him who has been transgressed against must be protected, lest the omission of punishment bring him into contempt, and lessen his honour'.[104] Who strikes you, or thrashes your slave, shows you up to the world as an impotent wretch, and to avoid contempt you must lash out, or the circling sharks will smell blood.[105] Not only violence but aggressive acts of almost any type could be construed as insults, even preventing a man from fishing or blowing smoke into his apartment.[106] Honour depends on having the power to defend it. It is important to be able to say, with Cicero, 'You will compel me to give thought to my own dignity: no one ever brought the tiniest suspicion on me whom I did not overturn and wreck,' and even more important, unlike Cicero, to be believed.[107]

dinner, Sen. *Ira* 3. 27. 4. Cf. honorific and dishonouring acts in Hobbes's world, *Leviathan* i. 10.

[102] Sid. *Ep.* 4. 5, 'indignum'.

[103] General horror of slander, e.g. Cic. *ad Fam.* 13. 24; Sen. *Ep.* 81. 27 (classed with exile, wounding, and poverty); Basil, *Ep.* 51. Debtor, *Dig.* 47. 10. 15. 32 (Ulpian), 47. 10. 19 (Gaius), 20 (Modestinus), and again 47. 10 *passim* for methods of insult. Emperors act to suppress lampoons, Tac. *Ann.* 1. 72; Suet. *Dom.* 8. 3; *CTh* 9. 34 *passim*. See esp. Sid. *Ep.* 1. 11, for the hysteria of Marcian's courtiers at the appearance of an anonymous lampoon; and cf. Pliny, *Ep.* 9. 27, where aristocrats try to convince an historian to suppress his work. Possibility of being humiliated by the poor, Artem. 2. 26; D. Chr. 66. 15, 18; Tac. *Ann.* 3. 36; *Dig.* 47. 10. 35 (Ulpian), 47. 10. 45 (Hermogenian). See Usener (1913 (1900)) on *flagitatio*.

[104] Aul. Gel. 7. 14. 3, 'cum dignitas auctoritasque eius in quem est peccatum tuenda est, ne praetermissa animadversio contemptum eius pariat et honorem levet'.

[105] Sen. *Ira* 2. 33. 1; *Clem.* 1. 7. 3 (of course the philosopher does not approve of such reactions); Dio 55. 19. 6. Violence as insult, *Dig.* 47. 10. 1, 47. 10. 7. 8 (Ulpian). For strong reaction to insult, refs. gathered by MacMullen (1986b), 515–18; cf. Pitt-Rivers (1966), 25–9.

[106] Fishing, *Dig.* 47. 10. 13. 7 (Ulpian); smoke, *Dig.* 47. 10. 44 (Javolenus). Cf. van Wees (1992: 107), 'the [Homeric] heroes . . . are strongly conscious of this symbolic dimension in all kinds of actions, including violent ones such as murder and theft. All such acts seem to them to imply a lack of respect for the victim.'

[107] Cic. *Sul.* 46, *dignitas*; on criticism of Cicero for failure to pursue his *inimicitiae*, Epstein (1987), 8.

Power into Honour

The perception that individuals could confer honour and dishonour on each other draws attention to the richly ambiguous relationship between honour and coercion in Graeco-Roman society. Some men—we think of emperors and their henchmen, but the same might be true of anyone with cash, contacts, or a burly retinue—could compel others not to slight them, and to go through the motions of honouring them. But surely, insincere honours, honours elicited by terror, don't actually add to their recipient's prestige? 'L'honneur que nous recevons de ceux qui nous craignent, ce n'est pas honneur'. So we naturally assume, and so ancient authors insist, adding that insincere honours, which are interpreted as a reproach and inspire mockery, actually destroy prestige, rather than contribute to it.[108] Yet it is perfectly clear that some men did coerce honour. Thus Cassius Dio on the tokens of respect shown to Sejanus, in command of the praetorian guard and for all practical purposes ruler at Rome while Tiberius sojourned on Capri: 'There was a crush and rivalry around his door, not only from fear of not being seen by him, but from fear of being among the last. For every word and sign was closely watched; especially those of the leading men.'[109] However insincere, coerced signs of honour at least offered a day-to-day gauge of the power to coerce, a quiet test of might politely concealed under an innocuous social function. As Cassius Dio goes on to say,

Concerning such men people are more punctilious than they are even towards emperors, so to speak, for the emperors, if anyone should offend them, deem it a virtue to excuse them, but to such men to pardon would seem to point up their weakness, but to assail and avenge is deemed proof of great power.[110]

To which one might compare the motive for the murder of a policeman in New York, 1989: 'Mr. Mason felt that the police—by putting him in jail and in other ways—had "disrespected" him in front of his workers. . . . Mr. Mason feared that loss of respect would lead to "loss of power" and, ultimately, to "loss of control" over his drug operation.'[111] To an evil potentate or a drug dealer, coerced honour, 'respect', is a minatory dis-

---

[108] Montaigne, *Essais* i. 42. 'Vera laus ornat, ita falsa castigat', Sid. *Ep.* 8. 10. 1, quoting Symmachus; Dio 52. 35. 2, 59. 25. 4.

[109] Dio 58. 5. 2; on the respect he was paid, also below, Ch. 3 n. 179.

[110] Dio 58. 5. 3; cf. Sen. *Clem.* 1. 21. 1. Thus Agrippina loses all her callers when she loses influence with Nero, Tac. *Ann.* 13. 19, 'nihil rerum mortalium tam instabile ac fluxum est quam fama potentiae non sua vi nixae'. Cf. *Hist.* 4. 11.

[111] Buder (1989).

play of power, scrutinized like the canary in the mine because if it dies, you die soon after.

But coerced honour is not merely a test, or a threatening parade, of strength. As much as Cassius Dio and other men of his sort hate the fact, it is real honour and it has standing in aristocratic society, as long as no one dares to laugh. It is possible for Tacitus to imagine a man like Vibius Crispus, 'whose money, power, and character ranked him among the splendid rather than the good'.[112] Why, Cicero asks, has Antony turned against the Republic? Not for any low motive, 'for I never saw anything sordid or base in you' (this is, clearly, the first *Philippic*), but for the highest, for honour. 'I fear that, ignorant of the true road to glory, you think it glorious to be more powerful alone than everybody else and to be feared by your fellow citizens.'[113] The secret is out: there is a low road to glory as well as a high one, as much as Cicero may splutter and deny it. Even Cassius Dio, in the same passage on Sejanus, must admit the force of coerced honours, although contrasting the quality of the distinction they create with the prestige that invests conventional aristocrats:

Those who are eminent from inherent prestige neither seek signs of approval from anyone, nor, should they be lacking, censure those who have failed to provide them, knowing full well that they are not being scorned. On the other hand, those whose grandeur is acquired seek such things very eagerly, as necessary to fill up their worthiness, and should they fail to get them, are as irritated as if they were being slandered, and as peeved as if they were being insulted.[114]

The honour of a man who has proper claims to honour, the man with 'inherent prestige', is strong and lasting. A truly great aristocrat 'is sprung from distinguished ancestors: whatever kind of a man he is himself, let him lurk under their shadow.'[115] He was largely armoured against the snubs of individual aristocrats if aristocratic opinion in general accepted his worth. But the inflated honour of Sejanus, by origin an equestrian, a 'small-town adulterer' as Tacitus sneeringly describes him, has less substance among the great of Rome. His honour is wobbly and insecure, and

---

[112] Tac. *Hist.* 2. 10, 'pecunia potentia ingenio inter claros magis quam inter bonos'.

[113] Cic. 1*Phil.* 33, 'vereor ne ignorans verum iter gloriae gloriosum putes plus te unum posse quam omnes et metui a civibus tuis'. On the motif of true and false glory in Cicero, Drexler (1962), 9–10 for refs.

[114] Dio 58. 5. 3, οἱ μὲν γὰρ οἰκείᾳ ἀξιώσει προύχοντες οὔτε τὰ δεξιώματα παρά τινων πάνυ ἀπαιτοῦσι, κἂν ἄρα καὶ ἐκλειφθῇ τι αὐτῶν, οὐκ ἐγκαλοῦσί σφισιν, ἅτε καὶ ἑαυτοῖς συνειδότες ὅτι μὴ καταφρονοῦνται· οἱ δὲ ἐπακτῷ καλλωπίσματι χρώμενοι πάντα ἰσχυρῶς τὰ τοιαῦτα, ὡς καὶ ἐς τὴν τοῦ ἀξιώματός σφων πλήρωσιν ἀναγκαῖα, ἐπιζητοῦσι, κἂν μὴ τύχωσιν αὐτῶν, ἄχθονταί τε ὡς διαβαλλόμενοι καὶ ὀργίζονται ὡς ὑβριζόμενοι.

[115] Sen. *Ben.* 4. 30. 4, 'egregiis maioribus ortus'.

he must use fear to maintain it by compelling constant individual signs of honour. If the power to coerce vanishes, so does the honour.[116] But it *is* honour: you can produce honour with fear.[117] This is possible because honour is a public thing; it is not a consequence of opinion merely, but of opinion publicly expressed. Men's secret views, however unfavourable, do not enter into the calculation of honour; and fear, greed, or toadying can make men express opinions they do not feel. Insincere honours are said to inspire mockery, but mockery too is a public thing, and it will not occur if it is death to laugh. Peaceable aristocrats naturally loathed such methods, but their own abandonment of violence over honour disarmed them against those who were prepared to threaten them with the weapons they had long before laid aside.[118] When we speak of men of gigantic power in society, it must be accepted that fear creates a great proportion of the honour they enjoy.

Yet it should be emphasized that although honour could be coerced, it was never merely a consequence, manifestation, or ratification of political power or wealth. Honour always remained conceptually quite distinct. Indeed, honour would be meaningless if this were not so: no one would want it any more. The possibility of the coercion of honour exists because it is possible to hijack a social function, honouring, which derives its legitimacy from other sources. The separateness of honour is emphasized by the fact that it was possible to have great power in the political realm without proportionate honour—Tacitus remarks on great incongruities in his obituaries of influential equestrians—and, then again, to be glorious in political eclipse and imperial displeasure, indeed, *because* of imperial displeasure:

Augustus accelerated Aetius Capito's consulship in order to set him ahead of Antistius Labeo, who was outstanding in the same [legal] studies as he, by the distinction of that magistracy. . . . But Labeo's inflexible independence rendered him more celebrated in reputation, even if Capito's obedience was more to the taste of princes. Labeo, stopping at the praetorship, won public commendation because of the insult inflicted upon him, Capito, who advanced to the consulship, won hatred through public ill will.[119]

---

[116] *Municipalis adulter*, Tac. *Ann.* 4. 3. Contrast the *gloria, vera, gravis,* and *solida*, which Cicero insists the young Octavian has, 5*Phil.* 50.

[117] Cf. van Wees (1992: 109–25, 153–6) on the coercion of signs of respect by Homeric heroes.

[118] Contrast the armed and armoured honour of 16th-cent. France, Neuschel (1989), 17–18.

[119] Equestrians, e.g. Tac. *Ann.* 3. 30, 'sine dignitate senatoria, multos triumphalium consulariumque potentia anteiit'. Cf. 14. 53. Quoted, Tac. *Ann.* 3. 75, 'dignatione eius

At the same time, as the case of Trimalchio shows, it was possible to have economic power without being honourable. And although loss of his fortune might inflict severe damage on an aristocrat's honour, it was possible to be thought poor and still be honourable, or so the senate under Tiberius believed, deeming Marcus Lepidus a man for whom 'nobility of birth borne without disgrace was to be deemed an honour, not an ignominy, given his ancestral poverty'.[120] Strength of other types could manifest itself as honour and potentially could create honour, but honour was something quite separate.[121]

HONOUR INTO INFLUENCE

Honour among aristocrats, once acquired, was not a passive possession, like an engraved watch or an honorary degree. Rather, those who had honour were able to exert power in society by virtue of the desire of others for it, and the concern of others not to lose it. The techniques they used, important both in society and for the working of government, will be examined next. Valerius Maximus' definition of the word *maiestas* is suggestive:

The *maiestas* of illustrious men is, as it were, a censorship held by private individuals: it is powerful at maintaining its own grandeur without a high tribunal, and without the help of assistants, it slides welcome and happily received into the souls of men, veiled in a cloak of admiration.[122]

The word *maiestas* can express a form of prestige with compulsive force.[123] By virtue of his honour, an illustrious man was capable of influencing the conduct of those around him. He could get his way by praising or blaming; the mere fact of his honour made others defer to him; by virtue of his honour he could get his way by participating, to his profit, in the exchange of reciprocal favours. The strength, social significance, and complex interplay of these methods is a function of the twofold composition of Graeco-Roman honour, of its being attributed both by the aristocratic community as a whole and by individual aristocrats.

magistratus anteiret. . . . Labeo incorrupta libertate et ob id fama celebratior . . . commendatio ex iniuria . . . odium ex invidia'. Cf. 4. 26, 6. 27.

[120] Loss, Tac. *Ann.* 6. 17, 'eversio rei familiaris dignitatem ac famam praeceps dabat'. Lepidus, Tac. *Ann.* 3. 32, 'nobilitatem sine probro actam honori quam ignominiae habendam'. See also 4. 44; Cic. *Quinct.* 49.

[121] Cf. Hatch (1989), who debunks crude materialist analyses of honour.

[122] Val. Max. 2. 10. pr., 'est et illa quasi privata censura, maiestas clarorum virorum . . . potens in sua amplitudine obtinenda'.

[123] Appendix, pp. 275–6.

Influence from Honour and Dishonour

Persons of great distinction could simply honour those whose conduct they liked, while dishonouring those whose conduct they disliked, and others' expectation of such treatment would drive them to obey these great men's wishes. Dio Chrysostom compared the life of one vulnerable to such treatment to that of a slave who must serve many masters, all of whom gave different commands.[124] Plutarch describes the plight of the tribune Octavius, who had vetoed Tiberius Gracchus' agrarian legislation in 133 BC. At Gracchus' behest the tribes of Roman citizens began to vote to strip him of his tribunate. When seventeen of the thirty-five tribes had voted, and the vote of one more would return him to private life, Tiberius begged him to yield. Octavius was moved and wept. 'But when he looked towards the men of wealth and property who were standing in a mass, his awe of them, I think, and his fear of ill repute among them, led him bravely to undergo every risk, and order Tiberius to do as he pleased.' The senate could get its way simply by glowering. The threat of the massed disapproval of the senators was overwhelming.[125] And the threatened criticism of a few—or one—was effective enough: 'Say two or three words and you've hurled him into misery and woe,' as Dio Chrysostom said. Atilius Crescens wanted a loan returned: 'You know the man's jokes,' wrote Pliny to the middleman whom he hoped would arrange it; 'make it your business that his humour does not become angry and vicious because of his injury.'[126] A sharp tongue artfully used, like that of the famous Severan wit Auspex, made its owner powerful in society, 'able to do favours for friends, and avenge himself upon foes'. At a lower level, a man could make a meagre living in second-century Athens by threatening to revile the famous rhetoricians who made their homes there unless an occasional jug of wine or garment or coin came his way.[127]

The flip side of calculated abuse was the strategic honouring of those who did, or could thus be induced to do, what a great man desired. Chiefly to gain Cicero's praise, Q. Fufidius, a Roman knight of Arpinum, ran an errand for their mutual home town—all the way to Cisalpine

---

[124] D. Chr. 66. 13.

[125] Plut. *Tib. Gracch.* 12. 3, αἰδεσθεὶς δοκεῖ καὶ φοβηθεὶς τὴν παρ' ἐκείνοις ἀδοξίαν. Cf. Plut. *Caes.* 10. 11.

[126] Woe, D. Chr. 66. 17. Crescens, Pliny, *Ep.* 6. 8. 8. Cf. Mart. 6. 64. 24–8.

[127] Auspex, Dio 76(77L). 9. 3. Abusing sophists at Athens, Philostr. *VS* 2. 10 (587). For insults getting things done, see also Caes. *BC* 1. 2; Cic. *ad Fam.* 12. 25a. 2; and esp. Lucian, *Nigr.* 13. A ghost driven off by insult is natural to the Graeco-Roman imagination, Philostr. *VA* 2. 4.

Gaul. Assist Bassus, wrote the famous sophist Libanius to a correspondent, and 'I will praise you, for you do everything in every way for praise; on this account your name will be glorious.' The eloquent and well-born bishop Gregory (for the Cappadocian Fathers were masters of this art) asks the influential pagan Themistius for a favour, as both his friend—and eulogist.[128] The Roman world preserves letters from important men which begin with high praise and end with a request. This was not simply arid rhetorical *captatio benevolentiae*: in a world where letters from such men were proudly shown around, the praise was payment in advance for the deed.[129]

Desirable conduct from others included honour, and a distinguished man might therefore honour another to induce the other to honour him, or to secure for him honour in the wider aristocratic community. Thus Cicero to an historian: 'The excellence of your writings, although I always expect much, is even better than my expectations,' and much in that vein. 'I am not afraid that I might seem to fish for your favour with this small screed of flattery'—but that was exactly his purpose, for he wanted the historian to abandon his current project and instead turn his pen to a grovellingly favourable account of Cicero's struggle against Catiline, and thus to augment Cicero's glory. 'And thus I openly beg you again and again that you praise my acts with even more enthusiasm than perhaps you feel: ignore the laws of history . . . and if bias in favour of me urges you strongly, scorn it not! Bestow upon our love more than truth allows.'[130] Letters from the magnificent bishops of late antiquity lauded the recipient's virtues and requested a reply. The fortunate recipient, it can be assumed, showed the letter around to his acquaintances and added it to his file because it increased his status in the world, and then wrote back in kind, to the benefit of the original writer.[131] This may seem curious, but since praising someone and thus increasing his honour cost none of one's own, a great man would carry on any number of mutually laudatory correspondences. Indeed, one of the chief purposes of friends was to praise.[132] Letters survive from antiquity which seem to have no

---

[128] Fufidius, Cic. *ad Fam.* 13. 12. 2. Bassus, Lib. *Ep.* 693. 5, τοὔνομα λαμπρόν. Themistius, Greg. Naz. *Ep.* 24. 6; cf. 83. See also Pliny, *Ep.* 5. 17; J. Chr. *Ep.* 50; in parody, Apul. *Met.* 6. 28–9, 7. 14–15. Letters of recommendation note a protégé's praise of addressee, Cic. *ad Fam.* 13. 24; Fronto, *ad Am.* 1. 6, 10, 26 (van den Hout).

[129] e.g. Greg. Naz. *Ep.* 103, 134; Basil, *Ep.* 74; Lib. *Ep.* 268.

[130] Cic. *ad Fam.* 5. 12. 1, 6, 3; cf. Pliny, *Ep.* 7. 33, 9. 8.

[131] Basil, *Ep.* 63, 163; Greg. Naz. *Ep.* 234; Aug. *Ep.* 229–31, 260–1; Sid. *Ep.* 3. 11.

[132] Friends, D. Chr. 3. 109; Philo, *Leg. Gaium* 272; Lib. *Ep.* 810; Theodoret, *Ep.* XXXI (Azéma).

content at all, except praise; but praise *is* content.[133] The letters formed part of a great network of men honouring one another—honouring one another to get things done, and to elicit honour in return.

An aristocrat was not free to exalt just anyone with his praises; nor could he lay about himself with insults and drive all before him. He who lauded the unworthy—the flatterer—or blamed the worthy—the slanderer—was a wretched and hated creature in aristocratic society. Plutarch expected these vices in the same person, and no wonder: they were symptoms of the same cancer, the failure to give to each his due. Aristocratic opinion demanded that the honour or dishonour bestowed upon a person be appropriate to his claims; that is, that the ascription of honour to a person by an individual should accord, at least roughly, with the ascription of honour to him by the aristocratic community. If there was no such accord, the honour of the one who praised or blamed inappropriately suffered.[134] This is one reason why the spectacle of coerced honour—whether bestowed upon monstrous emperors or their creatures: 'on such scum! on such filth!'—was so painful to an aristocratic Roman observer.[135] An aristocrat's ability to work his way by honour and dishonour was thus hedged around by a thorny aristocratic code, over whose bounds he crossed at his peril. And this rule of appropriateness, this law that each must be given his due, this deference, was no less vital than strategic praise and blame to the working of influence in the Roman world.

Deference

Status in the Roman world carried a great variety of privileges: public donations were regularly organized such that important townsmen, or members of a guild, received more money or oil or biscuits; the unimportant, less. The big man was punished less severely than the little for the same crime.[136] Where there were conflicting witnesses, the jurist told the judge to give greatest credence to prestige, and in Cicero's courtroom it was remarkable when the testimony of men of the greatest dignity was

---

[133] e.g. Basil, *Ep.* 64; Sid. *Ep.* 5. 11.

[134] The flatterer and slanderer, Plut. *quom. Ad. ab Am. Int.* 59d–60f, 66d, 67e–68b; *de se Ips. cit. Invid. Laud.* 547a; Amm. Marc. 28. 4. 12.

[135] Quoted, Pliny, *Ep.* 7. 29. 3, of the praetorian insignia conferred by the senate on Claudius' freedman Pallas; see also *Ep.* 8. 6. Severus' attitude was far better, Dio 76(77L). 6. 1–2.

[136] Donations, Mrozek (1987), 83–102. Punishments, see Garnsey (1970). In general, MacMullen (1974), 109–10, 118; (1988), 64–5.

disregarded.[137] To the most distinguished volunteer went the right to prosecute when there was more than one candidate for the job.[138] In sum, as Pliny expressed the norm to a governor, 'Conduct yourself so that you maintain a distinction between ranks and honours.'[139]

Alongside familiar social codes requiring deference to parents, husbands, and age, ancient aristocrats were especially bound by one requiring deference to honour. On the streets of Rome men uncovered their heads when a distinguished man passed. They greeted him first, dismounted at his approach, kissed his hand, or chest, or knee. They mentioned him with respect and praised him in speeches and writing, and offered him hospitality, since 'it is very appropriate that the houses of illustrious men lie open to illustrious guests'.[140] When Cato the Younger departed from the theatre to avoid seeing an actor undress on stage, such was his *maiestas* (in Valerius Maximus' view) that the rest of the audience followed him out.[141] Prestige elicited, indeed required, honour from those around it.[142]

The honorific implications of a great deal of conduct can only be understood when the relative distinction of the two parties, and thus their duty of deference towards one another, is known. For if a man did more than deference required, that could be an honour; less, an insult. Thus an act of deference appropriate to a superior performed for an inferior was honorific: when the great Sulla rose and uncovered his head for the young Pompey, this was meant and perceived as a tremendous hon-

---

[137] Credence to go to *existimatio* and *dignitas*, *Dig.* 22. 5. 3. 1 (Callistratus); 'dignitas et auctoritas', 22. 5. 3. 2 (Callistratus); cf. *CTh* 11. 39. 3 (334). Cicero, Cic. *Font.* 23–4; cf. Val. Max. 8. 5. 1–3; Dio 74(76L). 9. 5. On honour in the law I am indebted to E. A. Meyer.

[138] *Dig.* 48. 2. 16 (Ulpian), first of a list of criteria; cf. Cic. *Div. Caec.* 64.

[139] Pliny, *Ep.* 9. 5, 'discrimina ordinum dignitatumque custodias'. Cf. Cic. *Rep.* 1. 43; *Rhet. Her.* 3. 3; Theodoret, *Ep.* 91 (Azéma); Ch. 4 n. 158. It is remarkable when the ἔνδοξοι do not have precedence over the ἀδόξων, Philo, *Leg. Gaium* 13.

[140] Uncovering, Plut. *Quaest. Rom.* 266c, f. Greeting, Plut. *Pomp.* 23. 2; *quom. Ad. ab Am. Inter.* 62d; Mart. 3. 95. Dismounting, Apul. *Flor.* 21; Dio 45. 16. 2. Kisses, Lucian, *Nigr.* 21; Amm. Marc. 28. 4. 10. Mention respectfully, Cic. *Rosc. Am.* 15; *Rosc. Com.* 18; *Clu.* 118. Praise, Cic. *Rosc. Am.* 33. Hospitality, quoted, Cic. *Off.* 2. 64, 'valde decorum patere domus hominum illustrium hospitibus illustribus'; cf. 2 *Verr.* 4. 33. Also giving up one's seat at table, Plut. *quom. Ad. ab Am. Inter.* 58b; Sid. *Ep.* 7. 13. 4. Going to meet on the road, Cic. *ad Fam.* 3. 7. 4; standing behind, Sid. *Ep.* 1. 6. 4.

[141] Val. Max. 2. 10. 8, 'populus . . . confessus plus se maiestatis uni illi tribuere quam sibi universo vindicare'.

[142] Duty to honour prestige, Cic. *Inv.* 2. 166; Livy 24. 44. 10; Val. Max. 2. 10. 2; Sen. *Ep.* 102. 10; Jos. *AJ* 19. 52; Plut. *Cato Min.* 9. 5; Cyp. *Ep.* 76. 1 (*CSEL*); Sid. *Ep.* 7. 4. 1; and see Drexler (1988 (1961)), 62. Deference to parents and prestige can conflict, D. Chr. 49. 13.

our.[143] On the other hand, for Julius Caesar to refuse to rise at the approach of the massed senate and magistrates was to snub them, for his act implied superiority.[144] An inferior insulted a great Roman whose invitation to dinner he refused: 'Better to kill a man's brother than to refuse his invitation,' as Ammianus Marcellinus put it.[145] Relative position defined where one kissed the great man: if he offered hand or knee to one whose honour entitled him to kiss the lip, that was an insult, as was to offer only half the lip. Indeed, to avoid insulting people, a great man would necessarily submit to being kissed by many repulsive and diseased lips. Postumus thought he was honouring Martial highly by offering him his lips to kiss, but Martial preferred to kiss his hand, not liking where the lips had been.[146]

In addition to defining the degree of honour one man owed to another, the deference demanded by prestige also included obedience. Why did one man obey another? Among other reasons, 'on account of his being outstanding in prestige', said Cicero (or his ancient glossator).[147] Naturally, therefore, in obedience to the dignity of those who asked him, Cicero took up the defence of Sextus Roscius of Ameria. In obedience to their honour as *nobiles* it was expected that Cicero would admit Lentulus and Cethegus into his house; thereupon they would kill him at Catiline's orders.[148] When evil Romans tried to kidnap the daughter of Philodamus, 'by birth, office, wealth, and prestige easily the first of the citizens of Lampsacus', it seemed to Cicero that it was Philodamus' *dignitas*, and the greatness of the insult to it, that moved the citizens of the town to defend his house.[149]

---

[143] Sulla and Pompey, Plut. *Praec. Ger. Reip.* 806e; *Pomp.* 8. 3. Cf. Plut. *Cato Min.* 14. 1; *Brut.* 4. 3. Also honorific, a superior greeting first, Hor. *Ep.* 1. 7. 64–6; dismounting, Plut. *Pomp.* 8. 2; visiting inferior in his house, Lib. *Or.* 1. 166. See also Plut. *Pomp.* 19. 5; Pliny, *Ep.* 4. 17. 6; Amm. Marc. 14. 6. 2.

[144] Plut. *Caes.* 60. 4–5; cf. *HA Maxim.* 28. 1.

[145] Amm. Marc. 28. 4. 17; see also Hor. *Ep.* 1. 7. 62–4; Lib. *Or.* 1. 75.

[146] Offering unsatisfactory portions to kiss, *HA Maxim.* 28. 7; Amm. Marc. 28. 4. 10; Lucian, *Nigr.* 21; kissing with half the lip, Mart. 2. 10, 'basia dimidio . . . labro', 2. 22; compelled to accept kisses, Mart. 7. 95, 11. 98, 12. 59. Postumus, Mart. 2. 21; cf. Sen. *Ben.* 4. 30. 2. Conspectus of insults to an ex-consul: no one approaches him, salutes him, or does him any honour, Cic. *Pis.* 96, and see *Clu.* 41; see also MacMullen (1988: 69 n. 33) for the insult of ostentatiously ignoring those to whom acts of deference are due.

[147] Cic. *Off.* 2. 22, 'dignitatis praestantia'. Cicero's authorship of this passage has long been doubted, see Dyck (1980) for the controversy. Some think it Cicero's own addition, others an interpolation. No matter: it is in the text by the 4th cent., Dyck, p. 205.

[148] Cic. *Rosc. Am.* 4, *dignitas, auctoritas*; Catiline, App. *BC* 2. 3, ἀξίωσις; cf. Apul. *Met.* 8. 2.

[149] Cic. 2*Verr.* 1. 64, 'genere, honore, copiis, existimatione facile principem Lampsacenorum'; 67, 'Philodami dignitas tum iniuriae magnitudo movebat'. See also Cic. *Rosc. Am.* 119; *Pis.* 8; 2*Verr.* 2. 67; Herod. 4. 3. 3; [Victor], *Vir. Ill.* 72. 9; Sid. *Ep.* 7. 8. 2.

Why honour and obey prestige? At the conscious level, to refuse due deference was shameful; that is, the opinion-community of the aristocracy punished the perpetrator with dishonour. Plutarch warned against holding a dinner where places were not assigned: if everyone scrambled for seats, the eminent might fail to get places appropriate to their honour, they would be offended, and the host would seem gauche.[150] At the same time, zealous deference—say, putting up a statue of a distinguished man—was esteemed in aristocratic society: it was a public virtue that was perceived to confer honour upon its practitioner.[151] But deference was not, fundamentally, calculating. It was inculcated early, vigorously enforced in the household, and operated for the most part at an unconscious level. Bad conduct in the presence of prestige raised a blush, and, psychologically, it was much more difficult to refuse the requests of distinguished men than those of the obscure.[152] When Scipio Nasica, surrounded by senators, rushed from the senate building to kill Tiberius Gracchus, no one dared oppose them, as Plutarch has it, 'because of the worthiness of the men'. Instead, onlookers turned and fled, trampling one another. There is no calculation here, just ingrained—almost instinctive—action in the face of distinction.[153]

The concept of *auctoritas* lay at the heart of this pattern of influence. One meaning of the word was that aspect of honour which required deference in aristocratic society. And whether deference was conscious or unconscious, it is not hard to see how a distinguished man could use it to get others to do his bidding: when a freedman, terrified by his patron's anger, secured the intercession of the celebrated Pliny the Younger for his forgiveness, Pliny wrote to his patron, 'I fear if I were to join my pleas to his, that I should seem to compel you rather than ask you; I do so none the less.' The recipient of the letter did as he was bid, and received another note, in which he was praised for 'yielding to my *auctoritas*, or, if you prefer, indulging my prayers'. Although he is civil enough to suggest a more flattering colour for the patron's act, Pliny clearly had a right to give orders and be obeyed in a matter such as this. A man in Pliny's position was perfectly capable of being his own enforcer, by praising or

---

[150] Seating at dinner, Plut. *Quaest. Conviv.* 616b–c. Similarly, order of admission at *salutatio* should be by honour; Juvenal rails when money jumps the queue, 1. 99–111. Disgrace for failure of deference, Cic. *Mur.* 8; Plut. *Cato Min.* 39. 2; Dio 45. 16. 1–2 with Val. Max. 8. 5. 6.

[151] Statue, Pliny, *Ep.* 1. 17. Cf. Sen. *Ep.* 102. 10.

[152] Inculcation of deference in the young, Plut. *de Vit. Pud.* 529b–d; Pliny, *Ep.* 2. 18, 6. 6. 3. Blush, ibid. 3. 12, cf. Val. Max. 4. 5. 4. Refusing requests, Plut. *de Vit. Pud.* 534b–535b.

[153] Plut. *Tib. Gracch.* 19. 4, ἀξίωμα; see also Jos. *AJ* 19. 102.

blaming his target's conduct: 'Accept my applause and my thanks—but, in the future, be forgiving to your erring servants.'[154] Praise for the moment, but with a chilling undertone.

In practice, when the individuals involved were not well known to each other, the compulsive power of honour was invoked by directly signifying, often in letters of recommendation, the honour of the individual for whom a favour or honour was desired, and thus to whom, according to the code, other aristocrats ought to defer. Thus one's protégé was 'honoured most highly', or 'worthy of the greatest respect'.[155] Or the letter might indicate the importance of the recommendee by some recognizable standard (and thereby hint at the practical advantages of doing a favour for him): 'You will find him the chief man not only of his town, but almost of Achaea'; 'His father was a distinguished member of the order of knights'; 'I have found him worthy of his father and grandfather; his is a family as noble as it is possible to be'; or even, literary culture being so honourable, 'He is a learned and eloquent man'.[156] Since moral excellence was part of prestige, and indeed, so many Latin and Greek words used to describe people were freighted with status and honour connotations—'liberal', 'grave', 'fair'—letters of recommendation signalled the dignity of recommendees to their recipients with a sophistication and finesse that cannot always be grasped two millennia later, just as a foreigner cannot taste the difference between the varieties of Japanese rice.[157] But to read 'he got what we wanted on account of his own renown' is to know that honour got its way in practice.[158]

'I do not deny that sometimes I do favours even for the unworthy in order to honour others.'[159] If a man's own distinction failed, the renown

---

[154] On *auctoritas*, and related terms, see Appendix. Quoted, Pliny, *Ep.* 9. 21. 3, 9. 24. Cf. Cic. *ad Fam.* 13. 12.

[155] τιμιώτατος, Greg. Naz. *Ep.* 169. 2, 174. 4, 227. 1; J. Chr. *Ep.* 51; αἰδεσιμώτατος, Greg. Naz. *Ep.* 127. 2. See also Cic. *ad Q. Fr.* 2. 14. 3; Greg. Naz. 38. 3; Theodoret, *Ep.* 29–36 (Azéma); Sid. *Ep.* 6. 5.

[156] Chief man, Cic. *ad Fam.* 13. 78. 1. Knights, Pliny, *Ep.* 2. 13. 4, 'pater ei in equestri gradu clarus'. Worthy, Cic. *ad Fam.* 13. 34. Learned, Fronto, *ad Am.* 1. 10 (van den Hout). See also Cic. *ad Fam.* 13 *passim*; Pliny, *Ep.* 1. 14, 7. 22, 10. 4; Syn. *Ep.* 18 (Garzya); Sid. *Ep.* 2. 4. 1. Emphasis on literary culture, Fronto, *ad Am.* 1. 2, 3, 4 (van den Hout); Greg. Naz. *Ep.* 37. 2; Lib. *Ep. passim*. Cf. Victorian confidence tricksters, Mayhew (1987 (1882)), 347–9, 355.

[157] *Liberalis* = of or relating to free men, gentlemanly, noble, generous (*OLD*); *gravis* = stern, grave, respected, august (*OLD*); for καλός, 'fair', and other overlap of morality and honour, n. 52 above. For baffling indications of status, compare a contemporary UK author's reference to 'men . . . who look as if they might be accountants of the claret-buying variety' (Malcolm (1990)). This is obscure enough to a North American reader. Imagine how obscure it will be in two thousand years.

[158] Cic. *ad Fam.* 13. 19. 1, 'ipsius splendore'.

[159] Sen. *Ben.* 4. 30. 1, 'in honorem aliorum'; cf. 5. 19. 8.

of others to whom deference was due might succeed. Letters of recommendation certify that the recommendee is extremely close—a relative, a boyhood friend, a hereditary connection—to the recommender (or other superior individuals). Such claims wrap the recommendee in the glory of others and bolster his chances of getting the favour.[160] They also signal the network of persons who will be placed under an obligation if the favour is granted, alluding to another way honour exerted power in the Roman world.

Reciprocity

'Receive this most honoured and highly sought-after man, and do not hesitate to show him hospitality, thereby doing what is meet for you and what will obligate me to you.' Thus a sample letter of recommendation in an ancient pattern book of letters. 'Honoured' and 'highly sought-after' signal that deference is due the subject of the recommendation. 'Obligate me to you' introduces another aristocratic code, based on reciprocity.[161] If a man does a favour for you, you must do one for him in return. In a passage of lyric didacticism, Seneca envisions a universe of circulating favours, represented by the Graces, Χάριτες, the word in Greek usually used to translate *beneficia* (favours).

Why is the chorus [of the Graces], hand in hand, a ring turning on itself? Because the course of a favour passing from hand to hand returns none the less to the giver, and the fairness of the whole is lost, if it is anywhere interrupted, and it is most beautiful if it holds together and preserves the chain.[162]

Favours are here envisaged as passing from hand to hand in a continuous unbroken circle, ending up at their original bestower. A favour deserved a favour in return; the greater the favour, the greater the return. One did a favour, when asked, in order to be able to call upon the recipient when one wanted a favour from him.[163] The value of a favour was its value to the recipient: 'At as much as it is worth to escape the necessities of famine, so much shall we value your favour.'[164] This value was envisioned as

---

[160] Kim (1972), 48–51; Deniaux (1993), 135–61; and e.g. Fronto, *ad Am*. 1. 1, 3, 10 (van den Hout); Basil, *Ep*. 35. Boyhood friend, Cic. *ad Fam*. 13. 5; Pliny, *Ep*. 2. 13, 6. 8. Relatives/hereditary connection, Cic. *ad Fam*. 13. 15, 39; Basil, *Ep*. 31, 137; Lib. *Ep*. 275; foster-brother (σύντροφος), Basil, *Ep*. 36, 37.

[161] [Lib.] *Char. Epist*. 55, τιμιώτατον καὶ περισπούδαστον. Cf. Cicero's implicit definition of political power under the Roman Republic, *auctoritas et gratia*, Hellegouarc'h (1963), 307–8.

[162] Sen. *Ben*. 1. 3. 4.   [163] Saller (1982), 1–39, and esp. Cic. *Off*. 1. 47–9.

[164] Quoted, Basil, *Ep*. 86; see also Sen. *Ben*. 1. 5. 1 for the clearest statement of this common view. Sen. *Ep*. 81. 5–6, *Ben*. 1. 5. 2–7. 3, and Cic. *Off*. 1. 49 are polemical against this

quite finely measurable. Cicero urged his contemporaries to be 'good cal-culators of favours, to see by adding and subtracting... what we are owed by each and what we owe to each'. Accordingly, there was a technical, bookkeeping vocabulary in Latin, *officium*, *beneficium*, *meritum*, all words signifying 'favour' with various complex undertones.[165] A favour that one failed to reciprocate in life was expressed in money terms and paid off in one's will; or, failing that, the obligation was handed on to one's children. A very powerful man like Trajan, at the centre of a huge network of favours given and owed and who might therefore have trouble remembering what was owed him, totalled up the favours he had done in notebooks.[166]

This mental machinery made the principle of reciprocity a powerful tool for accomplishing one's will. It made it possible, for example, for favours to be exchanged between men who enjoyed no very intimate association, or indeed were on bad terms, by sending a letter listing favours already performed for the recipient by the sender, and demand-ing a favour in return, quid pro quo.[167] More commonly, however, a favour would be asked, and the asker's willingness to reciprocate sig-nalled: 'Just as you would eagerly embrace chances to oblige me, there is no one to whom I would rather be obligated.' Formulae of this type in let-ters of recommendation are the ubiquitous traces of the economy of favours at work; they are found in the Latin West and the Greek East from the first to the fifth century AD, and at every social level that has left records.[168]

Reciprocity operated between men, women, humans and the old gods, and man and the God of the Christians.[169] The recipient of a letter

system of valuation, insisting (*inter alia*) that the state of mind in which the favour is bestowed should be considered as well.

[165] Calculators, Cic. *Off.* 1. 59 (Sen. *Ben.* 1. 2. 2–3 is polemical against this). But the *bene-ficia* of the Christian God are so great that they cannot be calculated, Musurillo (1972), 14. 13. For technical vocabulary, Hellegouarc'h (1963), 152–70; Saller (1982), 7–22.

[166] Wills, A. Wallace-Hadrill (1981*b*), 66–70; Saller (1982), 71–3, 124; and esp. Mart. 6. 63. For favour-debts handed down generations, e.g. Sen. *Ben.* 4. 30. 2–3; D. Chr. 31. 62; Syn. *Ep.* 20. Trajan, *ILS* 1792; see MacMullen (1986*b*), 521.

[167] List of favours, Cic. *ad Fam.* 13. 77. Reciprocity among men on bad terms, ibid. 5. 5; between men not well known to each other, Fronto, *ad Am.* 1. 8 (van den Hout).

[168] Quoted, Pliny, *Ep.* 2. 13. Formulae of indebtedness in letters of recommendation, Kim (1972), 66–8, 90–4.

[169] Women, Tac. *Ann.* 13. 20; Pliny, *Ep.* 7. 19. 10. Pagan gods, a truism, see e.g. MacMullen (1981), 52–3. So deep-set is this reciprocal ethic in the ancient mind that Cicero (*Off.* 1. 58) can argue that duty to parents and country derives from the fact that we are 'beneficiis max-imis obligati' to them; Val. Max. (5. 3 ext. 3) refers to 'dandi et accipiendi beneficii com-mercium, sine quo vix vita hominum esset'. See also Sen. *Ben.* 1. 4. 2.

begging help in a tax matter was advised, 'In return for this benefaction
. . . God will grant you, your house, and your line his accustomed aid,'
and, even more explicitly, 'as much honour and freedom of speech as you
grant us . . . we pray that the same degree of increase of your fame, nay
more! be granted to you from our Good Lord during your whole life.'[170]
As St Basil here reveals, the principle of reciprocity applied to honours as
well: the value of a favour, and the favour in return, might be partly or
wholly honorific. Thus a purely practical favour could be paid back partly
or entirely with praise, or, for example, by putting up a statue of the benefactor. Practical (to the modern mind) and honorific favours were not
easily distinguished.[171] Thus the relative quality of the men involved can
determine who should be grateful to whom. When Smyrna was destroyed
in an earthquake, its people had to camp in neighbouring cities. 'Who did
not regard it as his own good fortune, who did not think he had received
a favour rather than bestowed one, when he took such leading men into
his house?' If a man is grand enough, to have him as a guest is honorific:
he is doing you a favour.[172]

The extensive reach of this pattern of influence was a result of the quite
complicated patterns of debt that could be put together in pursuit of a
favour. The author of a letter of recommendation writes to a man with a
desirable favour in his gift—help in business, help in court, an official
post—on behalf of a protégé (who thereby incurs a debt to the writer by
virtue of the writer's effective intervention), saying that both he and the
recommendee will understand themselves to have incurred a debt if the
addressee of the letter does that favour for the recommendee. If the recipient of the letter agrees, the recommendee has received two favours and
now owes two, the letter's recipient has performed two favours and is
now owed two, and the recommender has done one favour and owes one.
This system was stable, and ensured that everyone got an equal return for
his favour—it was capable of infinite repetition, elaboration, and extension among men who understood it, and it did not require charity on
anyone's part, as long as everyone's obligation was clear.[173] The weakest
link in the system was evaluating the favour owed by the recommendee

---

[170] Basil, *Ep.* 36 and 110, τιμή and περιφάνεια. Cf. Aug. *Ep.* 57, 206.

[171] Duty to reciprocate honours, Cic. *Inv.* 2. 66; Herod. 2. 3. 6–7; Dio 67. 12. 3. Praise as
favour or return, Cic. *ad Fam.* 10. 24. 1; Pliny, *Ep.* 3. 11, 3. 21; Apul. *Flor.* 16. Individuals honour their benefactors, *ILS* 946, 1110; *IGR* iv. 1215. Honour returned for tangible favours in
16th-cent. France, Neuschel (1989), 76.

[172] Aristid. 20. 17 (Behr); trans. adapted from Behr.

[173] Conventional three-party scenario, Cic. *ad Fam.* bk. 13 *passim*. For more complicated
scenarios see e.g. Cic. *ad Fam.* 13. 6a–b, 13. 22.

to the recommender, since the latter's role was chiefly that of a mediator, and indeed one whose efficacy could not always have been evident. What did the recommendee owe to a specific recommender if his was just one of a fat sheaf of recommendations, or if the recommendee had some other attribute—perhaps he and the recommendation's recipient were intimate of old—which might have gained him the favour even without a recommendation?[174] For this reason a recommender might indicate in his letter that the addressee of the recommendation should make clear to the recommendee exactly how weighty his recommendation has been, thus allowing the recommendee to place a value on the favour-debt he owed to the recommender.[175]

The fact that relations of reciprocity were perceived to operate with perfect efficiency even where no equal return for favours was possible extended the range of such patterns beyond persons of roughly equal power to men of many types and conditions. Indeed, where a favour was valued at the point of receipt, but where there was a significant disparity of power between the giver and the recipient of a favour, it regularly occurred that an inferior recipient was entirely unable to pay back the favour—he was, in Cicero's phrase, 'unable to sustain the favours'.[176] How could a Romatius Firmus, whose fortune was quadrupled through Pliny's beneficence, ever do anything for Pliny as valuable to the distinguished senator as elevation to the equestrian census had been for Romatius? He could not. Humble men were limited to returning gumballs for diamonds, what Fronto called 'everyday favours': showing up in the morning, forming a retinue through the day, constituting, as a member of the *corps de ballet*, a tiny part of the great man's prestige.[177] All an inferior could do was be 'grateful', that is, he could remember, and hold himself in readiness to repay, for ever.[178]

This made him, in the Roman lexicon, a client, whether so called or referred to by a euphemism (since the term *cliens*, or the suggestion that one had a patron, *patronus*, was considered degrading).[179] Clientage

---

[174] Multiple recommendations: Cic. *ad Q. Fr.* 1. 2. 11; Basil, *Ep.* 112; Aristid. 50. 74–8 (Behr).

[175] Cic. *ad Fam.* 13. 20, 25, 35; Basil, *Ep.* 149.

[176] Cic. *ad Fam.* 2. 6. 2. On this situation, Sen. *Ben.* 5. 2–6.

[177] Romatius Firmus, Pliny, *Ep.* 1. 19. 'Everyday favours', Fronto, *ad M. Caes.* 1. 3 (van den Hout); see also Cic. *Mur.* 70; *Comment. Petit.* 34–8; and for these duties see Hellegouarc'h (1963), 160–3; Rouland (1979), 483–8, 515–17; Saller (1982), 128–9.

[178] Cic. *Off.* 2. 69; *ad Fam.* 10. 11. 1; Publilius Syrus, S41 (Friedrich); Sen. *Ben.* 5. 4. 1, 7. 14–16.

[179] Degrading, Saller (1982), 8–11, and esp. Cic. *Off.* 2.69; thus the exiguity of ancient material clearly relating to the patronage–clientage of the freeborn.

should be considered a form of chronic (and sometimes hereditary) favour-debt, one in which the client could never, and was never expected to, repay the favours done him.[180] This makes freeborn patronage/clientage identical in rationale to the clientage which existed between a freedman and his former master, by far the most common use of the terms. A slave's former owner enjoyed patronage—lifelong (indeed, heritable) and enforceable under the law—and the services which derived from it, because no favour a freedman could bestow could ever pay an adequate return for the master's favour of setting the slave free. Should a free-born client find himself in a position powerful enough to repay, patronage ceased—which is what Marius meant when he remarked that a magistracy freed him from the bonds of hereditary clientship.[181]

Patronage, in the Roman sense, exists when true reciprocity of favours has ceased. In the fullness of time, even the necessity of counting favours given or owed also lapsed, as Fronto said, comparing the services of a young protégé with those of a client:

He did not grudge it (nor did I feel ashamed) that he should pay me the same obedience which *clientes* and faithful, devoted freedmen yield; this is not through arrogance on my part or flattery on his, but our mutual affection and true love have removed from both of us any hesitation in doing favours.[182]

There was, then, no end to the duties of a client. After the patron's favours had become such that the client was unlikely to be able to reciprocate, he was simply expected to obey for ever. All he could do was dream of a disaster befalling his patron: only then, by some imagined act of derring-do, could the client perform such great service as would free him.[183]

But how could an aristocrat rely on another aristocrat's repaying a favour? And why could he depend on a client's obedience? First, because

---

[180] Cic. *Off.* 2. 69–70; cf. Plut. *Fab. Max.* 13. 3; Johnson and Dandeker (1989), 225.

[181] Freedman and patron, *Dig.* 38. 2. 1. pr. (Ulpian). A freedman's lack of respect for his patron, or failure to perform such duties as his former master may have stipulated, is prosecuted as 'ingratitude', see Treggiari (1969), 68–81. Marius, Plut. *Mar.* 5. 4–5; Plutarch argues that Marius was not correct in this, and that only curule magistracies relieved one of hereditary clientship. On personal patronage under the Republic, Brunt (1988a), 382–442; Deniaux (1993); empire, Saller (1982) and Rouland (1979), 493–617.

[182] Fronto, *ad Ver.* 1. 6. 2 (van den Hout), 'oboedire . . . officiis'; cf. Cic. *ad Fam.* 7. 29, 31 (see Wistrand (1978), 21–2). Similar is the willingness of close friends to stop counting favours, Cic. *Amic.* 58; *ad Fam.* 3. 5. 1. On *amicitia*, Hellegouarc'h (1963), 41–90, 142–70; Brunt (1988a), 351–81; Saller (1989).

[183] Clients' obedience, Sen. *Brev. Vit.* 19. 3: not even their love and hate are under their own control. Clients' duties likened to slavery, Mart. 10. 82. Dreaming of disasters, Sen. *Ben.* 6. 25–43.

the duty of reciprocity was inculcated from an early age. Of children Cicero said, 'What a remarkable memory they have for those who have done well by them; how eager they are to make return.'[184] Yet reciprocity worked at a conscious level as well. He who failed to make return would get no further favours. 'According to the duty of friendship, a giver need not give more, but must be repaid,' says Pliny.[185] A humble man 'needs the help of many', and it was disastrous for him to become known—among the set who were able to give—for not paying what he owed, or not trying to do whatever lay within his power, however insignificant.[186]

Failing to get further favours was a by-product of the more general destruction of the ingrate's position in society. Returning favours was part of one's moral reputation, and one's moral reputation, in turn, was part of one's social prestige. To be known as an upright trader of favours, as a grateful man, contributed to one's honour.[187] And the moral ghastliness of the man who failed to make return for favours he was given was never in question. He was castigated for his forgetfulness and ingratitude—'You have said everything possible when you call a man an ingrate.'[188] From the man to whom he had failed to make return he might expect stentorian abuse; people would stare at the miscreant; his erstwhile friends would cheer at his funeral.[189] And a man owed a favour could flourish the club of public opinion at his debtor to get his favour in return.[190] Gratitude may well have been a private emotion among the Romans, but its great strength in Roman society depended on its status as a prominent public virtue, frozen under the pitiless glare of opinion.[191]

---

[184] Cic. *Fin.* 5. 61.

[185] Pliny, *Ep.* 7. 31. 7. By contrast, Publilius Syrus, B8 (Friedrich), 'beneficia plura recipit, qui scit reddere'.

[186] Cic. *Off.* 2. 70.

[187] Gratefulness a moral virtue, Cic. *Planc.* 80–1; Val. Max. 5. 2; Sen. *Ben.* 4. 24. 1, cf. Wistrand (1978), 11. Contributes to honour, Sen. *Ben.* 4. 16. 3; *Ira* 2. 32. 1; Dio 8. 36. 13.

[188] Quoted, Publilius Syrus, D4 (Friedrich). For denunciation of 'bad memory', 'ingratitude' = not paying what one owes, see also Cic. *Off.* 2. 63; Sen. *Ep.* 81 *passim*; *Ben. passim* and esp. 1. 10. 4, 3. 1. 1; Val. Max. 5. 3; D. Chr. 31. 39.

[189] Public abuse, Sen. *Ben.* 5. 22. 1–23. 2, 7. 28. 3, 7. 30. 1 (Seneca is against this); stared at and subjected to *publicum odium*, Sen. *Ben.* 3. 17. 1–2; cheer at funeral, Juv. 1. 144–6 (dying intestate, he thus fails to express his gratitude in his will, cf. Pliny, *Ep.* 8. 18. 3). For the disgrace of ingratitude see also Dio 8. 36. 14.

[190] Cic. *ad Fam.* 5. 5. 2; cf. *ad Att.* 9. 7b. 2.

[191] Fear for reputation, Sen. *Ben.* 6. 42. The moralizing purposes of Cicero's *de Officiis* and Seneca's *de Beneficiis*—indispensable sources for the operation of reciprocity—somewhat occlude the grounding of reciprocity in public shame; Seneca intends, *inter alia*, the transfer of its enforcement from the realm of shame to that of conscience, *Ben.* 4. 21, 6. 42. 1–43. 3, so one must carefully distinguish the world they inhabit from the world they would

Finally, even when a favour was returned the transaction had honour consequences, consequences which depended upon the relative distinction of the parties. A favour from a great man, it was perceived, could add to one's prestige as an honour, but accepting a favour could also detract. For to beg a favour was embarrassing: 'When asking, a respectable man shuts his mouth and blushes.'[192] Not only did getting a favour imply that one could not do what was required by oneself; it obligated one, and debt was dishonourable—'Who accepts a *beneficium*, sells his liberty.'[193] It was excruciating to have one's debt mentioned or, worse, cast in one's teeth. 'Give me back to Caesar!' cried a man saved from proscription by one of Octavian's friends, for it was better to die than have one's benefactor continually harp upon the debt: 'in a triumph I would only have had to march once!' But the honour overcame the humiliation when the benefactor was very much greater than the recipient: the honour consequences of a favour cannot be determined without estimating the disparity of prestige between the men.[194]

Honour as Power

Valerius Maximus insisted that *maiestas*, 'eminence', was powerful in getting its way, and some of the methods it used have now been illustrated. Coming into existence both from ascription by the aristocratic community and by individual aristocrats (whose ascription the community as a whole accepted), honour played a variety of roles in society. First, honour was a source of value: it constituted some or all of the value of men's actions, which might be honorific or dishonouring. Inextricably mingled with the exchange of goods and services, honour could be traded for goods, services, and further honour. Second, honour was a source of legitimate social authority, that is, of an authority people were brought up to obey. Deference, including obedience, to acknowledged possessors of honour was required in Graeco-Roman society. Third, honour was a social sanction. Fear of loss of honour—disgrace—enforced social norms and some of those norms, including deference (and the appropriateness of praise and blame) and the duty of gratitude, the reciprocity of favours and honours, could be used to work one's will in society.

---

like to; see Wistrand (1978), 12, 20–1. For credit in a system of reciprocal favours being grounded in honour, cf. Neuschel (1989: 93) for 16th-cent. France.

[192] Sen. *Ben.* 2. 1. 3, cf. 2. 2. 1.   [193] Publilius Syrus, B5 (Friedrich), cf. R15.
[194] Quoted, Sen. *Ben.* 2. 11. 1. Also, accepting a favour proves one's weakness and inferiority, Dio 59. 23. 2–4, cf. Saller (1982), 20. Having persons in debt for favours is prestigious, Sid. *Ep.* 3. 5. 1.

It is possible to see all three of these roles that honour plays at work harmoniously in a common social institution like the Roman will. A Roman was expected to pay off outstanding favour-debts in his will. But powerful men, and especially the emperor, regularly received legacies in the wills of men they had never met or done anything for.[195] How curious, also, that Pliny could write to Tacitus, 'You must have noticed how in wills, unless perhaps someone is the particular friend of either of us, we receive identical legacies.' How many people could have felt *exactly* the same personal debt to Pliny and Tacitus? What was similar, as Pliny insisted elsewhere in his letter, was their prestige, particularly as littérateurs; the legacies that came to them were an aspect of their right to receive as distinguished men, a nice compliment from one aristocrat to another.[196] But there was a final element. It was a terrible insult to be cut out of the wills of other aristocrats. So wills could serve, finally, as an after-death attack on the renown of others, as when the distinguished matron Junia mentioned in her will almost all the leading men at Rome, but left out Tiberius. A good strong dose of abuse in the text of the will avoided the danger of being thought to have excluded someone through inattention. A legacy, finally, perhaps accompanied by a passage of praise in the will, was an honour.[197] With a large enough estate, all of honour's claims could be satisfied.

At the same time, the tension between the attribution of honour by the community and its attribution by individuals manifested itself constantly in social relations. For when one man had substantially more prestige than another, he could use the overwhelming strength of his praise and blame to twist communally sanctioned relationships of reciprocity and deference to his benefit. Ancient aristocrats comfortably viewed their system of reciprocal favours as equitable. But since the value of favours could never be measured objectively, and there might well be differences of opinion about a favour's practical and honorific value, the system was

[195] Receipt of legacies from persons unknown to legatee, Cic. 2*Phil.* 40–1; Suet. *Aug.* 66. 4; Tac. *Ann.* 2. 48; *HA Hadr.* 18. 5. Obviously legacies to 'bad' emperors can be made in order that the terms of the rest of the will will be upheld (Suet. *Gaius* 38. 2; Tac. *Ann.* 16. 11), but 'good' emperors received such legacies as well. On legacies to emperors see R. S. Rogers (1947); for a list, Champlin (1991), 203–4.

[196] Quoted, Pliny, *Ep.* 7. 20. 6; for like prestige of Tacitus and Pliny see also *Ep.* 9. 23. Cf. Tac. *Ann.* 1. 8, and esp. the *Testamentum Dasumii, CIL* vi. 10229.

[197] Wills used to honour, dishonour, Champlin (1991), 12–17, 146–7. Insult, Junia, Tac. *Ann.* 3. 76; cf. 6. 38; Fronto, *ad Ant. Pium* 3 (van den Hout). Under Augustus a law was proposed to prevent such libel, Suet. *Aug.* 56. 1. Honour, Cic. *Quinct.* 14; Pliny, *Ep.* 7. 24. 8; Fronto, *ad M. Caes.* 1. 6. 8 (van den Hout); cf. Lib. *Ep.* 115. 1.

necessarily inexact.[198] The possibility of profiting from the ambiguous value of favours was clearly understood in antiquity, and that is why much is heard of 'investing' or 'sowing' favours. At one point Seneca even says, 'A man is an ingrate who returns a favour without interest.'[199] To get the best return on your favour, you plant it in the most fertile soil, you invest it with the most 'grateful' recipient. He will place a high value upon the favours done him, and pay them back many times over in action or praise.[200] What good judgement, then, what admirable Roman cunning, to do a favour for Artemidorus, 'who is of such a benign nature, that he talks up the favours of friends—he publishes around my favour to him at above its true value'. One tried to avoid, needless to say, investing one's favour with an ungrateful recipient: nothing is more base than a recipient who valued the favour too low.[201]

But men of high status tended to be ungrateful, as Cicero indicates: 'Men who consider themselves wealthy, distinguished, and fortunate do not even want to feel that they have been obligated by a good deed. In fact, when they have willingly accepted even a considerable favour, they think they have bestowed it.'[202] These grandees are men who can indulge themselves in the many reasons for not returning favours properly: 'The bother discourages one man, the expense another, the danger a third, and vile shame, lest the return of a favour admit that one accepted it in the first place.'[203] But how can they get away with this without damage to their reputation? Because who owes what is a matter of opinion, and some people's opinions are stronger than others. The unrequited creditor, a superior in honour, booms, 'He is ungrateful for the greatest favours!' 'I wish I'd never given him anything!' He sends for his pattern book of letters and copies out elegant epistles of reproach—no need for such care over private letters; these insulting letters are published through the town.[204] But the accusation's target does not lie supine, he

---

[198] Saller (1982), 16–17, citing Cic. *ad Fam.* 2. 6. 1–2.

[199] Quoted, Sen. *Ep.* 81. 18. For the metaphor see also Cic. *ad Fam.* 13. 22. 2, 28a. 3; Pliny, *Ep.* 4. 4. 3; and *TLL* ii. 1881, vi¹. 476. 82 ff. for more Latin refs.; Basil, *Ep.* 118. Moralists disapprove, Cic. *Amic.* 31; Sen. *Ben.* 1. 2. 3.

[200] 'Gratefulness' in this sense, Cic. *ad Fam.* 13. 4. 1; Pliny, *Ep.* 2. 13. 9; Sen. *Ben.* 5. 1. 3; this and allied concepts spring from the Latin *gratia*, which has a range of meaning extending from 'gratitude' to 'favour paid back' to 'influence', see Moussy (1966), and briefly, Saller (1982), 21.

[201] Pliny, *Ep.* 3. 11. 1. Ungratefulness in this sense, Sen. *Ep.* 81. 23.

[202] Cic. *Off.* 2. 69, 'locupletes, honoratos, beatos'. Cf. Amm. Marc. 14. 6. 13.

[203] Sen. *Ben.* 7. 26. 3.

[204] Sen. *Ben.* 4. 16. 2, 7. 26. 2. Letter pattern book, [Lib.] *Char. Epist.* 53, 64. Letters to third parties accusing persons of ingratitude, Cic. *ad Fam.* 8. 12 (one complains before their friends); *ad Att.* 8. 4.

heaps abuse upon his abuser in turn. Rumours start: 'how curious that he can't put up with a man to whom he owes so much . . . maybe a good reason underlies this?' Each assails the other's reputation. Who wins? The lesser man is at a fatal disadvantage. He can merely 'bespatter' the *dignitas* of the greater; but by implication the greater can 'defile' his. In the end, the honour of the little man is eclipsed, that of the great man only clouded.[205] The weight an individual could bring against another's honour, his ability to mobilize opinion, was proportional to his own. At the same time, the vulnerability of individuals to the honorific or insulting acts of others varied: as Cassius Dio's discussion of Sejanus showed (above, p. 53), the honour of those higher up was apt to be less subject to the opinion of individuals. Thus a very great aristocrat was both sovereign over his inferior's prestige and little vulnerable to his inferior's opinion. Where there was a substantial gap between the prestige of the two parties, on questions of what he owed and what he was owed, the greater man was judge in his own cause by virtue of his ability to destroy the reputation of the lesser. Indeed, the specific gratefulness or ungratefulness of lesser men—their attractiveness as recipients of the favours of the powerful—was established by the opinion of the most distinguished, who reported to each other about prospective protégés: 'I can protect my favours to him in no way better than by adding to them, especially since he has rated their value so high that he earns new ones as he accepts the old.'[206]

A marked disparity of prestige tended to transform the ideally equitable system of reciprocity into the enslavement of the lesser man to the untrammelled power of the honour of the greater: he must do as he is told, or take the consequences. This was the true plight of the Roman client. Once he got in debt to his patron, only his patron could say when that debt was paid off. Similarly, Pliny was a judge in his own cause when it came to the deference owed him. He stated his claim, and then praised compliance. A man like Cicero, a consular but no *nobilis*, should have calculated carefully before failing in deference to the magnificent Metelli: you should not have insulted me and attacked my brother, Q. Metellus Celer wrote to him; the honour of our family (*inter alia*) should have dissuaded you. You have failed to act in accord with the conduct of our

---

[205] Sen. *Ben.* 7. 30. 2, 'nemo non superioris dignitatem querendo, etiam si non inquinavit, adspersit'.

[206] Quoted, Pliny, *Ep.* 2. 13. 9; for reporting see also *Ep.* 7. 8, 7. 15. 3; Cic. *ad Fam.* 5. 11. 1, 6. 11. 2, 13. 25, 13. 27, 13. 42. 1, 13. 54, 13. 64. 1; Deniaux (1993), 184–6. The humble man must strive to show himself grateful, Cic. *Off.* 2. 70.

ancestors (no surprise that, riff-raff!): you will live to regret this. And one must imagine the bearer of this letter to Cicero carrying others to proud friends and allies of the Metelli, beating the drums of aristocratic opinion. Poor Cicero had to write back a crawling letter to Metellus.[207] Honour, again, was a form of power.

THE CITY

In the blink of an eye, the ancient aristocrat estimated the quality of those he met, and just as the gaze of the artist turning from the carefully arranged elements of the still life to everyday reality continues to distinguish the essentials of form and colour, so did the inhabitant of the Roman empire, trained to reckon up exactly the honour of men, naturally assign honour to things other than human. The gods had their prestige; the sky-coursing eagle rejoiced in his, and looking down might gaze upon an honourable province, a famous Roman legion, a distinguished island, a glorious mountain, or an illustrious building, all in an empire which itself had honour.[208] Honour was a filter through which the whole world was viewed, a deep structure of the Graeco-Roman mind, perhaps the ruling metaphor of ancient society. To us value is a consequence of price; the Greeks, needing a word for 'price', borrowed τιμή from the realm of honour. Every thing, every person, could be valued in terms of honour, and every group of persons: the honour of the Roman senate, of the equestrian order, or of a court of law, waxed and waned according to who its members were and their conduct.[209] The most significant collectivity in the Roman world was, however, the city. A grasp of the honour and influence of cities is helpful for an understanding of Roman government, and is particularly well illuminated by the norms of civic benefaction.

[207] Pliny, see n. 154 above; Cicero and Metellus, paraphrasing Cic. *ad Fam.* 5. 1, 'familiae nostrae dignitas'; 5. 2.

[208] Gods, Cairns (1993), *passim*, and other objects, 210. Eagle, Fronto, *de Eloq.* 2. 13 (van den Hout); cf. for ranking the natural world by *dignitas*, Sid. *Ep.* 7. 14. 8. Province, see n. 359 below; legion, pp. 250–2, 262–3 below; island, Philo, *Leg. Gaium* 282; mountain, Verg. *Aen.* 12. 135; building, Cic. *ad Q. Fr.* 3. 1. 1; Pliny, *Ep.* 7. 24. 9; even sewers, Cass. *Var.* 3. 30. 1. Empire, Cic. 2*Verr.* 4. 25; *Manil.* 11; Herod. 2. 8. 2. Cf. Yavetz (1974), 36–7, 47–8. Honour vocabulary is also used in a technical sense in rhetoric, for weighing words, Fronto, *de Eloq.* 2. 1 (van den Hout), and describing style, Herm. *Id.* 1. 5–6, 9.

[209] The Roman senate, Cic. 2*Verr.* 1. 5; Florus 2. 5. 3. Equestrian order, *Rhet. Her.* 4. 47; Mart. 5. 8. A court, Cic. 2*Verr.* 1. 18; *Clu.* 61. See Yavetz (1974), 37.

The Honour of Cities

The elements of the honour of a city were parallel, and in many respects similar, to those of human honour, and cities used influence grounded in honour to effect their will in similar ways. Great age and famous deeds in the past contributed largely to a city's honour, just as being sprung from a famous line did among men: indeed, the coins and inscriptions of an old and proud city might style it εὐγενής, 'well-born', and Dio Chrysostom said of Nicaea,

it is, in the nobility of its line, and the make-up of its people, inferior to no prestigious city elsewhere . . . [it is] made up of the most illustrious families—not trivial numbers of trivial men gathered together higgledy-piggledy—but the first among the Greeks and the Macedonians, and what is most important, it had as its founders both gods and heroes.[210]

Also contributing were natural advantages:location, the wealth of the land, presence of rivers, harbours, the beauty of the spot; population and sheer size; the possession of subject cities; the public revenues; and the works of man: structures public and private, notable temples, religious festivals, and games.[211]

Moreover, the city must act well: a city had a moral character just like a man, and the city's prestige rested in part upon widespread perception of that character. An orator praising a city might boast that the neighbouring peoples 'deem our city the very definition of justice, and come here to handle their litigation; just as the Athenians have inherited their Areopagus as an arena for justice, so do our neighbouring cities regard

---

[210] Nicaea, D. Chr. 39. 1, οὐδεμιᾶς ἡττωμένη τῶν ὁποίοτε ἐνδόξων γένους τε γενναιότητι. Cities' prestige in general, D. Chr 31. 40, 126, 159; Men. Rhet. 398. 23–6, *CIL* viii. 14394, 14728; Robert (1977a), 17 n. 76 for coins bearing types like σεμνῆς ἐνδοξοτέρας. Conspectus of the elements of cities' prestige, see esp. the elements praised in panegyrics on cities, n. 241 below; and more briefly, D. Chr. 31. 146; Aristid. 18. 3–6, 23. 13–26, 24. 45–56, 27. 5–15 (Behr); [Aristid.] 25. 3–8 (Behr). Especially for age and deeds, [Julian], *Ep*. 198 (Bidez), 407b–408a (on which see B. Keil (1913); Spawforth (1994): really a speech dating to the 1st cent. AD); Cic. *Mur*. 22; D. Chr. 31. 117, 32. 92–3. Age, Robert (1937), 302–5; (1980), 204–5. Deeds, Robert (1937), 247–8; D. Chr. 31. 66. εὐγενής, Robert (1977a), 17; and see Strubbe (1984–6) for the bases of the claim. For perceptions among modern Greek shepherds of the prestige of the nation as similar to that of family, J. Campbell (1964), 317.

[211] See conspectus in previous note, and esp. for size and location, D. Chr. 32. 35–6, 35. 13–14. Population, Pliny, *Ep*. 7. 32. Subject cities, D. Chr. 34. 47, 35. 14; public revenues, D. Chr. 48. 11. Structures, Vitr. 1. pr. 2; *Gk. Const*. 138; Aristid. 23. 68–9 (Behr); Philostr. *VS* 1. 25 (532); which must be kept in repair, [Aristid.] 25. 2 (Behr). Tumbledown structures are σημεῖα . . . ἀδοξίας, D. Chr. 40. 9. Walls, Dio 74(75L). 14. 4.

us.'²¹² In general the Rhodians (for example) conducted themselves with propriety—their gait was admired, as was the trim of their hair and their manner of dress. Their manners lent the city dignity. And even more unusual and distinguished, they sat in silence at public spectacles, and applauded with a sedate clucking. But vitiating these claims to renown was their alarming habit of honouring new benefactors by changing the labels on old statues, a cheese-paring practice destructive of the proud islanders' reputation. The citizenry of Tarsus, given to emitting a characteristic snort, were sharply advised by Dio Chrysostom that they were snorting away their city's lustre.²¹³ And a reputation for internal concord was likewise vital to prestige: 'who are more equal in honour to their rulers?' asked the same Dio rhetorically, castigating the Nicaeans for their disharmony.²¹⁴

To the Graeco-Roman observer the honour of a city was not different in kind or incommensurable in quantity with the honour of a man. Cities tended to have more prestige than private citizens, but this was by no means invariably the case: Scipio Africanus the Younger, the destroyer of Carthage, seemed to Cicero to have as much *auctoritas* as Rome, and the sophist Polemo 'addressed cities as if he were their superior'.²¹⁵ Thus it is predictable that 'citizens [of cities] bring distinction upon them, just as children do upon parents', and that 'the greatest distinction a city has is the praise given its citizens'.²¹⁶ A city could derive prestige not merely for its aggregate deeds and morals, but also from the present or past accomplishments of individual inhabitants. Especially valuable under the empire were famous practitioners of honourable intellectual pursuits like rhetoric: since Polemo could sneer at whole cities, his residence at

---

²¹² Men. Rhet. 385. 10–14. In general on cities' character, Plut. *Praec. Ger. Reip.* 799b–800b; D. Chr. 31. 5–6. Widespread perception, D. Chr. 32. 40–1, 86. Conspectus of cities' moral virtues, D. Chr. 34. 48, 44. 10. For virtuous cities see also Pliny, *Ep.* 1. 14. 4, 6; D. Chr. 41. 9.

²¹³ Rhodes, D. Chr. 31. 162–3, 32. 52 (they even reproach visiting foreigners for walking badly); Aristid. 24. 56 (Behr). Rhodes' statues, D. Chr. 31 *passim* and esp. 31. 2. Tarsus, D. Chr. 33. 34, 38, 51, 55; and for being 'difficult' with governors, D. Chr. 34. 9. See also for disgraceful conduct of Athens, D. Chr. 31. 116–23; Philostr. *VA* 4. 21; Alexandria, D. Chr. 32. 41, 47 *et passim*; and other cities, D. Chr. 31. 158; [D. Chr.] 37. 37; Pliny, *Ep.* 4. 22. 7.

²¹⁴ D. Chr. 39. 4, ἰσοτιμότεροι; see also Aristid. 23. 76 (Behr).

²¹⁵ Cities have more prestige, Aristid. 24. 12 (Behr). Africanus, Cic. *Mur.* 58. Polemo, Philostr. *VS* 1. 25 (535); and cf. Apul. *Flor.* 16.

²¹⁶ Quint. *Inst.* 3. 7. 26, *decus*; and D. Chr. 48. 4, κόσμος . . . ἔπαινος; see also Aristid. 29. 27 (Behr); Roueché (1993), no. 72; Sid. *Ep.* 7. 9. 23. Thus one needs to attend closely to the quality of members of city councils: Gk. *Const.* 184. 2. 57–61; Lib. *Or.* 11. 133–49.

Smyrna glorified her, 'for a city not only gives a man a great name, but can acquire one from a man.'[217]

In time of civil war the residents of one Italian town could easily be imagined creeping by night to fill their neighbour's amphitheatre with flammables, driven by jealousy at their rival's possession of the largest building in Italy: as between men, competition between cities for honour was keen.[218] A pecking order was clearly understood—a city's coins might, for example, proudly proclaim it the sixth or, failing that, the seventh, city of the province of Asia—and citizens were eager to advance their home towns.[219] They chanted their city's praises—its claims to honour—in public meetings, and they chanted abuse of a rival city in the theatre.[220] The impression visitors received of a city was carefully attended to: a native could earnestly assure a visitor, 'We easily excel all the other cities with our temples, baths, and public buildings.' When distinguished men visited, the city's morals improved, or her vices were at least hidden, for fear of giving a bad impression.[221] And the citizens of rival cities seized upon any vice, especially one as repulsive as the Tarsians' snorting, and castigated it, to hurt a rival's reputation and thus improve their own relative standing.[222] Just as citizens adored to hear speeches in praise of their city and attacks on their rivals, they loathed to hear their rivals

[217] Polemo, Philostr. *VS* 1. 25 (532). Citizens who confer distinction on their cities: Cic. *Planc.* 19–20, 22; Pliny, *Ep.* 7. 22. 2; Aristid. 30. 1–2, 32. 5, 20–1 (Behr); [Apol. Ty.], *Ep.* 47; Greg. Naz. *Ep.* 207. 2; Theodoret, *Ep.* 30, 32 (Azéma); Sid. *Ep.* 4. 4. 1. A woman confers distinction, *AE* 1910. 203. Liberal pursuits, Mart. 10. 103; Men. Rhet. 360–1, 364; Lib. *Or.* 1. 52. The humiliation of a townsman can also detract: thus Alatrium begs Cicero to defend a citizen's freedman on behalf of the town's *dignitas*, Cic. *Clu.* 49; see also 196, for conviction of a townsman in court.

[218] Burning amphitheatre, Tac. *Hist.* 2. 21, cf. *Dig.* 50. 10. 3 (Macer) for buildings erected 'ad aemulationem alterius civitatis'. On rivalry, Nörr (1966), 48–50; Robert (1977*a*); Merkelbach (1978); Syme (1988 (1981)). See esp. D. Chr. 38. 34 (explicitly compared to a rivalry between ἐπιφανεῖς . . . ἄνδρες); 31. 120–7, 34 *passim*, 38. 24, 29; 41. 2, τῶν πόλεων φιλοτιμίαν; Aristid. 23. 12 (Behr); Philostr. *VS* 1. 24 (529); and *MAMA* vi. 6 with Robert (1969), 287–8, a fragmentary Roman decree concerning rivalry. For violence, also Tac. *Hist.* 1. 65, 3. 57, 4. 3, 50; Herod. 3. 2. 7–9, 3. 3. 3. Cf. rivalry between towns in modern Mediterranean, Bourdieu (1966), 203; Pitt-Rivers (1971), 9–12.

[219] Pecking order, esp. Lib. *Or.* 20. 40; Aus. *Ord. Nob. Urb.*; also Cic. *Flac.* 74; D. Chr. 38. 5 (called a τάξις), 43. 1; Aristid. 23. 23 (Behr); Men. Rhet. 433. 23–32. Coins, Robert (1977*b*), 64–8 (but see Mitchell (1993), i. 206). See below, pp. 170–1, for the relationship of this order to the imperial cult.

[220] Chanting praises, Roueché (1989*b*). Abuse of others, in theatre D. Chr. 40. 29; in general, D. Chr. 31. 124, 154–5, 34. 14, 38. 41, 48. 4–5; Aristid. 23. 12 (Behr); *ILS* 6443.

[221] Quoted, Apul. *Met.* 2. 19. Attention to visitors' opinion, D. Chr. 7. 39, 32. 41–3, 51. 2. Improved conduct, Philostr. *VS* 2. 26 (613); concealing vices, D. Chr. 48. 2. Cf. modern Andalusia, Pitt-Rivers (1971), 26–7.

[222] D. Chr. 33. 38, 51, mentioning the Cilician towns of Aegae and Adana as detractors.

praised, thinking that praise of others dishonoured them.[223] An orator will appeal to this rivalry to get a city to do what he wants.[224] Just as with individuals, the greater a city's prestige the more closely and the more jealously it was watched, and just as the conduct of a distinguished man was imitated by ambitious protégés, an orator could urge a city to imitate the prepotently magnificent city of Rome.[225] Another symptom (and one of which, as will be seen, the emperors took advantage) was the eagerness of cities to stack up honorific titles. By the early third century as modest a town as Gaza was 'sacred, inviolable, autonomous, trustworthy, reverent, brilliant, and great'.[226]

Because cities were perceived to exist in the world of honour, relations between them could be conceived of in honour terms, as when Argos complained that Corinth's treatment of her was 'unworthy of her ancient power and renown', or Ephesus complained to the emperor of being insulted by Smyrna. 'I think that it was by mistake that the Smyrneans left your titles off the decree concerning the joint sacrifice,' wrote Antoninus Pius to the furious Ephesians, pouring oil upon turbulent waters, for the cities were old rivals. 'I am sure that they will act better in future, as long as you in your letters to them mention them appropriately in accord with what has been decreed.'[227] Sounding the same note, Aelius Aristides urged the rival cities of Asia to praise each other; and cities did honour one another with statues.[228] Not only did cities honour and defer, they traded favours. If Nicomedia really wished to be more highly esteemed by the cities of her region, said Dio Chrysostom, she should grant them as a benefaction the free use of her port.[229]

---

[223] Love of panegyric, D. Chr. 32. 37–8; hatred of criticism, D. Chr. 32. 11, 48. 4–5; love of attacks on rivals, Aristid. 23. 5 (Behr); praise of rivals hated as ἀτιμία, Aristid. 23. 7, 29 (Behr).

[224] D. Chr. 31. 157–60, 38. 30–1.

[225] Watched, D. Chr. 31. 39–40; [Aristid.] 25. 40–2 (Behr). Imitation, D. Chr. 41. 10.

[226] Gaza, *IGR* i. 387. See pp. 136–7 below .

[227] Argos, [Julian], *Ep.* 198 (Bidez), 409*b* (see n. 210 above), ἀρχαίας δυνάμεώς τε καὶ δόξης ἀνάξια. Ephesus and Smyrna, *Gk. Const.* 135 A. 10–15. And see Spawforth and Walker (1986: 95, 102), for cities claiming kinship with Sparta and Argos to participate in their fame.

[228] Aristid. 23. 7, 29 (Behr). For cities honouring one another, Liebenam (1900), 125 n. 3; and e.g. *IK Eph.* ii. 236; Höghammar (1993), no. 53; Roueché (1993), nos. 58–63; and for the Hellenistic background, Gauthier (1985), 162–4.

[229] Nicomedia, D. Chr. 38. 32, interpreted by C. P. Jones (1978), 87. For relationships of clientship (i.e. indebtedness for favours) between Rome and other states during the Republic, Badian (1958), esp. 1–13, 33–115.

Men and Cities: Influence

Since the honour of cities and men was commensurable, men could deal with cities, and cities with men, in honour terms. Just as the praise of a man was valuable to the recipient's prestige in proportion to the praiser's celebrity, so too were the prestige-bestowing honours of a city. To the citizens of the ancient, powerful, and rich city of Rhodes, which could claim to be second only to Rome in distinction, an orator could say, 'It is more prestigious to be invited to take a seat of honour once among you than it is to get a statue in other cities. And to be praised by your assembly is glorious; others seem not to honour enough if they burst their lungs with cheering.'[230] Comparing his city to others in the East, a Rhodian might say, 'The Roman [governors] don't care very much about being given statues among those people, but they are not heedless of the honour here.' By the late Republic the honours and testimonials of Greek cities carried great weight at Rome.[231]

'The monument, the inscription, and the bronze statue are thought great things by noble men,' as Dio Chrysostom said; 'Crowns and proclamations and seats of honour, costing nothing to those who give them, are worth everything to those who receive them.'[232] And citizenship, testimonials from a city, titles like 'Best Men, and Olympians, and Saviours, and Foster-parents', speeches by notables, acclamation in the city assembly, and being escorted by the crowd were honorific too, as were appointments to embassies to the emperor and other cities.[233] After death men

---

[230] Second only to Rome, D. Chr. 31. 62. Quoted, D. Chr. 31. 110, σεμνότερόν ἐστι τὸ παρ' ὑμῖν κληθῆναι εἰς προεδρίαν ἅπαξ τῆς παρ' ἑτέροις εἰκόνος. καὶ τὸ μὲν ὑμᾶς καθημένους ἐπαινέσαι λαμπρόν· ἄλλοι δὲ οὐδὲ ἂν διαρραγῶσι κεκραγότες οὐ δοκοῦσιν ἱκανῶς τιμᾶν; and, of course, one must not cheapen honours by giving them out too widely. Honour from a city proportional to city's honour, see also Cic. *Flac.* 74; Apul. *Flor.* 16; D. Chr. 39. 1.

[231] D. Chr. 31. 106, τιμή (also giving the context for 31. 110 in the previous note). Testimonials carry weight, Cic. *Flac.* 74; *ad Q. Fr.* 1. 1. 42; *ad Fam.* 12. 25a. 2.

[232] D. Chr. 31. 20, 75. 7; see also for conspectus of civic honours, Tac. *Dial.* 8; Plut. *Praec. Ger. Reip.* 820d; D. Chr. 31. 108, 66. 2–4; Apul. *Flor.* 16; *TAM* ii. 905. On civic honours, Liebenam (1900), 121–33, 379–82; for women, van Bremen (1996), 155–90; for the origins of the regime of civic honours in the Greek world, Gauthier (1985). For the sheer mass of honorific monuments in a city of the Roman period see Geagan (1967: 140–59), for Athens. A substantial proportion of all surviving inscriptions record, or form part of, such honours.

[233] Citizenship, [Apol. Ty.], *Ep.* 62; D. Chr. 41. 10 (here conferring Roman citizenship as well, an additional honour). Written testimonials, D. Chr. 77/78. 26; Robert (1965), 207; Reynolds (1982), no. 14. Titles, quoted, D. Chr. 48. 10; see also J. Chr. *de Ian. Glor.* 4; they are given by honorific acclamation, Robert (1949a), 74–81; (1960a), 569–76; (1981), 360–1; Veyne (1990), 125. Speeches, D. Chr. 51. 1–3; *IGR* iv. 1756. 52–62. Acclamation, cheering, D. Chr. 66. 2–3; Aristid. 30. 9 (Behr); *Sel. Pap.* 239; Colin (1965), 112–32; RouEché (1984). Escorted, D. Chr. 77/78. 33. Embassies, D. Chr. 51. 9; Philostr. *VS* 1. 25 (539).

might be honoured with public funerals, funeral games, and even shrines.[234] Each of these honours was ranked in relation to the others: the best of honours in life was a statue of wrought gold erected in 'the most distinguished shrines'.[235] The Romans adopted this nuanced and sophisticated system of Greek civic distinctions for use in their own cities.[236]

The city could also dishonour: as Dio Chrysostom said to the Alexandrians, 'If one of the better people should do something disgraceful where everyone is watching, you will pour contempt upon him and deem him worth nothing, even if he has a thousand times your authority.' Such contempt could take the form of abusive chanting or jeering in public meetings.[237] To a visitor, an insult could be offered by a town's failure to receive him with the ceremony due his prestige, or, indeed, by refusal to admit him at all; he could also be jeered on his way.[238] If the man to be censured had previously been honoured, his statues could be pulled down, or any other public honours taken away.[239] The ancient mind also classified acts of overt mob violence—stoning, or rushing at a man's house with burning brands—as acts of dishonour. At Sena, not only was a Roman senator beaten by order of the magistrates, but the townsfolk performed a mock funeral complete with satirical lamentation and abuse.[240]

By the same token—and the modern mind finds this somewhat curious—a man, particularly a very distinguished man, could honour, or

[234] D. Chr. 44. 3–4; Cic. *Flac.* 75; *ILS* 139–40.

[235] Ranking of honours, D. Chr. 31. 22, 108; Philostr. *VS* 1. 25 (530). Gold statue set up ἐν τοῖς ἐπιφανεστάτοις ἱεροῖς, D. Chr. 44. 2; cf. D. Chr. 31. 87–8; *IGR* iv. 1236. 27–8. The honour conveyed by a statue varies especially according to its material and placement in the city, Ward-Perkins (1984), 9; for the placement of statues in the forums of two North African cities, Zimmer (1989). Rhodes, D. Chr. 31. 9, 107–8 (and perhaps other cities, D. Chr. 31. 116; [D. Chr.] 37. 40; Cic. *ad Att.* 6. 1. 26), only sculpted the likenesses of those honoured highest; for lesser mortals, including some Roman governors (D. Chr. 31. 43–4), they relabelled old statues, sometimes quite inappropriate ones (D. Chr. 31. 155–6). Notice also that a town's civic bodies, the popular assembly and the councils (some cities had more than one), may honour together or separately, Geagan (1967), 140–59. Other civic honours (with no attempt to be complete): gilded portrait plaque, *IGR* iv. 1756. 48, 129; coins, Harl (1987), 28–9; meals at public expense, Philostr. *VS* 2. 15 (595); honorific banquets, Plut. *Cato Min.* 14. 3; meeting approaching honorands far from the city, D. Chr. 45. 4; and for elements of honorific reception by a town, *IGR* iv. 145. 18–25.

[236] A. Wallace-Hadrill (1990); see esp. Cic. *ad Brut.* 24.

[237] D. Chr. 32. 31; see also, for shouted abuse, 7. 25–6; 32. 11, 22.

[238] Failure to receive properly, Plut. *Cato Min.* 12. 2–5; refusal to admit, Cic. *Clu.* 193; *ad Fam.* 12. 15. 2–3; jeering visitor, Cic. *Clu.* 192; Philo, *Flacc.* 33–4, 153.

[239] Statues, Philostr. *VS* 1. 8 (490); [D. Chr.] 37; Cic. *ad Brut.* 24. 9; honorific inscriptions, D. Chr. 31. 28.

[240] Mob violence, D. Chr. 46. 6. Sena, Tac. *Hist.* 4. 45. Other insults, D. Chr. 31. 29; Philo, *Flacc.* 36–40; Jos. *AJ* 19. 357.

dishonour, a city. In his speech upon taking leave of a city, a notable was expected to proclaim to its people that he would 'never forget them, spreading news of them everywhere in admiration of their excellent qualities'. Panegyrics upon cities survive, and rhetorical handbooks gave instructions about how cities were to be praised; an orator might promise to circulate his panegyric through the provinces as a pamphlet, and the city praised might beg a copy. A great man's praise contributed to the city's honour.[241] So did his decision to defend it in court or to associate himself with it as its patron. Moreover, when a distinguished man made a gift to a city, he honoured it.[242] On the other hand, the blame of individuals was disastrous to a city's honour:

> And yet I have heard from many people that when, some time before, one of the governors sent us an unfavourable reply about our finances, and our goal was not achieved, many people ridiculed the city—not our neighbours, for that would have been less terrible [rivals' gloating being expected], but our own citizens . . . feeling no shame, when they said those things, that they were lacerating their own homeland and thoughtlessly ruining its reputation; for if they are among the city's first men, or among those held in honour, they ruin themselves, as leaders in a city which is weak and without prestige; but if they are of the base off-scourings, then they make their own dishonour greater and more severe, as the most wretched inhabitants of a most wretched city.[243]

With cities as with men, although the praise of the lower orders was worth little, their blame was destructive.

The key to understanding relations between man and city in the ancient world is the realization that cities were fully anthropomorphized: they were thought to act just as humans did.[244] Thus cities set out to control the acts of men, and men those of cities, just as men dealt with other men: employing—among other methods—honour-based forms of influ-

---

[241] Quoted, Men. Rhet. 431. 25–7. Panegyrics on cities, Aristid. 1, 17, 26 and see 21 (Behr); D. Chr. 35, 50; and esp. Lib. *Or.* 11. For instructions on how to deliver them, Men. Rhet. 346–67, 382–9; Quint. *Inst.* 3. 7. 26–7; Pernot (1993), i. 178–216. Pamphlet, Apul. *Flor.* 16; begging a copy, Hall (1992). Panegyric an honour to cities, Aristid. 1. 2, 17. 7 (Behr).

[242] Honorific: defence in court, *ILS* 6680; patronage, *AE* 1937. 119; benefactions, EJ 236; *CIL* viii. 4418; *IG* xii. 5. 946.

[243] D. Chr. 45. 6, καὶ ταῦτα λέγοντες οὐκ ᾐσχύνοντο διασύροντες τὴν αὐτῶν πατρίδα καὶ καθαιροῦντες ἐν τοῖς λόγοις οὕτως ἀνοήτως. εἴτε γάρ εἰσι τῶν πρωτευόντων ἐν αὐτῇ ἢ τιμωμένων, αὐτοὺς καθαιροῦσιν ἀσθενοῦς καὶ ἀδόξου πόλεως προεστηκότες· εἴτε τῶν ἀπερριμμένων εἰσι καὶ τῶν ὑστάτων, ἔτι μείζω καὶ χαλεπωτέραν ποιοῦσι τὴν ἀτιμίαν αὐτοῖς, εἰ τῆς ἐσχάτης πόλεως ἔσχατοι τυγχάνουσιν ὄντες.

[244] Thus a city may not only have a mother (*metropolis*) but children, and siblings, Robert (1937), 247–9; even a soul, Syn. *Ep.* 31 (Garzya). Appian urges men to model their conduct on that of cities, Fronto, *Add. Epist.* 4 (van den Hout).

ence. Naturally the ancient observer considered a regime of honours vital to the prosperity of a city, for a city used its honours to procure services from individuals.[245] First, 'Cities praise both those who have given them something or who can give them something.'[246] Prusa, for example, honoured influential men, in the hope that they would use their influence to get a package of concessions from the governors.[247] Others noticed the honours cities conferred, and this impelled them to act on the city's behalf. 'What mark of honour have you not enthusiastically bestowed?' Dio asked Prusa rhetorically, 'Have you not given portraits, statues, posts on embassies to cities and the emperor? Have you not honoured publicly, and privately by greeting? . . . Who then would not be eager to do whatever good he could for you?'[248] And a man used the power of his honours to manipulate cities. The orator simply assumes that a distinguished and skilled panegyrist would use his talent to elicit grants of citizenship from Greek cities.[249]

Cities should defer to the honour of men. A great philosopher, 'inferior to none of the Romans in birth, and possessed of more glory than anyone had for ages', castigated the Athenian people for viewing gladiatorial combats in the Theatre of Dionysus; far from ceasing, however, they drove him from the city. Such treatment of a man of his distinction, we are told, brought disgrace upon Athens.[250] Sardis was not about to make the same error: it honoured a man 'on account of his distinction in every respect'.[251] At the same time, the fame of a city demanded acts of deference from important men. Pliny leapt to represent the Firmani in court: their *splendor* prompted him.[252] Cicero expected his Roman jury to respect distinguished towns, and look favourably upon litigants they supported.[253] Troy, now a very tiny place, felt the awful wrath of

---

[245] D. Chr. 31. 25, 39. 7.

[246] Ibid. 51. 3. Cf. Cic. *ad Fam.* 10. 10. 1; *ad Brut.* 24. 9; D. Chr. 31. 108.

[247] D. Chr. 45. 4; cf. 41. 7. Honours for those who *did* influence important Romans, Robert (1960*b*), 326–9. Also, honorific decrees of invitation, Lib. *Or.* 1. 48; D. Chr. 41. 1.

[248] D. Chr. 51. 9, τί γὰρ τῶν σεμνῶν . . . οὐ κοινῇ τιμῶντες;

[249] Ibid. 38. 1; see also Julian, *ad Ath.* 268b–c.

[250] D. Chr. 31. 122, δόξαν δὲ τηλικαύτην ἔχοντα ἡλίκης οὐδεὶς ἐκ πάνυ πολλοῦ τετύχηκεν. For the disgrace, D. Chr. 31. 120–1, 123. Other civic failures of deference, Cic. *ad Fam.* 12. 15. 4; [D. Chr.] 37. 37.

[251] *IGR* iv. 1756. 46–7, ἐν πᾶσιν σεμνότητα. Cf. Cousin and Diehl (1886), 49; *IGR* iv. 144. 17 (a woman); *AE* 1937. 121; Cic. *Arch.* 10. Also, a man made city patron (see below) 'pro splendore dignitatis', *ILS* 6110, also 6114.

[252] Pliny, *Ep.* 6. 18; cf. Cic. *Scaur.* 27.

[253] Cic. *Cael.* 5; *Font.* 14; and esp. *Flac.* 61–4, 100–1, where the prestige of Athens, Sparta, other cities of Achaea, and Massilia, all supporting Cicero's client Flaccus, is set against that of towns in Asia Minor accusing him.

Augustus' lieutenant Agrippa when Julia, Agrippa's wife and Augustus' daughter, was nearly left to drown in the swollen Scamander by Troy's citizens, who were unaware that she was coming to visit. Agrippa fined them one hundred thousand drachmae, rendering them destitute. Agrippa was persuaded to relent by King Herod; he in turn was involved in the case because it was brought to his attention by the historian Nicolaus of Damascus, to whom the Ilians had appealed: Nicolaus 'very eagerly gave his support to them because of the city's fame'.[254] Civic distinction yielded honours as well as practical help. Given the magnificence of Pergamum, 'who . . . would not act wisely in meting out to it as much praise as possible?'[255]

Cities and men used the prospect of honours to control each other, and were bound to defer to each other's distinction. Predictably, relations of reciprocity also operated between man and city. So claimed Aelius Aristides, assuring Rhodes that many would come to her aid in the wake of an earthquake—some to repay her for benefactions received, some to cultivate a hedge against fortune by placing Rhodes in debt to them.[256] A city could be in debt to a man for a benefaction, and could feel that debt vividly. Thus the odd triumph of Scipio Africanus the Elder, victor in the second war against Carthage, under tribunician prosecution at Rome. 'On this very day, tribunes and citizens,' said he, 'I brilliantly defeated Hannibal and the Carthaginians in Africa,' and then he simply walked out of the court to sacrifice on the Capitoline followed by the whole assembly, leaving the thwarted tribunes gnashing their teeth. Such was the debt of gratitude owed to Scipio by Rome that the very bringing of a prosecution against him was widely thought disgraceful.[257] In accord with this way of thinking, a man whose family had performed many services for his city, Dio Chrysostom, listed them before Prusa's ominously rumbling assembly, and remarked, 'being descended from men such as these, you'd think I'd be worthy of some respect on their account, even if I were a rat myself, rather than stoning or burning alive!'[258] A city's creditor could therefore call in his debts, and he expected that the city would requite him with honour as well. Thus Aquileia raised a statue to Gaius

[254] Troy, *FGH* 90 F 134, δόξα (trans. Sherk); cf. D. Chr. 33. 46.

[255] Aristid. 23. 18 (Behr). Cf. D. Chr. 32. 52. A commonplace in panegyric is that the speech must be in proportion to the prestige of the town, Aristid. 1. 5–6, 26. 2 (Behr).

[256] Aristid. 25. 55 (Behr).   [257] Livy 38. 50. 4–51. 14; quoted, 38. 51. 7.

[258] D. Chr. 46. 4. For city debts to individuals cf. Cic. *Sest.* 9–10 (the city passes a resolution of thanks); *ad Fam.* 12. 14. 6; Pliny, *Ep.* 6. 18. Since cities must pay back their favour-debts, it is explicable that cities sometimes refuse great gifts, Fronto, *Add. Epist.* 5. 2 (van den Hout).

Minicius, who, in a long official career, was often the city's advocate before the emperor, 'that it be clear that there is no other way to repay our debts to so great a man, than by glorifying him publicly'.[259]

A city's gratitude was guaranteed by concern for the city's reputation. The voting of honours to requite a benefactor 'pertains to the dignity of the city'. A benefactor was honoured 'not so that he will be even more well-disposed towards us . . . but so that we may seem grateful to those who decide such things'.[260] 'Those' were the great men who reported to one another on exactly how grateful individual towns were, just as they did of protégés. Gratitude was, again, a public virtue. Ingratitude was as signally destructive of a city's prestige as it was of a man's: the ungrateful Rhodian practice of changing the labels on statues was widely mocked, their statues compared to actors.[261] Properly grateful cities might expect more favours in future, while an aspect of the collapse of an ungrateful city's honour was that it would enjoy no more favours. 'No one will judge those who insult their benefactors worthy of a favour. Your danger is that no one ever again will do you a benefaction.'[262]

Since the honour of cities permitted them to participate fully in relations of reciprocity, their taking of patrons, just as men might, becomes intelligible. Some great man had done the city a benefaction; incapable of equal return, the city senate voted to co-opt the benefactor as their patron.[263] Such co-option was highly honorific, and since the town of Bocchoris in Spain, for example, could not very well escort her patron into the Roman forum, the relationship was advertised on a plaque in the great man's house, there keeping company with the busts of his ancestors and other marks of his status. Thus the patron would continue protecting the city, representing her in court, funding public buildings.[264] Civic

[259] McC. & W. 336; cf. Pallas *et al.* (1959) (= *SEG* xviii. 143), col. 3. Also Cic. *ad Fam.* 10. 10. 1; D. Chr. 31 *passim*; Apul. *Met.* 3. 11. In this sense the benefactor can metaphorically be viewed as buying honour, D. Chr. 31. 59–61.

[260] *AE* 1947. 53, 'pertinere ad municipi [*sic*] dignitatem', and *ILS* 6680. See also Small. *Gaius* 404. 26–36.

[261] Reporting, Cic. *ad Fam.* 13. 4. 1, 13. 7. 5, 13. 11. 3. Disgraceful failures of civic gratitude, Val. Max. 5. 3. 2; Sen. *Ben.* 5. 17. 1–2. Rhodes' ingratitude, D. Chr. 31. 154–5 *et passim*.

[262] D. Chr. 31. 65; cf. 31. 22. More favours from proper gratitude, D. Chr. 31. 7.

[263] Individuals' patronage of cities, Harmand (1957), esp. 222–84, 309–28; Krause (1987); Nicols (1990a). Co-option from gratitude, Cic. *Sest.* 9, and see refs. in Harmand (1957), 357–8; Duthoy (1984), 145 n. 4. A city admits to an unrepayable moral debt, *ILS* 6680.

[264] Honorific, *ILS* 6110; *AE* 1937. 119, 121; often accompanied by other honours as well, Harmand (1957), 345–53. For *tabulae patronatus*, conveniently *ILS* 6093–116, discussed (with a complete list) by Nicols (1980a). For the aristocratic house as a museum of honour, Wiseman (1987), 393–6; Rawson (1991 (1990)), 583–5. Functions of the civic patron, Harmand (1957), 358–96, 432–47; Nicols (1980b); Duthoy (1984).

patronage seems to have carried little stigma for the client city—indeed, having important patrons was something to boast of.[265] The client city's sense of indebtedness to the patron may therefore sometimes be more rhetorical than real, a nod to the norms of patronage necessary to establish a relationship advantageous to both parties.

A city could be in debt to a man; so also a man to a city. 'I want you to believe me when I say that there is no city to which I owe more than to this one,' wrote Cicero, explaining his intervention with C. Cluvius on behalf of Atella. Julius Civilis, in rebellion from Rome, was restrained from turning Cologne over to his soldiers to sack by his gratitude for a favour the city had done him; the citizens had treated his son well when he had been arrested there at the beginning of the troubles.[266] Dio Chrysostom found himself facing a vast debt to the city of Prusa that his family had accumulated over many generations. The city had honoured his ancestors for their good intentions rather than for the benefits they actually managed to bestow, and thus the gap between the family's benefactions and the city's honours had grown great. Said the orator, 'I owe you favours for these honours, and I pray to the gods that I may be able to pay the debt.'[267] Luckily for Dio, favour-debt to a city could be repaid with honour: indeed a speech was expected of any distinguished man departing from a city, and in it he should 'announce his gratitude to the city . . . and praise whatever respects admit of encomium, whatever is distinguished about its history, its weather, or the beauty of its appearance.' The problem Dio confronted in chipping away at his debt to Prusa with a panegyric was that to praise so modest a city under the heading of the virtuous actions of its leading men would have compelled him immodestly to hymn the deeds of his own family. Perhaps he should have consulted Plutarch's work *On Praising Oneself Inoffensively*.[268]

City Finance and Public Benefaction

There is no better illustration of the power, ubiquity, and complexity of the honour relations between man and city than the financial arrangements for the day-to-day running, adornment, and entertainment of the

---

[265] On municipal albums, for example, *ILS* 6121–2.

[266] Atella, Cic. *ad Fam.* 13. 7. 4. Civilis, Tac. *Hist.* 4. 63. Cf. Cic. *ad Fam.* 13. 76; D. Chr. 41. 5, 50. 5; Apul. *Flor.* 16. Ingratitude to city, Sen. *Ben.* 5. 16–17.

[267] D. Chr. 44. 4–5 (evidently viewing the direction of the moral debt differently than at 46. 4: above, n. 258); very similar is Hall (1992), ll. 4–8.

[268] Panegyric from gratitude, quoted, Men. Rhet. 430. 30–431. 3, σεμνόν; see also Aristid. 1. 1–2 (Behr); Apul. *Flor.* 16, 18; Lib. *Or.* 11. 1–2, 9 (compared to a public benefaction). Dio in Prusa, D. Chr. 44. 5–6.

cities of the Roman empire. The capital aside, the great expenses of the cities—the provision of wood and oil for the baths, the elaborate religious festivals with public banquets and games, the building of temples, aqueducts, and great public structures—were met only in part by taxation. Instead, wealthy individuals, usually men but sometimes women as well, undertook these expenses themselves, spontaneously or as a function of the unsalaried magistracies of their towns—posts which were, moreover, time-consuming and which came to require a large upfront payment. Thus the financial provisions of the cities of the empire resemble less those of modern municipalities or states (although some indirect taxes were collected) and more those of provincial American art galleries and opera companies, which draw part of their funding from government grants (thus taxes) and receipts, but the bulk of their funds from the generosity of wealthy benefactors.[269] Dio Chrysostom could say proudly of his grandfather that on Prusa he 'spent all the wealth he received from his father and his grandfather, so that he had nothing remaining at all'. And he was by no means unique in having beggared himself for his city.[270]

This civic ethos flourished from the beginning of the empire to its end. There had always been notables unwilling or unable to be the benefactors of their cities, and thus corresponding legislation to compel them to pull their weight; perhaps the ranks of these notables swelled in late antiquity. Yet on the evidence, even in the face of economic confusion and increasing burdens imposed by a ponderous imperial government, over large areas of the empire the spirit of civic generosity waned little, even if poverty sharply restricted its late-antique expression. Yet why did the rich of the cities of the empire act in this way?[271]

[269] For a list of the various *munera* a town handed out to its wealthy citizens, Lepelley (1979–81), i. 207; discussion, Neesen (1981). For the size of the phenomenon of benefaction in the East and the range of possible benefactions, Quass (1993). On the financial aspects, Duncan-Jones (1990: 174–84), whose analysis of public buildings in North African towns has 58% built by benefactors, the rest from public funds. And by the 2nd cent., perhaps the largest source of a city's 'public' money was *summae honorariae*, the required payments made to the city upon election to the city council, a magistracy, or a priesthood (Duncan-Jones (1982), 82–8; (1990), 176–8). On female benefactors, Boatwright (1991), on the magnificent Plancia Magna of Perge; but see van Bremen (1996) for the limits of female participation.

[270] Dio's grandfather, D. Chr. 46. 3 (almost certainly untrue). Ruinous outlay, cf. D. Chr. 66. 2; J. Chr. *de Ian. Glor.* 7; *Dig.* 50. 2. 8 (Hermogenian); Harmand (1957), 385.

[271] Against the old view that this spirit of benefaction declines through the centuries of the empire: for the 3rd cent. see Jacques (1981); (1984), 351–78, 719–65; Duncan-Jones (1990), 163–73; 4th cent. and later, see Mrozek (1978), 366; Lepelley (1979–81), i. 293–318; Roueché (1989a), p. xxv; Veyne (1990), 26–9. It can still be seen as the barbarians close in: Sid. *Ep.*

In Greek, one of the usual terms for a public benefaction was *philo-timia*, an act of 'glory-love'. It was in honour terms that the rich man's motivation, involving so much trouble and expense, was chiefly under-stood: he devoted to the city his money and effort and got honour in return—cheering in the assembly and the voting of honorific decrees and monuments. Men who were willing to serve their town as magistrates were those who strove 'for accretions to their reputation and honours and greater power than others and crowns and seats of honour and pur-ple garments, and having fixed their gaze upon them and hanging upon them, they do and say those things which will gain them reputation.'[272] 'Bait', an orator termed the honours a city had to offer its benefactors, for they lured citizens into performing civic magistracies and benefac-tions.[273] Late third-century papyri from Egypt permit us vicarious atten-dance at the meetings of the city senate—where magistrates and liturgists were chosen—to see how this worked. A candidate was nominated and the city senate cried out in unison, 'Upright, faithful Nilus! Ever-hon-ourable is Nilus! Success to him!' If a candidate proved reluctant to take an office—'the office is beyond my powers'—he might be chivvied into it: 'Upright, faithful Ptolemaeus!'[274] And in the West honorific acclama-tion was used to elicit benefaction as well. When, in the arena, successful beast-fighters appealed through a herald for a gratuity, the crowd chanted at Magerius, the benefactor who had paid for the games, 'Let future givers of games learn by your example! Let past ones learn of it! Where, when, will we get such games again? You will give games as if you were quaestor! You will give games from your own money! This will be your day!' Magerius yielded. The crowd shouted, 'This is what it means to own property! This is what it means to be powerful!' Magerius was so

---

5. 20. 2, 6. 12. Of course the type of projects undertaken evolved over time and the kind of building inspired changed as the empire became Christian, Ward-Perkins (1984). For an economical review of current approaches to the phenomenon of public benefaction, G. M. Rogers (1991*a*: 29–30); and note particularly Veyne (1990: 5–156), for a less reductionist approach than mine.

[272] D. Chr. 34. 29, δόξας καὶ τιμάς (a good passage for bringing out the disproportion between the desire for power and the desire for prestige). See also Philostr. *VS* 2. 1 (551–2), 2. 25 (610); D. Chr. 34. 35; Pliny, *Ep.* 5. 11; *IGR* iii. 68. Honour from games, Apul. *Met.* 10. 18; Dio 53. 27. 6; Aug. *Conf.* 1. 10. 16; Robert (1940*a*) *passim*, for *philotimia*, pp. 276–80: its mean-ing stretches from the competitive emotion which gives rise to a civic benefaction to the benefaction itself, especially games; φιλοτιμεῖσθαι can be the verb used for giving an exhi-bition of gladiators.

[273] D. Chr. 66. 2.

[274] *P.Oxy.* 1413. 13 and 1415. 25, 27 (trans. Grenfell and Hunt). Cf. *P.Oxy.* 1414. 25–7; Aristid. 50. 101 (Behr). On election procedure in Egypt, Bowman (1971), 98–107. Honour for benefactors in patristic authors, Robert (1960*a*), 570–3, and esp. J. Chr. *de Ian. Glor.* 10.

delighted by the whole episode that he had the occasion immortalized in mosaic. Such focused honorific cheering was extremely hard for a Greek or Roman to resist.[275] And, as Magerius' crowd had called upon them to do, other potential benefactors looked on in envy: honours stoked the roaring furnace of rivalry. A priest of the imperial cult at Xanthos was honoured for having given games 'out of rivalry in acts of love of glory with the high priests of the province'.[276]

Gratitude to one's town, whether for upbringing, services, honour, or office, also played its role in inspiring public benefaction.[277] 'In order to make return for the honour Rufinus gave hand-outs to the town councillors . . . wine to the people, and produced games.' On a grander level, the town of Tifernum Tiberinum honoured Pliny, when he was a young man, by naming him their patron. He felt a debt, and built them a temple at his own expense.[278] And the town's own gratitude required honours for benefactors. Thus a statue went up, with an inscription on the base:

The whole people . . . put this up and dedicated it as a perpetual witness to their gratitude to L. Rasinius . . . Saturninus Maximianus . . . on account of . . . his giving games, and his zealous liberality towards individual citizens.[279]

The appropriate degree of gratitude was carefully reckoned, and honours doled out accordingly. Another worthy, L. Postumius Felix Celerinus, gave his townsmen three days of gladiatorial games, and in turn was voted not one statue, but one for each of the town's civic *curiae*, 'in order that his extraordinary goodwill be equalled by the number of statues— such great honours—with their dedicatory plaques'.[280]

Finally, a benefactor might act because the town's honour simply demanded benefaction. It naturally displeased L. Silicius, the curator of Lambaesis, that the council chamber should be tumbledown and that the

[275] Magerius, Beschaouch (1966). For the people as an active partner in setting the terms of benefactions, G. M. Rogers (1991*a*), 19–30; (1991*b*), 94–5. Irresistible strength of acclamation, D. Chr. 66. 2–3.

[276] Xanthos, *IGR* iii. 631, διημιλλῆσθαι ταῖς τῶν τοῦ ἔθνους ἀρχιερέων φιλοδοξίαις. Honours inspire rivalry, *IK Eph.* i. 27. 8–12; J. Chr. *de Ian. Glor.* 4–5.

[277] Benefaction inspired by gratitude for upbringing, Robert (1948*a*), 133–5; office, Apul. *Met.* 10. 18; for honour, *ILS* 6559; Buckler (1937), B. 18; in general D. Chr. 31. 63; *ILS* 7196 (an unrepayable debt).

[278] Rufinus, *ILS* 6839. Tifernum, Pliny, *Ep.* 4. 1.

[279] Rasinius, *CIL* viii. 11349 (Sufetula). See also *ILS* 6113; *CIL* viii. 14785–6; *IRT* 543; D. Chr. 31 *passim*; Sid. *Ep.* 6. 12. 8–9; Robert (1955), 58–62.

[280] Celerinus, *CIL* viii. 5276, 'singulae curiae singulas statuas de suo posuerunt ut eximiam voluntatem eius tanti honoris titulis adaequarent'. Cf. *IRT* 117; *CIL* x. 4725; Hands (1968), 51.

water supply to 'so distinguished a city' should be defective, so he made repairs 'appropriate to the prestige of a most fortunate city'.[281] At the same time, the benefactor was honoured because he was a man whose prestige entitled him to honour by virtue of the deference owed him. Thus Postumius Felix Celerinus, whom we have just met, was honoured not only from gratitude, but 'for his high morals and distinction' as well. The fact of public benefaction revealed a number of prestigious virtues in the benefactor, not least of which were generosity and magnificence; these were honourable qualities, and their possessor was honoured for them.[282]

To attribute the gigantic phenomenon of public benefaction entirely to honour and its workings is far too simple: religious feeling played a role as well, when the benefaction had sacred associations; so did fear, for the poor resented the rich, particularly if they seemed ungenerous to the city, and the poor's displeasure might be made patent by jeering or rioting.[283] The gracious world of *philotimia* may in part be concealing altogether more ruthless social relations: benefactions as the ransom the rich pay for the untroubled enjoyment of their wealth. But for a town's citizens (although public benefactors were by no means always local men) the most important admitted motivation for public benefaction besides love of glory was patriotism, devotion to the town for its own sake. 'Some rejoice in one thing, some in another; some in horses, some in arms: but I love my homeland; I love it as much as the rays of sun rising out of Ocean.' Thus the rhetorician; and the assent of the Greeks and Romans is overwhelming.[284] In modern terms, the ancient patriot combined in his devotion to his home city our familiar loyalty to nation and the fierce local loyalty so strong in inhabitants of Brooklyn, say, or Glasgow. Conventional opinion expected this loyalty to be more powerful than the

---

[281] *ILS* 5520, 'in tam splendidissima civitate . . . omnia pro splendore felicissime [*sic*] urbis'; see also *TAM* ii. 905, col. 5. 104–5 (ch. 20); col. 9. 91–3 (ch. 32); the emperor, Suet. *Aug.* 28. 3. Constructions appropriate to the dignity of the city, D. Chr. 47. 15; Jacques (1984), 715–17. Also, an embassy to the emperor conducted ἀξίως τῆς πόλεως, *IGR* iv. 1756. 32–3.

[282] Celerinus, n. 280 above, 'innocentiam splendoremque'. Prestigious moral qualities which benefaction reveals: Veyne (1990), 101 n. 106; Greek, Robert (1965), 222–8; Latin, see Forbis (1988), esp. 289–90, 298, or open Wesch-Klein (1990) at nearly any page. Greek and Latin honorific inscriptions are formulaic, and often list the honorands' attributes and virtues (for which deference is owed) and then the particular gifts for which the inscription (often the base of a lost statue) is also a reciprocal honour, see e.g. *IGR* iv. 1756. 63–74; *CIL* viii. 26590–1.

[283] Religious feeling, Veyne (1990), 86–7. Fear, Plut. *Praec. Ger. Reip.* 822a; Suet. *Tib.* 37. 3; Philostr. *VA* 1. 15; see C. P. Jones (1978), 20.

[284] Men. Rhet. 382. 19–23. Patriotism and eugenitism, Giardina (1988); Veyne (1990), 88–90, 108–10; Mitchell (1993), i. 206–7.

instinct for self-preservation: 'dulce et decorum est pro patria mori'.[285] And while there were perfectly practical reasons for a provincial in the empire to be concerned about the status of his city—Roman citizenship, and thus standing under the law, and tax obligations were usually consequences of that status—ancient loyalty to city cannot be reduced merely to pragmatic considerations, any more than modern patriotism can. It was an emotion at the basis of the ancient character.

But this emotion was inextricably bound up with considerations of honour. What did it mean to love one's city? The ancient patriot concerned himself with his city's honour, and the duty of civic patriotism was, in part, the duty to honour one's city. 'First, men need the gods . . . secondly, their cities: for cities must be honoured next after the gods,' Apollonius of Tyana is said to have written.[286] Why did ancient men love their cities? 'What is it to be a good citizen, what is it to deserve well of one's country in war and peace, if not to remember the benefactions bestowed upon one by one's homeland?'[287] And part of the devotion of citizens was a response to the city's honour: 'Glorious and great is my homeland and worthy to be longed for,' said the traveller.[288] Their city's prestige made up a part of its citizens' own individual honour, and the very love of the city was admired. To be *philopatris*, 'a lover of one's home city', was an admirable quality which, when demonstrated by public benefaction, was duly recognized with honours. And indeed, the value of the honours given to a citizen was increased in his heart by the fact that they were given by his native place.[289] The workings of patriotism, then, cannot easily be separated from the workings of honour. And public benefaction, so vast and characteristic of Graeco-Roman civilization, although it had no single cause and responded to no single need, cannot be understood without an understanding of honour.

CHALLENGES TO ARISTOCRATIC HONOUR

Even very humble citizens participated in, and were expected to be anxious about, the reputations, and rivalries, of their cities: it was hardly the

---

[285] Hor. *Od.* 3. 2. 13; cf. Cic. *Leg.* 2. 5.

[286] [Apol. Ty.], *Ep.* 11; see also Aristid. 1. 330 (Behr); D. Chr. 47. 2. Patriotism directed towards city's honour, D. Chr. 40. 10, 43. 1, 44. 8.

[287] Cic. *Planc.* 80; cf. *Off.* 1. 58; Sid. *Ep.* 4. 21. 3–4.

[288] Men. Rhet. 432. 17–18, λαμπρὰ καὶ μεγάλη; cf. D. Chr. 44. 6.

[289] City's prestige contributes to its citizens', see n. 28 above. Glory from patriotism, Cic. *ad Fam.* 10. 5. 2; 1*Phil.* 29. Patriotism an honoured virtue, Robert (1965), 215–16; Giardina (1988). Value of honours increased, D. Chr. 44. 1.

mayor of Nuceria who crept over to Pompeii to scratch on a wall, 'luck to all Nucerians; for Pompeians, the hook!' When city rivalries turned violent, as the one between Pompeii and Nuceria did, it was mass violence.[290] A city's honouring and dishonouring, as has been seen, was also often a mass affair: 'The theatre is filling, and the whole of the commons sitting high up offers a brilliant spectacle, made up of so many visages that often . . . neither tiles nor stones can be seen, but all is the faces and bodies of men—' and then they begin to acclaim their benefactor.[291] At least in this limited way, then, the commons contributed to the world of honour inhabited by their social superiors. But commoners also formed communities of opinion which attributed honour to their members. Indeed the Roman world was made up of innumerable communities of honour, many of which honoured qualities and achievements that aristocrats (whose standards varied from place to place, and who formed multiple communities themselves) might find strange or repulsive, and which constituted challenges to the way grandees conceived of honour. One such community of honour was the Roman army, where, as we shall see in Chapter 5, a fiercer, bloodier, more Homeric honour held sway; there aristocratic officers had a tenuous, even ambiguous, membership. There were, moreover, other outlooks which denied the value of honour—those of pagan philosophers—and other communities—we know the most about the Christians—whose singular conceptions of honour also had the potential, never entirely fulfilled, to challenge and change aristocratic honour. The definition—the recipe–of honour, and to a lesser extent its very value, was always in contention between rival communities of opinion in the Roman world, and the aristocratic conception of honour, broadly conceived, exerted a profound influence on how the rest of society conceived of honour.

Philosophers and Christians

Some denied the value of honour altogether. It was a commonplace of philosophers that the quest for honour was vain. Contemplate the vast extent of the world and of time: it reduces to utter insignificance even the greatest reputation.[292] The philosopher is a man who 'will bid *adieu* to honours and dishonours and to the praise and blame of foolish persons, whether they be many, or few but powerful and rich. Repute he will

---

[290] Commoners' concern for civic reputation, D. Chr. 32–3. Hook, *ILS* 6443c (good luck to the citizens of Puteoli as well). Nuceria and Pompeii, Tac. *Ann.* 14. 17.

[291] J. Chr. *de Ian. Glor.* 4.   [292] e.g. Cic. *Rep.* 6. 20–5; cf. Boeth. *Consol.* 2. 7, 3. 6.

regard as no different than a shadow.'[293] Glory is not a worthy end in itself. At best (in some views) it may be a subsidiary good, or offer a guide to virtue to persons of inferior wisdom, but (others would argue) no very reliable one since it is conferred by the opinion of the ignorant rather than the wise.[294] Indeed the powerful lure of honour can draw men away from the pursuit of virtue, and inspire failures of self-control, and foolish, dangerous, even evil deeds.[295] When the philosophical rigorist took to the roads of the empire, abandoning city and social convention, with only his dark cloak, wallet, and staff to mark him, it was not least the all-enveloping nets of honour that he was fleeing.[296] Yet however bristly his beard, however intimidating his stare, he could not escape honour. Greeks and Romans could not take off the spectacles of honour, and thus the admiration contemporaries felt for philosophers' virtue, freedom from convention, free speech, or miracles (since philosophers were the holy men of later paganism) was necessarily expressed with honour—by escorting and even civic tributes like statues.[297] 'Philosopher' even became a civic title, used to acclaim—to honour—civic benefactors.[298] To describe the intellectual prominence and following of philosophers, the terminology of honour was perforce employed.[299] And the influence of philosophers was conceived exactly in terms of the honour they enjoyed: 'If there should be any', Cicero avers, 'who may be moved by the distinction of philosophers, then let them briefly pay attention and listen to those whose distinction and glory are the greatest among learned men.'[300] As much as philosophers might reject the personal pursuit of honour, they no more than any other members of their society could reject honour as a deep structure by which to conceive, understand, and interact with their world. They had no alternative paradigm to honour to offer their contemporaries, not even a compelling alternative rhetoric of admiration for their own ideas and way of life. Philosophers were doomed to be honoured for their scorn of honour.

Even philosophers' personal rejection of honour was by no means unproblematic: accusations of hypocrisy from outside the world of phi-

---

[293] D. Chr. 67. 3, δόξα. For philosophical attacks on glory, cf. Epict. *Ench.* 19. 2, 24. 1; Sen. *Const.* 19. 1; *Ira* 3. 41. 1; Lucian, *Nigr.* 4; and Brunt (1974*b*: 20) gathers a crop from Marcus Aurelius' *Meditations*.

[294] Cic. *Fin.* 5. 69 and Plut. *Agis* 1–2 vs. D. Chr. 67.   [295] D. Chr. 66.

[296] For the wandering philosopher see Philostratus' idealized portrait of Apollonius of Tyana; for the philosophical outfit, Hahn (1989), 33–45.

[297] Lucian, *Demon.* 11, 58, 63; *Peregr.* 18; Philostr. *VA* 5. 24; [Ap. Ty.] *Ep.* 11, 47, 53, and esp. 62; Eunap. *VS* 477. For philosophers as holy men, Fowden (1982).

[298] Hahn (1989), 161–4.   [299] Eunap. *VS* 460, 462, 464.

[300] Cic. *Rep.* 1. 12, *auctoritas, gloria.* Cf. Eunap. *VS* 504.

losophy were common, and within that world, among philosophical rivals, furious charges of *philotimia* were exchanged.[301] Cicero observes, not unjustly, that 'philosophers inscribe their own names on those very books in which they write that glory should be scorned.' The Epicurean Lucretius is a case in point: he admits that he yearns for praise of his poem, a work in which he sternly advocates scorn for praise.[302] But perhaps hypocrisy is too hard a term. Extirpation of the lust for honour was the hardest tenet of philosophy to live up to. As Tacitus notes of the Stoic Helvidius Priscus, 'Even among wise men the lust for glory is the last one rooted out.'[303] Relations between philosophers and honour illustrate above all how powerful aristocratic conceptions of honour were in Graeco-Roman society.

Potentially more significant in its consequences, perhaps, than the philosophers' critique of aristocratic honour was the reinterpretation of honour by the fathers of the Christian Church. The Christian does not properly seek glory in this life: as Augustine puts it, the Christian does good deeds not to gain himself glory, but to glorify God.[304] John Chrysostom expressed the Christian paradox: 'To us gentleness, scorn for wealth, scorn for reputation, mockery of honour from the many . . . this is respectability, this reputation, this honour.'[305] In theory this Christian honour was conferred by God and was enjoyed in heaven; St Basil imagines the virtuous man upon Judgement Day meeting with a celebration similar to the one a public benefactor enjoyed in the theatre: 'God will congratulate you, the angels will acclaim you, all of humanity from the beginning of the world will cast blessings upon you.'[306] It was a topos to describe martyrs as the athletes of Christ, winning a glorious crown by their deaths, or as soldiers whose martyrdom was a glorious victory.[307] In principle, then, Christian views of honour offered the starkest possible challenge to aristocratic pagan attitudes. Activities prompted by the lust

---

[301] Hypocrisy, see esp. Lucian, *Peregr.* Accusations between philosophers, Julian, *Ep.* 12 (Bidez); [Ap. Ty.] *Ep.* 10.

[302] Cic. *Arch.* 26; cf. Plut. *an Rect. Dict. Lat. Viv.* 1128b. Lucretius, wants glory 1. 922–3, 4. 4, but attacks the pursuit of glory, 3. 59–78, 5. 1120–35.

[303] Tac. *Hist.* 4. 6, 'cupido gloriae'; cf. Lucian, *Peregr.* 38.

[304] Aug. *Serm.* 54; in general on profane glory, *Civ. Dei* 5. 12–20. For a less cursory treatment of patristic views of honour, von Müller (1977), 39–87.

[305] J. Chr. *de Ian. Glor.* 15, τοῦτο εὐσχημοσύνη, τοῦτο δόξα, τοῦτο τιμή.

[306] Basil, *Hom. in Ill. Dict. Evang.* 3 (= *PG* 31. 268). Christian glory after death, e.g. Cyp. *Ep.* 76. 2 (*CSEL*); Musurillo (1972), 19. 3; Tert. *ad Mart.* 4. 9.

[307] Athletes, Musurillo (1972), 5, esp. 5. 36, 8. 10; Weismann (1972), 111–14; soldiers, Cyp. *Ep.* 28, 58. 4 (*CSEL*); Harnack (1981 (1905)), 60, cf. 50.

for honour in this life were ruled out; ideally the whole proud, competitive, jostling ethos of the ancient city was abandoned.

In practice, however, Christian glory could also be enjoyed before death in the community of believers. Suppose some Christians, imprisoned for their faith, should happen to be released rather than executed, thus being denied the martyr's 'glorious road to God'? They would enjoy glory from their very imprisonment, and then 'flourish in the praise of the Church'. So much might they flourish in this earthly glory, indeed, as to become unmanageably puffed up, and thus require the intervention of Bishop Cyprian, who wrote that if they wished to maintain their high reputation, they must continue to be humble and modest despite their distinguished deeds.[308] Clearly, Christian honour, although it arose from the praise of quite different qualities, could work very much like pagan honour. Indeed, the distinction of a bishop's congregation (the confessions of its martyrs) reflected glory upon him, just as the distinction of an aristocrat's city did upon an aristocrat. Christian glory could be imagined to adhere to families, just as profane glory did: the descendant of martyrs gained glory from them, and if he was martyred in his turn he conferred glory upon his ancestors. Christian glory could even be conveyed by letters of recommendation.[309] Flourishing especially in the praise of the Church militant were monks and holy men, athletes of Christ winning glorious victories by their piety and feats of asceticism.[310] Holy men scorned earthly honour, but were honoured for their piety, so much indeed that the excess of honour could be viewed as the reason why St Symeon took refuge on a pillar.[311] Just as ancient pagans grappled with the unusual distinction of philosophers by honouring them, so Christians reached inevitably for the same intellectual tools to deal with those who were outstanding in their eyes.

Nothing could be further from the traditional definition of aristocratic honour than the Christian holy man, half-naked and stinking atop his pillar. But once the possibility of Christian honour in this world was admitted, the way was open for a *rapprochement* between Christian honour and the pagan honour of the aristocracy. Wayne Meeks argues that members of even the early Church largely respected honour as it existed

---

[308] Cyp. *Ep.* 10. 5 (*CSEL*); intervention, *Ep.* 13, 14. 2.

[309] Bishop, Cyp. *Ep.* 13. 1 (*CSEL*), 'ecclesiae enim gloria praepositi gloria est'. Families, *Ep.* 39. 3. Letter of recommendation, Aug. *Ep.* 230.

[310] Athletes, Weismann (1972), 114–17; Theodoret, *Religiosa Historia, passim* (on the agonistic quality of this asceticism esp. *PG* 82. 1468b–d). On Christian holy men, esp. Brown (1982 (1971)).

[311] Theodoret, *Religiosa Historia, PG* 82. 1473a; cf. 1316a–b, 1412a, 1417a.

outside their community.[312] In practice what can be seen in late antiquity is the two recipes of honour blended together: instead of the Christian definition of honour replacing the pagan definition as Christianity spread, we see instead the superaddition of the Christian qualifications for honour to the old pagan set, at least at the top of society. The spirit of the age is well evoked in the Christian Sidonius Apollinaris' epitaph on his grandfather, a great official:

> Here lies the Prefect Apollinaris,
> received after his just prefecture over the Gauls
> into the bosom of his mourning homeland.
> Wisest and most advantageous husbandman
> in field, war, and public business,
> and a free man under tyrannical despotism
> (an example—but dangerous—to others).
> But this is esteemed his greatest dignity:
> he cleansed his brow with the cross, his limbs with the font.
> He was the first of his line
> to renounce the sacrilegious rites of paganism.
> It is a singular glory; a proud virtue,
> to surpass by hope those equal in honour,
> and ancestors, equal in standing here,
> to excel from beyond the grave.[313]

Sidonius begins with a conventional set of pagan accomplishments: they confer *dignitas* upon his grandfather. Yet, in Sidonius' view, his reception into the Church also confers distinction, boosting him above his own very distinguished forebears. It does not surprise us to see the same author recommending a priest as 'a nobleman, in his home town', and 'my brother', not in Christ, but 'in the equality of our birth'.[314] Churchmen seamlessly mix and mingle Christian and profane claims to consideration in their letters of recommendation. Of course Celestiacus, for whom Theodoret solicits the help of the bishop of Antioch, has a 'wealth of faith', but he is introduced to the bishop as a man 'to be wondered at and magnificent to the greatest degree', a citizen of 'famous

---

[312] (1993), 49.

[313] Sid. *Ep.* 3. 12. 5, 'haec sed maxima dignitas probatur | quod frontem cruce, membra fonte purgans . . . hoc primum est decus, haec superba virtus | spe praecedere quos honore iungas | quique hic sunt titulis pares parentes | hos illic meritis supervenire' (trans. adapted from Anderson). Sidonius may indeed be a bishop when he writes this letter. Cf. *ILCV* 1067 and 1070 for bishop's epitaphs.

[314] Sid. *Ep.* 4. 4. 1.

Carthage, and of a family become glorious in that place'.[315] In short, not even for churchmen, despite their sermons, did the old claims to honour cease to function. Indeed, their writings frequently provide the best examples of profane honour in action.

Predictably, ecclesiastical offices were assimilated to pagan offices. They became 'dignities' to be competed for and boasted of, and an aristocrat's line might be praised as 'flourishing illustriously with both bishops and prefects'.[316] Bishops were viewed as magnates, to be toadied to with assurances that 'however great you are in reputation, and unmatched in rank, you are not to be lauded more for your distinction than for your condescension'.[317] Bishops cultivated their reputations, were furious if they were not treated appropriately to their high social position, and adopted the insignia and garb of the highest Roman dignitaries. They conducted themselves, in short, like the pagan aristocrats many of them had been before their appointment to the episcopacy.[318]

It is a testament to the structural role of honour in the Graeco-Roman outlook that Christians conceived their heavenly reward so largely in terms of honour. It is a testament to the everyday prominence of honour in ancient life that Christians could not keep their honour confined to heaven, but created a scheme of Christian honour—parallel to profane honour—on earth. And it is a testament to the overwhelming influence of aristocratic conceptions of honour in Graeco-Roman society that when Christian honour and aristocratic honour came together in the minds of late-antique Christian aristocrats, those aristocrats lived with the contradictions that are so striking to us. Aristocratic honour quietly expanded to incorporate Christian honour; Christian aristocrats were more aristocrat than Christian.

Communities of Honour beneath the Aristocracy

As a magistrate of Fundi discovered when he turned out in his official robes to greet some important travellers on the road to Brundisium, the

---

[315] Theodoret, *Ep.* 31 (Azéma), τῷ θαυμασιωτάτῳ καὶ μεγαλοπρεπεστάτῳ Κελεστιακῷ πατρὶς μὲν ἡ πολυθρύλητος Καρχηδών, γένος δὲ τὸ ἐν ἐκείνῃ γεγενημένον περίβλεπτον.

[316] Dignities, Cyp. *Ep.* 48. 4 (*CSEL*), *dignitas*; Basil, *Ep.* 239, ἀξίωμα, cf. *Ep.* 98. Competed for, Sid. *Ep.* 7. 5, *dignitas, honor.* Quoted, Sid. *Ep.* 7. 9. 17, *inlustris*; cf. 7. 9. 24.

[317] Sid. *Ep.* 7. 4. 1, 'cum sitis opinione magni, gradu maximi, non tamen esse vos amplius dignitate quam dignatione laudandos'.

[318] Reputations, Basil, *Ep.* 73; Sid. *Ep.* 4. 3. 2, 8. 6. 1–3; furious, Greg. Nys. *Ep.* 1. 30–5; Syn. *Ep.* 41 (Garzya); insignia and garb, Klauser (1974). On the outlook of late-antique bishops, see Brown (1992: 118–25) and Van Dam (1986) for the East; Heinzelmann (1976) and Mathisen (1993: 89–99) for Gaul. For the (usually curial) social origins of 4th-cent. bishops, Gilliard (1966).

upper reaches of Graeco-Roman society were subdivided by finely graded barriers of snobbery and hauteur. Fundi was a substantial town, and he was one of its most distinguished citizens, at the top of its social pyramid; he thought he deserved respect in the greater aristocratic world as well. The travellers, who included a consular, thought otherwise, and hooted with laughter as they passed.[319] A sixth-century notable of Gaza vividly realized that he would be beneath contempt at Antioch, to say nothing of Constantinople.[320]

When a great aristocrat peered down into society beneath him, there was a threshold beneath which, to his mind, honour did not exist; there were people, a great many people, without honour, and best kept that way. Thus the great Metellus Numidicus (*cos.* 109 BC) dismissed a turbulent tribune with the remark, 'I account him neither a friend nor an enemy . . . for I deem him not only unworthy to be praised by men of position, but even unfit to be abused by upright persons. For if you even name a wretch like him, when you can't punish him, you confer honour rather than insult upon him.'[321] Even to criticize such a man was to imply his membership in the opinion community of the aristocracy, so one ignored him. This category of persons without honour in aristocratic eyes included those defined in the law (by aristocratic jurists) as 'infamous'— brothel-keepers, actors, gladiators, convicted felons—persons whose conduct revealed that they had no sense of shame, and thus could have no honour.[322] The slave is the archetype of the man without honour, the comparative historian notes, and the line between slavery and freedom the elementary division in slave societies between those who possess honour and those who do not. Thus it is not surprising to see the jurist Ulpian puzzling about whether it is possible to commit *iniuria*, a legally defined insult to honour, upon a slave. Certainly if you thrash a slave, or sing an abusive song about him, it is an insult to his master, but is it an insult to the slave? Perhaps. The natural assumption of men of the status of the jurists was that slaves had no honour. So utterly beneath consideration were they that one might put up with jocularities from slaves that one would never endure from free men.[323] But at the same time, men of

---

[319] Hor. *Sat.* 1. 5. 34–6. On the duty to snub those who get above their station, MacMullen (1974), 104–13, and esp. *CTh* 6. 5. 1. Cf. J. Campbell (1964), 273, 305.

[320] Dorotheus Gazensis, *Doctrina* 2. 6 (= *PG* 88. 1645d–1648a).

[321] Aul. Gel. 7. 11. 3, 'indignissimum . . . a viris bonis benedicatur. . . maiore honore quam contumelia adficias'. Cf. Sen. *Ira* 2. 32. 3; Plut. *Cato Mai.* 25. 3.

[322] On *infamia* in the law, *Dig.* 3. 2 with Levick (1983), 108–14.

[323] Slaves without honour, Patterson (1982), 10–13 *et passim*; in the Roman context Saller (1994), 134–9; and *CTh* 14. 10. 1. 3 (382) on their inability to feel shame. Law of *iniuria*, see

high status understood that slaves could have honour, of a sort. 'There are ranks in a household,' wrote Claudian, 'and its members have their own prestige; he who has had but one master has the least stain upon his condition.' 'The imperial slaves themselves—those to whom there is a more illustrious rank in slavery—grumbled at such an associate, and, haughty, for a long time scorned' Eutropius the eunuch.[324] And Dio Chrysostom expected to see 'fellow slaves wrangling with one another over glory and precedence'.[325] An agricultural writer suggested that the estate manager 'should conduct festal days by rewarding each who is strongest and most frugal [of the field-hands] with gifts, sometimes even admitting them to his own table and being willing to grant them prestige with other honours'.[326] Here the slave bailiff of an estate is to use honorific dinners to get better work out of his labourers, slaves as well. If this is to be practical they must hanker after the honours he has to bestow. The slaves of farm or household thus constitute their own community of honour, although at a vast social distance from the community of the aristocracy above. And aristocratic authors, even if they grant slaves no honour in aristocratic eyes, realize that slaves grant each other slavish honour in slavish eyes. For 'There is no baseness so great', wrote Valerius Maximus, 'that it cannot be touched by the sweetness of prestige.' Or, poetically, 'Glory drags along the obscure no less than the nobly born bound to her shining chariot.'[327]

The existence of communities of honour far beneath the aristocracy can be illustrated in many contexts. Members of the lower classes naturally structured religious sodalities, trade guilds, and burial insurance clubs on the same basis as their social betters organized cities, relying on the better-off members to underwrite the expenses of the organization out of *philotimia*, in exchange for honour in the form of an ostentatiously higher-piled plate at club banquets, and statues, and honorific decrees

---

esp. *Dig.* 47. 10. 15. 34–45 (Ulpian). Jocularities, Sen. *Const.* 11. 3, 'et ut quisque contemptissimus et vel ludibrium est, ita solutissimae linguae est'.

[324] Claudian, *In Eutr.* 1. 29–31, 'discrimina quaedam | sunt famulis splendorque suus, maculamque minorem | condicionis habet, domino qui vixerit uno'; 1. 148–50, 'ipsi quin etiam tali consorte fremebant | regales famuli, quibus est inlustrior ordo | servitii, sociumque diu sprevere superbi'. Cf. Cic. *Parad.* 37; Stat. *Silv.* 3. 3. 64–78.

[325] D. Chr. 34. 51, περὶ δόξης καὶ πρωτείων.

[326] Columella 11. 1. 19, 'nonnumquam etiam mensae suae adhibeat, et velis aliis quoque honoribus dignari'. Cf. Eunap. *VS* 467 (with free labourers).

[327] Val. Max. 8. 14. 5, *gloria*; and Hor. *Sat.* 1. 6. 23–4, 'sed fulgente trahit constrictos Gloria curru | non minus ignotos generosis'.

passed by the members of the organization.[328] Abuse of a fellow member carried a twelve-sesterce fine in the Association of Diana and Antinous, a burial club at Lanuvium. But insult the *quinquennalis* (the club's highest officer) at dinner, and the fine is twenty sesterces: his greater honour must be the more protected.[329] The way standards of honour in such associations differed from those of the aristocracy can be seen from the kinds of people they elected to office. Aristocrats fastidiously excluded freedmen from positions of honour in their realm, from the town senate, from being mayor or aedile. Very grand persons even sneered at freedmen's free-born sons.[330] But freedmen (although not slaves) are extremely common as honoured officials in Italian trade guilds under the empire, guilds with many free-born members.[331] The dishonouring taint of servile origin was felt less in communities of honour lower down in society; in a burial society even a freedman benefactor might have attributed to him the supreme prestige embodied in *maiestas*.[332]

Indeed, aristocrats' own standards of honour were particularly vulnerable to contamination by far different, and fiercely held, conceptions of honour among professional communities of the legally infamous, far down the social ladder, for such communities might draw in aristocrats, even emperors. To act, to compete with the lyre, as Nero did, or as a gladiator, as Commodus did, was profoundly offensive to Roman aristocratic mores; to do such things was to be dishonoured in aristocratic eyes.[333] But such conduct was less a manifestation of absolute contempt for honour than the unwise pursuit of honour among a different, and wrong,

---

[328] On *collegia* in general, Waltzing (1895–1900); for refs. on their honour-for-money organization, iv. 299–430 and esp. 676–85. Banquets, i. 323–8, iv. 685–99, and *ILS* 7212. 2. 25–6 levies a fine on anyone who changes his seat during a banquet: surely seating was honorific, as at aristocratic banquets. For comic effect, Apuleius has bandits act like a *collegium* (*Met.* 7. 7): when one is elected chief, he is clad in a splendid robe, kisses the members one by one, and takes his seat on the highest couch, *Met.* 7. 9. Villages also work in the same way, MacMullen (1974), 23.

[329] *ILS* 7212. 2. 26–8; cf. *CIL* viii. 14683.

[330] Scorn of freedmen's sons, Hor. *Sat.* 1. 6. 5–6.

[331] Royden (1988), esp. 229–58.   [332] *ILS* 7889.

[333] To the Roman aristocratic mind stage performers are 'ex . . . faece progenit[i]', *CTh* 15. 7. 9 (381); Ducos (1990); gladiators even lower, Ville (1981), 339–43; for legal *infamia*, n. 322 above. But Roman aristocratic attitudes towards gladiators were complex, since gladiators displayed admirable physical courage, Wiedemann (1992), 34–9. And the status of some performers was higher in the East: athletes (see p. 43 above) might be of gentle birth, as might musicians on traditional instruments like the *cithara*, Nero's joy (Roueché (1993), no. 68–9); actors as well might rise to civic prominence. The West took fitful notice of the different standards of the East: Ulpian (*Dig.* 3. 2. 4. pr.) liberates athletes and musicians from legal *infamia*.

set.[334] Of gladiatorial combat Bishop Cyprian of Carthage wrote, 'For the secular combat men are trained and prepared, and reckon it a great glory for their honour, if it should happen to them to be crowned in the sight of the people and in the presence of the emperor.'[335] 'The bold Polynices has glory in arms,' reads one gladiator's epitaph; 'I was by no means inglorious among the living,' reads another.[336] Despite the epitaph of a beast-fighter which insisted that he was of a 'conspicuous and glorious line', the qualities—strength of body, boldness, skill at arms—which contributed to the prestige of gladiators (a savage and desperate breed, many of them slaves) were predictably different from those which exalted an aristocrat.[337] It was exactly the simplicity and brutality of this rude honour, and the ferocity with which it was pursued in the hothouse atmosphere of the gladiator training-schools and amidst the frantic adulation of the crowd, which could make it attractive even to the great. For Commodus was by no means the only Roman aristocrat to practise as a gladiator and be delighted to receive a gladiator's honours and titles.[338]

Nor was Nero the only Roman aristocrat to be attracted by the rivalries of professional musicians, actors, mimes, the turmoils of the theatrical *demi-monde* so vastly despised by the Roman aristocracy.[339] All of these skills were practised competitively—as contests in public games—and the victors crowed and gloried in their triumphs. The storage rooms of performers glower at one another across a passage in the theatre at Aphrodisias, an inscription proclaiming the 'unbeatable equipment of the unbeatable Autolycus, victor at Nemea' facing 'the unbeatable equipment of Kapyras and Philologus, Olympic victor'. Their owners were probably mimes. Proud as well was 'Ulpius Apolaustus, the greatest of the pantomimes, crowned in competition with actors and all performers

[334] Commodus seeks an ἀνδρείας δόξαν, Herod. 1. 13. 8. Nero, Tac. *Ann.* 16. 4, 'se aequum adversum aemulos et religione iudicum meritam laudem adsecuturum'; and in general, Suet. *Nero* 55, 'erat illi aeternitatis perpetuaeque famae cupido, sed inconsulta'. On Nero's sense of competitiveness: Suet. *Nero* 53–4; he was rumoured to have killed the actor Paris out of rivalry.

[335] Cyp. *Ep.* 58. 8 (*CSEL*), 'magnam gloriam conputant honoris sui'. Cf. Sen. *Prov.* 3. 4; Pliny, *Paneg.* 33.

[336] Robert (1940a), nos. 169, δόξα, and 260, οὐ . . . [ἄδ]οξος.

[337] Ibid. no. 25. 2, εὐσήμου δὲ γένους καὶ ἐνδ[όξου]; beast-fighting was less *déclassé*, Roueché (1993), 74–5. Gladiators' honour and qualities, Robert (1940a), 302–5; see also *ILS* 5150; re-emphasized by many of the professional names they took: Hector, Pugnax, Ferox, etc., see Ville (1981), 308–9.

[338] For gladiators' honours, Ville (1981), 313–18 and esp. *ILS* 5083–83a. Commodus' gladiatorial honours, *HA Comm.* 11. 10–12, 12. 11–12, 15. 8; Dio 72(73L). 22. 3; Herod. 1. 15. 8–9. Aristocrats as gladiators, Ville (1981), 255–62; and esp. Juv. 8. 199–210.

[339] Leppin (1992), 142–7; and esp. Juv. 8. 185–99; Tac. *Hist.* 3. 62.

twelve times'; indeed, the rivalries of pantomimes were so intense, and so keenly supported by their fans, that they gave rise to repeated riots at Rome.[340]

A few eccentric aristocrats aside, it was not likely in the long run that such competing definitions of honour would have much effect on aristocratic standards. Studies of decoration of the walls of houses at Pompeii and of tombstones in imperial North Africa vividly illustrate the tendency of the empire's lesser inhabitants to adopt upper-class status symbols.[341] As small men aped the ways of their betters, cultural influence flowed overwhelmingly downwards in Graeco-Roman society, rather than up. Martial bitingly reflected on snobbery of this type:

> Torquatus has a mansion four miles from the city:
> Otacilius bought a tiny farm at the same place.
> Torquatus built heated baths shining with many-coloured marble:
> Otacilius organized a kettle.
> Torquatus laid out a laurel grove in his grounds:
> Otacilius sowed a hundred chestnut trees.
> When Torquatus was consul, Otacilius was street-warden,
> and in so vast a dignity did not think himself a jot the lesser man.
> Just as a great ox once caused a toad to burst himself, I think
> Torquatus will burst Otacilius.[342]

Such emulation, besides being natural to a strongly hierarchical society, also brought rewards. The concentration of wealth and power in the hands of a narrow élite discouraged communities of honour beneath from setting themselves up in opposition to the values of those above. Associations of humble men emulated aristocratic institutions as closely as possible and used the honours they could bestow to attract generous and influential aristocratic benefactors. The adherence of these benefactors and patrons helped to confirm them as corporate entities with claims to honour in aristocratic eyes, just as cities were, and thus render them worthy of further benefaction.[343] When an association could catch a man

[340] On competition among performers in the West, Leppin (1992), 123–6, and cf. Jory (1988); in the East, Herz (1990), and for musicians see esp. Roueché (1993), nos. 67–9. Aphrodisias, Roueché (1993), p. 17, and 19–25 for discussion. Apolaustus, *ILS* 5184. Pantomime riots, Cameron (1976), 223–4; Jory (1984). It took mimes and pantomimes time to work their way into the more distinguished festivals, Roueché (1993), 23–4.

[341] Pompeii, A. Wallace-Hadrill (1994), 143–74; North Africa, Meyer (1990), 83–91; and esp. Cic. *Leg.* 3. 31–2.

[342] Quoted, Mart. 10. 79, 'consule Torquato vici fuit ille magister | non minor in tanto visus honore sibi'.

[343] Patronage of associations, Waltzing (1895–1900), i. 425–46; as an honour, 445; from which other honours flow, 446. For practical benefits to *collegia*, Clemente (1972), 214–23.

'loaded with dignity and replete with the honour of rods of office', its members naturally offered him the position of patron, 'glorying and rejoicing'.[344] Their eyes were directed upwards, at what would please and attract their social superiors.

Finally, the independent vitality of communities of honour outside the aristocracy was sapped by the co-option of their most successful individual members by the aristocracy, by the eagerness of such persons for honour at aristocratic hands. The Romans knew no inflexible castes; a man could rise from the lowest ranks of the free-born to the highest offices of a provincial town, to *claritas* in the eyes of the local quality.[345] The openness of the aristocracy tended to discourage the growth of flamboyantly different conceptions of honour beneath it; unsurprisingly, the most distinctive conceptions of honour we can trace exist among people who were excluded *de jure* from entry into the aristocracy, such as gladiators, actors, and the like. But such men too were vulnerable to aristocratic condescension. Thus we see an honorific inscription for L. Aurelius Pylades, freedman of the emperor, 'First among the pantomimes of his day, crowned four times in sacred games, patron of the association of Apollonian Parasites [a guild for mimes]; priest of the Synod of Performers, honoured by decree of the decurions of Puteoli with the ornaments of the decurionate and the joint-mayorship . . .' for giving Puteoli a gladiatorial show.[346] Here the honour of two quite different worlds is on display: his distinctions as a pantomime in the world of players, and his distinction as a benefactor in the world of cities and aristocrats. To aristocratic eyes Aurelius Pylades was doubly base, a former slave practising an infamous profession. He was twice disbarred from being made a decurion, but he can be given a decurion's—even a joint mayor's—ornaments: the right to parade as if he were. The senate of Puteoli does not scorn his cash; nor does he, despite his eminence in another area of life, scorn civic honours which might appear to us to proclaim the contempt of those granting them. In general, the despised of the empire did not turn their backs on the aristocratic society that despised them. They were willing to spend freely to gain honours which publicized their stigma: ornaments, since they could not hold offices, or membership in the *Augustales*, a priesthood of the emperor much sought by rich

---

[344] *CIL* xi. 1354, 'dignitate accumulat(us) et honore fascium repletus . . . gloriosi gaudentesq(ue)'. Cf. *ILS* 6504, 7218. Like cities, associations adopt boastful titles, esp. σεμνότατος and *splendidissimus*, Waltzing (1895–1900), iv. 574–5.

[345] *CIL* viii. 11824 with MacMullen (1974: 47 n. 60) for other instances of similar social mobility.

[346] *ILS* 5186; cf. Leppin (1992: 103–6) for other honours to players.

freedmen who could not become members of the town senate. Petronius mocks this perverse ambition in Trimalchio, and Seneca shakes his head at slaves 'who think death or blows more tolerable than insulting words', ambitiously fearing the scorn of their masters rather than their power.[347]

The domination of a community of honour by the values of the aristocracy is nowhere more evident than in the case of the slave and freedman assistants of the emperor. They were a sharply anomalous group in Roman society: often rich and powerful, but hemmed in by their legal status and viewed with the greatest suspicion by aristocrats. This was a proud, stand-offish band, with a strong sense of solidarity, with its own school, its own clubs, its own graveyards, and even pride in birth: to be born within the emperor's household was something to be proud of, and was indicated on a tombstone.[348] But the reason we know so much about them is the vigour of their attempts to act like, and report the approval of, 'real' aristocrats, and to enjoy honour in the wider world. Their tombstones boast of posts achieved in the imperial service—sometimes listing post after post, just as a senator's might. If a freedman in the imperial service was chosen to assist a great aristocrat, then that aristocrat's name, signifying his approval, might be inscribed as well.[349] Just like an equestrian, a freedman might inscribe his imperial letter of appointment, in which—joy!—the emperor calls his post, Master of Jollities at the palace, 'distinguished', *splendidus*.[350] Their taste for distinction outside the confines of the palace made imperial freedmen frequent public benefactors, honoured by cities with plaques and statues and special seats at town banquets.[351] And, of course, imperial freedmen's thirst for honours from the emperor, and emperors' willingness to indulge them with public honours only suitable for men of free birth, was a running scandal under the empire.[352] The overwhelming impression we get of the emperor's slave-and-freedman staff is of aristocrats *manqué*.

[347] *Augustales*, Ch. 3 n. 300. Trimalchio, Petr. 71. Quoted, Sen. *Const.* 5. 1.

[348] School, 'a Caput Africae', de Ruggiero (1895), with proud alumni, *CIL* vi. 8987. Clubs, Waltzing (1895–1900), iv. 153–62, esp. *CIL* iii. 6077. Birth, indication of *verna* status, Weaver (1972).

[349] Hundreds of tombstones of imperial slaves and freedmen indicate their jobs, see *ILS* 1473–1850 or *CIL* vi. 8398–9101 *passim*, and Treggiari (1973). Freedman *cursus* inscriptions, see Boulvert (1974: 121–4) for a list and discussion (adding *AE* 1972. 574), but Burton (1977: 163–4) corrects Boulvert's conclusions. Names of high officials, Weaver (1972), 231–3.

[350] Letter of appointment, *CIL* vi. 8619, '[. . .] magistri tui hortantur ut te ad splendidam voluptatum statio[nem promoveam' (?).

[351] Imperial freedmen honoured by cities for benefactions, Boulvert (1974), 222–8; see esp. Reynolds (1982), 156–64; *ILS* 6579 for special seating.

[352] Bruun (1990), 282–3, and esp. Suet. *Claud.* 28; *Galba* 14. 2; Tac. *Hist.* 2. 57; Dio 67. 15. 1, and see n. 135 above.

The Roman world was, thus, made up of countless communities of honour, some better attested than others, the great preponderance no doubt lost to us. Standards of honour differed from place to place, between religions, social classes, professions; different conceptions of honour jostled against one another, and competed for loyalty. But over all the values of those highest up were bound to exert a disproportionate power. Those who scorned honour could make very limited headway chipping at the bedrock of the inherited principles which governed the conduct of most members of the Graeco-Roman upper class. If aristocrats admired such scorn they might honour its exemplar—the philosopher or holy man—and return to their lives of *philotimia*. The challenge of Christian honour (which the example of aristocratic honour had brought into being and helped to mould) was met by an expansion of the aristocratic definition of what was honourable: Christian honour was devoured rather than fought against. Aristocratic conceptions of honour exerted a profound influence on the values of those beneath them; and the superior honours aristocrats had in their gift exerted a profound influence even on those whom they half thought incapable of possessing honour. There was a hierarchy among communities of honour, just as there were hierarchies everywhere else in the Roman world.

Borrowing Honour

A final aspect of the ascendancy of the values of the Graeco-Roman aristocracy over their world was the way in which communities of honour could borrow honour from one another. Of course a great man, like Pliny the Younger, summoned his friends to honour along with him. He used the prestige of others to buttress his own, and was so used himself: thus when Calpurnius Fabatus built a portico for Comum, and promised a set of gates, the city no doubt conferred upon him their conventional honours, but the benefactor also received a letter of praise from Pliny, his fellow townsman and relation, a letter perhaps more productive of prestige than any number of statues at Comum.[353] Similarly, when Carthage voted Apuleius a statue, it was the flattering interest of the consular Aemilianus Strabo, who proposed the motion, who demanded that the statue be placed in a prominent place, and who said and did much in Apuleius' honour, which elicited the rhetorical question, 'What is lacking to place me on the summit, the peak of fame, upon the very pinnacle of praise?'[354] But this borrowing of honour more frequently worked in the

[353] Pliny summons a friend to honour, *Ep.* 4. 12; honours Fabatus, *Ep.* 5. 11; cf. 6. 34.
[354] Apul. *Flor.* 16.

opposite direction: when a man, or more usually an association, felt inadequate to honour a benefactor, the city was applied to for help. The association commissioned a statue, and applied to the local senate for permission to set it up in the forum, where the city's benefactors were honoured.[355]

Individuals and associations could make up for the inadequacy of their own prestige by borrowing that of their city. But if even a city's honours were inadequate to the merits of a benefactor, that city would endeavour to have the honours of the whole province added to its own. Representatives of the cities of many provinces met in provincial councils.[356] They had their own titles by which to acclaim their benefactors: 'First man of the province! First man of the race!' They erected statues and gilded portraits. Provincial assemblies honoured the officials of the league and its benefactors in the same way, and for the same reasons, that cities honoured theirs.[357] Provincial councils also stood ready to second the honours of individual cities of their province. Thus the Lycian league honoured a benefactor who had made vast contributions to the league's cities, 'with the result that he has been given the testimony of suitable honours by all the cities; thus it was voted that he be honoured annually by the province as a whole.'[358] This was possible because provinces too were perceived to have honour, to which the prestige of individual member cities contributed.[359] Indeed, in late antiquity some of the patriotic

---

[355] Individuals, *ILS* 1325, 5503. Associations, Waltzing (1895–1900), iii, nos. 109–10, 112, and many Latin inscriptions where the approval of the city is marked with 'l(ocus) d(atus) d(ecreto) d(ecurionum)'.

[356] Deininger (1965). Not all provinces had them in the first three centuries of the empire (pp. 33–5), and the cities from which these councils drew their members did not always fall within Roman provincial boundaries: the Romans made one province of Bithynia and Pontus, but they had separate κοινά; Greece had many small ones, while the three Gauls shared one, which met at Lugdunum. A preponderance of the useful evidence relates to the Lycian league (pp. 69–81): growing out of a pre-Roman institution, it enjoyed prestige by virtue of its age, and thus was relied upon heavily by Lycia's rather undistinguished cities. All its activities can, however, be paralleled elsewhere.

[357] Provincial honours: acclaimed titles, πρῶτος τῆς ἐπαρχείας, πρῶτος τοῦ ἔθνους, Deininger (1965), 156 (councils also may play a role in bestowing titles on cities, *IGR* 4. 1249). For provincial honours see esp. *TAM* ii. 905; *IGR* iv. 1756; for Lycia, also Deininger, p. 77 n. 7. Provinces honour their local officials and benefactors, Deininger, *passim* and esp. *TAM* ii. 905 chs. 20, 22–3 *et passim*; Pflaum (1948), col. 1; *Gk. Const.* 18; *IGR* iv. 1756. 75–119. Hadrian created a Panhellenic council, the Panhellenion, which acted similarly: see the dossier of testimonials for Eurycles of Aezani, *IGR* iv. 573–6 with Spawforth and Walker (1985), 89.

[358] *TAM* ii. 905 ch. 58, and see *passim*; Pallas *et al.* (1959) (= *SEG* xviii. 143) with Robert (1960*b*), 324–42.

[359] Prestige of provinces, Amm. Marc. 14. 8. 2–14; also Cic. 2*Verr.* 1. 10, 4. 90; Fronto, *ad Ant. Pium* 8 (van den Hout); *TAM* ii. 905 col. 3. 6–7 (ch. 7), col. 5. 77–8 (ch. 19); *CIL* iii.

loyalty once devoted to cities seems to have been transferred to the empire's provinces.[360] The honour of provinces was recognized at Rome: Cicero insisted that his jury should defer to the prestige of provinces, having lined up Gaul, Cilicia, Spain, and Achaea against a divided Asia accusing his client of extortion.[361] Reciprocity of favours also existed between man and province, as Pliny the Younger demonstrated when he was loath to plead against the province of Baetica, which he had 'attached to himself with so many favours and labours'. Possessed of honour, provinces were thus also capable of gratitude, and so came to appoint for themselves provincial patrons.[362]

Some of the ways in which individuals and institutions, from tiny clubs to cities to vast provinces, came to grips with the world around them were strangely similar; they all had honour, and all used honour's tools. Moreover, the way in which institutions could borrow honour from men and each other, and men could borrow honour from them, indicates that communities of honour were not only arranged hierarchically, but were interlocking, and honour could frequently flow between them. This confirms that the currency of honour was very similar from place to place and up and down the social order, reflecting not only wide societal consensus about the value of honour, but also the firm dominance of one set of standards of honour, that of the aristocracy. The uniformity created by that dominance was one of the factors which permitted honour to spread its tentacles so far over the Roman world.

CONCLUSION

Taken one by one, *testimonia* to the working of honour in the Roman world do not get us very far. We have seen Pliny offer an inferior two possible interpretations of his compliance: 'Yield to my *auctoritas*' or (more politely) 'Indulge my prayers'. There could perfectly well be a third level as well, wholly hidden: 'Do as you're told or suffer some harm to your purse or safety.' Honour and power of other types tended to be

---

8257. Make-up of province's prestige: Cic. 2*Verr.* 2. 2–8; *Flac.* 62; Aristid. 21. 7, 13 (Behr); *TAM* ii. 905 ch. 14.

[360] Province referred to as *patria*, Sym. *Ep.* 2. 63; Aur. Vict. *Caes.* 39. 26; cf. Nörr (1966), 65; Roueché (1989*a*), 34.

[361] Cic. *Flac.* 100. And a provincial assembly might honour a man, *IGR* iii. 473. 13–14, διὰ τὰ σεμνότητα, or as, *IGR* 4. 1236. 20–1, ἐν ἅπασιν ἐπίσημον. Cf. *IGR* iv. 1756. 85–6, 92.

[362] Pliny, *Ep.* 1. 7. 2; cf. 3. 4. 6. Also Caes. *BC* 1. 29; *TAM* ii. 905 col. 8. 13 (ch. 29); col. 9. 102–3 (ch. 32). Provincial patrons, Nicols (1990*b*) with a list; for their functions, Nicols (1980*b*), 370–7.

concentrated into the same hands, and the rhetoric of honour could certainly conceal other considerations, invisible to us because we lack the context for a three-dimensional view of events. A letter from one man making a request of another and alluding to honour as the grounds for granting it would bear an altered complexion if the man making the request were known to be the landlord or creditor of the other: suddenly honour becomes a form of politeness. The author of any given letter of recommendation may always be talking in code: for 'distinguished' and 'highly-sought-after' read 'dangerous' or 'filthy rich'. An inscription honouring a man for building his town a portico would appear in quite a different light if it were known that the townspeople had recently been burning rich men in their houses: honour can conceal fear. In any given case the status of an appeal to honour can never be known; but with enough cases it is possible to establish a pattern of what people expected to happen. The expectation was that what we call honour had great power in society, and at all levels of society.

Honour was not one form of power, but many. Honour was the subject of social rules, like deference, but it also enforced rules, like reciprocity. Yet since honour lay not only in the consensus of the honourable many but also in the utterances of a splendid few, it could be a corrupt enforcer of rules, and the praise and blame of individuals was a form of power in its own right. There were countless other ways to get things done in the Roman world which had nothing to do with honour. Honour draws our attention because of its strangeness to us, not because it eclipsed more familiar forms of influence. Indeed, aristocratic honour was not a form of power which could easily exist unsupported by other types. A man needed the power to hurt to defend his honour, to protect himself against slights and humiliations. Wealth was an honourable quality, and although it was possible to imagine an honourable but impoverished aristocrat, a huge discrepancy between honour and resources was hardly usual. The power to hurt could be converted into honour, by compelling men to praise and not to blame; money could also be converted into honour, by public benefaction. But at the same time honour could be converted into other forms of power, as when a city's honours opened a benefactor's purse, or when clients—creatures of the honour culture—were used as an armed mob. The bonds of influence that held Roman imperial society together were made up of many strands, and the power of honour was inextricably intertwined with many other forms of power.

3

The Emperor

WHEN Augustus learned of his daughter Julia's adulteries, he withdrew into seclusion, overwhelmed, observers thought, by shame.[1] Shame at his own disgusting lusts and repulsive appearance might explain Tiberius' lurking on Capri.[2] Even Nero's murder of Corbulo at Cenchreae could be put down to a fastidious unwillingness to be seen by his distinguished general while dressed to play the lyre.[3] Conjectures like these, whatever their worth, emphasize the emperors' participation in the wider values of Graeco-Roman society. People who knew expected the emperor to have the same sense of shame as everybody else, at least while he remained sane. The collapse of this sense of shame could be depicted as an essential part of an emperor's transformation into a tyrannical monster, and Domitian's ruddy complexion, which fortified him against blushing at his acts, might therefore be implicated in his tyranny.[4]

Yet the emperor's shame and honour had wider significance than those of other men. As Tacitus had Tiberius avow, 'While other men take counsel on the basis of what they believe to be in their private interests, the lot of princes is different: to them, all the most important matters must be considered with regard to public opinion.'[5] For the reputation of emperors was perceived to be not merely a private affair, but a fact of rule. The Roman emperor ruled his empire not only as head of state, head of government, and generalissimo, but also, in the eyes of contemporaries, as head of a society which defined rank by honour. This chapter examines perceptions of the emperor's honour and of the consequences of that honour: expectations about the measures he undertook to

---

[1] Suet. *Aug.* 65. 2, *pudor;* cf. 66. 4; Dio 54. 21. 6.
[2] Tac. *Ann.* 6. 1 and 4. 57, *pudor;* cf. 4. 42; Suet. *Tib.* 42. 1.
[3] Dio 63(62L). 17. 5; cf. Herod. 1. 17. 2.
[4] Collapse: Tiberius, Tac. *Ann.* 6. 24, 38, 51; Dio 57. 23. 1–4, 58. 25. 3–4; Nero, Dio 61. 5. 1, 61(62L). 16. 3; Suet. *Nero* 26–7, 39. 3; Domitian, Tac. *Agric.* 45. 2. On imperial shame see Kneppe (1994), 308–14.
[5] Tac. *Ann.* 4. 40, 'principum diversam esse sortem quibus praecipua rerum ad famam derigenda'.

augment and defend it; about how others strove to attack him and control him by exploiting his honour's vulnerability; about how he used his supreme prestige (and prestige borrowed from others) to rule his officials and subjects. It offers speculations on why it was useful, and even necessary, for emperor and subject alike to conceive of imperial rule in terms of honour, and finally examines honour as a mix of subjective reality, rhetoric, and ideology in the context of the imperial cult, grounding the emperor's supreme honour as much in the aspirations of his subjects as in his own.

IMPERIAL HONOUR

Tacitus describes the emperor Domitian's reaction to his general Agricola's successful war in Britain:

This turn of events, although not talked up in boastful letters by Agricola, was received by Domitian, as was his wont, with a glad face and an anxious heart. For he knew that his recent German triumph was mocked as false because he had purchased people on the market and had their clothing and hair arranged as if they were captives. But he knew that now there was a great and genuine victory, with many thousands of foemen slain, being celebrated with enormous glory. And he dreaded this especially: that the name of a private individual should be raised above that of the emperor. In vain had the practices of the forum and the prestige of civil accomplishments been driven into silence, if another commanded military glory: the rest could easily be ignored one way or another, but the excellence of a good commander belonged to the emperor. Occupied by such worries, and (this was a proof of his cruel purpose) indulging to the full his practice of seclusion, he decided that it would be the best thing for the moment to store up his hatred, until the first flush of Agricola's glory and the support of his army languished; for even now he still held Britain.[6]

The historian, gazing into the imperial mind and divining the emperor's motivation, presents Domitian as justifiably worried that a man with an army might have as much prestige as he, concerned because he perceives a threat to his power. Tacitus' view in this passage, that great honour made its bearer potentially imperial, was perfectly conventional. From the first century AD to the fourth the actions of the emperors, and the

---

[6] Tac. *Agric.* 39, 'nunc veram magnamque victoriam . . . ingenti fama celebrari. Id sibi maxime formidolosum, privati hominis nomen supra principem attolli: frustra studia fori et civilium artium decus in silentium acta, si militarem gloriam alius occuparet . . . ducis boni imperatoriam virtutem esse. . . . Optimum in praesens statuit reponere odium, donec impetus famae et favor exercitus languesceret'. Cf. Dio 66. 20. 3.

comments of Greek and Latin authors upon them, attest the same imperial necessity: that the emperors have as much aristocratic prestige as possible, and that no one have more than they have. If someone comes to do
so, or the emperor loses too much of his, the emperor's political position,
it is perceived, crumbles.

The Nature of Imperial Honour

Observers envisaged imperial honour as the conventional honour of
Graeco-Roman aristocrats: Tacitus points especially to glory in war, but
notes that Domitian also deemed dangerous in a potential rival, and thus
'drove into silence', the prestige derived from civil and legal accomplishments, 'civilium artium decus'. To the ancient observer the honour of the
emperor was little different in kind from that of his subjects; there was
simply more of it. As the same Tacitus had a speaker put it in his *Histories*,
in an analysis of the men jockeying for power in AD 69:

Verginius hesitated with good reason, for his family was equestrian, and his father
an unknown—if he seized the empire he would be unequal to it, if he refused it,
he would be safe. But for Vitellius, the fact that his father was thrice consul,
censor, and a colleague in office of the emperor [Claudius] both gave him the
dignity of an emperor already, and also deprived him of the safety of a private
individual.[7]

And Herodian described the just-acclaimed emperor Pertinax turning
restlessly in his bed at night because his birth was not equal to his new
position, 'despite the fact that his manner of life was praised for self-
control and that he had gained glory in military activities'. The morning
saw him enter the senate and offer to resign in favour of Acilius Glabrio,
whose prerogative was backed by the tattered ghosts of a line extending
back nearly four hundred years to the conqueror of Antiochus III, and
from there (it was claimed) back to Aeneas.[8]

When a Greek notable studied to deliver a panegyric on the emperor,
the handbook he consulted listed the topics he should cover, pointing out
every possible source of imperial honour. They were just those for which
one might praise any great man: his city, his birth, his literary accomplishment, his deeds in peace and war which illustrate conventional aristocratic virtues.[9] His virtues might be beyond the human scale (a view the

---

[7] Tac. *Hist.* 1. 52, 'imperatoris dignationem'.   [8] Herod. 2. 3. 2, εὐκλεής.
[9] Men. Rhet. 368–77; cf. Philo, *Leg. Gaium* 140–8. Men. Rhet. 371. 5–14 suggests that
prodigies which accompanied the emperor's birth should be adduced (or invented); but
these are also to be mentioned in a funeral speech over a private citizen, 419. 25–32. See also
the fragment attributed to Diotogenes, probably of imperial date, preserved by Stobaeus in

imperial coinage encouraged), but they were normal, human virtues.[10] The orator's purpose is to present the emperor as exceptional in profoundly conventional terms. Unusual elements are used only to stop up holes in the usual: the audience expects praise of the emperor's origins, but what if both the place of his origin and his family are undistinguished? Only then does one 'hide the disgrace with some ruse' by asserting that he was begotten in heaven.[11] There are, of course, exceptions to the ordinariness of imperial honour. The newly acclaimed Vespasian glorified himself at Alexandria by performing healing miracles. But Tacitus represents him as scoffing at the suggestion at first. Only after a consultation with doctors (and consideration of the honour consequences of success and failure) did he try, and succeed. Clearly the performing of miracles was not an expected part of the imperial reputation, at least in Tacitus' day.[12] However else the emperor's subjects may have seen their emperor—as the font of law, as a superhuman, charismatic leader, as military supremo, increasingly as God's chosen representative on earth—they saw him also as an aristocrat competing with other aristocrats for aristocratic honour.

The prize of this competition was the empire. 'Commodus slew also Salvius Julianus . . . who after the death of Marcus Aurelius could have done whatever he wanted against him, since he was enormously distinguished and in charge of a great army.' Thus Cassius Dio, echoing Tacitus' description of the positions of Domitian and Agricola. With honour equal to or greater than that of the emperor, and an army, a great aristocrat was perceived by the empire's ruling classes to be in a position to topple the emperor.[13] And to some observers, even an army was by no means vital: thus Plutarch described Galba as 'a man who did not give place to many Romans in lineage and wealth, and stood first in them among those of his own time. He lived through the reigns of five emperors with honour and distinction, and brought down Nero rather by his

his collection *peri Basileon* 61–2, for the conventional origins of σεμνότης. On these fragments, and those of 'Ecphantus' (*peri Bas.* 64–6) cited below, also of uncertain date, Delatte (1942); for a summary of the dating controversy, A. Wallace-Hadrill (1982), 34 n. 13.

[10] Men. Rhet. 376. 18; Philo, *Leg. Gaium* 143. Virtues on coins, Ch. 1 n. 41.

[11] Men. Rhet. 370. 31, μεθόδῳ τινὶ κρύψαι τὸ ἄδοξον.

[12] Suet. *Vesp.* 7. 2, *auctoritas* and *maiestas*; Dio 66(65L). 8. 1–2, ἐσέμνυνεν. Scoffing, Tac. *Hist.* 4. 81, *gloria*. See Henrichs (1968: 65–72) for the whole affair. Further on imperial miracles, see above, Ch. 1 n. 36.

[13] Salvius Julianus, quoted, Dio 72(73L). 5. 1–2, ἐλλογιμώτατος. Cf. Dio 62. 23. 5 (Corbulo), 65(64L). 8. 3–4 (Vespasian); Tac. *Ann.* 11. 1 (Valerius Asiaticus), 14. 57 (Plautus and Sulla); Herod. 2. 7. 4–5 (Pescennius Niger). Or to provide powerful support, Tac. *Hist.* 3. 4.

distinction than by his power.'[14] Men with great prestige were the emperor's natural rivals. In the early 370s, in an odd episode described by Ammianus Marcellinus, a group of officials consulted the black arts to discover who would succeed the reigning emperor Valens. They constructed a magic tripod, operating on the same principle as a Ouija board, to spell out the successor's name. '*Θ* . . . *E* . . . *O* . . . *Δ*', spelled the contraption—and there the dabblers stopped. There was no reason to go on, for the answer was obviously the notary Theodorus, a man 'born to an old and brilliant family in Gaul, liberally educated from the very beginning of his childhood, most distinguished by his modesty, wisdom, refinement, elegance, and learning, who always seemed superior to whatever office or position he was holding'. Alas, the infernal gods did not share the diviners' assumptions: the tripod had of course meant Theodosius, Valens' successor in fact, and the inquirers came to bad ends.[15] Willing or not, men celebrated in aristocratic circles were always perceived as potential candidates for the throne.[16]

Men of too much renown were dangerous to the emperor, and suspected by him, so contemporaries thought.[17] Men with a smaller portion were no threat.[18] Cassius Dio specifically advised the emperor to be careful of distinguished men: do not give them glorious positions and commands of armies too close together; do not give them too long a string of honourable posts or leave them in office too long.[19] And the historians saw other imperial reactions to the danger such men posed: emperors depriving them of the opportunity to accumulate further glory in war,

---

[14] Plut. *Galba* 29. 1, ἐμβιώσαντα μετὰ τιμῆς καὶ δόξης, ὥστε τῇ δόξῃ μᾶλλον ἢ τῇ δυνάμει καθελεῖν Νέρωνα; also 3. 1–2.

[15] Amm. Marc. 29. 1. 5–32, quoted, 29. 1. 8, 'claro genere . . . natus . . . modestia prudentia . . . litteris ornatissimus'. The story is also recounted in Zos. 4. 13. 3; Eunap. 39. 1 (Blockley (1983)). For a similar story, Tac. *Ann.* 14. 22.

[16] Cf. Vitellius, n. 7 above; and Nerva, Dio 67. 15. 5; Pertinax, Dio 73(74L). 1. 1., Herod. 2. 1. 9; Gordian I, Herod. 7. 5. 5, *HA Gord.* 8. 3; Balbinus and Pupienus, Herod. 7. 10. 3–4, 8. 8. 8, *HA Max. et Balb.* 2. 7; Aurelian, *HA Aur.* 16. 1 (probably fictional). And others who never became emperor, Jos. *AJ* 19. 251; Tac. *Ann.* 14. 47, 15. 48, 52, 65; *Hist.* 4. 11, 4. 39. By ironic contrast, Tacitus' description of Claudius, *Ann.* 3. 18. On this subject, MacMullen (1985), 67–8.

[17] Suspected, general statements, Tac. *Hist.* 1. 85; Plut. *Galba* 3. 3; [Aristid.] 35. 10 (Behr); Amm. Marc. 30. 8. 10; cf. Sen. *Clem.* 1. 9. 10. A tradition about autocrats, Arist. *Pol.* 1311ᵃ, 1314ᵃ. Suspicion of individuals for their honour, Tac. *Ann.* 1. 13, 4. 13; *Hist.* 3. 58.

[18] Bar to seeking, or keeping, the principate: Verginius Rufus, n. 7 above; Tac. *Hist.* 2. 76; Suet. *Vesp.* 4. 5; Dio 71(72L). 22. 1–2, 78(79L). 18. 4; Herod. 2. 3. 1, 5. 1. 5.

[19] Dio 52. 20. 3–5, 52. 23. 2–3, in the speech of 'Maecenas', which represents the historian's own view, Millar (1964), 102–18, and for literature, Reinhold (1988), 179–80. Note the statement of the problem at 52. 8. 4–5, in the speech of 'Agrippa'. Emperors did increasingly separate honour and responsibility, see p. 189 below.

exiling them, killing them.[20] And they also saw what men did who feared such fates, acting to decrease their own standing, banishing the crowds of clients from their morning *salutatio*, walking nearly alone in the street, humiliating themselves.[21]

This grim competition for honour manifested itself too in the emperors' frequent holding of the consulship, and the way they reserved to themselves, and walled off from others, certain elements of the Republican machinery of aristocratic prestige, particularly in the military sphere. The great military honour of the triumph passed beyond the reach of those who were not emperors or members of the imperial family, as did the repute which arose from being hailed *imperator* by one's troops, or taking a cognomen from a defeated people. Victorious generals could expect no more than triumphal *ornamenta*, or lesser honours.[22] Consequent upon this limitation of military prestige, pretentious public buildings in the city of Rome, in the Republic a prominent method of senatorial self-advertisement, became an imperial monopoly after the reign of Augustus. In this way the emperor's action against the overweening honour of others, taken through reserving to himself many of the opportunities for aristocratic prestige, also served to increase imperial prestige.[23] As Tacitus put it, since the founding of the principate foreign wars had 'brought worry or distinction to one man alone'.[24] But the emperor could share the distinction when necessary: in the historians' eyes, the grooming of a successor to the imperial throne included inflating the chosen with prestige—from offices, honours, and victories—like a great balloon. After Tiberius' adoption by Augustus, 'nothing was passed over which might be inclined to augment his majesty, and all the

[20] Generals deprived of the opportunity to accumulate more military glory, Tac. *Ann.* 2. 26, 11. 19; Dio 60(61L). 30. 5; Amm. Marc. 20. 4. 1–2. Emperors slay men of high honour, a topos, Tac. *Ann.* 3. 55, 'magnitudo famae exitio erat'; 6. 10, 14. 58; *Hist.* 1. 2; Dio 63(62L). 17. 2, 72(73L). 7. 3; Philostr. *VA* 7. 4; Herod. 5. 2. 1. Individuals killed or exiled, Tac. *Ann.* 14. 22, 15. 35, 16. 7; *Hist.* 3. 38–9, 4. 11; Dio 69. 2. 5, 72(73L). 5. 3; and see n. 13 above for the deaths of Valerius Asiaticus, Plautus, and Sulla.

[21] Seneca, Tac. *Ann.* 14. 52–6; Agricola, Tac. *Agric.* 40. 3–4; L. Vitellius, Dio 59. 27. 5–6; and Herodes Atticus restrains his longing to cut a canal through the isthmus of Corinth, Philostr. *VS* 2. 1 (551). Cf. Brunt (1988*b*), 51–2.

[22] For the consulship, see esp. John Lyd. *Mag.* 2. 8, and p. 182 below. Imperial military honours, J. B. Campbell (1984: 120–56), cutting off the aristocracy, pp. 348–62; last non-imperial-family triumph, Cornelius Balbus in 19 BC; *imperator*, Blaesus in AD 22; cognomen, Gabinius Chaucicus, under Claudius. For triumphs and their honour value under the Republic see Eck (1984*a*), 138 n. 72.

[23] Public buildings, Eck (1984*a*), 132–42; Veyne (1990), 202–3, 235, 361–4, 388–9; prestige to be derived from such building, Dio 56. 40. 5.

[24] Tac. *Hist.* 1. 89, *decus*; cf. 1. 79.

more after Agrippa [Postumus] was disowned and exiled, for it was certain that all hope of succession lay in him alone.' Tiberius was given an army, and accumulated 'a vast concentration of glory', and so was given a head start in the competition against potential rivals.[25]

Increasing and Protecting Imperial Honour

Leaving aside such tactics, the emperor's competition for honour against his aristocratic rivals was hardly fair. More than anyone else he could coerce, frighten people into honouring him. Cassius Dio—the historian most interested in the workings of imperial honour—imagines Caligula addressing the senate, and portrays him imagining in turn advice that Tiberius gave him about the senators:

Treat none of them kindly nor spare any of them. For they all hate you and pray for your death; and they will kill you, if they can. Do not put your mind to doing what gratifies them, nor pay any attention if they chatter: look to your pleasure and safety, as is most just. Thus no harm will befall you, and you will rejoice in all the greatest joys. And, besides, you will be honoured by them whether they are willing or not.

And the very next day the senate gathered to vote Caligula extraordinary honours.[26] Thus the phenomenon—so loathed by Tacitus, so profoundly offensive to aristocratic sensibilities—of *adulatio*: slavish and insincere praise by the senate, and especially on the part of the most renowned senators, whom the emperors most suspected, with laudatory passages wedged into every speech no matter what the topic.[27]

By and large, as Tacitus notes, the emperor knew that the praise he coerced was insincere.[28] No matter; this was honour according to the logic of force. Cassius Dio, with many insincere honours recounted and many to go, admits frustration by the reign of Domitian. 'Why should I have to mention the honours given to him then . . . or always given to other emperors, just as bad as he, since they are given in order that the emperors may not become angry from suspecting—as they would from

---

[25] Suet. *Tib.* 15. 2, *maiestas*, 17. 1, *gloria*. Cf. Dio 58. 8. 1; *HA Hadr.* 23. 12–13; *Aelius* 3. 1–3; *Marcus* 16. 1; and by contrast Dio 60(61L). 32. 5–6. When the emperor Galba contemplated whom to adopt in a crisis, Otho and Piso were attractive because of their pre-existing distinction, Tac. *Hist.* 1. 13–14; Plut. *Galba* 19. 1; cf. Tac. *Hist.* 2. 1.

[26] Quoted, Dio 59. 16. 5–6, τιμάω; honours, 59. 16. 9–11.

[27] Pliny, *Paneg.* 54. 3–4; Tac. *Ann.* 3. 57, 14. 64; Dio 72(73L). 20. 2; *Pan. Lat.* 2(12). 2. 3. Stress on adulation by those with great honour, Tac. *Ann.* 3. 65, 'primores civitatis, quibus claritudo sua obsequiis protegenda erat'; also 1. 7, 2. 32, 6. 2; *Hist.* 4. 4; Dio 61(62L). 20. 4–5.

[28] Tac. *Ann.* 4. 31.

few or trivial honours—that they are being treated with contempt?'[29]
This recalls his earlier description of the honours done to Sejanus (above,
pp. 52–3), honours which threateningly displayed his terrible power to
compel, honours which were the day-to-day proof of the working of terror.[30] Indeed, the problem with which such honours confronted a tyrannical emperor, as the historian tells it, was that they could point up the
fact that not everything was directly under his power. Thus Caligula's
paradoxical attitude towards the honours the senate conferred upon him:

> It vexed him if small honours were voted to him, as it implied he was being held
> in contempt; greater ones vexed him too, as robbing him of his power over the
> rest. For he certainly did not want it to seem that anything bringing him honour
> was in the senators' power to bestow, as that implied that they were superior to
> him and able to grant him favours as if their inferior. For this reason he often
> complained of honours bestowed upon him, that they did not increase his dis-
> tinction but instead destroyed his power.[31]

Yet coerced honour is treacherous: it evaporates if ever the power or will
to coerce wavers, and, if the emperor, like a Vitellius or a Nero, has
squandered his claims to uncoerced honour by atrocious conduct, the
contempt of the world will reduce him to nothing.[32] The author of the
Augustan History, no deep thinker, attributes rebellions and turmoil in
the reign of Gallienus to universal contempt for the emperor's lust and
depravity.[33] This is probably invention, but a useful invention, since it
reveals the expectation so clearly. That an evil ruler's bad morals and vile
acts would inspire scorn, and scorn his overthrow, was an old insight of
ancient political thinking.[34] Good fame, therefore, had great political
value, since it protected the emperor against such a fate. Winning uncoerced honour, 'an empty reputation, in words' which Caligula imagined
Tiberius warning him against, offered a powerful support to the
emperor's position.[35]

---

[29] Dio 67. 4. 1, ἵνα μὴ προσυποπτεύοντες ἔκ τε τῆς ὀλιγότητος καὶ ἐκ τῆς σμικρότητος τῶν
τιμῶν ἐλέγχεσθαι χαλεπαίνωσι. For a convenient list of honours bestowed on the emperors
by the senate, Talbert (1984: 354–71), adding, for senate's acclamations, Rou
ché (1984).

[30] And quite unnecessary, insist commentators who naturally dislike this way of ruling,
since the emperor's power is so obvious, Sen. *Clem*. 1. 21. 1; Dio 55. 19. 6. On coercing praise
to this end, Bartsch (1994), 176–7.

[31] Dio 59. 23. 3–4, οὐχ ὡς καὶ αὔξησιν τῆς λαμπρότητος ἀλλ' ὡς καθαίρεσιν τῆς ἰσχύος.

[32] Nero, Suet. *Nero* 45. 2; conspirators motivated by his disgraceful conduct, Tac. *Ann*.
15. 67; Dio 62. 24. 1–2, 63. 22. 3–6; cf. Tac. *Hist*. 1. 16; Vitellius, Ibid. 2. 87, 3. 39, 58; Dio
65(64L). 16. 6. For Macrinus and Didius Julianus, see below (pp. 121–2). Cf. Dio 59. 25. 5b.

[33] *HA Gall*. 5. 1, 5. 7, 10. 1; *Tyr. Trig*. 1. 1, 12. 1, 11. Cf. *HA Comm*. 3. 4–4. 1.

[34] Traceable as far back as Aristotle, *Pol*. 1312ᵃ–13ᵃ.

[35] Dio 59. 16. 7, λόγῳ δὲ δὴ δόξαν κενὴν λαβών.

Yet the emperor's very power to terrify put him at a curious disadvantage in securing a great reputation, since it inspired suspicion that all honours conferred upon him were insincere. As Cassius Dio advised the emperor:

So far as you yourself are concerned, permit nothing exceptional or prodigal to be given you, through word or deed, either by the senate or by anyone else. For whereas the honour which you confer upon others lends glory to them, yet nothing can be given to you that is greater than what you already possess, and, besides, no little suspicion of fraudulence would attach to its giving. No subject, you see, is ever imagined to vote such a thing to his ruler of his own free will, and as whatever a ruler receives he must receive from himself, he not only wins no praise but becomes a laughing-stock besides.[36]

The solution? The emperor must seek glory through his deeds.[37] While Domitian's German triumph could be mocked as false, the triumph the senate voted Septimius Severus for his sack of Ctesiphon could hardly be, even though the senators who voted them may well have hated both emperors equally.[38] Indeed, Cassius Dio's advice may arise from his insight into Severus' policy. Here was an emperor who treated the senate badly, killing a fair number of senators and openly threatening the rest; at times his principate showed signs of degenerating into a reign of terror.[39] His stark advice to his sons was 'Live in harmony with each other, enrich the soldiers, scorn everybody else.'[40] Honours to Severus could certainly have been deemed insincere, and mocked (if a safe opportunity presented itself) since his was a reign under which aristocrats had to conceal their true opinions.[41] But he avoided the insecure perch of a Nero, avoided living in the shadow of contempt, by pursuing, and gaining, a gigantic reputation in war.[42] His claims to honour were legitimate by the

---

[36] Dio 52. 35. 2, τοῖς μὲν γάρ ἄλλοις κόσμον ἡ παρὰ σοῦ τιμὴ φέρει (trans. adapted from Cary). Cf. Plut. *Demetr.* 30. 4–5. But the care with which the historians (Cassius Dio included) list honours conferred upon emperors by the senate indicates that we should not take this too literally.

[37] Dio 52. 35. 3, λαμπρότης; cf. Herod. 2. 3. 7.

[38] Domitian, p. 108 above; cf. Dio 59. 25. 4. Severus' honours, *HA Sev.* 16. 6 (his gout prevented him from accepting the triumphal procession); Herod. 3. 9. 12–10. 2; Dio 76(77L). 1. 3.

[39] Senators killed, A. Birley (1972), 279–80. Threats, Dio 75(76L). 7. 4–8. 3; *HA Sev.* 12. 8–9. Reign of terror, Dio 74(76L). 9. 5–6, 76(77L). 8. 1–9. 2. General estimations, Dio 74(75L). 2. 2–4; Herod. 3. 8. 3, 8; *HA Sev.* 18. 7. He inspired violently contradictory opinions in the historical record, Rubin (1980).

[40] Dio 76(77L). 15. 2.   [41] Dio 75(76L). 8. 5.

[42] Herod. 3. 15. 2, ἐνδοξότατα βιώσας. Cf. *HA Sev.* 19. 6. Glory his motivation for campaigning, Dio 75. 1. 1; *HA Sev.* 15. 1; Herod. 3. 9. 1, 12; 3. 14. 2.

senate's own code, and by the code of aristocrats all over the empire who did not share the senators' animus against him. Honour is a public, not a private, affair: in a case like this, what the senators who voted the honours actually thought does not come up; there were no grounds for mockery. Actually performing praiseworthy deeds makes the sincerity of honours conferred for them irrelevant.

Naturally, then, contemporaries perceived the emperor to be as vitally concerned as any other aristocrat to accumulate claims to uncoerced honour. Pliny could urge Trajan to undertake public works in the East for the benefit of his glory, and imperial building in the provinces was a large phenomenon indeed.[43] Tacitus could attribute to the same motive Tiberius' paying for the rebuilding of the Aventine after a fire; imperial disaster relief was another large phenomenon.[44] Emperors ostentatiously imitated the conduct of great emperors of the past—Macrinus even mumbled like Marcus Aurelius—or at least proclaimed their intention of so doing.[45] Those who imagined an ideal emperor included the quest for glory as one of his qualities.[46] Historians especially saw this motive in military campaigns. Septimius Severus' ambition can easily be paralleled: even the implausible Claudius invaded Britain, we are told, in search of glory; perhaps he needed to do so especially because he *was* implausible.[47] The emperor publicized his victories in great decrees, on monuments and coins, sometimes even published his autobiography (implying special concern for élite opinion), at least in part to make his claims to honour in all areas as evident as possible.[48]

At the same time as the emperors acted to increase their prestige, they took care to preserve it. Augustus, for example, went to the trouble of writing replies to anonymous lampoons, as did Vespasian; and a late fourth-century author could still imagine emperors doing the same.[49]

[43] Pliny, *Ep.* 10. 41; Mitchell (1987), 352–60.

[44] Tac. *Ann.* 6. 45; disaster relief, Millar (1977), 423.

[45] Macrinus, Herod. 5. 2. 3–4; Pertinax, Herod. 2. 4. 2; cf. Pliny, *Ep.* 3. 18. 2–3; intentions, Suet. *Nero* 10. 1; *Gk. Const.* 275.

[46] Sen. *Clem. passim*; D. Chr. 1. 27; Pliny, *Ep.* 10. 88; Dio 52. 33. 7; *Pan. Lat.* 2(12). 27. 5; *HA Tac.* 6 .6. An old idea, Arist. *Pol.* 1311ª. On the importance of σεμνότης, and how to increase it with personal conduct, 'Diotogenes', in Stobaeus, *peri Bas.* 62 (see n. 9 above).

[47] Suet. *Claud.* 17.1, *decus*; for other examples, Isaac (1990: 387–93), and cf. *HA Marcus* 9. 4–5; Amm. Marc. 31. 12. 1.

[48] On forms of imperial publicity, Ch. 1 n. 40; nor, of course, if they were willing to risk mockery, did they have to tell the truth. Note the motivation alleged for Hadrian's autobiography, 'famae celebris . . . tam cupidus fuit', *HA Hadr.* 16. 1.

[49] Augustus, Suet. *Aug.* 55; Vespasian, Dio 66(65L). 11. 1; late 4th–cent., invented documents in *HA Macr.* 11. 3–7, 14. Cf. Tiberius' attitude towards lampoons, Suet. *Tib.* 59. 1–2: 'oderint, dum probent'.

The historians frequently attributed imperial action to the protection of the imperial honour. Tiberius, it was said, decided against a sumptuary law because it would be impossible to enforce, and that would be humiliating.[50] Nero refused to permit Seneca to retire lest his act be interpreted as a reproach.[51] Marcus Aurelius, we are told, loaded the relatives and freedmen of the late Lucius Verus with money and honours. The philosophical emperor had seemed somewhat less than prostrate at his adoptive brother's death, and was consequently concerned for his *fama*, about which he was very tender.[52]

Cassius Dio's early third-century guide to imperial conduct, the speech of Maecenas on emperorship, placed preservation of honour squarely at the centre of imperial concern: against plotters move with care, he said, for it is essential that aristocratic opinion should actually believe them guilty.[53] The emperor is like the sun: what he does can hardly escape notice.[54] Indeed, if the emperors did not show sufficient concern for their own dignity, the historians castigated them. Thus the verdict on Claudius, for example, who, by eccentric conduct when holding legal hearings, 'so cheapened himself, that everywhere he was openly held in contempt', or criticism of Julian, who conversed with members of the lower classes.[55] And an emperor was praised who carried his position with suitable dignity and hauteur.[56] Emperors, in order to preserve their honour in aristocratic eyes, did indeed pay a great deal of attention to the norms that regulated aristocratic behaviour, while avoiding 'vices ill-bred and injurious to the soul, which destroy the imperial prestige': for proof, consider the extraordinary consistency with which the emperors, and members of the imperial family, practised literature.[57]

---

[50] Tac. *Ann.* 3. 52.
[51] Ibid. 14. 56.

[52] *HA Marcus* 20. 4–5; cf. Brunt (1974b: 14) on scorn for fame claimed in Marcus' *Meditations*: 'on fame he protests too much.'

[53] Dio 52. 31–5; plotters, 52. 31. 9–10 (cf. in practice Tac. *Ann.* 15. 73; Philostr. *VA* 8. 4). On this speech, n. 19 above.

[54] Sen. *Clem.* 1. 8. 1–5; the emperor's visibility was a topos, A. Wallace-Hadrill (1983), 173 n. 48.

[55] Claudius, Suet. *Claud.* 15. 3, cf. 40; Julian, Amm. Marc. 25. 4. 18. See also Suet. *Nero, passim; Vit.* 10. 1; Dio 58. 22. 1–4, 60. 13. 3; Herod. 1. 14. 8–9, 1. 15. 7–9; *HA Comm., Elag., Gall. passim.* For avoiding scorn by not acting like a commoner, 'Diotogenes', in Stobaeus, *peri Bas.* 62 (see n. 9 above).

[56] Suet. *Claud.* 30; Tac. *Hist.* 1. 71; Dio 74(75L). 5. 7; Amm. Marc. 21. 16. 1; cf. *Pan. Lat.* 2(12). 6. 2. On the proper carriage of 4th-cent. emperors, Matthews (1989), 231–7.

[57] Vices, D. Chr. 3. 133, ἀξίωμα; cf. 32. 32. Emperor's literary (and philosophical) efforts, Dilke (1957) down to Marcus Aurelius, and subsequently, e.g. *HA Sev.* 18. 5; *Gall.* 11. 6–9 (probably fictional, but shows the expectation); Eutrop. 10. 7. 2 (Constantine); Amm. Marc. 21. 16. 4 (Constantius); and a considerable *œuvre* of Julian survives. Emperors are criticized for lack of education or interest, Suet. *Dom.* 20; Dio 77(78L). 11. 3; Amm. Marc. 31. 14. 5, and

Of course not all acted well. Those who acted appallingly, like Caligula or Nero, defended their honour by terror. The reigns of emperors unwilling or unable to act in a praiseworthy manner saw great upsurges in *maiestas* prosecutions, in particular levelled against men who were deemed to have insulted the emperor. It is notorious that the *maiestas* statute, originally directed at treasonous acts against the Republic, came under the empire to cover not only plots and assassination attempts against the emperor, but also what we would call slander or libel of him.[58] But the stretch from assassination to slander is not so great in a society where honour is a question of publicized opinion, where imperial honour is viewed as vital to imperial rule, where insults unpunished can bring one into a state of contempt, and where contempt is perceived to lead to destruction.

It should, moreover, be emphasized that in defending their honour the difference between the practices of emperors of all stripes was only one of degree. Augustus fined Junius Novatus for circulating a slanderous letter about him, and the course of imperial history reveals the unhappy ends of a whole variety of versifiers, slanderers, and critical Stoics, like Helvidius Priscus, even under 'good' emperors—emperors who did not permit *maiestas* prosecutions under that name, but still used their power to put those who insulted them out of the way.[59] If an emperor permitted a slight to pass unpunished, or only mildly punished, this was mentioned with surprise, and to Cassius Dio an essential aspect of Augustus' tribunician power was the right to punish those who insulted him.[60] The man who delivered an abusive speech to the emperor, even to the virtuous Marcus Aurelius, could be viewed as one contemplating suicide.[61] Exactly how hard the emperor should press required judgement. Cassius Dio's argument against *maiestas* prosecutions for insult proceeded from the assumption that the emperor would naturally do everything else in

it is bad that Nero must borrow eloquence, Tac. *Ann.* 13. 3. Note Claudius' claim to the throne when Tiberius is considering the succession (according to Tacitus), 'quod is composita aetate bonarum artium cupiens erat', *Ann.* 6. 46; cf. *HA Tac.* 4. 4; Zos. 4. 54.

[58] On the law and its use in the principate, Bauman (1974).

[59] Novatus, Suet. *Aug.* 51; and Augustus was later seen as remarkably mild in this regard, ibid. 54–6; Sen. *Clem.* 1. 10. 3. Helvidius Priscus, esp. Suet. *Vesp.* 15; Dio 66(65L). 12. 2–3 with Bauman (1974), 157–9. None the less, Vespasian 'lenissime tulit' abuse, Suet. *Vesp.* 13. More harsh emperors, Suet. *Dom.* 10; Herod. 5. 6. 1; *HA Comm.* 3. 4; *Sev.* 14. 13; *Carac.* 5. 7; *Gall.* 9; *Trig. Tyr.* 9. 8 (the last two accounts both fictional, but showing the expectation); Eunap. 5 (Blockley (1983)); Amm. Marc. 21. 16. 9; *CTh* 9. 4 (393). And Caligula had those being executed gagged so they could not reproach him, Sen. *Ira* 3. 19. 3–4.

[60] Suet. *Nero* 39. 3; Dio 58. 19. 1–2, 59. 26. 9, 77(78L). 11. 1a; *HA Hadr.* 23. 4; *Pius* 11. 8; *Marcus* 8. 1, cf. 29. 3. *Tribunicia potestas*, Dio 53. 17. 9, cf. 49. 15. 5–6; Tacitus does not agree, *Ann.* 1. 2.

[61] Philostr. *VS* 2. 1 (561).

his power to defend his honour, and that such prosecutions were unwise only because they cost more prestige than they saved: the historian recommends haughtiness and pretended unconcern instead.[62] But all emperors pressed to a greater or lesser degree: their honour was just too important to allow people to attack it with impunity, important because of its salience in the political realm, and important because emperors were fully paid-up members of a society which considered honour, augmenting it and repelling threats to it, a deadly serious matter.

The tender vulnerability of imperial honour was no secret to enemies of the regime: they attacked it. Discussing the revolt of Avidius Cassius under Marcus Aurelius, Cassius Dio pointed out as curious the fact that neither claimant slandered the other.[63] This was indeed an oddity, since insulting letters and proclamations were a standard aspect of civil war. If prestige was vital to ruling, and moral reputation part of prestige, it must be assailed along with the opponent's legions.[64] This method of attack was available also to others who were not in armed revolt. Not only was crude verbal and written abuse of emperors an insult, but also to be interpreted in this light was the contemptuous withdrawal of aristocrats from active political life, as in the case of Herennius Senecio; similarly attacks on the emperor through literature, like that of Curatius Maternus (who composed subversive tragedies under Vespasian) and those of biographers of notorious enemies of the principate. These slights to the emperor hurt, a fact shown by the unhappy ends at the emperor's hands of the writers of such works (which is why anything is known about them in the first place).[65] They hurt especially because the men who thereby established themselves as the emperor's detractors were often very great aristocrats, and as often men whose aristocratic distinction was outstanding because of their great moral virtue. 'Even glory and virtue create their enemies,' as Tacitus put it, 'they arraign their opposites by too close a contrast.'[66] Ostentatious suicide could be a final attack on the

---

[62] Dio 52. 31. 5–8; cf. for the strategy, Tac. *Ann.* 4. 34; Bartsch (1994), 84–5; this logic in practice, Suet. *Nero* 39. 3; Dio 61(62L). 16. 3. Seneca goes a step further: clemency to those who insult will bring glory, *Clem.* 1. 20. 3.

[63] Dio 71(72L). 27. 1.

[64] Octavian and Antony, Scott (1933); Syme (1939), esp. 270–7. AD 68–70, Suet. *Nero* 41; Tac. *Hist.* 1. 74, 2. 30; Plut. *Otho* 4. 3. Later, *HA Clod. Alb.* 10. 1–2; Dio 78(79L). 36. 1, 79(80L). 1. 2–4; and Julian's *ad Ath.* is a manifesto against Constantius.

[65] Senecio (killed by Domitian), Dio 67. 13. 2, and, more notoriously, Thrasea Paetus (see pp. 142–5 below). Curatius Maternus, Tac. *Dial.* 2–3, see Frank (1937). Opposition biographies, see esp. R. S. Rogers (1960).

[66] Tac. *Ann.* 4. 33, 'etiam gloria ac virtus infensos habet, ut nimis ex propinquo diversa arguens' (trans. Jackson).

emperor's honour. Thus Silanus could be suspected of killing himself on the wedding day of Claudius and Agrippina to maximize the scandal.[67] Tiberius pleaded with his friend Cocceius Nerva not to commit suicide, because it would be interpreted as a reproach and damage the emperor's reputation.[68]

RULING THE EMPEROR

The vulnerability of the emperor's honour, and his desire to augment it, permitted the largest concentrations of prestige—chiefly the great cities of the empire, Rome especially—to influence him. Indeed, the emperor's treatment of the urban *plebs* of the city of Rome was perhaps the most remarkable manifestation of his concern with his honour: his giving of and attendance at games; his provision for these games of thousands of gladiators and whole zoos of the world's most curious and savage beasts; his ruinous doles of food and money; and his zeal in ensuring the supply of grain to the city at vast expense and labour. Constantine's decision to recruit for his new capital of Constantinople an urban mob, upon which was lavished the same care as upon the Roman mob (without depriving the eternal city), indicates that the urban *plebs* was not just a beast to be placated, but an important prop to imperial rule. It was a commonplace to rank it, alongside the army and the aristocracy, as an essential imperial constituent.[69]

In so far as the emperor drew strength from lingering constitutional sentiment, the *plebs* had a role to play as one of the ancient estates of the Roman Republic. But Eunapius attributes a different motivation to Constantine: he wanted to be praised and applauded by his new *plebs*.[70] This was an attraction of the Roman mob too: although its members were nothing individually, massed and chanting in the circus they were the voice of the city of Rome, much the most celebrated city in the world; corporately they embodied the awful and solemn *maiestas populi Romani*. Just as the honour of a nabob of Lycia depended in large part on his poorer townsmen shouting themselves hoarse with his praises, so (to a lesser extent) did that of the Roman emperor.[71] This explains, in part, the distributions of largess to the people on important imperial holidays

---

[67] Tac. *Ann.* 12. 8, 'delecto die augendam ad invidiam'; cf. Dio 58. 21. 4.

[68] Tac. *Ann.* 6. 26, *fama*; cf. 3. 16.

[69] Ibid. 1. 2, 14. 11; D. Chr. 1. 28–30; *HA Elag.* 17. 7. [70] Eunap. *VS* 462.

[71] Mob shouting praises, Cameron (1976), 245-58; Roueché (1984), 183-4. Wild cheering of the emperor was usual whenever he appeared, Tac. *Hist.* 1. 32, 90; Herod. 2. 6. 13; cf. Cameron (1976), 170.

like birthdays, the adoption of prospective heirs, and so on. Just as with triumphs, the emperor—with his family—increasingly monopolized the opportunities to be cheered by the plebeians; and the emperors were, naturally, suspicious of men too popular with the mob.[72]

The honour bestowed by the urban *plebs* was one reason for the emperors to cultivate it. But it could be dangerous as well: and not only in its violence (it could be—and regularly was—put down by the garrison when it got riotous[73]) but also by threatening imperial power with humiliation, with loss of face, with the public destruction of imperial honour. In the theatre the commons hooted and jeered at lines with double meanings. In vast crowds they shouted slogans in the streets and around the senate house, and, especially, they chanted, often abusively, at the games.[74] The threat that observers believed such derision posed to the throne in extreme cases was vividly portrayed by Cassius Dio in his account of the fall of Macrinus. The scene is the circus at Rome, the date 14 September AD 217.

The people, because they could escape notice at the games, and emboldened by their numbers, raised a great chant at the horse-race on the birthday of Diadumenianus [Macrinus' son] . . . complaining particularly that they, alone among all men, were leaderless and without an emperor. And they called upon Jupiter, that he alone should rule them, and added, 'as a master you were angry; as a father, take pity upon us!' Nor at first would they pay any heed to the equestrian or senatorial orders . . . who praised the emperor [Macrinus] and the Caesar [Diadumenianus] and even . . . said in Greek, 'O wonderful day today! O wonderful emperors!' desiring the people to agree. But the people raised their hands to heaven and chanted, 'This [i.e. Jupiter] is the Augustus of the Romans! When we have him we have everything!' So great among men is respect for superiority, so great contempt for inferiority, that from that moment they [the people] regarded Macrinus and Diadumenianus as nothing, but already trampled upon them as if they were dead. On this account especially the soldiers despised him [Macrinus] and accounted as nought what he did to cultivate them, and even more so because the Pergamenes, having been deprived of privileges that they had formerly received from [Caracalla], heaped upon him many and untoward contumelies.[75]

[72] Limitations on games, Eck (1984a), 142 n. 105 for refs. Suspicion, Tac. *Ann.* 1. 7, 6. 46.

[73] *Plebs* controllable by force, Griffin (1991), 40. After Constantine's abolition of the praetorian guard, when there were very few soldiers at Rome, the physical threat of the mob was more formidable (MacMullen (1990: 263)), and successive prefects were driven out; but of course the emperors had withdrawn from the city as well.

[74] Whittaker (1964); Bollinger (1969). Individually, the abuse of humble men posed less danger, Dio 59. 26. 8-9.

[75] Dio 78(79L). 20, αἰδοῦς ἐς τὸ κρεῖττον καὶ καταφρονήματος πρὸς τὸ χεῖρον. The manuscript is somewhat lacunose, but the meaning tolerably clear. The historian stresses events at Pergamum because he was there.

From the jeering of the people, contempt; from the contempt of the people, the contempt and disaffection of the soldiers. Given the order of events perceived by the historian, 'respect for superiority', which bolsters the emperor, is hardly just respect for his military power. The picture of how jeering brought about an emperor's downfall is completed by Herodian's eerily similar description of the fall of Didius Julianus:

The soldiers became angry, and the people, perceiving the soldiers' attitude, held him [Didius Julianus] in contempt, and heckled him when he came out and mocked him for his shameful and dubious pleasures. At the circus, where in particular the mob expresses itself *en masse*, they insulted Julianus, and called upon [Pescennius] Niger as the succour of the Roman empire and the protector of the august emperorship: they asked him to help them as soon as possible as they were suffering outrage. Niger . . . a consular . . . who governed the whole of Syria . . . had grown fairly old and had gained honour in numerous and important affairs. . . . [The people] called upon him continuously at their gatherings, insulting Julianus, who was present, and honouring him [Niger] who was absent with imperial titles. Being informed of the disposition of the Roman *plebs* and the continual cries at meetings, Niger was naturally persuaded to expect that he could easily bring things under his control, especially since Julianus was not being protected by the soldiers of the guard since he had failed to pay them their promised money, and because he was held in contempt by the *plebs* as unworthy of the empire which he had bought. Niger gave himself over to the hope of empire [and thus revolted].[76]

Here the disaffection of the soldiers (offered a huge bribe which the emperor proved unable to pay) egged the people on to gibes, as opposed to the people's jeering alienating the soldiers. But both Cassius Dio and Herodian point to two aspects of imperial power they thought vital: the obedience of the soldiers, and not falling into contempt—aspects that were related, but not identical. Contempt encourages a man like Niger, with unblemished honour and an army, to test himself against the emperor. The massed shouting of the people of Rome brings Julianus into contempt not only in their eyes, but in all eyes.

The danger that popular jeering posed to the imperial honour, and thus to the imperial position, made it perfectly natural for some emperors to react violently. When the crowd booed a charioteer whom Caracalla favoured, the emperor deemed it a dangerous insult to himself, and set the troops on them. Caligula likewise sent in the army; and when

---

[76] Quoted, Herod. 2. 7. 2-6, εὐδοκιμήσας δὲ ἐν πολλαῖς καὶ μεγάλαις πράξεσι; cf. 2. 12. 4. For other accounts of this incident, *HA Did. Jul.* 4; *Pesc. Nig.* 3. 1; Dio 73(74L). 13. 2–5. Cf. Herod. 2. 12. 4.

he ordered members of the crowd at the games to be thrown to wild beasts (there was a famine of convicts), he had their tongues cut out so that they could not shout abuse at him as they were being devoured.[77] But the emperors' usual reaction to such treatment, and prophylactic measure to prevent it, was bread, circuses, and money. An explicit connection between public embarrassment and consequently far more meticulous attention to the needs of the *plebs* was drawn by Suetonius in his description of an occasion in the reign of Claudius:

when the corn supply had grown tenuous because of a series of bad harvests, he [Claudius] was held fast in the middle of the forum by a mob and besieged with insults and hurled pieces of bread, and it was with difficulty that he won through even by a postern gate into the palace; thereafter he considered every possible option for the importation of food even in time of winter.[78]

And Fronto notes the same motive for the imperial provision of amusements: 'The Roman populace is held by two things in particular, grain distributions and spectacles. The rule is established no less upon amusements than upon serious things: to neglect serious matters causes the greater loss, to neglect amusements causes the greater raillery.'[79] An emperor suspected of a monstrous crime, killing four consulars, both cleared himself before the senate, and, we are told, gave a double largess to the people to suppress rumours: to discourage the shouted expression of rumours, we suspect.[80] The power of the *plebs* over imperial prestige is emphasized by the willingness of the emperor to satisfy their chanted demands: some just did whatever the assembled people asked for. Tiberius, by contrast, simply refused to go to the games, because it was impossible to resist the requests made there.[81]

Even looked at strictly in honour terms, exactly how to treat the urban *plebs* required a nice judgement. All things being equal, the more food and money and entertainment an emperor provided, the less jeering and

[77] Caracalla, Herod. 4. 6. 4, ὁ δὲ οἰηθεὶς αὐτὸς ὑβρίσθαι. Caligula, Jos. *AJ* 19. 24-7; Dio 59. 13. 3-4; tongues, 59. 10. 3. By contrast, Constantine's mildness, Lib. *Or.* 19. 19. On relations of emperor and *plebs* in public, Cameron (1976), 157-92.

[78] Suet. *Claud.* 18. 2; see also Tac. *Ann.* 12. 43. In general, in the 4th cent. it is an excellent Prefect of the City under whom 'querellae plebis excitari crebro solitae cessaverunt', Amm. Marc. 21. 12. 24.

[79] Fronto, *Princ. Hist.* 20 (van den Hout), *gravior invidia.*

[80] *HA Hadr.* 7. 3 (cf. Asc. 35); and Hadrian disliked chanting, Dio 69. 6. 1–2.

[81] Automatically giving when the *plebs* asks, Jos. *AJ* 19. 24; Suet. *Titus* 8. 2; cf. Dio 60(61L). 32. 2. Tiberius, Suet. *Tib.* 47. Byzantine emperors were less generous, Cameron (1976), 285–8; especially evocative is a dialogue between Justinian and the circus factions, ibid. 318–33.

the more cheering, the more honour bestowed upon him by the city of Rome he could expect. Yet in aristocratic eyes honour from popularity with the mob, and honour among the mob, were quite different things. Over-generosity to the *plebs*, or even worse, personal participation in performances (as in the cases of Nero and Commodus), although it might delight the commons, contravened a variety of upper-class norms, incurred a variety of aristocratic frowns, and consequently cost, rather than earned, aristocratic esteem. Aristocrats expected the emperor to be polite but firm in his relations with the commons; any other conduct was criticized by the historians, weathercocks of aristocratic opinion.[82] To indulge the *plebs* over-much, to participate as a musician or a gladiator in lower-class communities of honour, presupposed vigorous control of the expression of aristocratic views.[83] Thus Cassius Dio, desperate to resist laughing (and subsequent execution) gnawed on leaves from his laurel wreath while Commodus, having fought in the arena, made threatening motions at the massed senate with his sword and the lopped-off head of an ostrich.[84] In an odd way the conduct of a Nero or Commodus might be viewed as parallel to Septimius Severus' wars: an attempt to make the insincerity of aristocratic praise irrelevant by presenting the esteem of the *populus Romanus* as a real claim to honour. But such an interpretation may make art of foolishness. Bad emperors took bad advice: surrounded by flatterers, they failed to realize the degree to which they were offending against aristocratic opinion, or indeed that they were overstepping the bounds of what even the people found acceptable.[85]

It was not only to the praise and blame of Rome that the emperor gave heed. Great Alexandria had a genius for lampoons, and indulged itself fully at the expense of Caracalla. The result, a massacre at the emperor's orders, shows that the emperor attended to the opinions of distinguished cities other than Rome.[86] And the terror of the citizens of fourth-century Antioch in the wake of a riot in which they had insulted Theodosius by

---

[82] Frowns, Dio 59. 9. 7; D. Chr. 1. 28, 1. 33; Amm. Marc. 25. 4. 18. By contrast Titus, who walked the fine line of indulgence to the people 'maiestate salva', Suet. *Titus* 8. 2; cf. *HA Marcus* 23. 2; Amm. Marc. 21. 16. 1. Opinions of emperors performing: Caligula, Dio 59. 5. 4–5; Nero, Tac. *Ann.* 15. 65, 67, 16. 4–5; Dio 63(62L). 1. 1, 63(62L). 9. Commodus, Dio 72(73L). 17–21.

[83] For hints of this strategy, Herod. 3. 8. 8–10, 5. 5. 8 and 5. 6. 6 with 5. 6. 1.

[84] Dio 72(73L). 21. 2; Millar (1964: 132–3) on this episode.

[85] Bad advice, Plut. *quom. Ad. ab Am. Inter.* 56f; Herod. 1. 13. 8. Even the mob thought Commodus went too far, Dio 72(73L). 20. 2; Herod. 1. 15. 7.

[86] Caracalla and Alexandria, Herod. 4. 9. 2–3; Dio 77(78L). 22. 1–23. 3. Other cities' insults to emperors, and their responses, Dio 66(65L). 8. 2–7, 78(79L). 20. 4; Herod. 3. 3. 3–5; Eunap. 29. 1 (Blockley (1983)); and esp. Julian at Antioch, Lib. *Or.* 15–16; Amm. Marc. 22. 14. 3.

abusing his statues shows that this imperial attention endured through the centuries.[87] Great and distinguished cities were listened to, for better or for worse. When Aelius Aristides wrote to Marcus Aurelius and Commodus begging them to rebuild Smyrna after a disastrous earthquake, he sounded three themes: the glory that the emperors would gain from the project, the city's own prestige, and the acts of Smyrna in the old days on Rome's behalf, creating a debt which the emperors should requite.[88] So alongside praise and blame, cities expected to get their way with the emperor by deference and reciprocity. They expected to deal with him just as they did with their civic notables, by exploiting the tenderness of his honour.

In fact, emperors did defer to honour. As Constantine intoned (in the baffling official rhetoric of his age):

All things which tend to the protection of the society of the human race we embrace in the consideration of our watchful care; but it is of the greatest importance that we take foresight that all cities whose appearance and beauty set them apart and place them among the bright lights of the provinces and regions should not only preserve their old dignity, but indeed advance to a better state by grant of our beneficence.[89]

And Pliny offers confirmation that such an attitude had been expected for centuries: when Prusa asked for permission to rebuild a ruined bath, the governor sent the request on to Rome with his endorsement, noting to Trajan that the work was demanded by the city's *dignitas*.[90] A handbook of advice for speakers urged the ambassador presenting a request to the emperor to dwell in particular on the city's claims to honour; and so they did in practice.[91] In a city's case before the emperor, a favourable verdict might be encouraged by the presence of 'high-born advocates', and because 'the worthiness of the city would have had weight'.[92]

The mention of high-born advocates signals that emperors deferred to distinguished men as well as cities. In one case, the emperor conferred

---

[87] Zos. 4. 41; Lib. *Or.* 19–23, and for this insult cf. Lib. *Or.* 19. 48, 20. 30. Of course the destruction of imperial statues could also signify revolt, and be punished as such, Herod. 7. 5. 8 and *HA Gord.* 9. 3 with Herod. 7. 9. 11.

[88] Aristid. 19. 2–11 (Behr).

[89] *ILS* 705, 'non modo dignitate(m) pristinam teneant'. See also *Gk. Const.* 18. 28–9, 184. 2. 57–8; Small. *Gaius* 368. 29. Also, imperial deference to a guild of athletes, *Gk. Const.* 37.

[90] Pliny, *Ep.* 10. 23. 2, 'dignitas civitatis et saeculi tui nitor postulat'.

[91] Men. Rhet. 423; in practice, *Pan. Lat.* 6(7). 22. 3–4.

[92] [Julian], *Ep.* 198 (Bidez; on this letter see above, Ch. 2 n. 210) quoted, 410a, ἀξίωμα: imagining an appeal (not undertaken in fact) from the provincial governor, presumably to the emperor.

immunity from civic duties upon an orphan, noting that 'with ancestors like Asclepiades and a father like Nilus he is sprung from men who were glorious in athletics. So how could it be decent for him not easily to obtain whatever he asks for?'[93] And a violently anti-imperial author alludes to the same norm. 'You answer me audaciously,' he has Trajan say to an ambassador, 'trusting in your high birth.'[94] Herodian noted that the low-born Maximinus Thrax sent away from his camp all men of distinction upon becoming emperor, speculating that he did so in order that 'with no one present to whom he would have to pay respect he would be free to indulge himself in acts of tyranny'.[95] We hardly need share Herodian's conjecture to appreciate the strength of his expectation.

The emperors could also be counted upon to pay back favours done them. When they failed to do so, they felt the lash of aristocratic censure. Thus Caligula 'incurred blame' for killing Macro, 'failing to remember the benefactions Macro had bestowed upon him, and especially that he had joined in conferring the empire on him alone'.[96] It is remarkable to Ammianus Marcellinus that the general Silvanus revolted from Constantius, 'despite the fact that he held Constantius under an obligation of gratitude, for his timely defection to him with his soldiers before the battle of Mursa'. In Ammianus' eyes, this meant that under normal circumstances, Silvanus could rely on coming to no harm at the emperor's hands despite the intrigues of his enemies.[97] Nero's general Corbulo naturally suspected nothing when summoned to Greece by letters addressed to him as 'father and benefactor'; that was the end of him.[98]

Favours done for the emperor could be called in, or hoarded against bad times ahead. Octavian was greatly in debt to Tarsus for the damage that city had suffered in supporting the Caesarians in the war against the tyrannicides. The city's reward was 'land, laws, honour, and authority over the river and the sea'. But with those boons the debt was paid, and

---

[93] *Gk. Const.* 289, ἀ[ν]δρῶν εὐδοκίμων κατὰ τὴν ἄθλησ[ιν]. Cf. 154; Tac. *Ann.* 2. 48, 3. 8; *Hist.* 2. 48 (even *in extremis*), 2. 65; Pliny, *Ep.* 10. 4. 4–5; Philostr. *VS* 1. 25 (533); Herod. 2. 1. 4, 5. 1. 7; *HA Marcus* 24. 2; *Pesc. Nig.* 7. 2; Amm. Marc. 15. 5. 27; John Lyd. *Mag.* 3. 38, 3. 50. It is thus a *mirum* when Tiberius fails to yield to the claims of the grandson of the orator Hortensius, Tac. *Ann.* 2. 37.

[94] Musurillo (1954), 8. 44–5; cf. 11. 88–96.   [95] Herod. 7. 1. 3, νέμειν αἰδῶ.

[96] Dio 59. 10. 6; cf. Amm. Marc. 22. 3. 7–8; also Sen. *Ben.* 5. 25. 2; *HA Did. Jul.* 6. 2.

[97] Amm. Marc. 15. 5. 33; cf. Philostr. *VS* 1. 25 (534). For the expectation that emperors will requite services, also Herod. 2. 3. 6, 5. 1. 6; Fronto, *ad M. Caes.* 1. 3. 4 (van den Hout); 'Diotogenes' in Stobaeus, *peri Bas.* 62 (see n. 9 above). And failure to requite his benefactors can be imagined leading to an emperor's murder, *HA Aur.* 36. 6.

[98] Dio 63(62L). 17. 5.

Tarsus could not expect special treatment when it later got into trouble.[99] In contrast, Rhodes, said Dio Chrysostom, should feel itself in no danger of losing its privileged status, since it could boast centuries of services to the Romans. Likewise Mucianus, so vital to Vespasian's victory, was able to presume upon the emperor's gratitude to treat him impudently thereafter.[100]

Indeed, the certainty that the emperor would pay back favours done him was a source of his power, because his subjects spontaneously performed services for him in order to place him under an obligation. Herodian imagines a man sent to kill Septimius Severus betraying the plot thus: 'My Master, I am come to be your murderer and executioner—or so the man who sent me here thinks; for myself I pray and desire that I may be your saviour and benefactor.'[101] It is certain that in time of need, cities and individuals rushed to offer the emperor money, money he might be reluctant to accept.[102] Many of those contributing will have felt coerced, but Cassius Dio describes men buying used gladiators from Caligula at vast prices in order to put the emperor in their debt.[103] They are acting like the acquaintances of the rich man in Juvenal suspected of burning down his own house in order to build a better one with the gifts given him by those hoping to place him under an obligation.[104] Charged with acting the tyrant at Athens, the rich sophist Herodes Atticus defended himself before Marcus Aurelius, crying, 'This is what I get for my hospitality to Lucius Verus? And you sent him to me!' Having entertained the co-emperor, the plutocrat had a right to expect favours in return from Marcus.[105] Perhaps this expectation partially explains the willingness of great men all over the East to undertake the fabulously expensive task of offering hospitality to the emperor, and indeed to his passing army as well.[106] But one had to be careful when doing favours for the emperor: doing him a favour he could not requite—like preserving

[99] D. Chr. 34. 7–8, 25, quoted 8. Cf. Aristid. 19. 11 (Behr); *RDGE* 58, 60.

[100] Rhodes, D. Chr. 31. 113. Mucianus, Suet. *Vesp.* 13.

[101] Herod. 3. 12. 2 (probably fictional); cf. 7. 1. 10–11; Dio 71(72L). 33. 4². Tac. *Hist.* 2. 37 has the officers of Otho and Vitellius eager for civil war to put their emperors under an obligation to them.

[102] Millar (1977), 140–4.

[103] Coercion, Dio 55. 25. 3, 59. 21. 4, 62. 18. 5; but not always, 59. 28. 9. Gladiators, 59. 14. 1–4.

[104] Juv. 3. 212–22; cf. Mart. 3. 52.   [105] Philostr. *VS* 2. 1 (561).

[106] Ameling (1983), 68–73; Mitchell (1983), 140–3; Halfmann (1986), 79–81, 129–37; Quass (1993), 164–7. For the expense and inconvenience, Millar (1977), 29–35. Aristocrats also boasted of (or were praised for) having forwarded the *annona*, Ameling (1983), 70 n. 36; Quass (1993), 167 nn. 515–16; helped with their cities' taxes, ibid. 177–8; *ILS* 6960; and provided the emperor with local militiamen, *IGR* iv. 580.

the throne for him, as Gaius Silius boasted he had done for Tiberius—constituted an intolerable reproach to the imperial honour. It placed the emperor in the disgraceful position of being a lesser man's client, and the man who did such a favour had to be put out of the way.[107]

The emperor quailed at chanted slogans at the games, treated honourable men and cities with special consideration, and returned favours done him, because that is how he was brought up. In the first place, he acted as any other Greek or Roman aristocrat would in similar circumstances, with an uncalculating and automatic regard for his own honour and that of others: he was no less a creature of his culture than they were. Yet at the same time, imperial honour had a special political significance. The emperor was perceived to occupy a position that rested in part upon his honour in aristocratic eyes: to increase and defend it was, then, an affair of state. The rhetoric of honour was, moreover, a gaudy parade behind which other affairs of state could easily be hidden. The violence of the vast urban *plebs* was a real danger in a world without machine-guns and water-cannon; in times of turmoil the commons could play a role in politics, especially if the garrison at Rome was divided in its loyalties or could not make up its mind.[108] Much safer to yield to a *plebs* which flung gibes than to deal with one which had advanced to flinging rocks and firebrands. Usurpers based themselves in great provincial cities and summoned to their banner great Romans and provincials, exactly the places and types of people to whom the emperor ostentatiously deferred, and to whom he might feel (or say he felt) gratitude.[109] The crudest imperial *realpolitik* demanded a vast, ever-changing flow of bribes and inducements to concentrations of power in the empire, a flow which had to be managed by the emperor without seeming frightened or weak. No taint of weakness attached to punctilious adherence to high standards of aristocratic conduct. As Herodian tells it, Septimius Severus' concession of a share of the principate to Clodius Albinus—a desperate measure to keep him and his fearsome British legions quiet until Severus had dealt with Niger—was represented to his dupe as a longing to yoke to the throne a man of splendid birth, and subsequent honours as recognition for the favour conferred. The historian, in short, imagines Albinus bamboozled by a show of deference and gratitude.[110] Here Severus' spectacular perfidy soon revealed the trick, but the expectation that emperors did defer

---

[107] Tac. *Ann.* 4. 18-19.   [108] Whittaker (1964).

[109] On the sinews of revolt (and thus the powers the emperor needed to appease), MacMullen (1985).

[110] Herod. 2. 15. 4-5.

and did pay back debts of favours from day to day always created the possibility of using such tricks in time of crisis. The fact that emperors by and
large lived by honour's laws made honour something they could hide
behind.

RULING WITH IMPERIAL HONOUR

In his own account of his deeds, Augustus avowed that 'After that time
[27 BC] I surpassed all in respect of my prestige (*auctoritas*), but I had no
more legal authority (*potestas*) than any others who were my colleagues
in any magistracy.'[111] So Augustus expected people to believe that he
ruled the empire by virtue of his honour; and, as has been illustrated, the
historians, other aristocratic observers, and the emperors themselves all
considered honour in aristocratic eyes not only valuable in itself, and
worth defending and increasing, but vitally important to imperial rule.
The aim now is to explain this perception, to explain how the emperor
was believed to convert his honour into obedience from aristocrats and
cities, those upon whom, in large part, imperial rule rested. For it was the
great aristocrats who commanded the army and governed the provinces;
it was lesser aristocrats who officered the legions and came to preside
over much of the administration, and it was the cities, governed by councils of local aristocrats, who did the business of the empire on a town-by-
town and village-by-village basis. Observers perceived the emperor's
subjects as inclined to imitate him and defer to him; they noted the power
(and danger) inherent in the fact that nearly all relations with him had
immense honour consequences; finally, they saw him laying his subjects
under obligations with favours practical and honorific.

In the first place, their own outlook encouraged aristocrats to imitate the
emperor as the most honourable man in their world. 'Whatsoever is
scorned by our rulers is neglected by all; what is honoured by them, all practise.'[112] Emperors' appearance, diet, and hair-style were enthusiastically

---

[111] *Res Gest.* 34. 3, 'post id tempus auctoritate (= ἀξιώμ[α]τι) omnibus praestiti, potestatis (= ἐξουσίας) autem nihilo amplius habui quam ceteri qui mihi quoque in magistratu
conlegae fuerunt'. I will not join the venerable controversy about the exact sense of *auctoritas* in this context, which can be followed in Grant (1946: 443-5 with refs.) and Wickert
(1954: 2287); both the Latin and the Greek versions admit the rendering 'aristocratic prestige' in the sense used here. Also relevant is Augustus' choice of title for himself: *princeps*,
'first'. Leaving aside the position of *princeps senatus*, the term *princeps* is closely allied to
superiority in honour in Republican usage, Wickert (1954), esp. 2039-47. On the title
Augustus, see n. 284 below.
[112] Lib. *Or.* 18. 156; cf. Men. Rhet. 376, a venerable topos, Brunt (1988*b*), 46 n. 20.

copied by the great men of Rome and the provinces.[113] Indeed, it seemed to
Tacitus that Vespasian's example, through 'obedience to the emperor and
love of emulating him', had effected a great moral reform among the
Roman aristocracy.[114] Commentators urged the emperor to take advantage
of this tendency, to rule by setting an example.[115] And onlookers pointed
out occasions when he did so in fact: Nerva, Pliny notes, had stimulated
public benefaction in this way.[116] Imperial officials were seen as especially
inclined to imitate the emperor, and Severus Alexander used this expectation as an instrument of policy, remitting to his subjects the 'crown gold', a
tax due him on his succession, in order to set an example to his officials, so
that (in his words):

> those who will go out as governors of provinces will learn the zeal with which they
> should spare, and exercise foresight for, the provinces over which they have been
> appointed, when they see the emperor conducting all the business of the empire
> with such good order, self-control, and restraint.[117]

Where the tendency to imitate is strong, the tendency to defer to the
emperor's honour will be strong as well. According to Philo, in the ideal
government three things 'tend towards indestructible rulership—dignity,
terribleness, and benefaction. . . . Dignity inspires respect; terribleness,
fear; benefaction, goodwill. Blended and harmonized in the soul, these
render subjects obedient.'[118] So aristocratic dignity was useful. A man
imagined instructing a military tribune on how to murder Septimius
Severus and his son Caracalla cautions him particularly not to be confounded by the emperors' distinction. The almost physical power of
supreme prestige, the blinding light that drove away Marius' would-be
assassin, could, then, be viewed as a prop to the emperor's position.[119]
Seneca represents Augustus saving a man mobbed in the forum by virtue

---

[113] Friedländer (1907–13), i. 30–2.

[114] Tac. *Ann.* 3. 55, 'obsequium . . . in principem et aemulandi amor'; cf. Herod. 1. 2. 4;
HA Pert. 8. 10; *Sev. Alex.* 41. 2. Cities are urged to imitate the emperors, D. Chr. 32. 60;
Aristid. 23. 78-9 (Behr).

[115] Pliny, *Paneg.* 45; Sen. *Clem.* 2. 2. 1; Dio 52. 34. 1–3; 'Ecphantus' in Stobaeus, *peri Bas.*
65 (see n. 9 above).

[116] Pliny, *Ep.* 10. 8. 1, cf. Suet. *Tib.* 34. 1; Tac. *Hist.* 2. 82.

[117] *Gk. Const.* 275. For officials, cf. Small. *Gaius* 380. 2; *Pan. Lat.* 10(2). 3. 3.

[118] Philo, *de Praem.* 97, τρία . . . συντείνοντα πρὸς ἡγεμονίαν ἀκαθαίρετον, σεμνότητα
καὶ δεινότητα καὶ εὐεργεσίαν . . . τὸ μὲν γὰρ σεμνὸν αἰδῶ κατασκευάζει, τὸ δὲ δεινὸν
φόβον, τὸ δὲ εὐεργετικὸν εὔνοιαν. Offered in the context of a millennial vision, but the elements are conventional. For theory see also Plut. *Praec. Ger. Reip.* 801d; 'Diotogenes' in
Stobaeus, *peri Bas.* 62 (see n. 9 above).

[119] Herod. 3. 11. 6, μηδὲ τὸ τῶν βασιλέων ὄνομα ταραττέτω (probably fictional); cf. for
dazzlement, 'Ecphantus' in Stobaeus, *peri Bas.* 64 (see n. 9 above); Philo, *Leg. Gaium* 276.

of his *auctoritas*, the quality the emperor boasted of in his *Res Gestae*.[120]
With the same quality, and a stern judgement, Marcus Aurelius is
depicted putting down turmoils among the Sequani.[121] Otho relied upon
it too in his last hours to persuade his young partisans to flee and save
themselves.[122] A lack of honour, it was perceived, made it very hard for
the emperor to rule. Authors trying to explain the severity of Maximinus
Thrax put it down to his low birth: since he assumed that he would be
scorned by his betters, he strove to compel obedience through terror.[123]
Commentators expected reverence for imperial honour to play a role in
government, or at least liked to think it did.

Honouring

The business of governing, as described in the treatises written to advise
the emperor on how to conduct himself, was presented not least as the
practice of 'honouring' those, both servants of his government and others, who did what pleased the emperor.[124] 'Honour many, trust few,' the
sage Apollonius of Tyana advised the king of the Persians.[125] The historians also assumed that the emperor would act this way, and that the
emperor could gain the loyalty of vital subjects, and cities, by 'honouring'
them; and they add examples of the emperors 'dishonouring' those who
displeased them, something else the treatises suggest.[126] How exactly did
this form of rulership work? Suppose there was an earthquake (earthquake relief was a frequent imperial concern). For the repair of Smyrna,
as Aelius Aristides tells it, the emperors 'invited the aid of men who
would be ambitious through the hope of future honour'.[127] And that

[120] Sen. *Clem.* 1. 15. 1.   [121] *HA Marcus* 22. 10.

[122] Tac. *Hist.* 2. 48. Cf. Herod. 4. 3. 3. Deference to imperial prestige could have dangerous consequences as well: when Caracalla suffered from diarrhoea, and had to break from
his journey to relieve himself, his retainers all stood far off as a mark of respect, providing
his assassin with access, Herod. 4. 13. 4.

[123] Herod. 7. 1. 2; *HA Maxim.* 8. 8–11.

[124] Speech of Maecenas in Dio, 52. 33–7; D. Chr. 1. 17, 30, 3. 132; Fronto, *ad M. Ant. de
Eloq.* 2. 6; *ad Ver.* 2. 1. 12 (van den Hout). For collected literature on works 'on kingship' in
general under the empire, with wise remarks, Reinhold (1988), 183–4.

[125] Philostr. *VA* 1. 37 (fictional).

[126] Tac. *Ann.* 14. 53; *Hist.* 2. 100; Plut. *Otho* 5. 1; Dio (narrative passages) 56. 43. 1, 65(64L).
7. 1, 68. 6. 4, 76(77L). 6. 1; Herod. 1. 8. 1, 3. 15. 4; *HA Hadr.* 16. 8–11; *Marcus* 2; Amm. Marc.
21. 12. 24; Eunap. *VS* 463. Honouring cities, e.g. Dio 69. 10. 1; Herod. 4. 9. 5. Honouring
assumed to gain obedience, Herod. 2. 15. 3; Eunap. 57 (Blockley (1983)); cf. Lib. *Or.* 18. 160.
Dishonouring, in theory, Dio 55. 18. 4, D. Chr. 1. 44; in practice, Dio 67. 2. 1, 76(77L). 2. 4–5.
Honour and dishonour, Dio 63(62L). 15. 2, 77(78L). 5. 2–4, 78(79L). 22. 3.

[127] Smyrna, Aristid. 20. 8 (Behr; trans. Behr), τοὺς φιλοτιμησομένους ὑπ᾽ ἐλπίδων
ἐκήλουν. Emperors' interest in earthquake relief, Mitchell (1987), 345, 349–52. Cf. *IGR* iv. 1441
with Robert (1937: 137), a provincial honoured by the emperor for collecting imperial taxes.

honour might come in the form of an imperial letter (after a different earthquake):

Imperator Caesar Titus Aelius Hadrianus Antoninus Augustus, son of the divine Hadrian, grandson of the divine Trajan Parthicus, great-grandson of the divine Nerva, Pontifex Maximus, in the fourteenth year of his tribunician power (etc. etc.) . . . to the magistrates, senate, and people of Limyra, greeting! I have learned . . . that Opramoas conducted himself towards the cities [. . .] which suffered in the earthquake, in a manner concordant with his devotion to honour, yet again having given most fully the necessary revenues from his own resources, my excellent governor Rupilius Severus having entrusted him even with the accounts of your city.[128]

The hugely rich Opramoas relieved the disaster with his own funds. In return, the emperor wrote a letter praising him for his act (as Limyra, beneficiary of Opramoas' money and trouble, asked him to do) with a good deal more stress on imperial titulature than on what Opramoas did; perfectly sensible, for the point was exactly that no less a person than the emperor, no less than all those sounding titles, approved of Opramoas. And the approval implied by letters like this was a vast accretion to Opramoas' honour:

When the emperor looked benevolently upon his [Opramoas'] policy, and by the manner of his reply encouraged the other magistrates to the same zeal, and encouraged the man himself to increase his enthusiasm for virtue—for the praise of a mighty emperor can do this, who encourages the spirits of those who strive towards highest reputation, and thus provides for the cities an abundance of good men—then Opramoas, exalted by the divine replies, showed his generosity [with another storm of benefactions].[129]

A nod from the emperor, and the coffers of provincial gentlemen gaped open, to the delight of their beneficiaries. The texts of thirteen similar letters from the emperor about Opramoas survive. Because of their honorific quality, they were inscribed for eternity.

---

[128] *TAM* ii. 905 ch. 46, φιλο⟨τ⟩είμως. Restoration of much of this fragmentary text is speculative, but the overall sense is clear; cf. ch. 47. For governors' entrusting Opramoas with other tasks, see below, Ch. 4 n. 222. For similar letters from emperors, see esp. *IK Eph.* i. 41 (with Swift and Oliver (1962)); Julian, *Ep.* 81 (Bidez); *Gk. Const.* 247; Philostr. *VA* 8. 7; *NTh* 18. 1 (439); and Pliny, *Ep.* 10. 60. 1, the collection of Flavius Archippus, summed up as 'ad honorem eius pertinentia'; and see the confected imperial letters of praise in the later lives of the *HA*. References to such letters: *IGR* iv. 1129; *SEG* vii. 135; Aristid. 50. 75 (Behr); D. Chr. 77/78. 26; Artem. 4. 31; Dio 77(78L). 13. 6; Philostr. *VA* 8. 7; Euseb. *Hist. Eccl.* 10. 2; Julian, *Ep.* 40 (Bidez); *Lib. Or.* 15. 7. Also honorific, carrying on an extended correspondence with the emperor, *SEG* ii. 410.

[129] Quoted, *TAM* ii. 905 ch. 66, ἐπὶ δόξαν ἀρίστην . . . θειοτάταις . . . ἀντιγραφαῖς αὐτοῦ σεμνυνόμενος (after a different benefaction); see also chs. 38, 59, 68.

Moreover, if we turn our gaze from the provinces to Rome, or wherever the emperor might be, we can appreciate the multiplicity of methods of honouring which the prince had available. Even a cursory reading of the historians, for example, reveals that the Julio-Claudian emperors gave an astonishing number of dinners. At home, in the provinces, in camp, the round of dinners never ceased. Very well, the emperors had to eat. But Augustus, whose stomach was less obedient than his empire, often had to eat beforehand; he just reclined as his carefully selected guests dined.[130] He was there for another reason: a Roman dinner party was an honorific event *par excellence*. The value a provincial gentleman would place on the honour of an invitation can be quantified: a bribe of 200,000 sesterces, half the equestrian census, was entered to secure a place at Caligula's table.[131] 'Whose table is more honorific than the emperor's?' observes Dio Chrysostom in a discussion of how an emperor might gain loyal assistants.[132] Cassius Dio describes emperors using dinners to gain aristocratic adherents, and Zosimus can imagine Probus luring men to their deaths with the prospect of this honour.[133] So intimate was the association of dining and ruling that by the fourth century a grandee who invited high military officers to dinner could be suspected of imperial ambitions.[134]

Because of the emperor's vast repute, almost everything he did from day to day—and not just dining—had prestige consequences for those around him, and for those with whom he came into contact. 'Many are the kinds of honour, O Emperor,' said the sophist Libanius to the emperor Julian; 'anything whatever that you may give will glorify the recipient.'[135] Like a great whale moving through the ocean, the emperor's wake caught up flurries of smaller fish. Consider a letter of Fronto to the emperor Lucius Verus in the second century:

---

[130] Suet. *Aug.* 74, 'convivabatur assidue nec umquam nisi recta, non sine magno ordinum hominumque dilectu'. Did not eat, ibid. 76. For frequency, also Suet. *Claud.* 32; later, *Vesp.* 19. 1; *Dom.* 21; it is worth remark that Septimius Severus rarely invited guests, Dio 76(77L). 17. 3.

[131] Suet. *Gaius* 39. 2, the emperor's reaction when he found out: 'nec tulerat moleste tam magno aestimari honorem cenae suae', cf. *Vesp.* 2. 3.

[132] D. Chr. 3. 132, ἡ παρὰ τίνι δὲ εὐδοξοτέρα τράπεζα; Compare Louis XIV's table, Saint-Simon (1983-8), v. 603–4.

[133] Adherents, Dio 65(64L). 7. 1, 73(74L). 14. 1-2. Cf. *New York Times* (1993) for a US congresswoman agreeing to vote for a bill sponsored by the US President upon receipt of an invitation to dine at the White House. Luring, Zos. 1. 65. 1–2.

[134] Amm. Marc. 25. 8. 18. When trying to limit her power, Tiberius forbids Livia to give a dinner for the senate and equestrians, Dio 57. 12. 5.

[135] Lib. *Or.* 14. 24, κοσμήσει.

You ordered me to be admitted first into your chamber, and in that way you gave me a kiss without exciting anyone's jealousy . . . I reckon the weight of this honour which you saved for me as vast and heavy. On many other occasions, besides, I have observed that your conduct towards me, in both word and deed, was intended to honour me as much as possible. How many times have you supported me with your own hands, lifted me up when I could hardly rise myself, and almost carried me when, because of ill health, I could hardly walk! With what a happy face and delighted expression have you always spoken with me! How happily you've continued to chat, how long you've drawn out the conversation, how unwillingly you've broken it off! And I rate these things very highly. For just as in the examination of entrails, often the smallest and tiniest bits, when separated off, signify the greatest good things to come, and from portents from ants and bees the greatest things are predicted, thus, from the smallest and most trivial signs of favour and goodwill offered by the one, true emperor, are signified the things which are greatest and most hoped for among men, love and honour.[136]

Here a kiss, a conversation are honorific, and elsewhere seating a man beside the emperor, walking to a subject's left, visiting him, letting him ride in the emperor's carriage, all confer honour.[137] Compare Louis XIV: 'No man ever sold his words, smiles, even his glances dearer.' 'If he addressed anyone, even to ask a question or on trifling matters, all his retinue noticed. It was a distinction about which people talked, and which always granted a sort of esteem.'[138] As at Louis's court, there were also more formal honours at Rome: the emperor might erect a statue or deliver a speech of praise. A few imperial words said in an aristocrat's honour could proudly be carved on his tombstone.[139] Dio Chrysostom expects the emperor to use his praise to gain adherents; Tacitus describes Vespasian using his to urge on his loyalists in time of civil war.[140]

[136] Fronto, *ad Verum* 1. 7 (van den Hout), 'hunc ego honorem mihi a te habitum taxo maximo et gravissimo pondere. Plurima praeterea tua erga me summo cum meo honore et dicta et facta percepi sic . . . ea quae amplissima inter homines et exoptatissima sunt, amores honoresque'.

[137] Conspectus of imperial tokens of honour, in a dream, Aristid. 47. 46–9 (Behr), where the degree of prestige these actions confer is exclaimed upon; also Pliny, *Paneg.* 23–4; Plut. *de se Ips. cit. Invid. Laud.* 546e; *Pan. Lat.* 2(12). 20. 2. And see esp. for honorific imperial kisses: Dio 59. 27. 1; *HA Marcus* 3. 4; *Pan. Lat.* 3(11). 28. 4. Seating beside emperor, Jos. *AJ* 19. 264; Dio 73(74L). 3. 3. Walking on left of subject, going out to meet, Suet. *Claud.* 24. 3. Visits to others, letting them ride with emperor, refs. collected by A. Wallace-Hadrill (1982), 40. Cf. the honorific quality of being 'thrice honourably received' by the emperor, *OGIS* 513; a *hospes* of the emperor, *ILS* 2735, 7358; *IGR* iv. 1247; 'known to the emperor', Robert (1937), 228; a 'friend of the emperor', Robert (1948*b*), 31–2; Millar (1977), 115–16; cf. Tac. *Ann.* 13. 30. More generally, *IK Eph.* i. 41. 26–7, an official who, in the words of Constantius, 'amoris [nostri ves]citur gloria'.   [138] Saint-Simon (1983-8), v. 527.

[139] Statue, Lahusen (1983), 104 (in the 4th cent. often without pretence of senatorial approval). Speech, see esp. John Lyd. *Mag.* 3. 29. Tombstone, *ILS* 986.

[140] D. Chr. 3. 131-2 and Tac. *Hist.* 2. 82. Cf. Dio 71(72L). 34. 4; Pliny, *Ep.* 8. 6. 13.

In this context it is possible to understand the trend whereby the emperor's everyday dealings with those around him, which under the early empire had simply been a more crowded version of those of any great Roman aristocrat—*salutatio* in the morning, conversations and public business punctuated by kisses during the day, and dinner parties at night—came, as the empire progressed, to be surrounded by a more and more elaborate ceremonial, and by rank on rank of salaaming retainers.[141] At least from Diocletian's time it was the custom to adore the emperor on the model of an oriental potentate, and the great notables of the realm knelt to kiss the hem of his robe.[142] Certainly ceremony was awe-inspiring, serving to elevate the emperor above his subjects, but it had another function as well. When the emperor Constantius wished to bring back into favour, and present with a high command, the previously disgraced general Ursicinus, that general 'was summoned by the Master of Admissions—for this is the more honorific way—and having entered the imperial council was offered the purple much more ceremoniously than he had been before'.[143] Three hundred years earlier, Seneca would have understood perfectly: 'It is an old custom of kings . . . to divide up the body of their friends . . . and to deem crossing, or even touching their threshold as a great thing, and as an honour to grant that you might sit nearer to the door, or that you might be the first to step inside his house.'[144] A courtier of the *ancien régime* would have understood as well, reflecting on this aspect of Louis XIV's craft. 'The hopes to which these small preferments and distinctions gave birth, and the prestige deriving therefrom—no one was more ingenious than he was in inventing these sorts of things without cease.' 'Every night he named a courtier whom he wished to honour to hold his candlestick at his ceremonial retirement, always choosing among the highest ranking persons present.'[145] The elaboration of ceremony increased the emperor's ability to gain obedience by showing honour to others: if in Constantius' day there was a more honourable and a less honourable way of being admitted to the imperial council, this was an opportunity to honour (and potentially dishonour) which Hadrian had lacked, an opportunity to distinguish one

---

[141] First-cent. emperor's daily round, Alföldi (1970 (1934–5)), 25–8, 40–2, and esp. Suet. *Vesp.* 21.

[142] Study of the subject of imperial ceremonial in general, and its trends, begins with Alföldi (1970 (1934–5)), esp. 25–118. On *adoratio purpurae* see Avery (1940); Löhken (1982), 48–68, 86–90; and esp. Matthews (1989), 246.

[143] Amm. Marc. 15. 5. 18, 'et per admissionum magistrum—qui mos est honoratior—accito eodem ingresso consistorium offertur purpura multo quam antea placidius'.

[144] Sen. *Ben.* 6. 34. 1, 'pro honore'.   [145] Saint-Simon (1983–7), v. 523.

grandee from another. At the *adoratio purpurae* the order of admission was precisely regulated by ranks of honour, a far more nuanced arrangement than the old custom of first and second admission in the morning.[146] This type of ceremony reduced to complete clarity the degree of honour that was being bestowed. Moreover, a less formal imperial style would tend to cheapen imperial gestures of honour, just as, according to Tacitus, lassitude was induced in the imperial generals when triumphal ornaments were handed out too widely and thus lost much of their éclat.[147] Ceremony reduced waste of imperial honour. No kiss, no nod was squandered, and thus the value of each was increased. Louis XIV 'rendered all [his words, smiles, and glances] precious by his careful selection and majesty; the rarity and brevity of his speech added greatly to this.'[148] Imperial honour under the early empire was a great and undisciplined river, dousing both the worthy and the unworthy; late-antique ceremony was like a system of Roman aqueducts, piping imperial honours with minute economy to where they needed to be.

It was not only for individuals that the emperor had a great and varied selection of honours at his disposal. The bitter rivalry of cities for prestige made them eager for honours the emperor might bestow. Thyateira was entitled 'most brilliant, most glorious, and greatest by imperial decree'.[149] Even grander than being 'most brilliant' was to have imperial confirmation of one's claim to be 'metropolis', or 'first city', of one's province.[150] Julian sat in judgement over the claims of Laodicea and Apamea to be second city of Syria after Antioch: both cities adduced their beautiful public buildings and their philosophers.[151] Emperors granted parts of their own names to cities as well, and thus Tarsus was 'Gordianic, Severan, Alexandrian, Antoninian, and Hadrianic'. Outside Italy almost

---

[146] Order of admission by *dignitas*, *Pan. Lat.* 11(3). 11. 3; the old custom of two admissions at the imperial *salutatio*, Alföldi (1970 (1934–5)), 28; and note that the privilege of standing near and speaking to the emperor in private were noticed earlier, Plut. *Galba* 13. 1. Architecture reveals a parallel trend towards ceremony in late-antique private houses, Ellis (1991), 117-23.

[147] Tac. *Ann.* 13. 53; cf. Suet. *Nero* 15. 2.   [148] Saint-Simon (1983-7), v. 527.

[149] *IGR* iv. 1249, λαμπροτάτης καὶ διασημοτάτης καὶ μεγίστης κατὰ τὰς ἱερὰς ἀντιγραφάς.

[150] 'Metropolis', Bowersock (1985) and esp. D. Chr. 33. 46; [Dion. Hal.], *Ars* 3. 3, and on its continued importance in late antiquity, Roueché (1989*b*: 218–19), when, however, it often (but not always) signified the seat of the governor of a province, and thus conferred practical benefits. 'First', D. Chr. 38. 24, 28–9. On both titles, Magie (1950), 1496–7 nn. 17–20; Robert (1940*b*); (1977*a*), 1–6. Titles granted by emperor, *Gk. Const.* 135; *SEG* xvii. 315; Robert (1977*a*), 18.

[151] Julian, Lib. *Or.* 18. 187, προτέραν ἐποίησε τῇ τιμῇ.

six hundred recipients of such names are known.[152] There was a bewildering variety of other titles too, and as time went on cities increasingly granted titles to themselves without application to Rome.[153] But whatever the authorization of a title, a city was certainly a bigger thing in the world if the emperor confirmed its pretensions by using it. When a letter from the emperor was inscribed, the city's titles might be singled out in large letters.[154] Such letters were often inscribed, not least because communications (particularly laudatory ones) from the emperor were highly prized, and practical benefits aside, the known fact of imperial favour increased a town's honour.[155] An emperor could honour a city by assuming, *in absentia*, a local magistracy or priesthood.[156] And however expensive that rarest of events, an imperial visit, it was highly honorific for the city.[157] The emperor could dangle before cities those honours upon which he relied every day at Rome by bestowing them upon cities' frequent embassies: they might be admitted first, or invited to dinner.[158]

It is possible to see the Roman emperor using honours to rule the cities of his empire. Commodus wrote to Bubon, a city in Lycia:

I praised you for your zeal and bravery . . . that you hastened with such great enthusiasm to the arrest of the bandits, overcoming them, killing some, and capturing others. On this account the council of the province of Lycia acted rightly in rendering you appropriate honour and the right to one vote beforehand [sc. in the provincial council], with the result that you became more glorious yourselves and made even others more zealous for such acts of virtue. I myself ratified the vote of the council and bestowed upon you the right to be counted, henceforward, among the cities with three votes.

[152] Imperial names, Galsterer-Kröll (1972), with a magnificent catalogue; granted by emperor, McC. & W. 461; *ILS* 705; Dio 54. 23. 7–8 (by act of the senate, ἐν μέρει τιμῆς). Still desired in the late 4th cent., Lib. *Or.* 20. 46. Tarsus, *IGR* i. 133; and her coins add other imperial cognomina as well, Galsterer-Kröll no. 495.

[153] Cities increasingly grant titles to themselves, Dio 54. 23. 8. Other titles, Robert (1977a), *passim*; Harl (1987), 22, 68; and a conspectus, Ziegler (1985), 164. The Greek pursuit of city titles (as opposed to imperial cognomina) was viewed with some mirth in the West (D. Chr. 38. 38), and titles are rarer there, but by no means unknown: e.g. *CIL* iii. 1456, *metropolis*; Galsterer-Kröll (1972), nos. 23, 47, 54, *splendidissima*; no. 92, *fidelis*; no. 141, *claritas*; and see Rives (1995: 135–8) on the theophoric titles of North African towns.

[154] *Gk. Const.* 160 with J. Keil (1932), 25.

[155] Communications, *IGR* iv. 1756. 124-5. Imperial favour, D. Chr. 31. 149.

[156] Liebenam (1900), 261 n. 4; Robert (1938), 144–50; (1946a), 52; and esp. *Gk. Const.* 87.

[157] Athanasius, *de Incarn. Verb.* 9; and visits are celebrated on coins, Harl (1987), 53–8.

[158] Suet. *Nero* 22. 3; *Gk. Const.* 246. 36–9; cf. D. Chr. 40. 13–15. Attention to such details lives on in China. 'The Prime Minister received Martin Lee and then saw him to the door of No. 10. . . . The Chinese saw this as a mark of approval for which there was no precedent. No Hong Kong Chinese had ever before been bid farewell at the door,' Newhouse (1993), 97.

As the emperor indicates, augmentation of a city's voting rights in the council of the Lycian league was honorific. Such an honour encouraged behaviour useful to the emperor, the hunting down of bandits. The Lycian league had given Bubon the right to cast a vote first: the emperor praised the city and ranked it with those cities which had three votes; now, with any luck, even more bandits would be hunted.[159] Elsewhere too the emperor can be seen honouring cities which had given satisfaction. A large contribution of money to the imperial treasury from Nicopolis ad Istrum brought high praise from Septimius Severus: 'You have shown the most shining enthusiasm in your decree. You have demonstrated that you are well-disposed towards us and reverent men and keen that we should think well of you.'[160] The same emperor permitted cities which had assisted him in the war against Niger to take the title 'Severan', chief among them Nicomedia; and the coveted title of metropolis was stripped from Antioch, an opponent, and transferred to Laodicea, a supporter.[161] Smyrna was a veritable museum of imperial honours, which were called 'an exhortation to foreigners'—that is, visitors would be inspired by the honours Smyrna had received from the emperor to act so that their cities would receive such honours as well.[162] 'Many were the great deeds of your forefathers,' wrote Julian to Athens in time of civil war, adding that he desired '*not* to be thought to be honouring one city more than others in the matters in which they compete by recalling these things and balancing them against one another, nor to gain an advantage, praising those that proved inferior less, as the rhetoricians do.'[163] He had to deny the intention because such conduct was expected of emperors. To confirm Alexandria in its opposition to its exiled bishop, the quarrelsome Athanasius, Constantius wrote, 'I must rank you among the few, or rather must glorify you alone before the others, for the great virtue and wisdom . . . your deeds proclaim, which are hymned through nearly the whole world.'[164] Cassius Dio could look back over two centuries of empire and come to the conclusion that encourag-

---

[159] Bubon, Schindler (1972), no. 2, τειμὴν . . . ἐνδοξότεροι.

[160] *Gk. Const.* 217. 21–4.

[161] Nicomedia's assistance, Herod. 3. 2. 9; names assumed, Magie (1950), 1540 n. 21; as a reward for Nicomedia, Robert (1977a), 28. Antioch and Laodicea, Herod. 3. 3. 3-5 with Ziegler (1978: 494–5), among other punishments and rewards. For the political use of granting towns imperial names and other titles, in 2nd- and 3rd-cent. Cilicia, Ziegler (1985), 67–120.

[162] Smyrna, Aristid. 19. 8 (Behr). Cf. Tac. *Hist.* 1. 65; Aristid. 23. 79 (Behr).

[163] Julian, *ad Ath.* 268b–c.

[164] Athanasius, *Apol. ad Const.* 30 (= *PG* 25. 633), ὑμᾶς δέ με χρὴ μετ' ὀλίγων τάττειν, μᾶλλον δὲ μόνους πρὸ τῶν ἄλλων σεμνύνειν.

ing rivalry between the cities by granting and withholding titles created more problems than it solved.[165] But his was a voice in the wilderness; the emperors after his time honoured cities with at least the enthusiasm of their predecessors. So natural was this method of rulership that when rivalry between cities became such a problem that an emperor had to intervene, that emperor 'sent a letter undertaking that he would deem that city the most excellent and best which was the first willingly to practise harmony'. That is, even rivalry was regulated by an appeal to that same rivalry.[166]

Dishonouring

Those an emperor insulted might kill him. Nero was conspired against, and Caligula and Caracalla slain, by those whose honour they had crushed with their own.[167] An emperor must be circumspect, the historians note, and not insult people needlessly.[168] Thus in the elaboration of imperial ceremony lay a potential danger to imperial rule: when degrees of honour were so precisely distinguished, it was so much easier to offend. Witness the vivid fury of a fourth-century grandee on an embassy to the usurper Maximus, subjected to the insult of an interview in the consistory. 'Why do you want to kiss someone you don't know?' he snapped at the emperor who had risen to greet him, 'for if you knew who I was you would not see me in this place!' This was exactly the type of solecism that could create a dangerous enemy. Luckily the outspoken ambassador was no man of the sword, but a bishop, the tempestuous Ambrose.[169]

An imperial insult did not have to be a mistake; it could be fully intentional, to punish, destroy, or expose those who had displeased. Lepidus, Augustus' former colleague in the triumvirate, the emperor

insulted at various times in various ways. He ordered him to come into the city from the country when he did not want to, and he always took him along to the senate, that he might incur the greatest mockery and insult, both with regard to the collapse of his power and of his prestige. He treated him with contempt, and especially called upon him to vote last among the consulars.[170]

---

[165] Dio 52. 37. 10.   [166] Aristid. 23. 73, and see 27. 45 (Behr).

[167] Above, Ch. 1 n. 50.

[168] Tac. *Ann.* 2. 36, 3. 52, 54; Dio 52. 33. 7, echoing advice in Arist. *Pol.* 1314ᵇ–15ᵃ. In practice, Tac. *Ann.* 11. 25; Dio 56. 25. 4.

[169] Ambr. *Ep.* 24. 3.

[170] Dio 54. 15. 4-5, ὅπως ὅτι πλείστην καὶ χλευασίαν καὶ ὕβριν πρός τε τὴν τῆς ἰσχύος καὶ πρὸς τὴν τῆς ἀξιώσεως μεταβολὴν ὀφλισκάνῃ. For asking opinion last among the consulars 'ignominiae causa', Suet. *Claud.* 9. 2; cf. Dio 59. 8. 4–6.

Consider the fates of men who had been Hadrian's friends. Among the victims of confiscation, proscription, and compulsory suicide was one Heliodorus, whose ruin by Hadrian was encompassed, we are told, by his being 'assailed with the most slanderous writings'.[171] To be forbidden the imperial presence was another insult: Augustus barred the historian Timagenes, Tiberius did the same to Piso, and other emperors acted similarly towards those who displeased them, down through the fourth century AD.[172] And always, there were dinners. Those out of favour could be insulted by not being invited, by being abused by the emperor at table, or by being seated beneath their station.[173] The fifth-century emperor Majorian used a dinner to humble the ex-prefect Paeonius, who had been slandering the high-born Sidonius Apollinaris (also present, and from whom we have the story). By this date, not only was seating at imperial dinners by rank of honour, but so was conversation, the emperor directing remarks first to the consul seated in the most honourable place, then to the consular seated next, and so in descending order. But when Majorian reached Paeonius, he passed him over in favour of one Athenius, seated below him. This was a slight, presumably intended to show his displeasure. Paeonius could not bear the insult: he answered the question set to Athenius, pretending it was for him. This was, in turn, a slight to Athenius: now Paeonius had insulted two great men. The emperor was equal to the crisis: he laughed at Paeonius. This insulted Paeonius, and honoured Athenius. Then the rest of the diners turned upon the ex-prefect, and, with the emperor's continued help, thoroughly humiliated him. The outcome was glory for Sidonius and dishonour for Paeonius. In the vestibule, Paeonius begged Sidonius' pardon. Thus the emperor settled a conflict between two great notables.[174]

The emperor's terrible scorn could be directed also at cities which displeased. In AD 154 the inhabitants of Barca in Libya, of old the rivals of Cyrene, sent their own representatives to the Capitoline festival in Rome.

---

[171] *HA Hadr.* 15. 5; these writings are perhaps to be identified with Hadrian's letters to men's home cities stating that they did not please him, Dio 69. 23. 2. For an imperial letter of abuse, Julian, *Ep.* 82 (Bidez), where the emperor observes that he is publishing it (446b); cf. Lib. *Or.* 18. 198. And for other insults used as policy, Suet. *Vesp.* 5. 3; Philostr. *VA* 5. 38.

[172] On imperial renunciation of friendship, R. S. Rogers (1959), with evidence down to the 4th cent. Timagenes, Sen. *Ira* 3. 23. 4–8; Tiberius and Piso, Tac. *Ann.* 3. 12. See especially for Tiberius, Bauman (1974), 109–13, 117–18, 124–8: *renuntiatio amicitiae* could signal the circling sharks to bring *maiestas* charges or other forms of prosecution.

[173] Invitation, Arr. *Epict.* 4. 1. 48; abuse, Suet. *Claud.* 8; Sen. *Const.* 18. 2; seating, ibid. 15. 1; and for insulting tableware, Plut. *Galba* 12. 2–3; Tac. *Hist.* 1. 48 (to punish the thief of a precious cup).

[174] Sid. *Ep.* 1. 11; for laughter as an insult, see *HA Sev. Alex.* 18. 1.

The emperor promptly moved to squash them, writing: 'I am amazed that you who have never hitherto sent a delegation or shared in the sacrifice now for the first time send representation to this contest! . . . And know: making innovations of this type brings upon cities the charge of contentiousness!' Imagine the acute pleasure of the inhabitants of Cyrene at this: they inscribed the emperor's letter in their own city so that they could glory for ever in the humiliation of a rival. Cyrene was greater in the world because Barca was lesser.[175] Two centuries later, vexed by the Antiochenes' raillery at him and their opposition to his attempt to control prices, the bearded emperor Julian penned a satire on the city, the *Misopogon* ('The Beard-hater'; it survives), and threatened to winter in Tarsus, a rival of Antioch's. This double blow brought the citizens of Antioch to their senses, as Libanius observed.[176] For if an imperial visit was honorific, ostentatious departure, or refusal to visit, was humiliating. Thus did Marcus Aurelius punish Cyrrhus, native city and ardent supporter of the rebel Avidius Cassius.[177] The emperor could also punish by depriving cities of their titles: what an agony for Nicaea, after long years of rivalry with Nicomedia, to lose the title 'first', for supporting Niger against Septimius Severus; what an agony for Antioch to lose the honour of being a *metropolis* for insulting Theodosius' statues.[178]

Cassius Dio and Tacitus on Imperial Insults

The imperial historians offer a pair of instances which broadly illustrate the perceived importance of strategic insult to the emperor's rule. As Cassius Dio describes it, when Tiberius had withdrawn into isolation on Capri and his minister Sejanus was powerful at Rome, the emperor came to fear for his position because 'both the senators and the others treated [Sejanus] as if he were emperor, and held Tiberius in contempt'.[179] Yet he could not act openly against Sejanus because the prefect commanded the loyalty of the praetorian guard and dominated the senate, 'by benefactions, by hopes, and by fear'; he had even transferred the loyalty of

[175] Barca, *Gk. Const.* 124 (trans. adapted from Oliver, *Gk. Const.*, accepting Oliver's (1979) reading; for another reading, Reynolds (1978), 114). Cf. *Gk. Const.* 6; Philostr. *VA* 4. 33; Dio 69. 8. 1a; Julian, *Ep.* 60 (Bidez).

[176] Circumstances of the *Misopogon*, Amm. Marc. 22. 14. 2–3. Threat to winter in Tarsus, Amm. Marc. 23. 2. 4–5; Lib. *Or.* 16. 53-4. Success of Julian's tactics, Lib. *Or.* 15. 57–9; Zos. 3. 11. 5.

[177] *HA Marcus* 25. 12; cf. 25. 11, among Antioch's punishments.

[178] Nicaea, Robert (1977*a*), 24–5. Theodosius and Antioch, Lib. *Or.* 20. 6–7, 23. 26–7.

[179] Dio 58. 4. 1, Τιβέριον ἐν ὀλιγωρίᾳ ποιεῖσθαι. Sejanus' excessive prestige, Dio 57. 21. 3-4, 58. 2. 7-8, 58. 5. 1-5; and see p. 52 above.

Tiberius' familiars to himself.[180] As Dio sees it, the overt reins of power were all in Sejanus' hands. All Tiberius had left was his honour, and that is what he used to deliver himself. The emperor sent frequent letters from Capri, some praising Sejanus and some attacking him, some honouring Sejanus' creatures, others dishonouring them. Thus the Romans 'could neither admire Sejanus any longer, nor hold him in contempt', and so Tiberius was able to reduce Sejanus' overweening prestige without stampeding his powerful lieutenant into open revolt.[181] With Sejanus weakened, Tiberius increased the proportion of insults, insults which included leaving Sejanus' titles out of a letter to the senate, forbidding sacrifices to be made to mortals (obviously directed at Sejanus, since people were sacrificing to him), and forbidding the consideration of honours for himself, this also being interpreted as an attack on Sejanus, because it necessarily precluded honours for him as well.[182] Thus 'people began to hold him in contempt', began to slight him and avoid him, and Tiberius was able to have him arrested on the floor of the senate.[183]

The modern mind is puzzled at so strange an analysis of the workings of politics. From Dio's narrative we can, naturally, pick out more explicable elements: Tiberius' eventual attack on Sejanus' prospects by indicating that he intended Caligula—popular with the *plebs* as the son of Germanicus—to succeed him; and his attack on Sejanus' power to hurt by publicly thwarting a prosecution Sejanus had a hand in.[184] But to Dio's mind the main thrust of Tiberius' policy was to bring Sejanus into contempt, first by insulting him and eventually, when he had worn him down, also by humiliating demonstrations of his weakness. Addicted to looking through appearances to the realities of power beneath, we are surprised to see power dependent on, and attacked through, appearances. We may even conclude that Cassius Dio is deceiving himself; but certainly this is what he thinks was going on.

It would be interesting to know if Tacitus' understanding of the fall of Sejanus was similar to Cassius Dio's; alas, that part of the *Annals* is lost. But Tacitus employs very similar logic in his description of the struggle of the emperor Nero with the Stoic senator Thrasea Paetus, which he represents as a battle of insults.[185] In AD 59, Thrasea fired the opening salvo

---

[180] Dio 58. 4. 2, τὸ μὲν εὐεργεσίαις τὸ δὲ ἐλπίσι τὸ δὲ καὶ φόβῳ.

[181] Dio 58. 6. 3-5, quoted 5, καὶ μήτε τὸν Σειανὸν θαυμάζειν ἔτι ἢ καὶ καταφρονεῖν ἔχοντες.

[182] Dio 58. 8. 3-4.   [183] Dio 58. 9. 1, κατεφρόνησαν; Sejanus' fall, 58. 9-10.

[184] Dio 58. 8. 1-3.

[185] On this whole affair, Rudich (1993), *passim*; MacMullen (1966), 21-81; and on the legal aspects, Bauman (1974), 153-7.

in this conflict by walking out of the senate when it was voting, at Nero's behest, to condemn the memory of the emperor's mother Agrippina, whom Nero had just murdered. In the next year Thrasea refused to cheer at the Juvenalia, games in which Nero performed.[186] These events were worth recording because they constituted an attack on Nero's honour, signifying the disapproval of a man great in dignity, for Thrasea was (as Cassius Dio puts it) 'among the foremost in family, wealth, and every virtue'. A Stoic philosopher, as Cato the Younger had been before him, he was especially distinguished for his moral excellence; 'virtue itself', Tacitus calls him.[187]

Two years later Thrasea struck another blow. The praetor Antistius had composed some insulting verses about the emperor, and was prosecuted under the *maiestas* statute; this, it was believed, 'more to seek *gloria* for the emperor than death for Antistius', for Nero was expected to veto Antistius' condemnation by using his tribunician power.[188] Seneca had urged Nero to seek glory from clemency, but staging opportunities was hardly what he had in mind.[189] The senators all played their part in this farce and urged that Antistius be condemned to death—all, that is, except Thrasea Paetus who, prefacing his remarks with an encomium upon Nero and an attack upon Antistius, urged instead banishment to an island. When a division was called, 'the independence of Thrasea ruptured the servility of the others', and Thrasea's motion was carried. This was a serious matter; hardly an overt insult, but coerced honour becomes mockery if anyone dares to laugh, and Thrasea was making a great production of holding back a jeer. To save Nero's face, the consuls refused to complete the formalities of the senatorial decree, and wrote to Nero informing him of the vote of the house; Nero, in turn, was 'held between shame and anger', not because his ruse had been found out (it was not concealed) but because someone had called him on it. He wrote, finally, insisting that the senate was free to vote as it liked, and that he had intended to pardon Antistius anyway. The decree stood: the senate could not reverse itself without seeming to jeer in earnest; Thrasea would not withdraw his proposal because of 'his usual firmness and unwillingness to destroy the glory' he had gained.[190]

So, to Tacitus, this was a battle over glory; and Nero's response, in the next year, came in the form of insult: forbidding Thrasea to come when

---

[186] Tac. *Ann.* 14. 12, 16. 21; cf. Dio 61(62L). 15. 2 and 20. 4. At some (unknown) point in his career Thrasea also composed a *Cato* (Plut. *Cato Min.* 25. 1 and 37. 1).

[187] Dio 62. 26. 1; Tac. *Ann.* 16. 21.   [188] Tac. *Ann.* 14. 48–9 (AD 62).

[189] Above, n. 62.   [190] Tac. *Ann.* 14. 49, *gloria*.

the senate repaired to Antium to congratulate Nero's empress, Poppaea, upon the birth of a child. Thrasea's attack on Nero's honour was thus reciprocated in kind.[191] Perhaps in reaction to this, Thrasea boycotted meetings of the senate entirely, thus insulting Nero further by being absent for the vote of divine honours to Poppaea when she died in AD 65, and for the trials of Silanus and Vetus, in which the emperor had an interest. By 66 Thrasea was refusing publicly to vow or sacrifice for Nero's health.[192] The remarks attributed by Tacitus to an enemy of Thrasea, intended to whip up Nero against him, indicate the nature of the threat that the historian thought Thrasea posed to the emperor: 'Just as once upon a time this strife-loving city talked about Caesar and Cato, now it talks of you, Nero, and Thrasea. He has hangers-on and partisans who imitate . . . his aspect and bearing: they are stern and unsmiling, so as to castigate your moral laxity. . . . The gazette of the Roman people is read minutely through the provinces and the army in order to find out what Thrasea has *not* done.' To Tacitus, Thrasea's actions posed a threat not least because they were broadcasting Nero's honour-destroying vices to the world, and Thrasea's conduct posed an unbearable threat to the emperor's *dignitas*.[193]

Nero's response to Thrasea's actions was consistent with his previous conduct: another insult. Thrasea was forbidden to attend the crowning of King Tiridates of Armenia. He knew that charges were being prepared against him as well. But Nero did not want him dead. A note from Thrasea delivered at the ceremony was opened eagerly, Tacitus imagines, 'in the hope that in terror he had written something which would elevate the fame of the emperor, and damage his own repute'. What Nero yearned for, it seemed to Tacitus, was a clear victory over the honour of Thrasea. All Thrasea had to do was admit he was wrong, to humiliate himself. Much better for Nero's honour that the great Thrasea abase himself and praise than that Thrasea die. But Thrasea's note enquired what he was charged with, and asked permission for rebuttal; the note could easily be construed as insolence. Nero ordered the senate convened for Thrasea's trial.[194]

Now, says Tacitus, there was a meeting of Thrasea's friends at his house. What was to be done? Should Thrasea defend himself before the senate? 'He could say nothing but what would increase his prestige . . . let

---

[191] Tac. *Ann.* 15. 23, *contumelia* (AD 63, soon after reconciled).

[192] Ibid. 16. 21–2 (AD 66); cf. Dio 62. 26. 3–4. [193] Quoted, Tac. *Ann.* 16. 22.

[194] Ibid. 16. 24, 'per quae claritudinem principis extolleret suamque famam dehonestaret'. For over-prestigious aristocrats humiliating themselves to save their lives see n. 21 above.

the people see a man face death, let the senate hear words more than human—as if spoken by a god! Perhaps Nero himself might be moved by the astonishing act.'[195] In other words, Thrasea might overcome Nero by sheer weight of honour; 'shame for his crimes might seize him'.[196] The battle of honour that Thrasea had declared seven years before, Tacitus has his friends say, could still be won: the philosopher should fight it out in the great arena of aristocratic opinion, the Roman senate; Nero could be humiliated and forced to back down. But there was a counter-argument. A trial before the senate would necessarily involve 'mockery and insults'—attacks, in other words, upon Thrasea's honour. And the battle could not, in the end, be won, because Nero was so depraved that he simply could not be embarrassed. Thrasea's own honour, and reverence for that of the senate (which would otherwise disgrace itself by convicting him), demanded that he commit suicide.[197] In Tacitus' mind, Nero would have sided with the first set of advisers—the ones who believed that Nero could be beaten: he thought that he was in danger of losing this struggle, and the seriousness with which he viewed Thrasea's threat is indicated by his posting of several praetorian cohorts around the forum the next day; those by the senate doors wore togas, but made no attempt to conceal their swords. The notorious *delator* Marcellus prosecuted, along with Cossutianus. The senators took fright. Thrasea was condemned, and upon being informed, committed suicide.[198]

The true motivations of the men who appear as players in Tacitus' drama of Nero and Thrasea and Cassius Dio's of Tiberius and Sejanus are ultimately unknowable. But the historians' accounts offer a useful understanding of how two Roman senators of great knowledge and insight thought that politics under the empire worked. Deprived of the support of his praetorians, the senate, even his friends, Dio's Tiberius overcomes Sejanus with insults; in Tacitus' case, force appears in defence of imperial honour, first to terrify Thrasea into self-humiliation, and finally when it looks as if the emperor might, by losing a long-drawn-out duel of insults, be brought into contempt. To the historians force and honour are intimately related, and an emperor needs both to rule; when one flags, the other must come to the rescue.

[195] Tac. *Ann.* 16. 25, 'nihil dicturum, nisi quo gloriam augeret'.

[196] Tac. *Ann.* 16. 26, *pudor*, extracting this suggestion from its denial in the contrary case. Presumably they hoped for an outcome similar to Tiberius' being shamed out of a *maiestas* prosecution by the prestigious Gnaeus Piso, Tac. *Ann.* 1. 74; cf. Plut. *Cato Min.* 33. 2.

[197] Tac. *Ann.* 16. 26, 'ludibria et contumelias'. Other authors also speculated that Nero had arrived at a state of *contemptus omnis infamiae* (Suet. *Nero* 39. 3); see n. 4 above.

[198] Denouement, Tac. *Ann.* 16. 27–35.

Borrowing Honour

As the struggle between Nero and Thrasea indicates, the Roman senate, at once vastly distinguished by tradition and also made up of the most distinguished men in the Roman world, was a prodigiously powerful source of honour and dishonour in its own right. The emperor relied very heavily upon it to buttress his own regime of honour, praising protégés before it and calling upon it to bestow (at his behest) the ancient honours of the Republic, triumphs (or, after Augustus, their ornaments) and lesser military honours upon successful generals, and also statues, the *ornamenta* of senatorial magistracies, and public funerals. In time, the senate also came to acclaim successful officials.[199] When the senate granted praetorian *ornamenta* to Claudius' freedman Pallas, the emperor's words of praise for him before the senate and the senate's own resolution were engraved on a bronze plaque affixed to a statue of Julius Caesar, a place where 'those in charge of imperial affairs can be incited to imitation, and the example of Pallas' proven faith and incorruptibility may inspire zeal for honourable emulation'.[200] Granting a freedman such honours was outrageous, but the decree indicates how the senate's honours were expected to help the emperor rule the empire.

Similarly, although the emperor himself could and did punish malfeasant officials and those he considered his enemies, he could protect his reputation by making the senate perform this invidious function.[201] The senate's brief to punish peccant governors has excited the derision of commentators, first for the senators' unwillingness to convict the obviously guilty, and, also, when the evidence was overwhelming, for the triviality of their punishments: 'Marius in exile drinks and rejoices from the eighth hour, while the gods rage, and you, O Province, who won the suit, weep.'[202] But justice lay as much in the proceedings as in the sentence. Trials in the Roman world had always engaged and endangered the

---

[199] Prestige of the senate, see above, Ch. 2 n. 208. Imperial praise before the senate, Pliny, *Paneg.* 70. 1–5; *HA Pert.* 2. 8–9; *Gord.* 27. 4–8. Honours granted by the imperial senate, Talbert (1984), 362–71; still in the 5th cent. described as the 'iustus arbiter dignitatum', *ILS* 1284. For honouring at imperial behest, esp. Dio 60. 23. 2–3; Suet. *Aug.* 38. 1. Statues voted by senate, Lahusen (1983), 100–3; for their value Dio 75(76L). 14. 7; see also Pliny, *Ep.* 2. 7. 1. Acclamations, *HA Claud.* 18. 2–3 (showing 4th-cent. practice).

[200] Pliny, *Ep.* 8. 6. 13, 'studium tam honestae aemulationis'.

[201] Suggested, Dio 52. 31. 3–4, echoing Arist. *Pol.* 1315ª. In practice, Dio 58. 16. 3, 58. 24. 2. For proceedings before the senate, Talbert (1984), 460–80.

[202] Juv. 1. 49–50. Extortion proceedings, Talbert (1984), 507–10; Brunt (1961).

honour of the litigants.[203] This was doubly true of trials before the senate, the echo chamber of aristocratic opinion, the body before which, above all, honour was gained or lost. Characteristic of the senate's special honour was the method selected for punishing those of its members, especially delators, who acted vilely under Nero and Vitellius: each senator was called upon in the senate-house to swear openly that he had contributed to no man's peril, and had benefited in wealth or office from no citizen's destruction. The guilty muttered or changed the words of the oath, to their mortification.[204] At stake at a trial in the senate, as much as an official's fortune, was the good opinion of his social peers and superiors—his honour. A trial involved days of abusive rhetoric before an audience of those whose opinion mattered most. To be condemned was to be judged a bad man by one's aristocratic peers: away flew one's *dignitas*.[205] When a senator was convicted of extortion, Pliny could avow that it was a more severe punishment for him to be stripped of the right to draw lots for provinces than to be thrown out of the senate entirely:

for what can be more wretched than for a man to be cut off from and forbidden from the honours that accrue to senatorial rank, but not its work and bother; and what more severe than for one blotted with such a disgrace not be allowed to lurk in solitude, but rather to be offered up for inspection and pointed out, in the most visible position possible?[206]

'What matters infamy if the coins are safe?' asks Juvenal of justice of this kind.[207] But infamy did matter, desperately. Suicide had always been an accepted Roman way of saving one's honour, or escaping a life made intolerable by shame.[208] And it was to suicide that a number of those charged before the senate, even if facing quite light punishments (so it seems to us), resorted.[209] Their action recalls that of the peculating Japanese company executive throwing himself before a speeding train upon being found out. All have suffered disastrous loss of face.

The power of the senate to reward the emperor's protégés with

---

[203] Trials engage honour, Cic. *Quinct.* 99; Aul. Gel. 6. 3. 19; Fronto, *ad M. Caes.* 3. 3 (van den Hout); and esp., for a trial before Julian, Lib. *Or.* 18. 184.

[204] Tac. *Hist.* 4. 41; also, for the terrible power of the senate's disapproval, Cic. *Piso* 42–3, 45, 99; cf. Suet. *Tib.* 47; HA *Hadr.* 3. 1.

[205] Pliny, *Ep.* 5. 13. 2; Tac. *Ann.* 14. 40–1; Sid. *Ep.* 1. 7. 13. Fear of this, Dio 52. 31. 4.

[206] Pliny, *Ep.* 2. 12. 3; but see 4. 9 as a corrective to this extreme view.

[207] Juv. 1. 48, 'quid enim salvis infamia nummis?'

[208] Cic. *ad Q. Fr.* 1. 4. 4; Suet. *Tib.* 61. 4; Pliny, *Ep.* 3. 9; Tac. *Hist.* 4. 11; *Dig.* 49. 14. 45. 2 (Paul).

[209] Suicides, Brunt (1961), 224–7; to avoid ὕβρις and αἰτία, Dio 58. 15. 2–4, here deemed more important than preservation of the estate, another motive for suicide.

honours and to dishonour his enemies was, of course, a function of the senators' own corporate prestige. And this the emperor's own honour and power could to some degree raise or lower. It was not, therefore, only antiquarian feeling or a nod to the emperor's own constitutional legitimacy which encouraged the emperors to 'honour' the senate as a body by attending its meetings in person, by showing elaborate respect for the consuls and other magistrates, and by throwing out unsuitable members.[210] A Roman senate with as much corporate prestige as possible, prepared (or required) to wield it in the emperor's interest, could be thought a powerful prop to the emperor, described, in Otho's speech in Tacitus' *Histories*, as 'the order by whose distinction and glory we attack the baseness and obscurity of Vitellius' supporters'.[211]

Nor was it only the Roman senate whose honour the emperor put to his own use. To honour the sea captain Lucius Erastus, who had frequently transported provincial authorities and twice even the emperor Hadrian himself, the emperor arranged for him to be appointed to the council of his home place, the great city of Ephesus. Thus the emperor could also use other cities' honour to reward those who performed tasks useful to him.[212] But for the most part, the borrowing of honour between cities and the emperor ran the other way; that is, a city, or a provincial council, invoked the emperor's vast prestige to honour its own benefactors. In the face of huge benefactions, the honours of city and province could be wholly inadequate to make return. Only the congratulations of the emperor would provide 'a worthy requital'.[213] Thus the city wrote to ask the emperor to honour their benefactor for them, and the emperor replied with a gratifying boom:

Imperator Caesar Titus Aelius Hadrian Antoninus Augustus, son of the divine Hadrian, grandson of the divine Trajan Parthicus, great-grandson of Nerva, Pontifex Maximus, in the thirteenth year of his tribunician power (etc.), to the magistrates, council, and people of the Ephesians, Greeting! You revealed to me the lust for honour which Vedius Antonius displayed in his benefaction to you

---

[210] Honouring the senate, Tac. *Ann.* 14. 28, 'auxitque patrum honorem'; Dio 66(65L). 10. 6; *HA Marcus* 10. 2–9; *Pert.* 13. 2; *Pan. Lat.* 3(11). 24. 5, 'veterem reddideris dignitatem'; Lib. *Or.* 18. 154; for more refs., A. Wallace-Hadrill (1982), 38 n. 43; cf. Cass. *Var.* 1. 4. 1–2. Acts of imperial respect for magistrates, Suet. *Claud.* 12; Pliny, *Paneg.* 77. 4–5, 93; Dio 57. 11. 3, 69. 7. 1; *Pan. Lat.* 3(11). 30. 2. Expelling the 'unworthy', Suet. *Aug.* 35. 1 which restores the senate to *splendor* (= ἐσέμνυνε, Dio 56. 41. 3); cf. *HA Hadr.* 8. 7.

[211] Tac. *Hist.* 1. 84, 'splendore et gloria'; cf. 2. 32.

[212] Erastus, *Gk. Const.* 82a; cf. *IK Eph.* v. 1488; and Philostr. *VS* 1. 22 (524) for a sophist and imperial procurator appointed to the Museum at Alexandria.

[213] *TAM* ii. 905 col. 13. 78–79 (ch. 53).

although I already knew about it. He has already laid to his credit the favours he got from me towards the eternal adornment of your city. Flavius Titianus, my procurator, sent your decree.[214]

The provincial council of Lycia repeatedly reflects on the efficacy of such imperial letters in encouraging further benefactions.[215] The emperor's honour was great, ideally greater than any individual's, but not necessarily greater than that of the senate or the greatest cities of the empire. Thus he called upon others to honour for him, and others similarly called upon him. Imperial relations of honouring were not merely bilateral; rather, the emperor participated, from a position of great (but not unparalleled) strength in a vast network of honouring which encompassed the entire empire.

Honour and the Emperor's Bounty

To what extent are we to believe in this idyllic picture of an imperial rule as dependent upon pride and shame as it is on fear and greed? To pull apart this vision it is useful to look at imperial grants valued for more than the honour they convey. For honours did not begin to exhaust the boons the emperor had available. To individuals, everything the emperor had it in his power to give—sums of money, property, immunities, citizenship, political offices, priesthoods, legal judgements (and their overturning)—were given as *beneficia*. In less than two years as governor of Bithynia, Pliny submitted to the emperor Trajan six requests for special favours that we know of, and in the imperial biographers it is usual to read, even of good emperors, that Caesar 'enriched his friends'.[216] But even the mass of benefits which were desirable for reasons other than the honour they bestowed were perceived to have honorific qualities. Consider a letter from the emperors Marcus Aurelius and Lucius Verus to an official in Mauretania, granting Roman citizenship to a local chieftain:

---

[214] *Gk. Const.* 139, φιλοτιμία (with 138 to clarify the meaning). See also 81; *TAM* ii. 905 chs. 26, 30, 37, 38, 46–8, 50; *AE* 1931. 38; *ILS* 6680; Quass (1993), 160 n. 473. Also, praise of the donor in the context of confirming the terms of the benefaction, *Gk. Const.* 159; Wörrle (1988), lines 1–6. Provincial council: *TAM* ii. 905 *passim*; the Attic Panhellenion, *Gk. Const.* 155; guild of athletes, *Gk. Const.* 28.

[215] Above, n. 129.

[216] On offices, see pp. 185–6 below, and Tac. *Ann.* 2. 36 on the free ability of the emperor to dole them out an *arcanum imperii*. On imperial benefactions, Millar (1977), esp. 133–9, 465–549; Saller (1982), 41–78 (Pliny's six requests, p. 58). Friends enriched, Suet. *Aug.* 66. 3; *HA Hadr.* 15. 1; *Marcus* 3. 8–9; *Aur.* 45. 3.

We have read the petition of Julianus the Zegrensian that was attached to your letter, and although we are not accustomed to grant Roman citizenship by imperial indulgence to the men of these tribes unless they have performed extraordinary services, nevertheless, since you affirm that he is a leading man among his peoples, and utterly faithful in his prompt obedience to our affairs, and because we do not think that many clans among the Zegrenses can point to similar services, and because we hope that many will be inspired to emulate Julianus by the honour we have bestowed upon his house, we do not hesitate to grant Roman citizenship to him, his wife Ziddina, and also his children Julianus, Maximus, Maximinus, and Diogenianus.

The emperors here grant citizenship to a tribal leader in a wild march of the empire in order to inspire his rivals with loyalty to Rome. The emperors expected the honour of the grant to inspire emulation; it was honour from the emperors, rather than the legal rights conveyed by citizenship, that, they hoped, would protect the Roman borders.[217] And more than just citizenship could be considered honorific. The fourth-century emperors Arcadius and Honorius explained in a law that they conferred warrants for the use of the public post on persons of *illustris* rank as an honour only; such persons should not actually presume to use them.[218] And it is not unknown to hear of a person who was 'honoured with money'.[219] Moreover, in a trend parallel to the elaboration of imperial ceremonial, from the time of Diocletian grants of gold and silver to individuals came more and more to be made in the form of medallions, exquisite pins, or silver dishes inscribed, for example, 'a gift of our lord Valentinian Augustus'. Thus the form of the wealth—the object itself—came to stress the honorific quality of the gift.[220] 'A consul I am indeed,' said an appointee in his speech of thanks to the emperor Julian, 'and a most distinguished consul. For has there ever been a consul more distinguished than I—raised and made brilliant by the consulship you gave me? By the distinction you are conferring?' The consulship carried its

---

[217] Julianus Zegrensis, *AE* 1971. 534 with Sherwin-White (1973): 'nostris rebus prom[p]to obsequio fidissimum . . . plurimos cupiamus honore a nobis in istam domum conlato ad aemulationem Iuliani excitari'. Cf. Cic. *Balb.* 7, 22–3; D. Chr. 41. 10; *Gk. Const.* 10. 57; and Gauthier (1985: 151–2) for the tradition of honorific Hellenistic grants of citizenship.

[218] *CTh* 8. 5. 54 (395).

[219] Dio 59. 26. 4, χρήμασιν ἐτίμησεν; cf. 61. 6. 1; Suet. *Vesp.* 18; Lib. *Or.* 1. 80.

[220] MacMullen (1962); for a conspectus of gifts, the forged letters in *HA Claud.* 14, 17; *Aur.* 12, 13; *Prob.* 4. 3–7 (and earlier collections of grants were lovingly described as well, Philostr. *VS* 1. 25 (532–3), 2. 10 (589)). For the honorific quality of such gifts, *HA Claud.* 15. 4; *Prob.* 4. 5.

own traditional prestige, but achieving it was a sign of the emperor's favour, and that bore honour as well.[221]

Similarly, the emperor had in his power a great number of boons for cities, which are described as valuable for the same combination of reasons. It was, in the first place, the emperor who defined which collection of houses and men was to be recognized as a city and which was, for administrative purposes, merely a village dependent on a recognized city, and thus potentially subject to that city's levies. Once city status had been granted, it fell to the emperor to decide (before Caracalla gave citizenship to all free inhabitants of the empire) whether a city (and thus its inhabitants) was to be granted Roman citizenship, or the lesser but still substantial package of Latin rights. Some cities paid imperial taxes, others did not: immunity from taxation was also at the emperor's pleasure. And a hard-won status like any of these had to be protected over time: the accession of a new emperor was accompanied by flurries of embassies from cities asking that their rights and immunities be confirmed. The emperor could also give tax relief in the wake of a natural disaster, or forgive a city years of back taxes. He could intervene to alter the route his governors followed on their assizes, so that Roman justice would be convenient and cheap for the residents of one city, and awkward and expensive for others, thus also directing to favoured cities the profitable flocks of litigants and hangers-on that followed the governor. The emperor also gave gifts of money and grain to cities; he erected edifices for them, and reserved the right to approve major projects of their own and any changes in their constitutional arrangements.[222]

But again, honour was seen in such practical benefits. As Dio Chrysostom reminded his native Prusa:

Buildings and festivals, and independence in the administration of justice and exemption from standing trial away from home, and not being grouped together with others for tax purposes, like some village, if you'll pardon the expression— by all these things, as is natural, the pride of cities is inflated and their prestige becomes greater.

---

[221] *Pan. Lat.* 3(11). 29. 3, 'quis enim me fuit amplior consul, quem sublimat et inlustrat consulatus quem tribuisti, amplitudo quam tribuis?'; cf. Pliny, *Paneg.* 92. For the consulship, below, pp. 183–4. Other imperial grants described in honour terms: Eus. *VC* 4. 1. 1–2, for a conspectus; *Gk. Const.* 136. 3b–c. 20, a favourable judgement at law; Julian, *Ep.* 58 (Bidez), the restoration of a man from exile; *IGR* iii. 599, a doctor's immunity from civic duties.

[222] Millar (1977), 394–456. Profit from assizes, D. Chr. 35. 15. *IGR* iv. 1287, emperor makes Thyateira an assize centre; *Gk. Const.* 123, refuses to put Berenice on the assize route.

Dio left aside the practical utility of these imperial gifts, stressing instead the degree to which they increased the city's prestige. They were desired so that the city might 'enjoy greater honour from resident aliens and the Roman governors'.[223] Moreover, a grant officially recognizing a city as such might be referred to as an honour in an imperial letter.[224] Although the city statuses of 'colony' and 'municipality', granted by the emperor, had real legal value under the high empire, this value was lost by the fourth century, when the terms had long been legally meaningless. Yet cities continued to style themselves colonies and municipalities, and a man might undertake to repair his town's 'insignia' and 'ornaments' of colonial and free status.[225] The assignment of tributary lands was described as an honour, as was being granted the right to coin money.[226] Immunity from taxation was pictured as an honour, and the orator Aristides valued the emperors' rebuilding of Smyrna after an earthquake not least for the prestige thereby bestowed upon the city: before the earthquake, 'the degree to which it was held in honour was not clear'. Now the emperors had made their opinion known through their rebuilding project.[227]

So too, the emperor's punishments are described in honour terms. A city on the wrong side in civil war, or which had offended in some other way, could be punished with massacres, fines, and deprivations of territory and rights; it could even be stripped of city status and attributed to a loyal city as a possession.[228] But consider Herodian's description of how Septimius Severus punished Byzantium for supporting Pescennius Niger: 'It was deprived of its theatres and its baths and all its glory and honour, it was subordinated—as a village—to Perinthus.'[229] 'His

[223] D. Chr. 40. 10, ἀξίωμα; τιμή (trans. adapted from Crosby). Cf. D. Chr. 44. 10–11; Reynolds (1982), no. 48. 6–7; Tac. *Hist.* 1. 8; Lib. *Or.* 19. 22.

[224] *ILS* 6091, cf. *ILS* 6090.

[225] Fourth cent., Lepelley (1979–81), i. 128–31, and Kotula (1974); also given in 1st-cent. Italy where it was legally meaningless, Millar (1977), 408; as in the 3rd-cent. Near East, Millar (1990), 37, 52–6. Repair an 'arcum . . . cum insignibus colo[niae] . . . ornamenta liberta(tis)', *ILS* 5570.

[226] Lands, Dio 54. 7. 2; coining money, *SEG* xxxiv. 1306 with Weiss (1991), 381–84; Harl (1987), 23–4; and Robert (1960c).

[227] Immunity from tax, *ILS* 423; *Gk. Const.* 69; cf. *Gk. Const.* 212, for confirmation of the immunities of a society of Dionysiac artists as an honour. Earthquake, quoted, Aristid. 20. 9 (Behr); also 20. 5, she gains the emperors as distinguished founders.

[228] Punishments for cities, an imagined conspectus, Lib. *Or.* 19. 39. In practice, in civil war, Suet. *Galba* 12. 1; Dio 54. 7. 2; HA *Marcus* 25. 9; *Sev.* 9. 4–8; for other reasons, Suet. *Tib.* 37. 3; Dio 54. 7. 6, 57. 24. 6, 60. 24. 4. Also, for insulting the emperor, see n. 86 above.

[229] Herod. 3. 6. 9, παντός τε κόσμου καὶ τιμῆς, with Ziegler (1978), 494. Cf. Dio 74(75L). 14. 3, οὐδὲν ὅ τι οὐχ ὕβριζον.

destruction of their walls', said Cassius Dio, in the same context, 'caused them pain chiefly because it deprived them of the glory which they had reaped from displaying them.'[230] Pergamum lost the right to mint coins: Cassius Dio simply referred to the punishment as 'dishonour'.[231]

This expansive conception of imperial honours and dishonours has a double significance. First, it would be perverse to deny that the emperor and his subjects felt that all imperial grants could potentially be imbued with honorific quality, all imperial punishments with disgrace. This was a true secret of empire, for, by the nature of things, the emperor's treasury of honour was far richer than his treasury of money, offices, and immunities, all of which had to be paid for, directly or indirectly.[232] The emperor's treasure of honour did not have to be gouged out of the imperial taxpayers, nor did it have to compete with the needs of a ravenous army. Louis XIV's courtier notes that the king 'knew that the many favours he had to distribute were not nearly enough to create a continual effect. So he substituted notional for real favours, and through the force of jealousy little preferments filled all our days, one might even say all our moments, by his artifice.'[233] The logic of honours was quite different from the logic of bribes. A letter, a kiss, or permission for a city to style itself 'most brilliant' cost nothing. The emperor need only guard against giving out honours to the wrong sort of people—lest the honours become tainted—or granting them too widely, lest he cheapen the distinctions.[234] As the panegyrist of Theodosius remarked, when offices gave out, honorific chats, kisses, and dinners took over.[235]

Yet honour serves as a form of politeness as well. Hadrian exempted the citizens of Antinoopolis from performing liturgies elsewhere. Antoninus Pius confirmed that immunity, as did Marcus Aurelius. But his letter of confirmation dropped the financial details, and referred to the immunity simply as an honour. The fact that vulgar money is at stake has quietly vanished under a courteous euphemism.[236] Moreover, to describe a salary from the emperor as an honour was enormously

---

[230] Dio 74(75L). 14. 4, δόξα; which perhaps explains Prusa's ambition for walls in time of profound peace, D. Chr. 45. 12.

[231] Pergamum, Dio 78(79L). 20. 4, ἀτιμία, with Harl (1987: 24–5), listing other cities which also lost the right to mint.

[232] Potential lack of honours, offices, and money, Dio 52. 12. 2–5, and its gloomy consequences. Bad results of excess in giving out offices, rights, and exemptions, Tac. *Hist.* 3. 55.

[233] Saint-Simon (1983–7), v. 522.

[234] Cheapening honours, D. Chr. 31. 109–10; and see n. 147 above; tainting honours, Dio 52. 12. 6–7, 58. 4. 8; also (for offices) below, p. 182.

[235] *Pan. Lat.* 2(12). 20. 1–2.   [236] *Gk. Const.* 164–6, τιμή.

attractive to a Graeco-Roman aristocrat.[237] For otherwise it was a bribe or a payment for service, both shameful. The fact that 'honours' can serve as the simple and ample shorthand for all possible grants an individual might receive from the emperor signifies not only the power of imperial honour in society, but also the indispensability of the rhetoric of honour to a government largely made up of, and immediately ruling over, persons very finicky about appearing to be motivated by profit.[238] Honorific gold can be offered without risk of offending, and can be accepted without loss of face. A regime can operate by giving out things people want only to the degree that the *amour propre* of the recipients allows them to accept them: describing gifts and grants of all types as honours made it a great deal easier for them to do so.

The emperor too could hide shabby business beneath the penumbra of honour. Need to get rid of some overweening aristocrats? Send them out as governors to nasty, unhealthy provinces, 'as if honouring them greatly'. Need money? Then extend citizenship (and thus the associated taxes) to all free inhabitants of the empire and call it an honour to them.[239] It was not strictly false to call such things honours, and the emperor was just as pleased as his subjects to let his real goals hide behind honour.

Gratitude

'A man can be compelled to fear someone, but he must be persuaded to love him: and he is persuaded not only by what he himself receives, but by what he sees others receiving.'[240] An imperial boon, whatever the reasons for which it was valued, and however those reasons might be concealed, created obedience in two ways. First, those who desired it would act in a way calculated to gain it. The emperor emphasized that boons were bestowed on those who performed services for him, and not upon those who did not. In a letter to the Samians, for example, Augustus refused to grant them exemption from taxes, comparing their services invidiously to those of the Aphrodisians, to whom he had granted it; for Aphrodisias, 'having sided with me in the war, was captured because of its inclination towards us'. Samos could adduce no similar sacrifice—benefaction—to the emperor, and thus could not expect to receive 'the

---

[237] See esp. *Pan. Lat.* 9(4). 11–12, 16.
[238] 'Honours' as shorthand, Jos. *Vit.* 423, 428–9; Dio 52. 12. 2–7; Aristid. 30 (Behr); Men. Rhet. 420. 30–1.
[239] Dio 77(78L). 11. 7, πάνυ τιμῶν; 77(78L). 9. 5, λόγῳ . . . τιμῶν.
[240] Dio 55. 19. 4.

biggest benefaction of all'.[241] In time of rebellion anticipation of rewards was among the reasons for keenly supporting a claimant to the emperorship.[242]

But in writings from the Roman empire the use of imperial boons as a lure is overshadowed by the expectation that boons will produce gratitude, and gratitude, loyalty. The emperor Vespasian, 'warned by his friends to beware of Mettius Pompusianus because he was commonly said to have in his possession an imperial horoscope [a notorious sign of imperial ambitions] made him consul, guaranteeing that Mettius would in future remember the *beneficium*.'[243] Under the code of reciprocity, imperial *beneficia*, including purely honorific ones—say a kiss from Caligula—, created an obligation: and the emperor could call in that obligation or hoard it against future difficulties.[244] Herodian described Marcus Aurelius on his death-bed cashing in his account, recalling the honour he had bestowed upon his familiars, and requiring them to make return through loyalty to his son.[245] In sum, as Cassius Dio had Augustus express it in an address to the senate, 'It is possible for me to rule you for ever, you can see that yourselves . . . my supporters have been bound to me by exchange of benefactions.'[246]

Gratitude might be among the reasons dictating choice of side in civil war. Tacitus portrayed the cities of the Gauls as bound to Galba in AD 69 by his recent expansion of the Roman citizenship there, and by his lowering their tribute for the future.[247] Gratitude also appears in the day-to-day ruling of the empire. Caracalla needed animals, so he cancelled back taxes in Mauretania, thus conferring a *beneficium*. 'I am certain', he wrote to the provincials, 'that you will reciprocate my generosity . . . and do me a favour by virtue of your woods, which throng with celestial beasts.'[248] Alexandria was a chronic aggravation to the emperor, vast and notoriously prone to riot. The emperor gave the city a gift. 'Are you not aware

[241] Samos, *Gk. Const.* 1.
[242] Tac. *Hist.* 1. 57; Herod. 2. 9. 12; Amm. Marc. 26. 6. 16; cf. Herod. 4. 3. 2.
[243] Suet. *Vesp.* 14, 'spondens quandoque beneficii memorem futurum'; and see n. 267 below; cf. Dio 55. 21. 3–22. 2. And for the emperor calling his grants to cities χάριτες, *Gk. Const.* 44, 285; *beneficii*, Small. *Gaius* 368; *IK Eph.* i. 42. 3–4.
[244] Caligula's kiss, Dio 59. 27. 1; cf. Suet. *Vesp.* 2. 3; Herod. 6. 1. 9.
[245] Herod. 1. 4. 3, 6.
[246] Dio 53. 4. 1. The debt for favours continues down generations. Thus Vespasian can be deemed loyal to Nero from benefactions bestowed by Claudius, Philostr. *VA* 5. 29; also Zos. 2. 46. 3. When emperors ratify the *beneficia* of previous emperors *en bloc*, thus forgoing gratitude, this is remarked upon, Millar (1977: 414 n. 16), cf. Pliny, *Paneg.* 39. 3.
[247] Tac. *Hist.* 1. 8; also Herod. 2. 7. 9–10; cf. Plut. *Brut.* 6. 7; Cic. *ad Fam.* 10. 8. 3.
[248] *AE* 1948. 109. 10–14 with Corbier (1977).

of the care the emperor has lavished upon your city?' bellowed Dio Chrysostom over the roars of the Alexandrian populace, meeting the supreme challenge of a long career of giving advice to cities. 'You must repay the emperor's benefaction—not, by god, by building [honorific] fountains or triumphal arches—but by making your city better: by order, by good behaviour.'[249] It was thus vitally necessary that the emperor's favour be as well known as possible. A governor wrote to the Alexandrians: 'Since, because of its size, the whole of the city could not be present at the reading of [the emperor's] sacred and exceedingly benefi-cent letter, I deemed it necessary to publish the letter, so that each man, having read it, might wonder at the greatness of our divine Caesar, and have gratitude for his goodwill towards the city.'[250]

Just as opportunities for a humble client to make adequate return to his patron were extremely rare, so was it unusual for an individual or city to be able to offer any practical return for the emperor's benefactions.[251] Thus, like the client, they simply held themselves in readiness for ever: the emperor contemplating his empire might see a great many favours-wait-ing-to-happen, 'goodwill', the stuff of obedience in bad times.[252] But just as the poor client could chip away at his mountainous debt by appearing every morning and following his patron around (a tiny honour which, in the company of many such, made its recipient highly honourable), so too could a man or city attempt to square the account to some degree by honouring the emperor. Indeed, in addressing the Alexandrians, Dio Chrysostom had had to work against the presumption that the return for the imperial favour would naturally be honorific.[253] On holidays the speaker appointed by the city would rise and deliver a grateful oration in the emperor's honour—'Having, as we do, so many good things from the emperors, it is absurd not to return them our due and proper offering.'[254]

[249] D. Chr. 32. 95. [250] *Gk. Const.* 19. 1. 2–11; cf. *ILS* 423. 40.

[251] D. Chr. 34. 25; Sen. *Ben.* 5. 4. 2; Lib. *Or.* 20. 1.

[252] 'Goodwill', Greek *eunoia* towards emperor, Herod. 1. 4. 5, 1. 6. 6; *Gk. Const.* 157. 8, 217. 22, 276; and in loyalty oaths, see Herrmann (1968), 123–5 nos. 3–5. In Latin *voluntas, ILS* 140. 45. *Eunoia* related to gratitude, de Romilly (1977), 67; Dion. Hal. *Ant. Rom.* 2. 10. 4; D. Chr. 31. 7, 41. 4–7; Aristid. 23. 25 (Behr); Philo, *de Praem.* 97; Herod. 1. 4. 2; and more generally on the term, de Romilly (1958). *Voluntas,* Sen. *Ben.* 7. 15. 3–5.

[253] For presumption that τιμή and ἔπαινος will be the return for imperial benefaction, Dio 57. 17. 8; Philo, *Leg. Gaium* 284; for a variety of honours from gratitude, Men. Rhet. 377; cf. Philo, *Flacc.* 48, 97–8 (for the special case of the Jews). For *eunoia* expressed by honour-ing the emperor, *Gk. Const.* 35. 8.

[254] Men. Rhet. 368. 15-17 (trans. adapted from Russell and Wilson); and see [Aristid.] 35. 4 (Behr).

In the temples, markets, and public places of the towns of the empire, statues of the emperor arose, expressing gratitude for imperial deeds.

To the divine Imperator Caesar Augustus Vespasian, in the proconsulate of M. Fulvius Gillo, the Caesar-loving people of Aphrodisias, free and autonomous from the beginning of the empire by the favour of the emperors . . . dedicated this [statue] as their own favour [in return].[255]

Since the emperor's officials were expected to feel gratitude to the emperor for their appointment, they too honoured him in return, both in speeches of thanks before the senate, and with statues scattered through the provinces.[256] Nor were honours unsatisfactory requital for imperial benefits: their very inadequacy made them pledges of obedience against times of turmoil, when the subject could bear practical assistance to his emperor, and it was through the incessant honouring of his whole empire that the primacy of the emperor's honour among men was maintained.

In so far as obedience and honour to the emperor were founded upon gratitude for favours, they were founded on the strength of the social sanction which enforced gratitude upon aristocratic society. This is the fear that Zosimus attributes to Julian, contemplating rebellion against Constantius, that 'he would gain a reputation among many people for being ungrateful'.[257] This honour sanction was both strong and lasting: consider Herodian's description of Severus Alexander' amazed reaction to the revolt of Maximinus, whom the emperor had loaded with favours.

When Alexander had been informed of what had happened, he was utterly confounded and struck dumb by the unexpectedness of the news. And he came running out of the imperial pavilion like one possessed, crying and quaking, and accusing Maximinus of faithlessness and ingratitude, and listing all the benefactions which had been bestowed upon him.[258]

It was almost beyond belief to a Roman that someone thus bound to the emperor should revolt: as we have seen, a praetorian prefect was willing to die rather than seem ungrateful to Constantius.[259]

---

[255] Reynolds (1982), no. 42 (cf. *IK Eph.* ii. 237); also on statues from gratitude, Price (1984a), 174–5. From province, EJ 42; individuals, *IK Eph.* v. 1501; *ILS* 453.

[256] Expectation of gratitude for appointment, Amm. Marc. 25. 8. 11; Sym. *Rel.* 2; also Pliny, *Paneg.* 90 and *Pan. Lat.* 3(11). 15-32 (both in the context of speeches of thanks for appointment, cf. Dio 60. 11. 7); to be requited with honour, Philo, *Flacc.* 81; *Pan. Lat.* 3(11). 32; and in practice, for statues, *ILS* ch. 2 *passim*.

[257] Zos. 3. 9. 5, δόξα; cf. Dio 55. 21, αἰσχυνόμενοι . . . εὐεργέτας ἀδικῆσαι.

[258] Herod. 6. 9. 1.

[259] Prefect, above, Ch. 1 n. 48; cf. D. Chr. 1. 20; Dio 52. 34. 11, 55. 16. 5, for deprecating the

Well might Julian worry about his reputation if he revolted; Constantius had raised him up to be Caesar, junior co-emperor. 'Revere him who created you,' thundered the Roman senate.[260] And the emperor's own massive prestige stood ready to crush the ungrateful. Augustus raised Cornelius Gallus from a base origin and appointed him Prefect of Egypt. But the poet returned the favour by speaking ill of Augustus and vaunting his own achievements to an unseemly degree: he had his accomplishments carved on the Pyramids, littered Egypt with statues of himself, and inscribed for posterity in a trilingual inscription (he was taking no chances) little in the way of grateful or reverential mention of his benefactor. Utterly unsurprising, then, that the emperor diagnosed an 'ungrateful spirit', and barred the palace and the imperial provinces to Gallus, thus bludgeoning him with the immense imperial dignity.[261] And how would the obscure T. Marius Urbinas, an officer of Augustus' who (despite promises to the contrary) failed to express his gratitude to his benefactor in his will, ever have achieved the invidious distinction of inclusion in a book of examples for the use of orators, if the emperor had not trumpeted Urbinas' ingratitude in loud imperial tones?[262] At the same time the emperor himself encouraged gratitude with his honorific praise. In gratitude for some imperial grant, the city of Sardis voted to celebrate Gaius Caesar's assumption of the *toga virilis* as a holiday. An embassy was dispatched to advise his grandfather, the emperor Augustus, who replied in a letter, 'I praise you because you are honourably ambitious to show yourselves to be grateful in exchange for the benefactions you have received.'[263] In the face of a substantial differential in honour, the reciprocal exchange of favours tended to resolve itself into a form of extortion applied by the more prestigious party. Thus the emperor's great honour cast its shadow over all relations of indebtedness to him. The emperor, not least because the expressions of his opinion could make or destroy the reputations of those around him, had

danger of recipients of imperial benefactions acting ungratefully; but *contra*, Dio 66(65L). 16. 3–4.

[260] Amm. Marc. 21. 10. 7; cf. Tac. *Hist.* 3. 37.

[261] Suet. *Aug.* 66. 1–2, 'ingratum et malivolum animum'; Dio 53. 23. 5–7, ἠτιμώθη ὑπὸ τοῦ Αὐγούστου; he was then harried to suicide by his enemies. Inscription, EJ 21 (for Greek and Latin versions). Cf. Herod. 3. 6. 2–3, 3. 12. 10; Dio 71(72L). 27. 1; HA Gord. 30. 2.

[262] Val. Max. 7. 8. 6.

[263] Sardis, *Gk. Const.* 7, ἐπαινῶ . . . ὑμᾶς φιλοτειμουμένους; cf. 15. 2. He also rewards, with privileges and praise, *eunoia*, the goodwill which his subjects store up in return for his benefactions, since they cannot requite them: see *Gk. Const.* 13, 28, 35, 185, 246, 296; cf. Jos. *AJ* 16. 162. In Latin he requites *obsequium*, AE 1971. 534. 7, 1948. 109. 5 (and *fides*).

it in his power to say who was indebted to him, how much they owed him, and what they had to do to pay him back.

Gratitude was a real part of imperial power, both as something subjects felt (and were expected to feel by those around them), and because it was so useful as a disguise. Caligula, profligate and greedy, cancelled as 'ungrateful' the wills, and confiscated the estates, of chief centurions who had failed to leave Tiberius or him a legacy appropriate to the debt of gratitude they had incurred for reaching such high rank.[264] This was a tyrannical act, no question; but a well-chosen one, since the conduct of the *primipilares* was indeed disgraceful. Men were expected to feel gratitude on very general grounds: Claudius was forced to protect from prosecution provincials who received citizenship under him but failed to mention him in their wills.[265] Caligula's genuine claim to gratitude offered a decent cover for his plundering. Similarly, honour might mask a subject's fear. Domitian, made coheir by Agricola (who loathed him), considered it an honour, no doubt an expression of gratitude and deference. In fact, Tacitus strongly implies, Agricola did this for the usual reason that evil emperors were made heirs, to protect the rest of his estate. But obviously, given Domitian's reception of the will, Agricola was not so unwise as to say so. Tacitus thinks that Agricola succeeded in hiding his real views behind the machinery of honour because Domitian was blinded by ceaseless flattery.[266] But most of the time whether the emperor saw through the ruse will hardly have mattered. Just as cash from the emperor can be attractively presented as an honour to a subject, obedience to the emperor, often the consequence of fear or greed, is most safely and agreeably represented by all parties as an act of honour flowing from the subject's laudable sentiments of deference and gratitude. Indeed, the 'honours' that subjects direct at the emperor from gratitude can include almost anything. When Cassius Dio describes Vespasian's declawing of Mettius Pompusianus by making him consul, he has the emperor say, 'He will certainly be mindful of me and honour me in return.'[267] Not plot to murder me, that is. The emperor's subjects trumpet their profound gratitude to the emperor, honouring him not only as benefactor of individuals and towns, but as 'benefactor and saviour of the whole world'.[268]

---

[264] Suet. *Gaius* 38. 2; Dio 59. 15. 2; cf. Suet. *Nero* 32. 2. For soldiers' gratitude to the emperor, see pp. 255–7 below; on the obligations fulfilled in wills, p. 70 above.

[265] Dio 60. 17. 7; cf. Sen. *Ben.* 6. 19. 2.

[266] Tac. *Agric.* 43. 4, 'laetatum eum velut honore iudicioque'.

[267] Dio 67. 12. 2–3, πάντως μου μνημονεύσει καὶ πάντως με ἀντιτιμήσει; cf. *HA Maxim.* 14. 1.

[268] EJ 88; cf. 98b; Small. *Gaius* 135; McC. & W. 95; Small. *Nerva* 105; Aristid. 23. 54 (Behr).

Such abject indebtedness provided an explanation for any act of loyalty, whatever its true motivation: a way of describing one's deed which was safe before one's superiors, face-saving before one's equals and inferiors, and comfortable before one's self-opinion. That real gratitude was often present, and reciprocated with honour, can hardly be doubted: it was that fact that made it such an effective screen. To conceal the cruel and sleazy workings of empire as completely as possible in a dazzling light-show of praiseworthy emotion was in everybody's interest.

THE IMPERIAL CULT

The Roman imperial cult offers the most compelling insight into the complex relationship between honour as a practical way of getting things done in the Roman empire, honour as polite deception, and honour as self-deception. The cult—the practice of building altars and temples to the emperors, and performing, there and elsewhere, the activities of divine worship—was geographically and socially extremely widespread; it was carried on in public and in private, perhaps privately first, at least in Italy. It involved sacrifices, processions, games, and banquets; it seems to have included all the aspects of pagan religiosity of which testimony survives except dedications to divinity in exchange for a miracle. Provincials devoted vast resources to it: over eighty temples and sanctuaries associated with the imperial cult have been counted in Asia Minor alone.[269] And while perhaps in some areas the cult was an imperial project, or at least encouraged by the emperor's officials, and some emperors—Caligula in particular—took a considerable interest in it, over great spans of the empire and great tracts of time, the provincials offered cult spontaneously to emperors who were sometimes reluctant to accept it.[270] The imperial cult was a multifaceted institution and significant in different ways, perhaps surrounding the emperor with an aura of divinity which helped him rule, perhaps offering a symbol of unity to a divided and diverse empire, perhaps a way for subjects to understand their relationship with the ruling power, perhaps representing an early stage of the

[269] On the organization of the cult: in the East, Price (1984a), temples in Asia Minor, p. 135; West, Fishwick (1987–92). On private worship in Italy, Santero (1983). Is the imperial cult properly a religious phenomenon? The answer depends on one's definition of religion: Price, 7–16; Fishwick, 42–5.

[270] Officials' involvement: East, Price (1984a), 70–1; West, Fishwick (1987–92), 97–9, 141–5. Emperors, see pp. 168–9 below. The cult is usually deemed an imperial project in the West, at least at the provincial level: Fishwick, *passim*, but see Tac. *Ann.* 1. 78; EJ 100 on the municipal level; and Hopkins (1978), 209.

reconstruction of the emperor as a glittering Byzantine icon.[271] The relationship between the cult and honour is the limited subject to be addressed here.

Why Worship the Emperor?

Whatever their wider significance, it is well known that acts of divine cult for the emperors were honours, holding a place at the top of a continuum of honours which an individual, city, or provincial council might bestow. Thus Tiberius wrote to Gytheum in Laconia, which had voted the late Augustus and himself divine tributes:

> Decimus Turannius Nicanor, your ambassador . . . gave your letter to me, to which was attached your law concerning acts of piety towards my father, and honour towards me. For this I praise you, for I think it meet for all men in common and your city particularly to preserve . . . [for Augustus] exceptional honours appropriate to gods. I am well content with more moderate, human honours.[272]

Divine honours were only one kind (albeit the most honorific) among many. Cities and provincial assemblies of the empire erected numerous statues to the emperor (traces of more than fifty have been found in Ephesus alone); cities began their meetings with acclamations to him; they voted him complimentary decrees; they appointed embassies to convey their honorific sentiments to him.[273] They nominated the emperor, honorarily, to their highest priesthoods and magistracies (we have already seen the emperor honour cities by accepting such elections), minted coins in his honour, renamed their months in his honour, declared holidays in honour of his accession day and his successes, and held sacrifices on those days.[274] If he visited, there were processions with torches and flowers; the gates were sweet with incense; there was music.[275] And while the emperor might single out divine honours for

---

[271] For recent discussions of the wider significance of the cult, Hopkins (1978), 197–242; Bowersock (1983); Price (1984a).

[272] *Gk. Const.* 15. 2. 14-23, εἰς εὐσέβειαν μὲν τοῦ ἐμοῦ πατρός, τιμὴν δὲ ἡμετέραν. . . . ἐξαιρέτους . . . τιμάς; cf. *Gk. Const.* 23.

[273] Imperial statues at Ephesus, Price (1984a), 174; at Leptis Magna, over eighty; in late-antique Rome, close to four thousand, Hopkins (1978), 220. Civic acclamations, Roueché (1984), 184–6. Decrees and embassies, e.g. *Gk. Const.* 68, 115; Jos. *BJ* 4. 620; Pliny, *Ep.* 10. 43. 1-2. Provincial honours to emperor, Deininger (1965), *passim*.

[274] Emperor in civic posts, *Gk. Const.* 206; Lib. *Or.* 11. 269, and n. 156 above. Coins, Harl (1987), 41–9; *IGR* iv. 769. Months, Scott (1931), 207–19, 264–6. Holidays and celebrations, Herz (1978), and see e.g. EJ pp. 44–55.

[275] Reception of imperial visit, Halfmann (1986), 111–24; Harl (1987), 56; and above, Ch. 1 n. 43; and see esp. Herod 4. 8. 8; Amm. Marc. 21. 10. 1; *Pan. Lat.* 11(3). 10. 5, 5(8). 8. 1–4.

refusal, it seems that those doing the honouring saw no great conceptual gap between honours human and divine: they were voted in the same decree, muddled in with all the others. Alexandria voted to keep Claudius' birthday as a holiday, to erect numerous statues of him, to have a tribe take his name, and to dedicate sacred groves, a high priesthood, and temples to him; the priesthood and temples he declined.[276] 'The conclusion to be drawn is that divine and human honours differed in degree but not in kind; both belong at different intervals on essentially the same scale.'[277]

In the provinces, when the emperor's name was mentioned, his individual subjects rose, praised him, did him reverence, and offered a double prayer—to the gods for the emperor, and to the emperor himself.[278] They mingled human and divine honours too, without a second thought. Individuals' acts of worship for the emperor found their place naturally in a panoply of other honours: a man might erect to the emperor a statue, an amphitheatre, an altar, or a temple.[279] At private banquets, a libation was poured, with the cry 'blessings upon Augustus, father of his country'.[280] Upon the emperor's arrival, all rose and saluted him.[281] Nor was the emperor's absence a bar to honour, for his statues, or indeed his letters, could take his place.[282] The simple volume of honours directed at the emperor by provinces, cities, associations, and individuals was remarkable; even the Jews, singled out by ancient authors as grudging in this respect, erected in their synagogues shields, crowns, plaques, and inscriptions in honour of the emperor.[283]

So the puzzle is really twofold: why did the emperor's subjects honour him so intensively? And why, with such a great variety of honours available, were the emperor's subjects moved to honour the emperor with acts of cult?

---

[276] *Gk. Const.* 19.

[277] Fishwick (1987–92), 33; cf. Nock (1930), 50–1, and, for the Hellenistic tradition, Habicht (1956), 206–13.

[278] Aristid. 26. 32 (Behr).

[279] Statues, McC. & W. 138; *ILS* 411; *IK Eph.* v. 1504. Amphitheatre, EJ 236; or a fountain, *IK Eph.* ii. 424; a stoa, Small. *Gaius* 101; and on public buildings generally, Pliny, *Ep.* 10. 75. 2. Altar, EJ 103, 135; and see Price (1984a), 112. Temple, *IG* xii Suppl. 124; EJ 110, 121. For dedications *in honorem domus divinae*, Raepsaet-Charlier (1975).

[280] Fishwick (1987–92), 84 n. 10, 375; quoted, Petr. *Sat.* 60, 'Augusto patri patriae feliciter'.

[281] Suet. *Vesp.* 13; Philo, *Leg. Gaium* 352; Dio 59. 7. 6, 63. 28. 1: Nero's final flight from Rome was hampered by meeting on the road a person who saw through his disguise and automatically hailed him as emperor.

[282] Statues, Price (1984a), 200–5; letters, Philostr. *VS* 2. 10 (590).

[283] Associations, Waltzing (1895–1900), iv. 585–608. Jews, Philo, *Leg. Gaium* 133; for limitations on Jewish honouring, see p. 199 below.

The avowed reasons for the imperial cult are plain enough. 'Since men call him thus [sc. *Sebastos* = Augustus] in proportion to his degree of honour, they revere him with temples and sacrifices on the islands and continents, distributed through the cities and provinces. Thus they repay the greatness of his virtue and his benefactions to them.' Nicolaus of Damascus describes a dual motivation here. Cult was offered to the emperor because of the greatness of his honour, and because of his benefactions—in our terms, both from deference and reciprocity.[284] Nor was this an unusual view. Lucian too described the cult in terms of reciprocity: 'The emperor's greatest pay is praise, and fair glory in the eyes of all, and honour for his benefactions: statues and temples and holy precincts, so many as he has from his subjects. These things are pay for his consideration and forethought.'[285] And the Jew Philo, not one to view pagan practices with starry-eyed naïvety, discusses the cult in terms of deference owed to emperors' prestige. Nicolaus' judgement is confirmed.[286]

Yet why should deference to the emperor's honour and reciprocation for his favours take this form? Because, we are told, given their extent, no other recompense would be adequate. The friends of Caligula, whom he installed as client kings in the East, owed him a vast debt. 'The kings, even if they devoted themselves entirely to that end, being incapable of equally reciprocating the favour of such a god for the benefactions they have received', consequently repaired to Cyzicus, there to offer worship to Drusilla, Caligula's sister.[287] And if kings could not reciprocate otherwise, how could mere cities? What was the modest Greek town of Acraephia to do when Nero granted it, along with the rest of Greece, freedom, including immunity from taxation? Its inhabitants reinscribed their altar to Zeus the Saviour to 'Zeus the Patron of Freedom, Nero, for ever', and placed statues of Nero and Messalina in the temple of Apollo,

---

[284] Nic. Dam., *FGH* 90 F 125, ὅτι εἰς τιμῆς ἀξίωσιν τοῦτον οὕτω προσεῖπον . . . τό τε μέγεθος αὐτοῦ τῆς ἀρετῆς καὶ τὴν εἰς σφᾶς εὐεργεσίαν ἀμειβόμενοι. For the title *Sebastos* (= Augustus) see also Philo, *Leg. Gaium* 143; Dio 53. 18. 2. For this pair of motivations see also Cic. *ad Q. Fr.* 1. 1. 26, cult for Roman officials justified by *dignitas* and *voluntas* 'pro tuis maximis beneficiis'.

[285] Lucian, *Apologia* 13, ἔπαινοι καὶ ἡ παρὰ πᾶσιν εὔκλεια καὶ τὸ ἐπὶ ταῖς εὐεργεσίαις προσκυνεῖσθαι. Cf. *Gk. Const.* 15. 2, 17; Philo, *Leg. Gaium* 149–50; from individuals, Small. *Gaius* 142; *IG* xii Suppl. 124; thus the crime of Christians who refused to offer cult to the emperor might be seen as 'ingratitude', Eus. *Hist. Eccl.* 7. 11. 6–10. On divine honours from gratitude, see esp. Nock (1932), 517; and on the Hellenistic background, Habicht (1956), 160–71, 230–6; Gauthier (1985), 46–8, 60–6; Robert and Robert (1989), 84.

[286] Philo, *Leg. Gaium* 140–52.

[287] Small. *Gaius* 401. 5–6 (trans. Braund).

'so that our city might appear to have employed every possible honour and act of piety towards the house of the lord Nero Augustus'.[288]

The use of divine honours to fulfil the requirements of deference to the emperor is explained in the same way. Philo, describing a pogrom at Alexandria, endeavoured to prove that the Greeks' blasphemous installation of statues of Caligula in the synagogues—that is, transforming them into temples of the imperial cult—was not a consequence of a genuine desire to honour the emperor, but was intended instead to bait the Jews. Did the Greeks so honour the Ptolemies, whom they also hailed as gods? No, Philo imagines a Greek Alexandrian saying, 'but the emperors are greater than the Ptolemies in prestige and fortune, and thus it is necessary for them to receive greater honours'. Yet neither Augustus nor Tiberius was honoured in this fashion, Philo replies, and then proceeds to total up their claims to prestige to prove that they were superior to those of Caligula.[289] His argument rests upon the assumption that the establishment of temples to the emperor is an honour appropriate only to dignity so vast that no other honours are adequate. Similarly, in an inscription from Mytilene:

It is never possible to match [honours] humbler both in nature and frequency to those who have obtained heavenly glory, and who have the power and supremacy of gods; but if anything more honorific than these measures should turn up in later times, the zeal and piety of the city will not be found wanting in further deifying him.[290]

Divine honours are represented as the solution to a quandary: what is to be done when conventional honours are inadequate to the emperor's merits? When the deference and gratitude due him are so overwhelming? Only the best will do.

Yet if divine honours are conceived as the solution to a problem, the question of sincerity arises. Did this sense of inadequacy and *aporia* pass through the mind of every subject every time the loyal libation was poured? On each and every occasion did the emperor's subjects really think that the emperor had performed benefactions so vast, had

---

[288] Small. *Gaius* 64. 49–55. Expressions of bafflement as to appropriate civic recompense for imperial benefactions, [Aristid.] 35. 38 (Behr); EJ 98. And for appropriateness of divine honours to world benefactions, *Gk. Const.* 17.

[289] Synagogues to be imperial temples, Philo, *Leg. Gaium* 137. Emperors compared to Ptolemies, 140, ὅτι μείζους μὲν οἱ αὐτοκράτορες τὰ ἀξιώματα καὶ τὰς τύχας τῶν Πτολεμαίων εἰσί, μειζόνων δὲ καὶ τιμῶν τυγχάνειν ὀφείλουσιν. Augustus and Tiberius, 141–52.

[290] *IGR* iv. 39. b. 7–18, οὐρανίου . . . δόξης . . . ἐπικυδέστερον; see Price (1984a), 55.

distinction so great, that no other form of honour was adequate? But such questions misconceive the psychological status of gratitude and deference in the Roman world: they are public dispositions first, rooted in the sense of honour and shame. Since acts of cult were 'approved by all men everywhere', it was important to be *seen* to be properly grateful and deferential.[291] A town voting the emperors divine honours might specify in the decree that their officials shall 'erect a stone monument carved with this sacred law ... in order that standing ... in the open air for everyone to see, the law ... may testify to all men the gratitude of the Gythean people towards their rulers'.[292] 'Let the decree be inscribed and valid for all time,' voted Ephesus about a birthday festival proclaimed in gratitude to Antoninus Pius, 'so that the character of the city may be obvious to men now and in the future.'[293] And an individual built a temple to Augustus' adoptive sons, 'wanting to *show* his gratitude and piety towards the whole [imperial] house'.[294] Of course, publicly failing to show one's gratitude, one's loyalty, could be dangerous: Cyzicus was punished for failing to finish an imperial temple.[295] But the sense of display revealed here indicates that it is the desire for the esteem of those around one, not to seem to one's rivals (even to one's self) deficient in an important aspect of personal or civic character, that explains not only great public acts of imperial cult, but also the constant drumbeat of tiny, individual, private honours to the emperor. Gratitude and deference to the emperor drove the imperial cult not only because they were sometimes 'heartfelt', in the modern sense, but also because they were an ideology widely participated in and enforced by psychological structures of honour and shame.[296]

Yet this only pushes the question of sincerity back a step. Even if individuals' acts of cult were governed by the expectations of society, how could a broad expectation exist that every emperor, even the strange and rapacious Nero, even the gladiator Commodus, even the bizarre Elagabalus, was worthy of divine honours? Yet such an expectation was necessary to the men who were most influential in forming opinion on a city-by-city and province-by-province basis. For their own honour came

---

[291] Quoted, Philo, *Leg. Gaium* 152.
[292] *Gk. Const.* 15. 1. 34–40, εὐχαριστίαν; on this word, Robert (1955), 58–62.
[293] *IK Eph.* i. 21. 35–7.
[294] *IG* xii Suppl. 124, (trans. Price (1984a: 3), who accepts the restoration [ἐνδείκνυ]σθαι; my italics).
[295] Dio 57. 24. 6.
[296] 'To credit the princeps with *numen* is ... honour arising from heart-felt gratitude,' Fishwick (1987–92), 387.

to depend, in part, on the emperor's being worthy of divine honour. Gratitude in the Roman world was not only enforced by shame; it was a public virtue, to be publicly displayed as a claim to honour. To requite the emperor's benefactions with acts of cult was itself an act of *philotimia*, competitive ambition for honour.[297] So too were acts of cult inspired by deference. Mytilene did not modestly hide its extravagant reverence for Augustus' honour—noticed above—but sent copies of its decree to Pergamum, Actium, Brundisium, Antioch in Syria, Massilia in Gaul, and Tarraco in distant Spain. This last may have inspired Tarraco to the emulative construction of an altar to the emperor.[298]

The imperial cult was part of the world of *philotimia*. Priesthoods of the emperor were prominent perches from which to undertake glorious acts of public benefaction; priests and boards of priests performed the acts of cult and paid for the games, dinners, and public distributions in the emperor's honour at imperial festivals.[299] And since the imperial cult insinuated itself into a world where the municipal aristocracies already had a great many opportunities to exchange their money for civic honours, it was perhaps natural that the new imperial priesthoods attracted ambitions for glory previously constrained in their expression: in Italy especially, the substantial numbers of wealthy freedmen legally excluded from the municipal senates by their origin; in the provinces, men who had exhausted the honours of their own cities, and looked for higher honours as provincial priests of the imperial cult.[300]

The imperial cult was something to which important men looked for honour, and upon which their honour came to depend. Gratitude and deference to the emperor served also as an ideology forming the substructures of an arena in which subjects and cities struggled for honour among themselves. Thus the use of the term 'piety' (*eusebeia*), which the emperor's Greek subjects were expected to display towards the emperor, and which motivated acts of imperial cult.[301] In the specific context of the

[297] *IGR* iv. 1756. 26 (= *Gk. Const. 7*).

[298] See above, n. 290; for Tarraco, where Augustus was resident, Fishwick (1987–92), 171–2. For rivalry in deference cf. *SEG* xxiii. 206.

[299] Civic priests of the imperial cult in East, Price (1984*a*), 62–4. And for the place of the civic imperial priesthood in the career of notables in Spain, Étienne (1958), 223–31.

[300] Provincial imperial priests, Deininger (1965), 148–54; their glory, Firm. Mat. *Math. 4.* 21. 5; *IK Eph.* i. 43; their backgrounds and careers, Stein (1927); and see e.g. Alföldy (1973) on the flamens of Hispania Citerior. On the *severi Augustales, Augustales,* and *magistri Augustales* of the West, largely freedmen, for Italy, see Duthoy (1978): membership is an *honor* for which a *summa honoraria* is paid; they enjoy honorific garb, seating, etc., and perform benefactions; for spread in the rest of the empire, Duthoy (1976).

[301] Price (1984*b*), 88–9. Provincials understand it as a duty, *IK Eph.* vii. 3801. Cf. *eusebeia* for a governor, *SEG* i. 329. 48.

imperial cult the precise content of this attitude is difficult to make out, but *eusebeia* was felt towards the gods (its primary sense), and in those environs it combined a powerful reciprocal flavour with a proper reverence for the gods' *timē*, what has been called deference among men.[302] But this disposition towards the emperor also appears as something for which the emperors' cities and subjects competed among themselves, something which one acted 'to make not only the city but also the rest of the province witness to', something for which one was honoured by one's fellow citizens.[303] At the level of competition between cities, 'pious' or 'most pious' might be taken as city titles.[304]

A man who hopes to be honoured by his townsmen for his 'piety' towards the emperor, or a city which hopes to outdo a hated rival by displaying that quality, is in no position to question whether that disposition is justified by imperial behaviour. *Philotimia* could make the imperial cult's formal masters, gratitude and deference to the emperor, its servants instead. Eagerness to partake of the honour the cult offered required complicity in the ideology of the cult, even if that ideology wore thin at times, becoming no more than rhetoric under bad emperors. The mixture of lying, euphemism, and self-delusion involved we can only guess, but the necessity is clear: for if the emperor was admitted to be *un*worthy of cult, his priest was a ridiculous, rather than a glorious, creature; his splendid crown of office, festooned with tiny imperial busts, suddenly as ludicrous to him as it is to us.[305] The logic of the imperial cult required that the emperor be worthy of cult. The honour of his priests and cities required that the emperor be properly honourable, be worthy of the honours which it was an honour for them to bestow upon him. Thus the honour and civic patriotism of provincials could make the emperor honourable, rather than the other way round. Nor did the curious logic of *philotimia* drive the imperial cult alone. All forms of honour towards the emperor could be viewed as motivated by the subjects' *philotimia*.[306] And his subjects' competition with one another demanded that the emperor be worthy of honour. Did the people of the Latin town of

---

[302] *Eusebeia* to the gods, Rudhardt (1958), 12–17; Burkert (1985), 273–4; Cairns (1993), 208 n. 111. For *eusebeia* to emperor as reciprocal, Philo, *Flacc.* 48, 98, 103; *Gk. Const.* 15. 2; *IK Eph.* ii. 237.

[303] Quoted, *IG* xii Suppl. 124. 25–6 (trans. Price). Honour for *eusebeia* towards emperor, Price (1984b), 88 n. 79; (= *pietas*, *ILS* 6582c; and for rivalry in *pietas*, Pliny, *Ep.* 10. 100); *eusebeia* associated with φιλοδοξία, EJ 352. 9.

[304] εὐσέβειος, Robert (1940b), 58; εὐσεβεστάτη, Robert (1977a), 16. Cities honour one another for *eusebeia*, *IK Eph.* ii. 236.

[305] Crowns, Fishwick (1987–92), 477–8. [306] *Gk. Const.* 35; Herod. 4. 2. 9.

Treba Augusta really think Commodus 'supreme in all virtues'?[307] But they certainly could not honour him as bereft of all virtues. Commodus' subjects manufactured his virtues not so much to please him as to please themselves.

The great panoply of honours that his subjects directed towards the emperor has its roots in gratitude and deference as appropriate public dispositions. At bottom, the imperial cult arises from a sense that the emperor's honour is so vast, and his benefactions so great, that all other forms of honour are inadequate; it arises from the sense of humiliation before their peers that ancient persons felt if they could not act appropriately towards honourable benefactors. But while gratitude and deference towards the emperor were fundamental to the cult, they are less than a full explanation of it: for they also gave the cult (and other honours) their ideological legitimacy, enshrined them as a part of civic life, and thus as proper objects for individual, and civic, *philotimia*. This *philotimia* took on a life of its own, carrying the cult through the reigns of good emperors and bad. It is *philotimia* that explains the enormous resources devoted to the imperial cult in what seems to us a desperately poor world, and perhaps even explains its long survival under Christian emperors.[308]

Why Be Worshipped?

The Roman emperor never heard of the vast majority of acts of cult and other honours to him; when provincials rose and blessed his name, no one told him about it. But the grandest forms the cult took could be used by cities to influence the emperor. The embassies that cities sent to the emperor to request the granting of new privileges, or the confirmation of old ones, might offer him a temple.[309] As a form of honour from his subjects, at least, the cult was valuable to the emperor. All things being equal, it did add to his prestige.[310] It thus might be encouraged and assisted by emperors, not only by the mad Caligula, but even by the moderate Hadrian.[311] Upon the elevation of Caracalla to share the throne with his father, the town of Aezani voted a festival and sacrifice. In return, Septimius Severus wrote a letter praising her as 'prestigious and of great

---

[307] *ILS* 400. [308] Under Christian emperors, Bowersock (1983).

[309] *Gk. Const.* 19, 23, 39; more generally, acts of cult inspire *eunoia* in the emperor, Julian, *Ep.* 89b (Bidez), 293c; and cf. Philo, *Leg. Gaium* 137, for the Alexandrian Greeks' expectation of praise and benefits from Caligula for turning the synagogues into imperial shrines (an exceptional case).

[310] Philo, *Leg. Gaium* 153; Tac. *Ann.* 4. 38; but this is denied by Cassius Dio 52. 35. 4 (see Fishwick (1990b)) in the context of his discussion of insincere honours (above, p. 115).

[311] Price (1984a), 68–9.

service of old to the Roman rule'.[312] And the wider disposition, *eusebeia*—which gave rise to the cult as well as other loyal behaviour—, the emperor also requited with grants: it was for *eusebeia* that Nero said he freed Greece and that Gordian III confirmed the rights of Aphrodisias.[313] Moreover, the offering of divine cult to non-imperial persons died out under Augustus, the emperor who also confined triumphs to himself and his family; and later emperors were expected to be as suspicious of anyone who inspired cult as they were of over-glorious generals.[314]

Yet the realities of politics discouraged the emperor from accepting a temple from all who offered it. The offering of divine tributes to rulers was an old custom in the East, and largely unobjectionable there. But in the West, it was a slowly waning but powerful aristocratic conviction that direct worship of a living man was revolting, and an emperor who accepted it (if asked) offensive and vainglorious.[315] Indeed, Tacitus tells us that Tiberius used the refusal of an offer of cult from Hither Spain to dispel rumours about his growing taste for adulation.[316] A wise emperor, properly concerned for such rumours, carefully allowed himself only the honour that aristocratic opinion would bear. Thus at the outset of the principate, direct worship of the emperor was discouraged in the West, especially in Italy, and indirectness preferred. The emperor was therefore worshipped together with Roma; or the emperor's *genius* (tutelary spirit) was worshipped; or his *numen*, his divine spirit, or his personified virtues; or the emperor was worshipped in the context of a wider cult of divinized emperors past.[317] Certainly to compel worship, especially in the city of Rome as Caligula did, was monstrous. Yet one should not overemphasize imperial reluctance. High-profile public offers of cult the emperors might refuse, but it was under Augustus, despite his seeming fastidiousness, that public cult in Italy was organized; and public cult was strong enough to sap the vitality of purely private cult organizations by the end of his reign.[318] Cassius Dio claims that no emperor had ever dared to

---

[312] *Gk. Const.* 213. 19–21, [πό]λις ὄντες ἔνδοξος καὶ ἐκ παλαιο[ῦ Ῥω]μαίων ἀρχῇ χρήσιμος; see also *Gk. Const.* 15; *IGR* iv. 1756.

[313] Nero, *Gk. Const.* 296 (also *eunoia*); Gordian, *Gk. Const.* 279. For imperial grants prompted by subjects' *eusebeia*, see also *Gk. Const.* 18, 24 and 29 (both guilds), 218. Subjects' *eusebeia* also manifested by sending a gold crown, *Gk. Const.* 27; money, ibid. 217; or playing host to the emperor, *TAM* ii. 905 ch. 13.

[314] Price (1984a), 50–1. [315] Fishwick (1990b), 270–2.

[316] Tac. *Ann.* 4. 37.

[317] On the various dodges used in the West, and their trends, Fishwick (1987–92).

[318] Augustus and cult, Fishwick (1987–92), 83–93, and esp. 91 n. 55 on the cult in Italy. Decline of private *collegia* dedicated to imperial cult in Italy, Santero (1983), 123–5; the *Augustales* are a civic institution.

accept an offer of cult in Italy; this may be true of Augustus, but those who built shrines to him in Italy did not ask him, nor did he enquire.[319] And a long, slow trend can be discerned, whereby imperial insistence on various distancing mechanisms slowly faded: by the early third century direct public worship of the emperor was deemed appropriate even in the West.

Imperial acceptance of offers of public cult made in the East was also noticed in the West; this will have exerted a restraining influence on how many the emperor accepted.[320] There was, moreover, a considerable political advantage inherent in accepting only a proportion of the offers of cult that subject cities made. For while the cult itself was an honour directed by his subjects at the emperor, permission for large-scale public worship had to be elicited from the emperor, and this permission was part of the armoury of honours that the emperor used to rule his empire.

> Up with Perge, which alone has the right of asylum!
>
> .   .   .   .
>
> Up with Perge, temple-warden of the emperor since Vespasian!
> Up with Perge, honoured with the sacred standard!
> Up with Perge, honoured with silver coinage!
>
> .   .   .   .
>
> Up with Perge, treasury of the emperor!
> Up with Perge, four times temple-warden of the emperor!
>
> .   .   .   .
>
> Up with Perge, head of Pamphylia!
> Up with Perge, not false in any respect!
> All rights [are held] by the senate's decree![321]

Thus, shouting rhythmically, the citizens of Perge listed their city's claims to prestige. This inscribed acclamation indicates both the range of imperial honours that a city might enjoy and the prominence of those honours related to the imperial cult. Such honours were the object of rivalry: 'Lesser men and cities are eager to rival greater men and cities,' said Philo of the imperial cult.[322] The status of cities as 'first' or 'second' in the province was strictly observed in the order in which their representatives

[319] Dio 51. 20. 8; on the emperor's attitude, Nock (1930), 55.

[320] Claudius refuses cult at Alexandria as 'offensive to his contemporaries', *Gk. Const.* 19. 49; and Augustus preferred to be worshipped officially in both East and West only in the company of Roma, Fishwick (1987–92), 126–30.

[321] *SEG* xxxiv. 1306, acclamations selected from a longer document, translation adapted from Roueché (1989b). For a discussion of the various honours, ibid. 208–15; Weiss (1991).

[322] Philo, *Leg. Gaium* 338. For the place of the imperial cult in the rivalry between cities, Robert (1977a); Merkelbach (1978); Ziegler (1985).

marched in the processions that constituted an important part of the provincial cult of the emperor.[323] Cities begged permission to erect a temple to the emperor, to become the emperor's 'temple-warden'— *neocoros*. Thereby a city 'harvested honour', and would boast of the grant on its coins.[324] And the honour was keener when a city overcame others to get the privilege: in AD 26, Tiberius heard eleven cities plead their cause before the senate. As might be expected, they adduced their claims to prestige and the favours they had done for Rome.[325] When holding a neocorate became common, cities begged for a second, and a third, and a fourth.

Not only was permission to build a temple a sign of imperial favour, but one might ask as well for the right to hold games (an act of cult in both the Latin West and Greek East) for the emperor. Greek games had their own system of ranks, privileges, and titles, a system which was regulated by the emperor.[326] He might allow a city to found, say, 'Sacred Iselastic Iso-Pythian Œcumenical Augustan games'.[327] Or he might permit them to assimilate a traditional competition to the imperial cult, granting it an imperial name and raising its status. Thus the 'Great Sacred Iselastic Œcumenical Games of Zeus and Commodus'.[328] Of course prominent festivals and games had practical as well as honorific attractions: they attracted tourists with money to spend, and a city which held provincial observances for the imperial cult attracted liturgists, and could demand contributions from other cities of the province to pay for them.[329] But for most cities the profit will hardly have equalled the expenditure. The rivalry of cities for grants of the right to undertake acts of cult to the emperor was, at bottom, an outgrowth of their rivalry for

[323] Merkelbach (1978), 290–2.

[324] 'Harvest of honour', *Gk. Const.* 266. 22; also Aristid. 19. 13 (Behr). On the neocorate, Hanell (1935); Robert (1967), 48–57; Price (1984a), 64–7, 72–3: although the right might be voted by the senate, the decision was the emperor's in fact, p. 67. This honour died hard: in the 5th cent. AD Sardis is still 'twice temple-warden', Buckler and Robinson (1932), no. 18.

[325] Tac. *Ann.* 4. 55–6.

[326] Mitchell (1993), i. 217–25, arguing (p. 224) a trend in imperial cult away from emphasis on building temples (2nd cent.) to agonistic festivals (3rd); Harl (1987), 63–70; Ziegler (1985); Robert (1977a), 30–5: imperial authorizations as δωρεά, p. 33; imperial games as a source of prestige, Men. Rhet. 366 (and in general, on the prestige of festivals, 424–5).

[327] *IGR* iv. 1251 with Robert (1937), 119–23.

[328] *MAMA* vi. 11 with Robert (1969), 283–4. For such assimilations, Price (1984a), 103–4; the imperial cult may not always be implied by imperial titles, but the titles will in any event have been granted by the emperor.

[329] Crowds at festivals, MacMullen (1981), 18–26; liturgists from other cities, e.g. Étienne (1958), 143–9; cf. Reynolds (1982), no. 14; *ILS* 705. Contributions, Spawforth (1994).

honour, and it is hard to overstate the degree to which that passionate competition, over time, came to revolve around the imperial cult.[330]

If his subjects wanted the titles and honours and rights associated with the imperial cult, that was a source of power for the emperor, who could grant them as political prizes. Septimius Severus granted Nicomedia a second neocorate, presumably as one of the city's rewards for its help against Niger.[331] And after that same civil war the Tarsians awoke to discover in their province of Cilicia a rival city, Anazarbos, now also entitled to hold distinguished provincial games for the emperor. Perhaps Anazarbos shrewdly backed Elagabalus against Macrinus in 218, earning herself a second neocorate, and then deftly supported Decius in 249, thereby drawing ahead of Tarsus with three neocorates.[332] As a seismograph records the rumblings of distant earthquakes, so the grants of the privilege of cult games to the cities of Cilicia, an area crucial to Roman military communications, reveal the Persian wars of the third century in which their help was needed and rewarded.[333] The emperor could never grant permission to all who asked, or he would be squandering his capital; he could neither risk cheapening the honour by handing it out too widely, nor debase it by giving it to the unworthy. Tiberius naturally refused the request of Gytheum, a small town in Laconia; perhaps if famous Sparta had asked, the answer would have been different, for he did not scorn cult at haughty Smyrna.[334] Claudius was not so foolish as to reward Alexandria, gnawing crocodile-like on its long-suffering Jews, with the honour of building him a temple.[335] The emperor's decision to grant the honour of an imperial temple or games was carefully made, one of the thousands of political calculations about the distribution of honours that were part of ruling the Roman empire.

---

[330] Cf. *IK Eph.* i. 43. 2 (= line 15 Gk.) where the 'honorem Asiae ac totius provinci[a]e dignitatem' depends on the imperial festival at Ephesus.

[331] Robert (1977*a*), 34–5.

[332] AD 193, Ziegler (1985), 71–9: Anazarbos also received a neocorate, but Tarsus received a second neocorate, so Tarsus was not disloyal. Presumably Anazarbos adhered to Severus' cause earlier or more zealously. AD 218, Mitchell (1993), i. 221 (*pace* Ziegler (1985), 35); AD 249, Ziegler (1985), 99–108. For other suggestions of political grants, Mitchell (1993), i. 221–4.

[333] Ziegler (1985), 67–120; seismograph, p. 126. See also Harl (1987: 65–70), for games and politics in the rest of the East.

[334] Gytheum, see n. 272 above. Smyrna, Tac. *Ann.* 4. 15, 55–6; Price (1984*a*), cat. 45.

[335] *Gk. Const.* 19. 47–51; ill-treating the Jews, lines 73 ff.

CONCLUSION

There is an ancient definition of imperial power implicit in Tacitus' descriptions of Agricola and Domitian, Nero and Thrasea; in Cassius Dio's depiction of Tiberius and Sejanus and the jeering of Macrinus; in Herodian's picture of the revolt of Pescennius Niger. To such observers imperial power depended upon the loyalty of the soldiers and upon unequalled honour. We are certainly at liberty to conclude that the second half of this aristocratic definition of power is the pathetic self-delusion of a class desperate to reassure themselves of their own importance. After all, emperors could proclaim their scorn for aristocratic opinion, Caracalla writing to the senate, 'I know that my acts are not pleasing to you; but I have arms and soldiers exactly so that I can pay no heed to what is said of me.'[336] But that same emperor used those arms and soldiers to punish the jeers of Alexandria, hardly an act of blithe contempt for public opinion. The emperors and the historians were brought up in the same school, in a society in which the protection and expansion of renown were enormously important, in which renown was seen as significant in all areas of life, and in rulership especially. Honour exists only in the mind, depending for its existence on a widespread conspiracy of the imagination. But if everyone, including the emperor, partly shared in that conspiracy, honour was a reality to them, and played a real role in politics.

The Roman emperor and his subjects inhabited a world articulated in terms of honour and honouring, reciprocity and deference. The historians' fascination with imperial honour, their eagerness to entangle the emperors in a web of honour, indicates above all how such men were trapped themselves. This was a world of mirrors, a mixture of sincerity, deception, and vanity, the whole mix a source of power to the emperor. A subject's real desire for honours from his emperor to promote himself or his city in local competition for distinction was of the greatest utility to the ruler. It did not matter, however, if this eagerness was often no more than a cloak, as long as it could assist the working of other forms of imperial power—bribes and terror. A subject's heartfelt sense of gratitude or deference was obviously useful, as was that sense when he felt it on his city's behalf; but so were those sentiments if used as a blind, consciously or unconsciously, or as the ideological basis for institutions like the imperial cult, which contributed to the emperor's power. Imperial

[336] Dio 78(77L). 20. 2.

rule did well to put down roots in two of its subjects' strongest emotions, *philotimia*, the lust for honour, and civic patriotism, manifested in the lust for civic glory. The paradox that Tacitus has Marcus Terentius express, 'all that is left to us is the glory of obedience', is brought to life in the Greek provinces of the empire, where *philosebastos*, 'Augustus-loving', is a title that cities proudly boast of, and where loyalty to the emperor was an honourable virtue like generosity, competed in by civic notables, and honorifically acclaimed: 'Claudius-loving! Caesar-loving! Augustus-loving! Rome-loving!'[337] That overwhelming sense of competition that had once sent the Achaeans ranging over the fields of Troy now manifested itself in loyalty to the emperor. This was a deep well of imperial power.

The essential fiction involved in aristocratic conceptions of the emperor was not that emperors cared about their honour—they usually did—but that there was meaningful competition in honour between emperors and others. Emperors never competed for honour on a level field. The control of soldiers made it possible for the emperor to protect his honour, at least for a while, even if he had acted extremely badly. The imperial cult, moreover, reveals the way in which subjects connived in rendering their emperor honourable. Not only priests of the cult, but anyone whose city competed with another, or indeed who did not wish to set himself in shameful public opposition to the norms of his society, had a stake in the emperor's honour. The emperor's subjects insisted that their emperor was splendid and glorious as much for themselves as for him. And this conspiracy of loyal sentiment was reinforced by anyone who looked forward to receiving, or had received, an honour from an emperor. For the emperor's own honour defined the abiding value of his kiss or invitation to dinner, established how delightfully humiliated rivals would be that one man had a letter from him, and they did not. The more honour the emperor granted to the great men of the empire, the more they were complicit in upholding his honour: whatever the emperor's real qualities, whatever his actual worthiness for honour, an honourable emperor was necessary for the way his subjects went about their business.

The emperor's honour was in large part a creation of what his subjects wanted to believe. A new reign, especially that of the son of a popular

---

[337] Tac. *Ann.* 6. 8, 'obsequii gloria'; cf. Pliny, *Paneg.* 9. 5. φιλοσέβαστος as city title, Robert (1969), 288–9. φιλοκλαύδιον [erased and replaced with φιλονέρωνα, itself later erased], φιλοκαίσαρα, φιλοσέβαστον, φιλορώμαιον, Small. *Gaius* 262; cf. *IGR* iv. 1048. On the relation of such titles to acclamations, Roueché (1984), 182 n. 15 with refs.; for φιλοσέβαστος as a personal title, see Robert (1949*b*), 211–12; for φιλόκαισαρ (and others), see the indices of *IGR* iv, p. 682.

emperor, or the successor of a slain tyrant, inspired the brightest hopes.[338] A new emperor, if he did not ascend to the purple amidst rivers of blood, had the distinction his subjects thought he ideally should have, rather than the honour that he might properly have received if he had been subjected to the searching analysis usual in aristocratic circles. This happy presumption of glory—backed by the universal human longing for good overlords, perhaps by the incomparable distinction of imperial ancestors and by imperial pronouncements, and certainly by the distinction that the imperial office itself bestowed (discussed in the next chapter)—was very robust. It took a great deal for an emperor to disgrace himself: the yearnings of his subjects, on the one hand, and his ability to terrify, on the other, made sure of that. Imperial honour was not merely part of the shared fantasy of the Roman world. It was something fantastic within that fantasy, a glorious orchid imagined by the flowers of an imaginary garden.

---

[338] Suet. *Gaius* 13–14; *Galba* 14. 1; Dio 61. 3. 1; Herod. 1. 7; but see Suet. *Titus* 6–7 for an exception.

4

Officials

THE attractions of holding a high post in the Roman imperial government were manifold. Who would not be overjoyed to ruin, flog, or execute his more irritating acquaintances? 'Comandare e meglio di fottere', as the Sicilians say. An armed guard and the colour of authority could advance almost any end. 'I can have whomever I want clubbed to death!' an imagined governor gloats.[1] One of the roads the rods of an official cleared most frequently was that to fortune. Offices were remunerative because of the large salaries they came to carry, the gifts that were their holders' everyday expectation, the opportunities to convert public money into one's own, and the vantage they afforded for bribes and extortion.[2] It was worthy of remark when an official returned home no richer than when he left.[3] More and more, offices were also valued because of the delightful immunities from costly civic burdens they offered. Indeed, in late antiquity men can be seen seeking official posts solely to enjoy this last benefit, serving briefly or holding their posts in sinecure, and then getting on with their lives.[4]

Yet honour words provide the most common terms for office in the classical languages, *honor* or *dignitas* in Latin, and τιμή in Greek.[5] And these are not dead metaphors, technical expressions devoid of their original flavour: honour, prestige, lies absolutely at the heart of Graeco-Roman perceptions of office holding. A modern reader of constitutionalist disposition naturally has difficulty distinguishing the categories of municipal office and civic burden (*munus*, liturgy), since both required

---

[1] Arr. *Epict.* 3. 7. 32; cf. Juv. 10. 96–7.

[2] Salaries: Pflaum (1978), for the principate, including HS 1,000,000 (the senatorial census!) per annum for the Proconsul of Asia (Dio 78(79L). 22. 5); late empire, A. H. M. Jones (1964), 397–8. The salary might be a reason to seek a post, Fronto, *ad Pium* 1. 10. 2 (van den Hout); Plut. *Praec. Ger. Reip.* 814d. Conveniently on gifts, the perfectly legal pocketing of government money, and corruption, MacMullen (1988), 124–67.

[3] Philostr. *VS* 2. 29 (621); Lib. *Ep.* 359. 3, a topos.

[4] A. H. M. Jones (1964), 740–6; Liebeschuetz (1972), 174–8; Millar (1983).

[5] For Latin vocabulary see esp. Hellegouarc'h (1963), 384–5; Löhken (1982), 12–14.

an individual to undertake expenses for his town; not so the ancient jurist, who understood that offices conferred dignity on their holder while civic burdens did not.[6] Indeed, the accretion to prestige could be perceived as the essence of obtaining an appointment when everything more superficial was stripped away. Pliny, when begging an official post for a friend, makes it clear that he has no reason other than the desire to increase the friend's honour—he does not even care what the position is, so long as it is distinguished and does not require much work.[7]

Or so he says. For of course the association of office with honour permitted a great deal of flummery. A Roman aristocrat in an official position was no one's hired help. But would he perhaps be willing to accept a substantial stipend from the emperor as compensation for the sacrifice of his leisure and to augment his dignity?[8] Why, yes! Put that way it would be churlish to refuse. And so he really thought of it, no doubt. But when the corruptly gained perquisites of lowly fourth-century bureaucrats are casually referred to as their 'dignities', we have arrived at a world of polite pretence.[9]

It is to the realities and humbugs of office and honour that we now turn; first to investigate the symbiosis that existed in the Graeco-Roman mind between posts and honour, then to survey the consequences of that relationship for Roman government beneath the exalted sphere of the emperor: the power that honour allowed and assisted officials to exert over subjects, the power of subjects over officials likewise. Both are particularly well illuminated by the fourth *Sacred Tale* of Aelius Aristides. Finally, we consider the possible consequences for government when, as often in late antiquity, a preponderance of honour and authority did not lie in the same hands.

OFFICE AS DIGNITY

The intricacy of the association of honour and office is evident in an imperial constitution of AD 376 concerning the grain supply to the city of Rome, a decree regulating relations between the offices of the Prefect of the City of Rome and the Prefect of the Grain Supply, two great bureaux which were struggling to dominate this area of administration, perennially so vital to the civil peace of the great, hungry city.

---

[6] *Dig.* 50. 4. 14 (Callistratus), 'cum dignitatis gradu'.

[7] Pliny, *Ep.* 3. 2; cf. 4. 4. 2.

[8] Dio 52. 21. 7, ἕνεκα . . . τῆς ἀξιώσεως; cf. Tac. *Ann.* 4. 16.

[9] *Dignitates*, *CTh* 6. 30. 11 (386), 13 (395); also, immunities intended for the *scriniorum gloria*, *CTh* 6. 26. 14. pr. (407 or 412).

The Office of the Prefect of the Grain Supply has control over its own functions, but in such a fashion that, when the Prefect of the City undertakes a public procession in accordance with ancient tradition, there be a distribution of bread in recognition of his rank and dignity. Nevertheless, we desire that the Prefecture of the Grain Supply yield to the lofty dignity [of the Prefect of the City] only to the extent that it does not thereby yield the duty of provision. And the officers of the Urban Prefecture shall not insinuate themselves into the office of the Grain Supply, but the officers of the two bureaux will put aside their rivalry. The Prefecture of the Grain Supply shall do its own work, not as subject to authority, but rather, by being diligent in its own business it shall protect itself from contempt in so far as it does not insult the superior office. The Prefecture of the City shall have precedence over all magistracies in the city, and shall take from the province of all other magistrates only so much as can be taken without injury and hurt to the honour of others.[10]

A 'masterpiece of ambiguity'?[11] But only if viewed in twentieth-century terms; by the forgiving standards of late Roman law, clear enough. The two offices have come to blows over the supply of bread for distribution during public appearances of the Prefect of the City. The Grain Supply is to provide this bread, the emperor insists, as an act of respect for the Prefecture of the City. Relations of reverence between officials, sometimes explicitly distinguished from strict relations of obedience (as here), are a frequent concern of late-antique law:

Nothing whatsoever is to be common and shared by any governors with the palatines of our clemency, as many as are directed by the counts of the consistory [i.e. members of the staffs of the Counts of the Sacred Largesses and the *Res Privata*]. Except for the reverence which is owed and offered to governors of provinces, not only by their inferiors but also by their superiors, each will go about his own business.[12]

---

[10] *CTh* 1. 6. 7, 'suis partibus annonae praefectura moderatur, sed ita, ut ex veterum more praefecto urbis per publicum incedente honoris eius et loci gratia expensio panis habeatur. Eatenus tamen praefecturam annonae cedere volumus dignitatis fastigio, ut curandi partibus non cedat. Neque tamen apparitoribus urbanae praefecturae annonarium officium inseratur, sed apparitorum aemulatione secreta ministerio suo annonae praefectura fungatur, non ut potentiae subiecta, sed ut negotii sui diligens tantumque se a contemptu vindicans, quantum non pergat in contumeliam superioris. Praefectura autem urbis cunctis, quae intra urbem sunt, antecellat potestatibus, tantum ex omnibus parte delibans, quantum sine iniuria ac detrimento alieni honoris usurpet'. Trans. adapted from Pharr. See Chastagnol (1960: 297–300) for the background, but with a different interpretation of this law.

[11] A. H. M. Jones (1964: 690), describing a previous imperial intervention, *CTh* 1. 6. 5 (365), as well.

[12] *CTh* 6. 30. 4 (378 or 379), *reverentia*; cf. *CJ* 1. 55. 4 (385).

Here the emperor explicitly ruled out any relations of legal authority between the provincial governors and financial officers dispatched from the palace.[13] Relations of respect would, of course, still exist. Ammianus Marcellinus praises the strict separation of military and civil authority in the reign of Constantius, and then the fact that great officials both civil (his subordinates) and military (not) showed proper reverence for the praetorian prefect.[14] And other laws stipulated the acts of reverence that one official owed another: governors shall under no circumstances bar the clerks of the imperial court from their morning *salutationes*, for example, and members of the imperial bodyguard are to be permitted to kiss vicars.[15]

For the Grain Supply to fail in its reverence for the Prefecture of the City is to insult it; it shall not do so. At the same time the lofty Prefecture of the City has acted arrogantly in attempting to seize functions from offices with lower standing, thus insulting them; it too shall desist. Nothing unusual here: an official's failure to perform public acts of respect for another was an insult and punished under the law, as all improper insults between officials might be.[16] Certainly 'the *corrector* of the province of Augustamnica deserved to be punished, along with his office staff, for his insult to the *dux*.' Although, again, the one was not technically subordinate to the other, for a *corrector* was a civil governor, and a *dux* a high military officer, in a generation which kept civil and military chains of command separate.[17] This imperial insistence on officials not insulting one another could create difficulties when the duties of reverence and those of honest administration conflicted. Suppose an inferior official's investigations were to uncover something discreditable to a superior?

Appropriate reverence is to be shown by inferior judges to those of higher rank. But where the public interest is involved, and the lesser governor is investigating the truth, no insult is done to his superior. Yet it is certain that anyone who exercises his office so as to afflict with unworthy insults those in official authority will not escape the sting of our indignation![18]

[13] Cf. *CTh* 6. 30. 6 (383 or 384).
[14] Amm. Marc. 21. 16. 2, 'sed cunctae castrenses et ordinariae potestates, ut honorum omnium apicem, priscae reverentiae more, praefectos semper suspexere praetorio', with Matthews (1989), 253. Cf. Greg. Naz. *Ep.* 143. 5; Cass. *Var.* 7. 43.
[15] *CTh* 6. 26. 5 (389), *reverentia*, and 6. 24. 4 (387), *honorificentia*; cf. 6. 26. 16 (410 or 413).
[16] Above, n. 15.
[17] *CTh* 1. 7. 2 (393), *contumelia*, with A. H. M. Jones (1964), 376. The case came to the emperor's attention because the *corrector* had been punished by the *magister militum*, a high military official. The punishment was just, the emperor said, but the praetorian prefect ought to have inflicted it. [18] *CJ* 1. 40. 5 (364), *reverentia, iniuria*.

The emperor carves the narrowest possible exception to the duty of reverence, while sternly reasserting it.

Placed in its context of careful imperial regulation of kissing and greeting and elaborate legal safeguards against officials insulting one another, the law of the quarrelling prefectures reveals that due reverence between officials could be considered part of government, something that made things happen. It was not merely a polite way of describing relations of obedience (although in a world where aristocrats so hated to be seen to obey it will frequently have served as that) because it was expected to exist, and operate, where obedience, explicitly, did not. It is a second stream of power alongside strict obedience, usually flowing down the same course, but sometimes not; it was useful both ways. More than a simple resolution of administrative confusion, the law of the prefectures may allude to terrible events: the legal persecution of Roman senators in the later years of Valentinian by his creature Maximinus, Vicar of the City of Rome and former Prefect of the Grain Supply. Gratian, Valentinian's successor, may be trying to placate the wounded senatorial aristocracy by exalting the Prefecture of the City, traditionally their bailiwick. But whether or not this is so—or whether the emperor is here discussing due reverence as a way of making a veiled threat—he is using an aspect of relations between officials with a very long history. Junior officials had long been commended for their reverential disposition towards their superiors, whether or not those superiors technically had the right to command them, and however inept those superiors might be.[19] Old too were acts of reverence from an inferior towards his superior, like lowering his *fasces* upon his approach, or going to meet him, still the custom in the fourth century. Venerable as well was the outraged sense of personal insult if such acts were neglected.[20] Suetonius reports only a few details about Nero's grandfather, but one of them is that as aedile, he forced a censor to give way to him in the street, a disgraceful reversal of the natural order of things.[21] Investigation of the consequences of this aspect of relations between officials for the internal working of government is

[19] Maximinus, Amm. Marc. 28. 1. 8–56; for suggested connection with this law, Matthews (1975), 66. Long history, Plut. *Tib. Gracch.* 5. 1; *C. Gracch.* 2. 1; Cic. *ad Fam.* 5. 19. 1; Pliny, *Ep.* 10. 86a (cf. 4. 15. 12, 10. 26).

[20] *Fasces*, Plut. *Pomp.* 19. 5; cf. Vel. Pat. 2. 99. 4; meeting, Cic. *ad Fam.* 3. 7. 4–5 (an old custom); and still in the 4th cent., Lib. *Or.* 1. 69; Amm. Marc. 21. 16. 2; cf. Cic. *ad Att.* 6. 3. 6 for escorting.

[21] Suet. *Nero* 4; such acts of deference are enforced by the 'honos . . . et dignitas' of the one performing them, Cic. *ad Fam.* 3. 7. 4.

impossible, since the necessary evidence has not survived. But clearly the origins of this official culture of respect need to be understood.

Honour from Obtaining Office, 1: The Independent Honour of Offices

To which exactly is the insult or reverence, the office or its holder? To both, in fact.[22] The honour of a man was inextricably bound up with the office he was holding and the offices he had held. To gain an office in the Roman world was to enjoy an accretion to one's honour. Fronto asks Antoninus Pius for a procuratorship to 'enhance the dignity' of an elderly acquaintance—and promises that if it is offered it will be declined: the old gentleman wants the honour of having been granted it, not the associated powers and duties.[23]

Receiving an office was perceived to confer honour because, in the first place, every political position, from that of the emperor down to the petty official of a provincial town, every civic pagan priesthood, and, by the mid-fourth century, every high ecclesiastical position itself rejoiced in a certain traditional degree of honour, honour made patent to the world by special attire, seats at public events, and by the accompaniment of appropriate retainers.[24] Offices, like men and cities, were perceived to be independent entities in the world of prestige, and an office had its prestige wholly apart from that of the person who might be occupying it at a given moment. Thus a corrupt governor could be deemed to have failed in reverence towards his own office.[25] An office conferred honour upon its holder, just as a great man or a distinguished city might by honouring him; similarly, the degree of honour conferred depended on the relative honour of the post and holder. A very distinguished man gained no honour from a lowly post, just as he would gain little from a lowly praiser; it might even degrade him.[26] At such a juncture he is described as being 'above his office', a revealing phrase, in that it implies the precision with which the honour of men and of offices could be totalled up and compared.[27] If an official were cashiered, the honour of his post nevertheless lingered about him for a while, like smoke.[28]

[22] Cic. *ad Fam.* 3. 7. 4–5; Vel. Pat. 2. 99. 4; Sym. *Rel.* 23.

[23] Fronto, *ad Pium* 1. 10 (van den Hout), 'dignitatis . . . ornandae causa'.

[24] Magistracies, see esp. Plut. *Brut.* 7. 1; Pliny, *Paneg.* 77. 5; John Lyd. *Mag.* 2. 7–9; Cass. *Var.* 6 passim. Emperorship, Tac. *Hist.* 2. 48; John Lyd. *Mag.* 1. 6. Ecclesiastics, see p. 95 above. Insignia: Mommsen (1887–8), i. 372–435; Löhken (1982), 80–6; retainers, Mommsen (1887–8), i. 320–71.

[25] *De Reb. Bell.* 4. 1, 'despecta reverentia dignitatum'.

[26] Plut. *Praec. Ger. Reip.* 811b; cf. Lib. *Ep.* 34. 4. Degrade, *HA Comm.* 3. 3.

[27] Amm. Marc. 29. 1. 8; cf. Plut. *Praec. Ger. Reip.* 813c; Sym. *Rel.* 12. 3.

[28] Sid. *Ep.* 1. 7. 4.

The honour of a post could change over time. Looking back from his sixth-century prison cell, Boethius could point out the decline in the honour of the praetorship and the Prefecture of the Grain Supply.[29] An office's prestige was to a great extent a function of those who had held it in the past. If persons of high honour had held it, they conferred their honour upon it, as, for example, when the emperor held the consulship; if a base person held it, he dishonoured and polluted it. Pliny (especially touchy because a former praetor himself) insisted that the praetorship was contaminated when Claudius' freedman Pallas was given praetorian insignia—he professed himself amazed that anyone could be persuaded to seek the praetorship after it had been thus dragged through the mud.[30]

The conduct of the holders of an office also had an impact. The austere justice of Cato the Younger was expected to raise the status of the praetorship, just as his reform of the office of the quaestorian clerks had that of the quaestorship. Yet because his eccentricity led him to preside without tunic or shoes over the trials of prominent men (or so some reported), he could be held to have disgraced, rather than adorned, the office.[31] In this respect the emperorship was no different from any other office. It too had an independent prestige, and could be disgraced, as for example by Commodus' fighting in the arena. Naturally, it might be viewed (at least rhetorically) as 'a disgrace, rather than a source of praise, to be named emperor after Vitellius'.[32] Not the least of Augustus' achievements was to instil honour so vast into the imperial office that he embodied and invented that it could prop up, at least for a while, many of his odd or evil successors.

Finally, forces exterior to the post itself could have an impact on its prestige. Cassius Dio assumes that the emperor has the honour of offices under his power; it is important to maintain them, he says.[33] For the emperor could damage the honour of a position by depriving it of insignia and august ceremonies; or he could add to it, as Gratian did when he allowed the Prefects of the City of Rome to crash through the

[29] Boeth. *Consol.* 3. 4.

[30] Offices honoured by their occupants: Sall. *Jug.* 4. 7–8; Plut. *Praec. Ger. Reip.* 811b; Basil, *Ep.* 98; J. Chr. *Ep.* 147; John Lyd. *Mag.* 3. 50. Emperor in the consulship, Pliny, *Paneg.* 60. 2; Lib. *Or.* 12. 10, 21. 29; honorific for his colleague, Pliny, *Paneg.* 92. Dishonoured by holder: Pallas, Pliny, *Ep.* 8. 6. 16; cf. Sall. *Jug.* 63. 7; *HA Elag.* 11. 1; *CTh* 9. 40. 17 (399); Jer. *Ep.* 66. 7; Claudian, *In Eutr.* 1. 8–28, 284–370.

[31] Quaestorship, Plut. *Cato Min.* 17. 1; praetorship, 44. 1. Cf. Plut. *Pomp.* 47. 3; Boeth. *Consol.* 3. 4.

[32] Commodus, Herod. 1. 15. 7. Vitellius, Tac. *Hist.* 2. 76, 'a contumelia quam a laude'. Cf. ibid. 1. 37, 3. 58; Suet. *Vit.* 10. 1; Philostr. *VA* 5. 29, 32; *HA Macr.* 15. 2.

[33] Dio 52. 20. 3, τιμή, ἀξίωμα.

streets in a great carriage agleam with silver, their new official con-veyance.[34] When the praetorian prefect deprived the chief clerks in his bureau of their venerable right to a siesta, he was deemed to have dis-honoured their office.[35]

The emperor could also grant or withdraw a post's practical functions, which, as the law of the Grain Supply indicates, were considered part of its honour.[36] A governor, entitled to enforce his will by violence, enjoyed 'a dignity adorned by terrors'.[37] To take functions away from an office (as the Prefecture of the City was trying to do) was to insult the office, and thus its holders past and present, who derived their own honour from it; in the wider world of aristocratic opinion, this was to lay oneself open to the accusation that one was not paying the office the deference it was due. To the familiar jealousies and turf-wars of bureaucratic life the Romans added a whole additional level of prickly intransigence.[38] By the fourth century, no fewer than three great bureaux were involved in the raising and spending of government revenues, a situation to the modern mind 'gratuitously complicated'.[39] But all administrative changes had honour consequences, and systematic reorganization of the structure of govern-ment along modern, 'rational' lines was unimaginable. It could take cen-turies for posts with no function at all to vanish: the old senatorial offices of tribune and aedile finally disappeared in the late third century, when senatorial feelings were not at a premium; but the tribunate had seemed functionless to many in Pliny the Younger's day, and soldiered on none the less for at least a century and a half after that.[40]

Although the powers and functions of an office were part of its hon-our, the honour of offices was only partly contingent upon their practi-cal power (just as was the case with aristocratic individuals), or indeed upon their having any function at all. The ordinary consulship main-tained and even increased its glory in the fourth century despite the fact

[34] Hurt honour, John Lyd. *Mag.* 2. 17, 19; cf. Amm. Marc. 26. 6. 16; Plut. *Tib. Gracch.* 15. 1; *Fab. Max.* 10. Carriage, Sym. *Rel.* 4, 20; Symmachus thought it vulgar, but it was used, Chastagnol (1960), 203–5. Cf. for addition to honour, John Lyd. *Mag.* 2. 30, 3. 39; also Cass. *Var.* 6. 5. 1.

[35] John Lyd. *Mag.* 3. 15; the prefect can also honour his own bureau, 3. 49.

[36] Cf. Suet. *Tib.* 31. 2; Cass. *Var.* 6. 18. 1; responsibilities appropriate to honour, *CTh* 1. 12. 2 (319); Cass. *Var.* pr. 6.

[37] Cass. *Var.* 7. 1. 1, 'tua . . . dignitas a terroribus ornatur'.

[38] Cf. John Lyd. *Mag.* 3 *passim*; to maintain them is to maintain offices' *maiestas*, Suet. *Tib.* 30. Office owed deference by emperor, John Lyd. *Mag.* 3. 50.

[39] A. H. M. Jones (1964), 411.

[40] Tribune and aedile vanish from *cursus* inscriptions, Christol (1986), 84–5. The tri-bunate may have maintained some shadowy existence even in the 4th cent., Kuhoff (1983), 28. Tribunate pointless, Pliny, *Ep.* 1. 23 (Pliny tried to take it seriously).

that its incumbents had next to no duties (besides giving games), and suffect consulships (held for short stretches of the later part of the year) declined in prestige.[41] In part, the honour of offices was self-perpetuating entirely within the world of honour. For those who had passed through offices had the most prestige and thus the greatest ability to confer prestige on what they believed to be worthy, and it was 'natural for a man to want to have deemed most important those offices which he has held'. So Pliny had a 'greater reverence' for the consulship.[42] In part, too, offices' tradition sustained them. For, to determine the honour owed a post, aristocrats looked over their shoulders into the past, even the distant, semi-mythical past. Whatever one's opinion of recent holders of the consulship or its political impotence, its glory was maintained by memory of the heroes of the early and mid-Republic. From this arose the sense that the consulship was so lofty an office that few of those who actually held it were worthy of it.[43] Necessarily, in such an environment, polemic that aimed at improving the honour of an office manufactured for it a tradition. Thus the sixth-century John Lydus, in his treatise on magistracies, emphasized (quite wrongly) that the praetorian prefect, in whose office he held a post, was descended from the Master of Horse, second in power to the kings of exceedingly ancient Rome. If he could convince his contemporaries of that origin, his office would enjoy, by virtue of tradition, a certain prestige which an office of lesser lineage would not.[44]

The honour of a post was fairly clear, whatever its origins, and whatever the reasons for its longevity. Tacitus, for example, could easily suggest this with a simple phrase like 'the consuls and the praetors enjoyed their appropriate prestige'.[45] Indeed, the weight of consensus allowed the prestige conferred by posts to crystallize to such an extent that terms organically grew up to describe it. The holders of high equestrian procuratorships under the principate came to be called 'most perfect men', *viri perfectissimi*. A senator was an 'extremely brilliant' man, a *vir clarissimus*, soon abbreviated to *v.c.*; in time, these descriptive terms hardened into titles.[46]

---

[41] Consulship, Bagnall *et al.* (1987), 1–4, and cf. John Lyd. *Mag.* 2. 8.

[42] Pliny, *Ep.* 4. 17. 3, 'maior . . . reverentia'.   [43] *Pan. Lat.* 3(11). 15. 4.

[44] John Lyd. *Mag.* 1. 14–15, 2. 3; cf. 1. 34, also Cass. *Var.* 6. 3. 1–2, for a fanciful tracing of the praetorian prefecture to Joseph and Pharaoh.

[45] Tac. *Ann.* 4. 6, 'sua consulibus, sua praetoribus species'.

[46] Hirschfeld (1901); under the principate, Pflaum (1970) and Alföldy (1981), 190–4; for late antiquity, A. H. M. Jones (1964), 525–30. For *perfectissimus*, Ensslin (1937a); note also *spectabilis* (first seen applied to a proconsul, *CTh* 7. 6. 1 (365)), Ensslin (1929), 1554; *illustris*, to Prefects of the City, Berger (1914), 1072.

It was not only the great official who partook of the honour of the office he held: the lesser employees in the bureau of such an office in late antiquity were ranked in honour among themselves, and they also shared in the éclat of the great office. If its honour declined, to be a clerk in its employ would cease to confer honour, and might instead confer disgrace. John Lydus confirms the impression drawn from the imperial law about the Grain Supply: the view from a great late-antique bureau, perhaps with over a thousand authorized employees and even more supernumeraries, was very similar to that from an ancient city. The keen rivalry between the functionaries of the Prefect of the City and those of the Prefect of the Grain Supply (which the emperor had to step in to forbid), just as if they were the citizens of Nicaea and Nicomedia locked in a struggle for civic honour, is wholly consistent. And if a great office was similar to a city, it is not surprising to note that its prestige suffered if its functionaries could not keep up appearances.[47]

Honour from Obtaining Office, 2: Benefactions and Competition

The honour that each office enjoyed independently of its holder, and of which its incumbents and associated lesser functionaries partook, was not the only reason why obtaining an office conferred prestige in the Roman world: posts were at the same time favours, *beneficia*. In a world where one was appointed to posts by high personages, the receipt of an office publicized the esteem of the great man who had given it. 'He quitted his retirement for a short time, with great praise, and was appointed by our friend Corellius as his assistant in buying and distributing lands under the generosity of the emperor Nerva—for how great is the honour of having been selected by so great a man who had so wide a field to choose from!'[48] It is, therefore, unsurprising that an equestrian officer will mention who appointed him: an inscription which describes his career will list him not merely as a *praefectus fabrum* (a first step in the equestrian *cursus*), but as the *praefectus fabrum* of, specifically, emperor Claudius.[49]

---

[47] Rank among lesser employees, John Lyd. *Mag.* 3. 4, 22; partake of rank of high office, 2. 17; for outlook, ibid., *passim.* esp. 3. 1; cf. *CE* 744. Numbers in late-antique offices, A. H. M. Jones (1964), 1412. Keep up appearances, *Mag.* 3. 14.

[48] Pliny, *Ep.* 7. 31, *laus, gloria*; cf. 4. 8. Posts are *beneficia*: refs. collected, Saller (1982), 42 n. 6; add (later) *HA Sev. Alex.* 46. 4–5; Sym. *Rel.* 1. 1.

[49] *Praefecti fabrum*, Saddington (1985), 537–42. Mention of who appointed or promoted senators and *equites*: e.g. *CIL* iii. 726, 6687; *ILS* 1740; McC. & W. 288; *AE* 1956. 124; Pflaum (1948), col. 1. A letter of appointment might be carved on stone for the admiration of posterity, *AE* 1962. 183a, with Pflaum (1971). For honour from being appointed by the emperor, see also above, Ch. 3 n. 221.

Moreover, official posts, particularly junior ones, were traded openly on the basis of reciprocity: 'You will have both me and him as your most grateful debtors,' says Pliny, begging an equestrian post for a friend.[50] Indeed, equestrian offices were simply given to Pliny to hand on to whomever he liked—the identity of the final recipient was of no interest to the original bestower of the office.[51] An office gained in such a way signified the esteem of the man who applied his influence, the *suffragator*; he was a great man, and that esteem was honorific. Thus Junius Septimius Verus Hermogenes announced on an inscription that he was 'adorned with a [military] tribunate paying sixty thousand [sesterces] a year by his influence', 'his' being, in this case, the consul Balbinus Maximus'.[52]

Finally (and this is perhaps the key to this whole galaxy of perceptions), to a considerable extent the prestige enjoyed by holders of offices derived not from the post itself, or who had given it or exerted influence to gain it, but from the fact that the competition for posts was perennially viewed as a contest, a contest won by honour. 'For a man who is rich and a grandee,' as Artemidorus baldly put it, 'to dream that one is a god portends the greatest office: one in proportion to his dignity.'[53]

In Cicero's time, if a less 'worthy' candidate won an election, that fact was proof prima facie of electoral corruption. Defending Gnaeus Plancius against just such a charge, the orator had to describe at length how it was possible for a man of merely equestrian birth to overcome a blue-blood in an election for aedile.[54] Under the empire, when elections were transferred to the senate, the same ideal was maintained. Tacitus believed that until the reign of Claudius (when, he sneers, the imposition of expensive games made an auction of it), the quaestorship had been allotted 'in accordance with the dignity of the candidates or by the indulgence of the electors'.[55] Pliny, looking back from the same era, could affirm that before his own corrupt generation 'the worthy usually prevailed over those with the most influence', and he makes it clear that 'worth', as he sees it, was conventional aristocratic prestige, birth, and morals, achievement attested to by men of distinction, and the fact of

---

[50] Pliny, *Ep.* 3. 2; cf. 4. 4; *ILS* 2941. On this subject Saller (1982), *passim* and esp. 41–6, 75.

[51] Pliny, *Ep.* 3. 8, 7. 22.

[52] *ILS* 1191, 'suffragio eius ornatus'; cf. *CIL* v. 4332; *ILS* 4928–9 (where the *suffragator* is a vestal virgin). On the distribution of military tribunates, Cotton (1981).

[53] Artem. 3. 13, κατὰ τὸ ἐπιβάλλον τοῦ ἀξιώματος; cf. Apul. *Met.* 10. 18.

[54] Cic. *Planc.* 6–15 and esp. 18; also *Mur.* 36, 76; Hellegouarc'h (1963), 398 esp. nn. 4–5; and cf. Dio 56. 40. 4; Hor. *Sat.* 1. 6. 15–17.

[55] Tac. *Ann.* 11. 22, 'ex dignitate candidatorum aut facilitate tribuentium'; trans. Jackson. On elections in the senate, Talbert (1984), 341–6. For the waxing and waning number of offices the emperor left to the senate to elect, Saller (1982), 42–3.

distinguished supporters; perhaps, he says, the secret ballot will restore those happy times.[56]

Doubtless those who lived in Tacitus' and Pliny's honest days of yore would have looked back even further for honest days, shaking their heads about the corruption of their own present. No matter. The ideal of offices going to honour lived on, largely unhampered by reality. And the ideal applied to the emperor too, and anyone else who had positions in his gift, there being no objective system of appointment or promotion to high posts.[57] It was a point of deference to appoint the most honourable candidate, and emperors were lauded when they did so. In praising the early years of Tiberius' administration, Tacitus observed:

> In giving out offices, he considered the nobility of the candidate's ancestors, his glory in war, and the lustre conferred by his civil accomplishments, to establish that there was not anyone better. . . . The imperial property was entrusted to such as were most distinguished—sometimes to men he had not met, on account of their reputation.[58]

Best, in Tacitus' eyes, to sift through the candidates and to give the office to the most honourable—his honour being consequent both upon achievement in the imperial service and other qualities, like high birth. To such a mind, even competence was mediated through honour. Trajan is praised by Pliny for giving 'to youths of most distinguished line the office owed to their birth'.[59] And not unnaturally in such circumstances the 'splendour of his birth' led Accius Sura to hope that he might be given a vacant praetorship.[60] Prosopographers note the advantage that the sons of consuls enjoyed in advancing to the consulship themselves.[61] When

---

[56] Pliny, *Ep.* 3. 20, 'ita saepius digni quam gratiosi praevalebant'.

[57] Criteria of appointment and promotion, Saller (1982: 79–117) on this much-vexed question; cf. J. B. Campbell (1975) and (1984: 325–47) on military positions; Brunt (1975*b*) on the Prefect of Egypt (an especially intricate job). The chooser's latitude was restricted by law (which an emperor might always flout) and custom, producing the characteristic shapes of imperial career paths (conveniently, E. Birley (1981: 4–35) for senators; Pflaum (1950) for equestrians); but there was no prescriptive, objective system, no civil-service exams; it was all very informal. Outstanding ability was hardly scorned, Tac. *Ann.* 13. 6–8; *Agric.* 9. 5; but, like the men sent to rule British India, Roman aristocrats were assumed to be equal to all appointments.

[58] Tac. *Ann.* 4. 6, 'mandabatque honores, nobilitatem maiorum, claritudinem militiae, inlustris domi artes spectando ut satis constaret non alios potiores fuisse. . . . res suas Caesar spectatissimo cuique, quibusdam ignotis ex fama mandabat'. See also Plut. *Otho* 1. 2; Herod. 6. 1. 4. On the ideology of choosing officials, cf. Brunt (1988*b*).

[59] Pliny, *Paneg.* 69. 4, 'iuvenibus clarissimae gentis debitum generi honorem'; also 58. 3.

[60] Pliny, *Ep.* 10. 12. 2, 'natalium splendor'.

[61] Alföldy (1977), 95–110; Leunissen (1989), 90–1; the degree of this advantage is controversial, Hopkins (1983), 127–46; sons of *consules ordinarii* have an advantage over sons of *suffecti*, and, of course, much more goes into this advantage than pure distinction of birth.

Pliny recommends young men to great officials for appointments he recommends them not as skilled soldiers or efficient bureaucrats, but as individuals whose qualities were as estimable as possible in aristocratic eyes. The attributes wanted in a military tribune and in a bridegroom were identical: good family, a good fortune, skill in rhetoric, and good morals—all the contributors to aristocratic honour.[62]

If offices were expected to go to the worthy, to pass over the most honourable candidate was to deem him unworthy, to insult him. Cicero cast about to find someone to watch over Cilicia after his departure: he chose Coelius Caldus since, as his quaestor and a *nobilis*, none of the more experienced, willing, candidates could be preferred to him without *contumelia*, 'insult'. Cicero's letters express grave concern about Coelius' youth and competence for so tremendous a responsibility, but Cicero's primary concern was to avoid making an enemy by violating Coelius' rights in aristocratic eyes, and the provincials be damned.[63] Insulting important men was dangerous, even to emperors: Tacitus represents Tiberius complaining about the ill will he created when he passed men over.[64]

Not only were the insulted themselves angry. Aristocratic society as a whole condemned such failures of deference; when the emperors (about whom the most is known) gave offices to less distinguished candidates, they were castigated by aristocratic opinion. According to Cassius Dio, 'many blamed' Macrinus for appointing one Adventus consul, a baseborn creature 'who was not even able to talk properly to anyone in the senate, and thus, on the day of the elections, pretended to be ill'.[65] Preferring an undistinguished candidate to nobles for the praetorship, Tiberius excused his action: 'It seems to me that Curtius Rufus', he joked, 'was born from himself.'[66]

There was plenty to complain about. In all generations emperors were capricious, in all generations loyalty might be rewarded to the disadvantage of standing. In late antiquity bribery (never absent) came to play an increasing role in appointments even to the highest offices, as, slowly and

[62] Pliny, *Ep.* 2. 13, 3. 2, 4. 4, 15, 7. 22. Cf. bridegrooms, Pliny, *Ep.* 1. 14, 6. 26; Tac. *Ann.* 6. 15.

[63] Cic. *ad Fam.* 2. 15. 4; *ad Att.* 6. 6. 3–4 (with L. A. Thompson (1965); Marshall (1972) on the constraints on his choice; and cf. *ad Fam.* 2. 18. 2). Cf. Aristid. 50. 73 (Behr).

[64] Tac. *Ann.* 2. 36; cf. Dio 79(78L). 22. 3.

[65] Dio 78(79L). 14. 1–3; cf. 71(72L). 22. 1, 78(79L). 13. 1–4; for historians' disapproval, Suet. *Tib.* 42. 2; Herod. 5. 7. 6–7.

[66] Tac. *Ann.* 11. 21, 'Tiberius dedecus natalium eius velavisset'.

inconsistently, did religious affiliation.[67] But perhaps most important, using honour as a criterion for appointment flew in the face of what gradually became a fundamental policy of empire: great honour and responsibility, especially the control of soldiers, were to be kept apart. Even under Augustus the seeds of this policy were sown: the commander of his guard, the praetorian prefect, and the Prefect of Egypt were not senators, but equestrians. Nero, we are told, appointed Vespasian to command in the Jewish War since he was 'of tried energy and not to be feared in any way because of the humbleness of his line and name'.[68] The destruction of Nero by the distinguished Sulpicius Galba will have confirmed the wisdom of this choice of humble competence. Certainly under the principate the luxurious express-elevator to the highest offices to which those of patrician birth were entitled usually carried them right past the floors on which spears and swords were stored.[69] In the chaotic late third century all senators were increasingly excluded from responsible positions, an exclusion which became virtually (but not absolutely) complete under the low-born Diocletian.[70] Subsequent emperors gradually reversed this trend, but never entirely.[71] The return of the old aristocrats was especially limited in the army, which was increasingly dominated by barbarians at all levels, men who had to cut their nostril hairs daily.[72] The preserve of the aristocrats was, instead, the civil side—although even at higher levels special skills (such as shorthand-writing and knowledge of the law), rather than the traditional aristocratic rhetorical education, were increasingly valued, and although seniority (mingled with corruption) came increasingly to regulate advancement in the lower reaches of the late-antique civil service.[73]

Yet all this had little effect on the ideology of aristocratic office-holding. Symmachus avowed that honour and glory would throw open the door to the highest ranks, and Ammianus Marcellinus noted with

---

[67] Corruption: not overwhelming in principate, Eck (1982), but much greater at all levels in late antiquity, Ste Croix (1954), 39–48; Liebs (1978). Religion, von Haehling (1978).

[68] Suet. *Vesp.* 4. 5.

[69] Patricians, Eck (1974), 217–19; there were, of course, exceptions. See Hopkins (1983) 171–4 for the growing bifurcation between the 'grand set' and the 'power set'.

[70] Third cent., Christol (1986), 39–54. Diocletian, Arnheim (1972), 39–48; Barnes (1981), 10, with (1982), 140–74.

[71] Arnheim (1972), 49–102, and see pp. 223, 231 below.

[72] Liebeschuetz (1990), 7–47, and esp. 23; but Elton (1996: 136–52) has questioned the extent of this barbarization. Nostril hairs, Sid. *Ep.* 1. 2. 2—a description of Theoderic.

[73] Law and shorthand, Liebeschuetz (1972), 242–55. Seniority, A. H. M. Jones (1964), 602–3; but there were no such objective criteria for the short-serving powerful *dignitates*, ibid. 378–96, esp. 388, 391–5.

approval when it did, and snorted with contempt when the unworthy pushed their way in.[74] The rights of high birth were still respected, if not always by the emperor. When an unsuitable person was advanced to govern several provinces as vicar, grumblings could be heard among the fifth-century *jeunesse dorée* of 'birth trampled underfoot'.[75] The ideal might become reality particularly where aristocrats themselves had latitude to choose—in the Gallic Church, for example. It was not at all foolish for a candidate for the episcopacy to stress his lineage.[76] Sidonius Apollinaris selected as bishop of Bourges one Simplicius, a man of distinguished birth whose wife's splendid family contributed to his lustre, a former official, a performer of civic duties, one who ranked among the *spectabiles*, a man of good education. Sidonius made the selection knowing that among the clergy seniority was much esteemed; knowing also that people would complain at the choice: 'Sidonius . . . is swollen up with his own high birth, elevated by the glories of his offices; he scorns the poor of Christ.' No matter. Sidonius' regret was that the canons of the church forbade him from appointing the even higher-ranking *illustres* Eucherius and Pannychius; alas, they had married a second time.[77] If one had issued Cicero or Pliny with a bishop's staff and a copy of the canons, they would have made the same choice; reading Sidonius' praise of his candidate, it is easy to forget that it is the product of a Christian century.

We cannot trace the degree to which the expectation that office would go to honour was vindicated in reality; clearly, always less than some would have liked, and sometimes more than was prudent. Upon Cicero's mention of a patrician, his imperial commentator notes, 'The brilliance of this race has advanced even incompetents to the highest honours.'[78] Perhaps he was thinking of Mamercus Scaurus, consul under Tiberius, the descendant of Cicero's patrician; despite his vile morals, memory of his great family secured him support.[79] In fact, how much of a role

---

[74] Sym. *Ep.* 9. 67, 'macte igitur primi honoris auspiciis et ad honorem et gloriam felices tende conatus, ut et tibi ad celsiores gradus ianuam pandas'. Honour gains office (with the sources of the distinction noted), Amm. Marc. 23. 1. 4, 27. 11. 1, 28. 3. 9; cf. Eunap. *VS* 490; Sid. *Ep.* 1. 4; Cass. *Var.* 1. 3–4; and for the assumption, Amm. Marc. 15. 5. 14; Lib. *Or.* 4. 20. Unworthy gain office, Amm. Marc. 18. 5. 5, 21. 10. 8, 28. 1. 42.

[75] Sid. *Ep.* 1. 3, 'calcata generositas', cf. Firm. Mat. *Math.* 3. 5. 34, 38; A. H. M. Jones (1964), 388.

[76] Sid. *Ep.* 4. 25. 2. For the high standing of 5th-cent. Gallic bishops, Mathisen (1993: 91–2), but Gaul may be an extreme case, Barnish (1988: 138).

[77] Sid. *Ep.* 7. 9; Sidonius, bishop of Clermont and former Prefect of the City of Rome, made the choice because the locals were deadlocked.

[78] Asc. 23, 'quae generis claritas etiam inertes homines ad summos honores provexit'.

[79] Sen. *Ben.* 4. 31. 3–5; cf. Tac. *Hist.* 3. 86.

honour actually played in the distribution of offices was not very important. The ideal, the expectation, was extremely robust regardless, for it drew less on observation of contemporary circumstances than upon the psychological need of those involved, a need manifested (as so frequently in the ancient world) in an imagined past where things had worked as they ought. The enduring belief that office went to honour was a consequence of Graeco-Roman aristocrats' yearning for contests over honour with clear winners and losers. They had the competitive outlook of Homeric heroes, but no Trojan War to settle who was the best of the Achaeans. There, the Trojan Pandarus, having struck the great Diomedes with a spear, and thinking the blow mortal, shouts to him, 'You are struck right through the flank, and I don't think you'll hold up much longer: you have given me a great claim to glory.'[80] Instead it is Pliny's 'Julius Naso seeks an office. His opponents are both many and excellent. To overcome them is as glorious as it is difficult.'[81] In a world where posts were perceived to go to the candidate who enjoyed the greatest aristocratic esteem, to gain them was to prove to the world that you had honour greater than those you defeated, and as great as that of your colleagues in office. Especially glorifying then, if your consular colleague was a great general.[82] The contest for honour among aristocrats pervaded all areas of life, but political life especially, and realities of politics yielded in the mind to the demands of honour.

Honour While in Office

Not only did honour flow from the fact of receiving office, but offices also permitted the accumulation of more honour during their holder's tenure. Advice to a governor: 'By the immortal gods! Apply your care and consideration to those things which will bring you the highest dignity and glory!'[83] And Tacitus remarked at the death of the distinguished Lucius Piso that 'his particular glory was the way in which he tempered his authority as prefect of the city'.[84] Official position placed one in the public, the aristocratic, and even the imperial eye, and this permitted its

---

[80] *Il.* 5. 284–5, ἐμοὶ δὲ μέγ' εὖχος ἔδωκας.

[81] Pliny, *Ep.* 6. 6, 'petit honores Iulius Naso; petit cum multis, cum bonis, quos ut gloriosum sic est difficile superare'.

[82] *Pan. Lat.* 3(11). 15. 2; a veil, since the colleague, the barbarian Nevitta, was thought by Ammianus (21. 10. 8) a disgrace to his position, but the principle is plain; cf. Pliny, *Ep.* 5. 14.

[83] Cic. *ad Fam.* 10. 3. 3, 'summam dignitatem et gloriam'; cf. *ad Q. Fr.* 1. 1. 3, 41–5.

[84] Tac. *Ann.* 6. 10, *gloria.* Cf. Cic. *ad Fam.* 2. 11. 1; Tac. *Agric.* 8; Herod. 2. 7. 5; *HA Sev.* 4. 7; Amm. Marc. 29. 2. 16; *IK Eph.* i. 41; Greg. Naz. *Ep.* 104. 1; *CTh* 8. 8. 5 (395).

holder to show off his native virtues.[85] If Marcellinus the quaestor, who returned to the treasury public money that he certainly could have pocketed, had performed some similarly upright deed in private life, it is unlikely that Pliny would have written to a distant friend in praise of him.[86]

By and large, office illuminated conventional aristocratic virtues—wisdom, justice, self-control, courage.[87] But office also permitted some kinds of fame—like military glory—not available in the everyday round of forum or agora. There was honour in winning battles, honour in advancing the boundaries of one's province.[88] And it was easier to get a reputation for being just if one had been a judge; it was impossible to get a reputation for using one's power moderately, like Lucius Piso, if one had never had power to abuse.[89] The great fourth-century senator Praetextatus, we are told, gained increased *gloria* in aristocratic eyes from the useful measures he enforced as Prefect of the City: forbidding balconies, knocking down private buildings built leaning against temples, and reforming the weights and measures.[90] Naturally, even at the same level of authority, some posts offered more opportunities for distinction than others.[91] Observers expected a lively competition for glory between officials in office. Vitellius' general Caecina was impelled to imprudent activity by the approach of his rival Fabius Valens, for he feared that the latter would gobble up all the glory from the civil war.[92] Cicero expected to be able to goad his brother, governor of Asia, into better conduct by reminding him of the excellent reputations of the governors of Sicily and Macedonia.[93]

The danger, of course, was that the spotlight focused on the holder of an official post might illuminate vice rather than virtue. If legal controls over a governor's conduct were slight, it was because of the high confidence placed (often misplaced, we think) in social controls. It was not

[85] Public eye, Cic. *ad Q. Fr.* 1. 1. 9, 41–2; 2 *Verr.* 5. 35; cf. Hellegouarc'h (1963), 372–3; Pliny, *Ep.* 8. 24, 10. 26. 2; Cass. *Var.* 7. 7. 1.

[86] Pliny, *Ep.* 4. 12.

[87] Catalogue of governors' virtues, Men. Rhet. 415–17. Display of virtues in office, Cic. *ad Q. Fr.* 1. 1. 9, 18, 37, 45; *ad Fam.* 2. 18. 1; Pliny, *Ep.* 10. 86b; Tac. *Hist.* 3. 75; Zos. 5. 2. 2; and on countless honorific inscriptions.

[88] Military glory, J. B. Campbell (1984), 348–62, and esp. Juv. 10. 133–41; Tac. *Ann.* 4. 26; Lib. *Ep.* 972. 2. For the Republican background, Harris (1979), 17–34; Drexler (1962), 12, and esp. Cic. *Off.* 2. 45; *Mur.* 22, war the most glorifying activity of all. Expanding province, Tac. *Agric.* 14.

[89] Justice, Pliny, *Ep.* 9. 5; Piso, n. 84 above.

[90] Amm. Marc. 27. 9. 8–10, 'adulescebat gloria praeclari rectoris'.

[91] Cic. *Mur.* 18, 41–2; *Planc.* 64–5.

[92] Tac. *Hist.* 2. 24; cf. 3. 8, 52–3, 64; Zos. 4. 51.   [93] Cic. *ad Q. Fr.* 1. 2. 7.

only punishment that governors feared, but scandal, loss of honour, arising from revelations of conduct that their peers deemed unacceptable. When a governor departed for his province a friend, with tears in his eyes, might commend to him the governor's own reputation, and sigh with relief when he returned with it intact.[94] A letter asking a favour from a governor asks for help not so far as his duty permits, but 'in so far as is consistent with your dignity'.[95] For it is primarily an official's dignity that will suffer if he does wrong. As Juvenal reminds an (imaginary) aristocratic governor,

If your corps of assistants is honest, if no long-haired youth sells the judgements of your tribunal, if your wife commits no crimes, if on your assizes through all the towns no harpy stands ready to grab money with curved claws, *then* you can number your line from Picus: if high names delight you, place the whole battle of Titans, and Prometheus himself among your ancestors . . . But if ambition and lust whisk you away, if you break rods in the blood of allies, if the blunt axes of a weary lictor delight you, then the nobility of your ancestors will rise up against you and hold a brilliant torch over your crimes.[96]

This was a doubly serious penalty because, as Pliny remarked in exactly this context, 'it is more uglifying to lose, than never to get, praise'.[97] One of the dangerous qualities of lowly late-antique functionaries, their superiors thought, was their lack of any sense of shame; very well, said the emperor, if they are shameless like slaves, they will have to be subjected to slaves' punishments.[98]

The norms that bound aristocratic officials were not a special set of professional ethics. Rather, officials were expected simply to conduct themselves by the everyday code that regulated aristocratic behaviour, adapted to their new surroundings—not to act 'ill-bred', as Dio Chrysostom puts it.[99] They should not, of course, practise extortion and plunder the provincials, and should place a limit on their ire and avarice.

[94] Cic. *ad Att.* 6. 1. 8, 'flens mihi meam famam commendasti'; and a stream of letters sounding the same theme follows. Intact, Cic. *ad Fam.* 13. 73. 1, 'incolumi fama'. Cicero refers to 'nostros magistratus, qui et legum et existimationis periculo continentur', 2 *Verr.* 5. 167. Cf. ibid. 4. 56–7, for extravagant behaviour to protect reputation.

[95] Cic. *ad Fam.* 13. 22. 2 (and *passim* in bk. 13), 'pro tua dignitate'; and cf. 13. 73. 2, *existimatio, fama.* See also ibid. 15. 7, 15. 12. 1; Fronto, *ad Am.* 1. 1. 2 (van den Hout).

[96] Juv. 8. 127–39. Cf. Cic. *ad Q. Fr.* 1. 1. 37–8; Amm. Marc. 28. 4. 2–3; Lib. *Or.* 12. 21–2; Boeth. *Consol.* 3. 4; Cass. *Var.* 12. 2. 3–4. And a good governor humiliated a bad predecessor or successor, Cic. 2 *Verr.* 2. 139–40; *ad Att.* 6. 1. 2; Cass. *Var.* 1. 4. 8. On scandal, MacMullen (1988), 135–7.

[97] Pliny, *Ep.* 8. 24. 9, 'multo deformius amittere quam non adsequi laudem'.

[98] Amm. Marc. 22. 4. 4, 'nullus existimationis respectus'; emperor, *CTh* 14. 10. 1. 3 (382).

[99] D. Chr. 32. 32; cf. Cic. *ad Q. Fr.* 1. 1. 18–19.

They should respect the laws and decrees of the senate. They are advised 'to take nothing from anyone's prestige, liberty, or pride'. They should respect literature and the gentle arts as well.[100] The same concern for repute encouraged an official to select and supervise his subordinates carefully. To choose a subordinate was to trust him with part of one's reputation, which his misbehaviour would besmirch, just as the misconduct of a governor or a general's disaster damaged the emperor's honour.[101] A good appointment, by official or emperor, contributed to the superior's honour, since both the appointee's own prestige and his good behaviour cast lustre upon his superior.[102] 'The governor is honourable of himself, but you render him more brilliant by your assistance,' wrote Bishop Gregory to the governor's assessor.[103]

Sources of Honour and their Consequences

Especially significant for the working of government was officials' harvesting of honour in the provinces, which they did by striving to secure the esteem of rich and pompous magnates (some of implausibly ancient lineage), of magnificent cities, and of the whole province, represented in its provincial assembly. Local honour assiduously cultivated its rulers. When the imperial governor, travelling around his province, arrived at a city, he was met with all due ceremony: the population was drawn up outside the gates, the ephebes marshalled in their cloaks, the magistrates in their robes of office, the priests in their crowns.[104] A local notable would be called upon to give an address in the governor's honour. Since 'the provincials consider this a point of honour', the jurist adjures him to listen politely.[105] (Those Greeks *do* drone on.) The topics to be covered in a speech of this type are expounded in a rhetorical handbook which survives, and one can well imagine the leading citizen of some rarely visited minor town desperately poring over it in the small hours of the night

---

[100] Pliny, *Ep.* 8. 24. 3, 'nihil ex cuiusquam dignitate, nihil ex libertate, nihil etiam ex iactatione decerpseris'. Also Cic. *ad Q. Fr.* 1. 1. 13; Juv. 8. 87–91.

[101] Cic. *ad Q. Fr.* 1. 1. 12–14; cf. 2*Verr.* 2. 28–9; *ad Att.* 5. 10. 2, 5. 11. 5, 5. 14. 2, 5. 17. 2. Emperor, Suet. *Aug.* 23. 1; Tac. *Ann.* 1. 80; Lib. *Or.* 18. 194.

[102] Pliny, *Ep.* 4. 15. 8–10; HA *Gord.* 5. 1; *IK Eph.* i. 41. 14–15.

[103] Greg. Naz. *Ep.* 156. 4, λαμπρὸν γὰρ ὄντα τὸν ἄρχοντα καὶ παρ' ἑαυτοῦ, λαμπρότερον αὐτὸς ἐργάζῃ τῇ συνεργίᾳ; *PLRE* i, s.v. Asterius 4 for the assessor. Cf. Cass. *Var.* 12. 1. 2.

[104] Liebeschuetz (1972: 208–9) with Plut. *Cato Min.* 13. 1 and cf. *Pomp.* 40. 1–3, τιμή, for more detail (but honouring a freedman of Pompey); Hirt. *BG* 8. 51, *honor*. The further out from the city an official is met, the more honorific, Jos. *AJ* 19. 340; similarly, the further he is escorted on departure, Amm. Marc. 28. 3. 9. Reception of those arriving by sea, Plut. *Pomp.* 78. 2–79. 3; Philostr. *VA* 5. 24.

[105] *Dig.* 1. 16. 7. pr. (Ulpian), 'cum honori suo provinciales id vindicent'.

before his appearance.[106] Such an honorific reception was only a sampling of the many honours that the governor could look forward to from the towns of his province. He would bear away, as an orator put it, 'a salary of praise'.[107] As the handbook urges a notable praising the governor to say,

Let the cities establish sacred choruses, let them sing and praise him. Let us prepare decrees for the emperors, praising and admiring him [the governor], and begging that his rule should last for many years; let us dispatch statues of him to Delphi, to Olympia, and to Athens; first, however, let us fill our own cities with them.[108]

And so it was: a city might erect a statue in its own market, or in the provincial seat of the governor, at a Panhellenic sanctuary, in the governor's home city, or at Rome.[109]

Thus the whole creaking machinery of civic honours was adapted to dealing with governors. What stands out is the care provincials took that the centre should know of the honours they bestowed, and the care the centre took to find out: people at Rome knew the number of statues an official received, even in the provinces, and judged him accordingly.[110] Cities were forever sending embassies to the emperor to give thanks for, or offer complaints about, their governors.[111] In late antiquity the provincial assembly of Asia reported its acclamation of a proconsul to the praetorian prefects, and they wrote back and congratulated him. Their honorific letter was inscribed.[112] The emperors also took measures to have such acclamations reported to them.[113] Local aristocrats and travellers carried on a vast, albeit slow, correspondence with the great men of Rome and Constantinople, and other grandees across the empire; great

---

[106] Handbook, Men. Rhet. 378–88, 389–90, 415–18.

[107] Aristid. 17. 21 (Behr), τοὺς μισθοὺς τῶν ἐπαίνων αὐτόθεν κομιεῖσθαι.

[108] Men. Rhet. 417. 27–31. Cf. for conspectus of honours to governors, Cic. *ad Att.* 5. 21. 7; 2 *Verr.* 2. 154. For a governor honoured by eight cities, Robert (1940c), 53. Under the Republic, festivals were voted as well, Price (1984a: 42–3, 46–7) and e.g. Cic. 2 *Verr.* 2. 51–2; but divine honours (ibid. 4. 151) were not usual under the empire, Price p. 51.

[109] Honours for governors at Rome, Eck (1984b), esp. 212–13; in their home cities, pp. 214–17. Individuals also erected monuments to officials, e.g. Dio 75(76L). 14. 7; *IG* ii². 4224–5; *IK Eph.* iii. 616, 620, vii. 3033.

[110] Statues, Suet. *Titus* 4. 1; cf. *Vesp.* 1. 2. For the reception of honours at Rome, above, Ch. 2 n. 231 and cf. Cic. *ad Fam.* 15. 14. 3.

[111] Millar (1977), 419; and for his replies, e.g. *Gk. Const.* 80; McC. & W. 460. Under the Republic an official was livid if his successor interfered with missions to Rome thanking him, Cic. *ad Fam.* 3. 8. 2.

[112] *IK Eph.* i. 44 with Roueché (1984), 186.

[113] *CTh* 1. 16. 6. 1 (331); by the public post, 8. 5. 32 (371). And officials reported on one another, Cic. *Mur.* 20; *ad Fam.* 13. 54; Pliny, *Ep.* 10. 86b.

men in the capital and the provinces eagerly questioned travellers from far away on how their governors were behaving.[114] Cities passed flattering testimonial decrees and presented the official with a copy, great men wrote praising letters, certain that the officials would publicize them themselves; when a panegyric upon an official was delivered by a famous orator, the official sent copies of it—so many as to require ten copyists— far and wide.[115]

Provincial opinion, then, had an impact not only upon an official's honour in his province (no great matter, perhaps, as he would soon go home), but also upon his honour at the centre of affairs, at the seat of honour. In Pliny's panegyric to Trajan, the expectation that offices were granted to honour even ramifies into an ideal that makes provincial honours—votes of thanks—a key to official advancement.[116] Whether or not this was often the case in reality, it was hardly surprising that governors extorted honours from provincials, just as they did money. In AD 11 this caused Augustus, extending Republican precedent, to forbid the voting of laudatory decrees to a governor during his tenure and for sixty days after he departed—so oppressive had the officials' solicitation of honour become. Honours to governors during their terms were still limited in the third century, and in the fourth.[117]

If the honours of their subjects were something that officials wanted badly enough to extort, then the provincials, who had those honours in their hands, had power over officials. Or so at least it seemed to Philo, who depicted the Greeks of Alexandria using that power to lay the groundwork for their long-meditated pogrom of AD 38. They secured the co-operation of Caligula's freedman courtier Helicon 'not only with money, but also with hopes of honours'. Helicon 'promised everything

---

[114] Letters to the great (frequently other officials) about officials, Basil, *Ep.* 96; Syn. *Ep.* 62 (Garzya); Theodoret, *Ep.* XXXIX–XL (Azéma). Travellers, natives of the province report, complain, Cic. *ad Fam.* 10. 3. 1, 12. 23. 1; *ad Q. Fr.* 1. 1. 37, 2. 4. 7; Fronto, *ad Am.* 1. 6, 2. 7. 1 (van den Hout). In general, Sym. *Ep.* 3. 34, 'Magnillus vicaria potestate per Africam functus testimonio omnium publice privatimque conspicuus'.

[115] Testimonial decree, EJ 320a; cf. Small. *Nerva* 243; Robert (1946b), 21–3. Letters of praise to officials, Basil, *Ep.* 63; Theodoret, *Ep.* 71 (Azéma); Sid. *Ep.* 8. 7; *HA Trig. Tyr.* 10. 9–13 (fictional); shown around, Lib. *Ep.* 1351. 2. Panegyrics publicized, Lib. *Ep.* 345; ten copyists, *Or.* 1. 113. Governors themselves also send private letters of self-praise, Cic. *ad Fam.* 15. 4.

[116] Pliny, *Paneg.* 70. 8–9.

[117] Republican stricture, Cic. 2*Verr.* 2. 146; Augustus' decree, Dio 56. 25. 6; 3rd cent., Paulus, *Fr. Leid.* 2; 4th, *CJ* 1. 24. 1 (398). On these regulations, Nicols (1979); Premerstein (1912), 215–17. On the corrupt extraction of praise, Cic. 2*Verr.* 2 *passim*; Amm. Marc. 30. 5. 8–9. A governor's successor is ideally placed to extort it for him, Cic. 2*Verr.* 2. 64, 139, 4. 140–1.

... dreaming of the moment when ... he would be honoured by the greatest and most prestigious city.'[118] Of course, Philo's accounts of secret conversations between his enemies do not merit much credit, but Tacitus might well have agreed that the power which provincial honours permitted subjects to exert over their rulers was both great and sinister. He depicts an occasion in Nero's day when it came to the attention of the senate that a Cretan magnate had boasted that the laudatory decrees of the provincial council were in his gift. As a consequence, under the terms of a soon-moribund *senatus consultum*, provincial councils lost the right to pass decrees of thanks, for Thrasea Paetus rose and demanded that the reputations of Romans not be in the power of provincials:

> As things are now we court foreigners, and we flatter them, and, as if at the nod of one or another of them, thanks or an accusation is decreed—the latter faster. Very well, let the accusation be decreed and let the provincials still have that way of showing their power. But let false praise and praise elicited by begging be restrained like evildoing or cruelty. .... The early days of our magistrates are usually better, and they decline as their tenures draw to a close when, just like candidates, we are gathering up votes: if such electioneering is forbidden, the provinces will be ruled both more fairly and with greater consistency, for just as avarice is controlled by fear of extortion proceedings, thus canvassing shall be limited by the prohibition of votes of thanks.[119]

Who can grant or refuse the province's vote of thanks, can rule the governor; Tacitus' Thrasea thinks this the usual state of affairs. So too can he who can grant or withhold the acclamations of a great city, say Antioch: in the fourth century a well-organized claque there ensured that upon a governor's first appearance in the theatre—an advent usually accompanied by tumultuous cheering—he would instead be met with profound silence. He paled. Negotiations ensued. Only when the required concession was granted would the crowd cheer him.[120] Not only was silence not the expected honour, it portended worse: unpopular officials were thunderously abused at great gatherings in the cities of the empire.[121] A wise fifth-century Prefect of the City of Rome schemed to avoid this, writing

---

[118] Philo, *Leg. Gaium* 172–3, τιμαί; ὑπὸ τῆς μεγίστης καὶ ἐνδοξοτάτης πόλεως τιμηθήσεται.

[119] Tac. *Ann.* 15. 20–2; cf. Jos. *AJ* 20. 215. Provincial honours for and condemnations of governors, Deininger (1965).

[120] Liebeschuetz (1972), 209–18 (with comparative material), 278–80, and esp. Lib. *Or.* 33. 11; for other acclamations of governors, Robert (1960d), 24–7. Cf. for cities' praise, D. Chr. 48. 2; Men. Rhet. 425.

[121] Cic. 2*Verr.* 5. 94; Philo, *Flacc.* 139; Herod. 1. 12. 5; Dio 72(73L). 13. 4; and see n. 165 below for some officials' violent reactions.

to a friend to ask him to intercede with the Prefect of the Grain Supply (so relations were *still* not good): 'Commend me to his vigilance; that is, the stability and defence of my reputation. For I fear the thunder of the theatre shouting, "The Roman people are starving!"'[122] In extreme cases the people could do more than shout: they could pelt the official with turnips, or destroy his statues.[123]

How exactly cities manœuvred to rule officials with honours is evident in a long Mauretanian inscription from the reign of Antoninus Pius in which the city of Sala described and explained the honours it had voted to Sulpicius Felix, prefect of the auxiliary cohort which formed the local garrison.

Inasmuch as C. Valerius Rogatus and P. Postumius Hermesander, the joint mayors [*duumviri*], have reported that a successor has been named for the most excellent and rare prefect Sulpicius Felix, to whom, because of the extraordinary example he has set, although he has already received public testimony, it is now necessary to offer even clearer tokens of our esteem, since it is proper at once to requite him for his new favours—both to the city and to individuals—with new honours, and to offer the hope of similar treatment to those of his successors who in the future may act similarly . . . [his acts are listed—prevention of raids, sorting out the city's public finances, thrifty work on the walls, etc.] . . . Now for those qualities which characterize a spirit of the greatest sincerity: he surpassed the degree attained by his predecessors in moderation, modesty, kindness, restraint, reverence for the local senate, love of the people, and zeal, in that he provided us with free access to our woods and fields . . . And the benevolence which he displays is delightful at present, and in the future a source of well-being for us, because of the example he has set. For his acts and morals we voted Sulpicius Felix the rank of local senator, to rank among the joint mayors, which decree the excellent governor received with delight. And now when we hear that a successor has been appointed to him . . . we beg the extremely indulgent governor, who takes delight in the praise and laudation of his prefects, and indeed himself makes them laudable, to favour us, since we wish to be grateful for this matter, by permitting us to put up a statue to the prefect . . . and . . . to send ambassadors to celebrate him before the most sacred emperor.[124]

An extremely popular official was about to leave. The city thus honoured him as highly and as explicitly as possible, so that his successors would know exactly what they needed to do to get similar honours.[125] Explicit comparison is also made to his predecessors, whose conduct was

---

[122] Sid. *Ep.* 1. 10. 2, *fama*; cf. Philo, *Flacc.* 41; McC. & W. 328. 5–7.
[123] Turnips, Suet. *Vesp.* 4. 3; statues, Cic. 2 *Verr.* 2. 158–63.
[124] *AE* 1931. 38 with Carcopino and Gsell (1931).   [125] Cf. *ILS* 1283.

inferior.[126] He who wants a statue must emulate Sulpicius Felix, rather than his predecessors. Since the city felt that its own honour was not enough, it previously asked the governor to add his, and now even contemplates sending an embassy to Rome to elicit the approval of the emperor.

Such an inscription explains many others, less prolix. The city which put up a monument (usually a statue) thanking an official for driving off barbarians, for recovering civic property, for getting their taxes lowered, for preserving the curial class of the province, or for building or repairing civic structures was not only rewarding the outgoing official with honour, acting out of gratitude for his benefactions and reverence for his virtues (perhaps even sincerely); it was promising honour to those who followed him, attempting to inspire rivalry. The statue was as much a bait as a reward.[127]

It is well, finally, to remember that there were those who could not put up statues. 'The nation of the Jews is by its law ill-disposed to such things [sc. honours], and is used to revere justice rather than glory.'[128] To work properly, the machinery of honours required not only graven images but full-fledged Graeco-Roman civic institutions, and those of Judaea, even before the destruction of Jerusalem, may have been rudimentary.[129] Judging by Josephus, the Jews confined themselves for the most part to honorific escorting and chaotic acclamations, either glorifying or insulting.[130] Perhaps this was among the reasons why they were so badly treated by the Roman authorities, who will have reacted just as King Herod is said to have: when the Jews proved unwilling to honour him with statues or temples, he favoured his Greek subjects, who were willing; and the Greeks were frequently the Jews' enemies.[131] Even where there was no cultural, religious, or financial bar to honouring, governors naturally valued the honours of some cities more than others, and civic

---

[126] Cf. *CIL* ii. 4112, vi. 1696, ix. 1576.

[127] Barbarians, *ILS* 2767; *IRT* 480, 565; property, Höghammar (1993), no. 57; taxes, Roueché (1989a), no. 24; *curiales*, no. 36; civic structures (very commonly, esp. in late antiquity), Robert (1948c), 60–76, 87–9. Rivalry, cf. Sym. *Rel.* 12.

[128] Jos. *AJ* 16. 158; cf. Tac. *Hist.* 5. 5: non-Jews noticed that Jews did not erect honorific statues.

[129] How rudimentary is controversial, see Tcherikover (1964) and Goodman (1987), 110–16, against e.g. Schürer (1973–87), ii. 184–226.

[130] Escorting, Jos. *BJ* 2. 297–300, 318–24. Acclamations: favourable, Jos. *AJ* 17. 200–5; *BJ* 2. 297; abusive, Jos. *AJ* 17. 206–7, 18. 60, 20. 108; *BJ* 2. 280–1 (before a superior official), 2. 326; and perhaps with much the same effect on Roman officials, huge crowds of weeping petitioners, *BJ* 2. 171–4; Philo, *Leg. Gaium* 225–43.

[131] Herod, Jos. *AJ* 16. 156–9, 19. 329; but Herod's alleged scorn for the Jews is not strictly true, judging by his building programmes in Jewish areas, Hengel (1989), 33.

discord was debilitating. A city must praise and blame with one voice, Dio Chrysostom says, for otherwise, there is feebleness in dealings with governors.[132]

Not only cities could deal with governors in this way. From day to day in the empire, honourable men offered their valuable praise to the governor in exchange for favours. 'When one of their friends gains an office like the one you now hold, you see most of the sophists hurrying along to him with an oration and a wallet, delivering the former and proffering the latter to be filled'.[133] A well-turned panegyric upon a late-antique praetorian prefect might earn the orator an official post as well as a bag of gold.[134] The distinguished St Basil begged an official to let off an admittedly guilty malefactor in this way:

and let this deed as well be added to the reports about you: give it to us, who desire to hymn your deeds, to surpass the songs of benevolence of earlier times . . . with as much power as we have, we will cry up your deeds, if we be not considered altogether too petty heralds for so great a man.[135]

Of course, he is not too petty a herald—that is exactly the point. And one can threaten to withhold praise as well. Libanius wrote menacingly that a governor should not have flogged a *curialis*; he should instead have treated him with kindness. 'I find that *such* governors enjoy high prestige,' he observed obliquely, referring to gentle rulers, 'I wish that you would be one of them, rather than the other sort.' 'If it were possible to undo what has been done [the flogging], it would be proper to do so. But since this is not possible, let your remaining time be gentler and may we offer a better basis for your fame.'[136] The ability of a distinguished man like Libanius to mould the governor's reputation allows him to mould his conduct too. Possibly Libanius hints at some other threat as well, but given the delicacy and indirectness of his letter it is hard to imagine that it was advisable to speak more bluntly. Even where honour is not at issue it provides the sophist with a safe way to threaten a dangerously powerful man.

Libanius was not always so restrained. Not only does his corpus preserve a number of speeches attacking the conduct of governors (no doubt

---

[132] Some more than others, D. Chr. 31. 110: see p. 78 above; feebleness, D. Chr. 48. 6–7.

[133] Lib. *Ep.* 552. 3; cf. 1053. 1 for the ways in which a rhetorician can advance the reputation of an official.

[134] John Lyd. *Mag.* 3. 27; cf. Sid. *Ep.* 1. 9. 6–8.

[135] Basil, *Ep.* 112 (trans. adapted from Deferrari); cf. 148; Cic. *ad Fam.* 13. 48; Greg. Naz. *Ep.* 21. 5, 140, 146; Lib. *Ep.* 195. 5, 359. 9; mobilizing local opinion, Basil, *Ep.* 72–3.

[136] Lib. *Ep.* 994 (trans. adapted from Norman), εὑρίσκω γὰρ τοὺς τοιούτους ἄρχοντας εὐδοκιμοῦντας. . . . καὶ παρέχωμεν ἀφορμὰς τῇ φήμῃ βελτίονας.

published when they were safely out of the province), but some officials whose conduct he did not approve he ostentatiously ignored while they were present—an insult; nor was he the first sophist to signify his scorn of a governor in this way.[137] It is at some similar drubbing that Fronto hints when he begins a letter to an official with warm assurances that 'my concern for your prestige is the same as that for my own', and then, just as warmly, castigates the official at length for demoting a protégé of his from the local senate at Concordia.[138]

OFFICIALS AND SUBJECTS

That subjects mobilized honours and dishonours to control their governors should hardly cause surprise, for it was by far the best method they had. An imperial governor was under no legal or constitutional obligation to pay the slightest attention to the wishes of those he ruled; he served at the emperor's pleasure, not theirs. A destructive whirlwind of rods and axes, he could be as arbitrary as a whirlwind too. It was, obviously, of the first importance to his subjects to control the governor's actions as much as they could, but their only legal recourse against him was to prosecute him after his term ended. Such prosecution was an uncertainly successful course and often dangerous, and even if it worked it was powerless to reward the good and thus encourage more good in future. Subjects' ultimate resort was violence, but that inspired savage reprisals, and under the high empire, at least, violence against officials was rare.[139] Bribery was a technique used as well—more and more, perhaps, over the centuries of the empire. Yet this was expensive; good governors refused to accept bribes; and those attempting to bribe might be punished.[140] Honour was legitimate and effective, and it was to honour they turned.

The position of the governor ruling over his subjects was far stronger.

[137] Speeches, Lib. *Or.* 4, 27–8, 33, 46, 54, 56–7. Ignoring, Lib. *Or.* 1. 168–9, 212, 223–4, 2. 7; also Nicetes, Philostr. *VS* 1. 19 (512), and the governor plotted vengeance; cf. Amm. Marc. 14. 7. 10–16. Under the Republic, individuals try to curb officials by challenging them (or their subordinates, in terms which reflect upon them) to a judicial wager, a *sponsio* (Cic. 2*Verr.* 3. 132–7; cf. Plut. *Tib. Gracch.* 14. 4), a type of action which particularly engaged the honour of those involved, see above, Ch. 2 n. 98.

[138] Fronto, *ad Am.* 2. 7 (van den Hout), 'qui existimationi tuae famaeque iuxta quam meae consultum cupiam'; cf. Lib. *Ep.* 217. 2.

[139] Prosecutions, see above, Ch. 3 n. 202. Reprisals, Cic. 2*Verr.* 1. 79, 3. 68; Jos. *AJ* 20. 113–14.

[140] Élite officials' attitude to bribery, MacMullen (1988), 127–35; their inferiors had always been corrupt. Punishment for attempted bribery, Cic. *ad Q. Fr.* 1. 1. 13.

To obey him, as we have seen, was the right thing to do: over much of the empire his authority was perceived to be legitimate. He had force—some at least—and the right to use it, the right to flog and execute those who disobeyed, if he could catch them, and if they did not belong to legally immune high-status groups. Literary evidence emphasizes the immunity of Roman citizens in the first century, and the jurists point to the 'more honourable', decurions and above, from the second.[141] It was an accepted fact (one which might be used to defend even a monstrous governor) that 'without fear and severity the Republic cannot be administered . . . Why else are the rods borne before the governors? Why are they given axes? Why is a dungeon built?'[142] And the governors' bloody power was used. 'How many brigands die every day?' asked Lactantius rhetorically, discussing crucifixion.[143] A late-antique school-book taught children essential vocabulary for getting on in their provincial world, specifically the tortures a governor might inflict on a suspected bandit. 'He is racked; the torturer thrashes him; his chest is beaten; he is hung up; . . . he is flogged with rods.' All this, naturally, with the maximum possible publicity.[144] Provincials walked in terror of their governors.[145] And that terror, combined with dark tales of what befell those whose conduct demanded the intervention of the emperor, the coming of vengeful armies, kept the Roman Peace.

Yet while the Roman provinces could not be ruled without terror, they were not ruled wholly by terror, or at least by terror unassisted. The cities 'undertake that the governors—willing or unwilling—should entrust everything to them, and use them alone, or at least chiefly.'[146] It appears that governors frequently enjoyed the willing co-operation of the cities and great men of the provinces. The governor's use of honour and its works to gain this co-operation—and the consequent ability of his subjects to rule him in turn—stands out in the most detailed description surviving from antiquity of a man dealing with his government at the provincial level. This is Aelius Aristides' remarkable account in his fourth *Sacred Tale* of his efforts to escape civic duties in the province of Asia in the year AD 153.[147] Matched against the Proconsul of Asia, the powerful,

---

[141] Governors' rights, Garnsey (1968); immunities, Garnsey (1970: 260–71), minimizing the contrast between centuries: social status was usually respected, Roman citizen or not. In practice decurions' immunity decayed in the 4th cent., MacMullen (1986*a*), 162.

[142] Cic. 2*Verr.* 5. 22; cf. Philostr. *VA* 3. 25; Cass. *Var.* 12. 5. 6.

[143] Lact. *Div. Inst.* 5. 3. 5.

[144] School-book, Dionisotti (1982), line 75; and see p. 4 above.

[145] Pliny, *Ep.* 3. 9. 15.   [146] Aristid. 23. 64 (Behr).

[147] On which, Behr (1968: 81–4), with more detail on the legal aspects.

distinguished, and subtle C. Julius Severus, only the deft application of gigantic influence secured Aristides' release.

Deference

Aristides' adventure began when the Mysian city of Hadriani sent to the proconsul a list of persons suitable to hold the office of *eirenarch*, a municipal post with police duties. But Aristides also owned property there, and although he was not on the list the governor chose him on his own initiative, because 'my rank was not among the undistinguished, and he overlooked and dishonoured the other names that had been sent'.[148] Aristides was chosen out of deference to his honour, then, at least as he represents it. But the hypochondriacal orator was unwilling to perform the office, and had two legal objections (of questionable merit): that his primary responsibility for such burdens was to Smyrna, and that he enjoyed immunity as a sophist.[149] Yet his situation was awkward: the governor, rather than the town, had made the appointment, and as a compliment. To object without giving offence was difficult.[150]

Aristides' strategy was to assemble a number of letters of recommendation, including some from a former Prefect of Egypt, from the emperor Antoninus Pius, and from the young Marcus Aurelius. These 'very splendid and honour-bestowing' letters, which (as Aristides noted) had not been solicited specifically for this undertaking, were presented to Severus. The emperor actually addressed the legal question: Aristides did merit a sophistical immunity, but only if he was actually practising rhetoric.[151] Since this was in doubt (Aristides' health prevented him from taking students) the legal situation remained clouded.[152] But these letters helped Aristides' case in another way. When it was time for a hearing, Severus did not even allow the advocates opposed to Aristides to speak, but immediately granted the exemption, 'because', as he put it, 'I marvel at his reputation, and I agree that he holds the first place in oratory, and these things have also been written to me by my friends at Rome'. The letters served to demonstrate—and increase—Aristides' honour. Under the shared code of governor and subject, honour commanded a favourable judgement.[153]

---

[148] Aristid. 50. 71–3 (Behr), quoted 73, μοι δοκεῖν τάξιν ὅτι οὐ τῶν ἀφανῶν, παριδὼν καὶ ἀτιμάσας ἅπαντα τὰ πεμφθέντα ὀνόματα.

[149] His excuses, Aristid. 50. 73, 75, 87 (Behr).

[150] Ibid. 50. 77 (Behr).   [151] Ibid. 50. 75 (Behr), καὶ μάλ' ἔντιμα καὶ λαμπρά.

[152] Ibid. 50. 87 (Behr).

[153] Ibid. 50. 78 (Behr), τῆς δόξης ἄγαμαι, καὶ σύμφημι πρωτεύειν περὶ λόγους, καὶ ταῦτά μοι καὶ παρὰ τῶν ἐν Ῥώμῃ φίλων ἐπέσταλται.

Severus is doing just what Cicero asked a governor to do in his time. 'Let the business be completed', wrote he on behalf of a protégé, 'appropriately both to the truth of his case and to his dignity.'[154] Four centuries after Cicero, Bishop Gregory's brother has died: official help is needed to protect the estate. 'He was', Gregory writes to Sophronius, the powerful Master of the Offices, 'one of the not obscure; indeed, unless my brotherly affection muddles me, he was one of the most distinguished; notable for his education, superior to the many for his gentlemanliness.' Letters asking favours of officials understandably stress the honour of the beneficiary in all its aspects.[155] Indeed, the jurist has to point out to proconsuls the need to grant lesser men court hearings as well, lest the honourable, those with eminent advocates, and the unscrupulous monopolize their time.[156] A distinguished ambassador, sent to give a speech inviting the governor to a city, should not fail to allude (delicately, but not too delicately) to his own standing, the rhetorical handbook notes.

If the summoner has a brilliant reputation, say something about this as well in a second prooemium: 'Many courted election to this embassy; many were eager to be chosen as ambassadors to Your Magnificence. Of its suitors the city chose perhaps not the worst: you, of course, will recognize the product of an Athenian education.'[157]

In short, as Fronto advised a governor: 'Treat the provincials appropriately to their honour.'[158]

A governor treated his subjects with deference not least because men like Fronto, in whose hands his reputation lay, were watching. Appalling failures of deference on the part of governors attracted unfavourable attention, perhaps even a blistering speech from Libanius.[159] Cicero too paid attention to how governors acted, supporting ancient Lacedaemon with his personal endorsement (for cities were owed the deference of

---

[154] Cic. *ad Fam.* 13. 57. 2, 'pro causae veritate et pro sua dignitate'. Cf. 13. 13–14 and bk. 13 *passim*; also 2*Verr.* 5. 156 (ironic, but indicating the expectation); and ibid 1. 126, 3. 61, for the combination of *auctoritas* and *gratia*, expected to be effective with officials.

[155] Greg. Naz. *Ep.* 29. 4, τῶν λίαν ἐπιφανῶν, γνώριμος μὲν ἐπὶ παιδεύσει, καλοκἀγαθίᾳ δ᾽ ὑπὲρ τοὺς πολλούς. PLRE i, s.v. Sophronius 3 for the recipient. Cf. *Ep.* 207; Lib. *Ep.* 275, 557; and for formulaic indications of honourableness (see above, Ch. 2 n. 155), Greg. Naz. *Ep.* 22. 2, τιμιώτατος; 21. 3, 39. 2, αἰδεσιμώτατος.

[156] *Dig.* 1. 16. 9. 4 (Ulpian), *honor, dignitas*.

[157] Men. Rhet. 425. 31–426. 5, ἐὰν ἀξίωμα ὁ καλῶν ἔχῃ λαμπρόν; trans. adapted from Russell and Wilson. For distinguished emissaries, cf. Philo, *Leg. Gaium* 300.

[158] Fronto, *ad Am.* 1. 20 (van den Hout), 'pro honore provinciales tractare'; cf. Pliny, *Ep.* 9. 5; Sym. *Ep.* 9. 40; and they do, Jos. *BJ* 1. 278.

[159] Lib. *Or.* 54 and 56; cf. Cic. 2*Verr.* 3. 61–2 *et passim*; Jos. *BJ* 2. 308–14; Sid. *Ep.* 1. 7. 3.

governors as well), 'although I do not doubt that they [the Lacedae-
monians] are commended to you sufficiently by their prestige and that of
their ancestors'.[160] Pliny paid attention as well, advising a man who was
going to be governor of Achaea, 'Revere their divine founders . . . their
ancient glory, and their age itself . . . Honour their antiquity, their great
deeds, even their legends.'[161] And so the Proconsul of Asia decreed the
days of the festival of Artemis at Ephesus to be sacred, 'in consideration
of the piety owed to the goddess and the honour of the most brilliant city
of the Ephesians'.[162]

Thus Severus the proconsul acted conventionally towards Aelius
Aristides, and Aristides overcame Severus in a perfectly conventional
way. The proconsul's initial choice of the sophist to perform the job,
however, reveals a darker side of the governor's deference. Offered something he did not want as a compliment to his standing, Aristides felt himself trapped. The provincials whose help a governor needed most were all
of high standing: he could give out any number of nasty jobs as compli-
ments, secure in the knowledge that it was ticklish to refuse what was
offered with a smile, however icy, for that was to insult the governor. The
future emperor Antoninus Pius, then Proconsul of Asia, naturally lodged
at the house of the absent sophist Polemo, 'as it was the best house in
Smyrna and belonged to the best man'. Polemo's reaction when he
returned, turning the proconsul out, was both astoundingly arrogant and
perilous.[163]

Everybody knew that insulting the governor was dangerous. It was
characteristic of Roman administration to employ the governor's power
of violent coercion in defence of the honour of man and office, and that
honour was expected to be extremely prickly.[164] Direct, open insult—say
shouted abuse—might be savagely punished, and stark measures were
taken to prevent it: convicts might be dragged away with a hook in their
mouths, so that, the rabbi tells us, they could not shout curses at the governor.[165] Indeed, a governor 'often has blameless men thrust in prison
because [he] is struck by a sense of gratitude [to such men's enemies] or

[160] Cic. *ad Fam.* 13. 28b. 1, *auctoritas.*
[161] Pliny, *Ep.* 8. 24. 3, 'reverere gloriam veterem . . . Sit apud te honor antiquitati'. And
such are among the many claims to distinction that the orator should cite when inviting a
governor to a city, Men. Rhet. 424–30.
[162] *IK Eph.* i. 24. a. 10–13, ἀποβλέπων . . . εἰς τὴν τῆς λαμπροτάτης Ἐφεσίων πόλεως
τειμήν.
[163] Philostr. *VS* 1. 25 (534).   [164] Touchiness, Lib. *Or.* 1. 207; Aug. *Ep.* 11*. 7.
[165] Abuse, Jos. *AJ* 18. 60–1; *BJ* 2. 295–302; Amm. Marc. 15. 7. 1–5; Cass. *Var.* 1. 27. Hook,
Lieberman (1944–5: 44–8), to prevent cursing of the 'king', who may be the emperor or a
governor, p. 11.

insult'.[166] Custom prescribed acts of reverence to Roman magistrates. One stood up for them, one yielded to them in the street, one went to meet them, one made way for them, one dismounted at their approach.[167] Nor did one fail in such things: the blind man, the jurist says, who cannot see to revere the insignia of the magistrate, cannot sue in court.[168] When the future emperor Septimius Severus was legate to the Proconsul of Africa, we are told, an old friend rushed up and embraced him, only to find himself flogged to the public announcement, 'Let no plebeian impudently embrace a legate of the Roman people.'[169] In short, as Pliny wrote to a governor, 'Do not fear contempt. For how can a holder of *imperium*, of the *fasces*, be held in contempt, unless, base and filthy, he first has contempt for himself?'[170] The governor walled his honour with his power to coerce.

It is this side of Roman provincial government that Aristides has in mind when he contemplates rejecting a proconsul's courtesy. Not that such a high personage, a Roman citizen, a man so well connected, would be flogged or executed (although chilling tales of governors exceeding their legal authority might be recalled at such moments), but some sort of reprisal might well be expected.[171] It was not a stratagem when a governor used his power to punish insults: governors were members of a society, and class, that took insults deadly seriously, and they had more power than most to deal with them. But it *was* a stratagem for a governor, like the cunning Severus, to manœuvre a subject into a situation in which he must obey—or insult him, with incalculable consequences. The governor's 'deference' to a subject could serve as a screen for power of other types.

The conception of the governor's honour and of insult to it, moreover, was very broad, and this too could be useful. Wherever we look, we see disobedience to an official's dictates, or resistance to him, viewed as a matter of disrespect, scorn, insult, or contempt.[172] The governor could

---

[166] [Pelagius], *de Div.* 6. 2 (= *PL* Suppl. 1, col. 1386), 'quia aut gratiarum aut iniuriarum pulsaris adfectibus'.

[167] Stand up, make way, Pliny, *Ep.* 1. 23. 2; Suet. *Tib.* 31. 2; cf. Herod. 3. 11. 3; meet, *HA Car.* 17. 2; dismount, Livy 24. 44. 10; Plut. *Fab. Max.* 24. 2.

[168] *Dig.* 3. 1. 1. 5 (Ulpian), 'insignia magistratus videre et revereri non possit'.

[169] *HA Sev.* 2. 6; the account goes on to say that legates went in carriages thereafter to prevent this happening again. Cf. Plut. *C. Gracch.* 3. 3.

[170] Pliny, *Ep.* 8. 24. 6.

[171] Governors exceed their legal authority in punishment, MacMullen (1986a), 149.

[172] e.g. Tac. *Ann.* 12. 54; Dio 54. 5. 1, 61. 6. 2; Philostr. *VA* 7. 23; *AE* 1960. 202; Sym. *Rel.* 23, 31; Cass. *Var.* 3. 8. 1. Continued disobedience was *contumacia*, a word closely related to *contumelia*, and the sense of insult to the official was felt, *Dig.* 11. 1. 11. 4 (Ulpian).

take offence at nearly anything. You wish to appeal his judgement? What insolence, what an insult! Although the emperor stepped in to guarantee the right of appeal, the thought that the governor would view an appeal in such a light will have been discouraging indeed.[173] There was nothing insincere in this outlook, but it did give an official room to manœuvre. A few years before Aristides' run-in with Severus, some neighbours had seized a property of his by force. Aristides brought influence to bear upon the proconsul at Pergamum, who took him by the hand, and promised, 'They will not scorn *us*'.[174] In an instant, whatever Aristides' greedy neighbours might do to keep the land is transformed into contempt for the governor, which was altogether more dangerous than a legal case over property. The governor could, to a degree, choose what to take offence at, and because he was so dangerous when offended, he could use his prickliness to threaten people, while not seeming to act outrageously. Who could blame him for defending his honour?

The vengefulness of officials in the face of insult should be kept in mind when deference to governors is considered as a form of rulership. Certainly failure to pay due deference could be painful, as Septimius Severus' old friend found. But ancient authors insist on a distinction between ruling by honour and ruling by force. Thus the emperor Hadrian 'sent Severus [Aristides' adversary, in another posting] to govern Bithynia, a task which needed no arms, but a ruler and manager who was just and wise and possessed prestige'.[175] Similarly, Cicero in his province, centuries earlier, undertook famine relief. 'Wherever I went, without violence, without legal proceedings, and without insult, but by my prestige and exhortation, I ensured that Greeks and Roman citizens who had stored grain should promise great quantities to the commons.'[176] Or again, Cicero asked a governor to assist a protégé 'not only with your legal authority, but also with your prestige and advice'.[177] So perhaps it is not ludicrous to imagine a fourth-century Proconsul of Asia asking a friend, Musonius, whom he technically outranked, to collect taxes in his stead: it was easy for Musonius on account of his enormous repute.[178]

Deference was certainly a comfortable way for officials to imagine their own bloody rule, and a flattering way for their terrified subjects to

---

[173] *CTh* 11. 30. 11. 1 (321), *contumelia*. Cf. Tac. *Agric.* 16. 2.
[174] Aristid. 50. 107 (Behr), οὐ μὴ ἡμῶν καταφρονήσωσι.
[175] Dio 69. 14. 4, ἀξίωμα.   [176] Cic. *ad Att.* 5. 21. 8, 'auctoritate et cohortatione'.
[177] Cic. *ad Fam.* 13. 26. 2, 'cum iure et potestate . . . tum etiam auctoritate et consilio tuo'.
[178] Eunap. 29. 2 (Blockley (1983)), εὐδοκιμῶν.

describe it back to them. But neither deference as a euphemism for fear nor deference enforced by threat of flogging can explain observers' practical concern that officials be of high status, lest they prove unable to perform their duties.[179] As Plutarch said, 'In actual affairs and in government, the rich and prestigious man makes little of and scorns a common and poor official.'[180] Titus Aufidius, who once held a trivial post in the late-Republican administration of Asia, was elevated to the proconsulship: 'Nor did the allies', the Tiberian author Valerius Maximus says in some surprise, 'scorn to obey the rods and axes of a man whom they had seen grovelling before others' tribunals.' A Roman expected disobedience in such a case.[181]

Nor can force explain the phenomenon of a governor's being eclipsed when an individual with greater prestige than he appeared in his province. Thus the words Philo has the Greeks of Alexandria address to his *bête noire*, the Prefect of Egypt Flaccus, about the visit of Agrippa, just created king in Judaea by Caligula: 'His sojourn here . . . will be your deposition: a greater weight of prestige and honour surrounds him than you . . . he ought to have pleaded and begged leave *not* to come here in order that the governor of the country not be overwhelmed and scorned.' In consequence, to even the odds, Flaccus permitted the Greeks of Alexandria to make embarrassing demonstrations against Agrippa.[182]

Nor, finally, can force explain the measures taken to bolster official honour. Desiring to leave Rome, Augustus wished to leave the city in the hands of Agrippa, his low-born general and friend; the emperor, we are told, 'wanted to bestow upon him greater prestige, in order that he be able to rule more easily', and thus married him to his own daughter Julia.[183] Vellius Paterculus offers the same interpretation for Agrippa's consulships, triumphs, and priesthoods. 'Great business needs great helpers', so it is necessary that they be 'eminent in dignity and their usefulness fortified with prestige'.[184]

Deference to officials was not optional. Failure was punished. But deference to honour was also something that men did feel in fact. Both the deference of subjects towards their rulers—even if coerced in specific

---

[179] Dio 52. 8. 6–7. [180] Plut. *Praec. Ger. Reip.* 817a, ἔνδοξος.

[181] Val. Max. 6. 9. 7.

[182] Philo, *Flacc.* 30–1, μείζονα τιμῆς καὶ εὐδοξίας ὄγκον; demonstrations, 33–40. In contrast, Pliny praises Trajan for managing not to have this effect on *legati*, *Paneg.* 19.

[183] Dio 54. 6. 5, ἀξίωμα; cf. 51. 3. 5.

[184] Vel. Pat. 2. 227. 3, 'dignitate eminere utilitatemque auctoritate muniri'. Cf. *HA Hadr.* 7. 3, Hadrian leaves Dacia for Rome, 'Dacia Turboni credita, titulo Aegyptiacae praefecturae, quo plus auctoritatis haberet, ornato'.

cases—and the deference of governors towards their subjects—however insincere in specific instances—were firmly rooted in social norms. That is what made deference such an effective tool for getting things done, whatever the spirit in which it was employed.

Gratitude

To return at last to the troubles of Aristides. Faced with the pile of letters glorifying the sophist, those overwhelming demands of deference upon him, Severus the governor had little choice but to grant Aristides' plea for exemption. Yet the proconsul was cunning and not so easily beaten. Having conceded the legal point, he instantly asked Aristides to perform the unwanted job anyway, as a personal favour.[185] Although the deftness of his riposte took the sophist by surprise, there was nothing unusual about a governor getting things done by the letting-out and getting-in of favours. A fourth-century governor was building a portico at Antioch: 'You have ordered some people to convey columns from Seleuceia, you have asked it from others as a favour'; and the orator Libanius expected that at least the richer of the town's *honorati* would be pleased to do such a favour for the governor.[186] And so—as favours—officials could get taxes in Egypt collected and the smithies of Antioch supervised.[187]

Favours one did for an official (or a man who eventually became an official), he had to pay back with potent favours of his own; thus the powerful were often delighted to place him in their debt. Send along the supplies, a late-antique praetorian prefect wrote to the Ligurians, 'for you efficiently constrain me to confer all benefits upon you, if you cheerfully carry out my commands'.[188] An official had any number of lovely favours at his disposal; indeed, anything he did could be viewed as a favour.[189] The imagined governor who flung innocent men into prison because they insulted him, imprisoned others out of a sense of gratitude to their enemies.[190] When Libanius was practising in Nicomedia, the friend of a rival of his called upon the Vicar of Pontica to arrest the sophist; the friend and the vicar had been fellow students at Athens, had performed many reciprocal favours for one another at that time, and saw no reason to stop merely because one had risen to great power.[191] As Josephus sees it, the course of Vespasian's campaign against the Jewish rebels in Galilee

---

[185] Aristid. 50. 78–9 (Behr), χάριν αἰτοῦντος.
[186] Lib. *Ep.* 196. 3; see also Cic. 2 *Verr.* 3. 44.
[187] Taxes, *P.Oxy.* 1490; smithies, Lib. *Ep.* 197. 2.
[188] Cass. *Var.* 11. 16. 4.
[189] Saller (1982), 150–9.
[190] Above, n. 166.
[191] Lib. *Or.* 1. 66; cf. Cic. *ad Q. Fr.* 1. 1. 35; Sid. *Ep.* 4. 14. 1.

was dictated in part by the general's gratitude to King Agrippa.[192] A city's orator did not neglect, when addressing a speech of welcome to a visiting governor, to allude to the services that the city had performed for the Romans; nor did a petitioner, if by some fortunate chance the official himself hailed from the city, fail to demand that he 'make just return' for his rearing.[193] Finally, favours, such as the honour of a statue, could be voted before the governor ever conferred a boon: best to place him under an obligation as soon as possible.[194]

Into the net of gratitude with which they hoped to entangle those who ruled them, subjects wove other officials as well. Please help an Antiochene notable gather savage beasts for games he is holding, Libanius wrote to the Proconsul of Asia. For Asia, he was certain, abounded with brutes of the largest size and the most delightfully fierce dispositions. 'Imagine that you are listening to the whole city [of Antioch], then to the worthy Salutius, third to the excellent Rufinus'— these were the praetorian prefect and Count of the East respectively, conveniently off fighting Julian's Persian War—'they will deem it as much a favour to them as if they had written themselves.'[195]

An official hardly needed to hawk his favours around; he was besieged by petitioners begging for help and offering to be laid under an obligation.[196] 'Charge to my gratitude whatever favour you accord her,' Symmachus casually reminds an official, asking for tax relief for a distinguished lady.[197] The official was hardly reluctant: once he did what was asked of him, he could use the resulting favours-in-return, gratitude, to rule.[198] 'I'm doing a *beneficium* for your brother,' said the Prefect of Egypt, manœuvring to get the high-born Bishop Phileas to recant his Christianity; 'return my favour.'[199] It didn't work: martyrs had other things on their minds than their aristocratic reputations. It was, however, expected to. When Cicero's brother Quintus governed Asia, the smooth administration of the province was hampered by a natural and seemingly irreconcilable conflict between the interests of the Roman tax-farmers and the Greek subjects. What to do? Cicero urged his brother, 'Set aside

---

[192] Jos. *BJ* 3. 445, 461. Cf. Cic. 2*Verr.* 1. 73.

[193] Allude to services, Aristid. 17. 7 (Behr). Just return, Basil, *Ep.* 75; cf. Roueché (1989a: no. 24), tax relief attributed to such a repayment.

[194] D. Chr. 31. 43 (θεραπεύεσθαι), also 105–6; cf. Cic. *ad Q. Fr.* 1. 1. 31.

[195] Lib. *Ep.* 1400. 7; cf. *Ep.* 308. 3; Jos. *AJ* 17. 222 = *BJ* 2. 17.

[196] e.g. Cic. *ad Fam.* 13. 18. 2 and bk. 13 *passim*; Lib. *Ep.* 205. 2, 810. 7; and on behalf of towns, Cic. *ad Fam.* 13. 4. 2, 13. 7. 5, 13. 11. 3.

[197] Sym. *Ep.* 9. 40.   [198] Willingness, Lib. *Ep.* 101. 1, 843. 2.

[199] Musurillo (1972), 27. a. 175–7; cf. Cic. 2*Verr.* 5. 82.

your right to command and the compulsion inherent in your office and *fasces;* join the tax-farmers and the Greeks by means of gratitude to you and your prestige.'[200] And four hundred years later Gregory of Nazianzus wrote to a governor asking him to remit a fine levied on the bishop's protégé, 'considering that this fine—the value of two horses—could not possibly profit the treasury as much as the favour we will save up for you, as if it were engraved'. For the moment, Gregory will get the fine remitted; for the future, the governor will be able to call upon him to employ his influence on official business.[201] Finally, men in high positions could lay such gratitude away, insurance against a change in the political climate. Nero's monstrous praetorian prefect Tigellinus escaped execution under Galba because he had placed Titus Vinius, Galba's intimate, under an obligation by saving his daughter. He had preserved her, Tacitus says, exactly 'to provide himself with a refuge in the future, for the worst men, distrusting their present fortune yet terrified of a change in it, accumulate private gratitude as a defence against public loathing.'[202]

In practice, the return for officials' favours was frequently honorific. 'We, the sustained and restored citizens of Lepcis Magna,' reads a statue base, 'thank him for his infinite benefactions, both those he bestowed upon us alone and those we have received in common with the rest of the province.'[203] Just as with the emperor, honours to officials might be offered with an apology as to their inadequacy to repay the debt. Thus 'the senate of Madaura voted to put up a bronze statue as an honorific mark of reverence, even though it is unequal to his benefactions.'[204] And whether or not they meant it, this sense of indebtedness made clientage— an honour to the patron, a pledge of further assistance to the client—a possibility. Here Madaura appropriately describes itself as the benevolent governor's client, and indeed cities very often formally co-opted officials as their patrons.[205]

Relations of reciprocity between officials and subjects were grounded in a shared culture of honour, and in a realistic understanding of the fact

---

[200] Cic. *ad Q. Fr.* 1. 1. 35, 'remoto imperio ac vi potestatis et fascium publicanos cum Graecis gratia atque auctoritate coniungas'. Cf. *Gk. Const.* 40. 20, illegal requisition of animals ἢ χάριτί τινων ἢ ἀξι[ω]⟨σ⟩ει.

[201] Greg. Naz. *Ep.* 198. 4.

[202] Tac. *Hist.* 1. 72; cf. Cic. *Font.* 45–6; Philo, *Flacc.* 23.

[203] *IRT* 562; cf. Roueché (1989a), no. 16, ἀμειβόμενοι; EJ 320a; Cic. 2*Verr.* 2. 137. Panegyrics in the case of orators, Lib. *Or.* 21. 3; John Lyd. *Mag.* 3. 27.

[204] *I.L.Alg.* 1. 4011, 'etsi impari beneficiis eius honorifico obsequio decrevit'; cf. *AE* 1931. 38. 30–2; Roueché (1989a), no. 36, ἀντ᾽ εὐργεσίων μικρὰ δίδουσα γέρα.

[205] Warmington (1954); Harmand (1957), 188–220, 290–309, 396–405; Krause (1987).

that both needed the favours the other could provide. For an official to attempt to disentangle himself from the ties of gratitude which connected him to his subjects would not only have been disgraceful (as 'ungrateful'), it would make him unable to do much of what needed to be done, and deprive him of the honours that the provincials gave him for doing things for them. Similarly, for a subject to stand aloof was dangerous: who knew when he might need the governor's help? This was one of the levels upon which Severus' fiendish request for a favour from Aristides operated, for one always thought carefully before refusing a favour to a governor. To turn down such a request, moreover, might be an insult. By asking Aristides to perform the office as a favour, the governor appeared to be 'establishing the beginning of a friendship'— so, then, did Aristides propose publicly to *scorn* the friendship of the Proconsul of Asia?[206] If he did, storms were forecast. Such a 'favour' had to be granted when asked, and the confirmation of Aristides' immunity was meaningless: governors in future could ask for favours too. Severus' asking of a favour is as minatory as his deference; aristocratic standards are manipulated so that an inferior must obey—or insult, and prod the porcupine. The rhetoric of gratitude elegantly disguises much more ruthless power relations.

Honour and Dishonour

Once again out-manœuvred by Severus, Aristides contemplated bribery; but the proconsul was as incorruptible as he was clever.[207] So the sophist had recourse again to influence. At Pergamum he enlisted the help of the great consular L. Cuspius Pactumeius Rufinus, who wrote to Severus 'and hinted concerning the future, what would happen if he did not willingly exempt me'.[208] This threat (of what exactly, we do not know) finally defeated Severus. At Smyrna, after he had read Rufinus' letter, he yielded with poor grace, sending Aristides on to the city council: if they would appoint him one of Smyrna's immune rhetoricians, Severus would dismiss the claims of Hadriani. The governor called Aristides 'first of the Greeks and the very height of oratory', yielding to necessity in fact, but covering his retreat by a pretence of deference. For Aristides included along with Rufinus' threatening note a new letter of recommendation from an old friend of the governor's, the distinguished Pergamene L. Claudius Pardalas, who praised Aristides' oratory: the sophist tactfully offered the governor a face-saving escape.[209]

---

[206] Quoted, Aristid. 50. 79 (Behr).   [207] Ibid. 50. 81–2 (Behr).
[208] Ibid. 50. 84 (Behr; trans. Behr).
[209] Ibid. 50. 85–7 (Behr; with Behr's notes); quoted, 87.

Yet Aristides' troubles were still not over. Before he could present his case before the council at Smyrna, he was nominated there to the post of *prytanis*, which he was just as reluctant to undertake as he was to be *eirenarch* at Hadriani. Far from being willing to grant him immunity, the council at Smyrna wished him to undertake duties for them. Thus Aristides and Smyrna's advocates inevitably found themselves before Severus' court at Ephesus.[210] Now Severus' situation was difficult: although firmly threatened by Rufinus, he did not wish to offend the great men of Smyrna, did not wish to fail in deference to the supremely proud city that would eventually style itself 'The First in Asia in Beauty and Size, Most Splendid, Metropolis of Asia, Thrice Temple-warden of the Emperors according to the decrees of the Most Sacred Senate, Glory of Ionia, City of the Smyrnaeans'.[211]

So an elaborate ballet was performed to secure Aristides his immunity. By pre-arrangement, the sophist was honorifically escorted into court by the governor's own lictors. Aristides came late: a retainer of the governor's called his name a second time, only to be quelled by Severus. He will come, the governor said courteously. The sophist's arrival was attended by marks of respect from proconsul, assessors, and advocates. Aristides spoke at length, and freely, pointedly giving the kind of speech one might before the emperor, not only demonstrating that he was the acme of oratory, but offering a reminder, if one was needed, of the men whose good opinion placed him on that peak. Those in court greeted his speech with the enthusiasm due a brilliant sophistic performance. The advocate for Smyrna (who had got the point, if the whole thing had not been agreed beforehand) made a few remarks in honour of Aristides, and then shut up. Finally, to honour the council of Smyrna, the proconsul referred the matter to them, sending Aristides along for their decision with an honorific letter of his own. The council, of course, confirmed Aristides' immunity 'with such honour and grandeur, as to make it seem that they had never done so for anyone else'. And without being asked, Severus wrote to Hadriani telling them to appoint someone else *eirenarch*.[212] Aristides got his immunity, and Severus dodged both the wrath of Rufinus and any disgraceful failure of deference to the brilliant Aristides or to the magnificent city of Smyrna.

---

[210] Ibid. 50. 88–9 (Behr).   [211] *IK Smyrna* 640 (3rd cent.).
[212] Aristid. 50. 90–3 (Behr), quoted, 93, μετὰ τιμῆς τοσαύτης καὶ σχήματος. For honouring with an armed escort, cf. Eunap. *VS* 490; applauding a speech, ibid. 484 (by shaking the toga).

What stands out in Aristides' account is the meticulous detail with
which the honours that the governor conferred are recounted, and the
craftiness with which the honours were used. Like the emperor—perhaps
to a degree in imitation of the emperor—governors were used to ruling
with honour. Tacitus describes Agricola, the governor of Britain, taking
salutary measures for the internal peace of his province:

> So that men at once scattered and savage, and thereby ready for war, might be
> habituated, through pleasures, to peace and quiet, he privately exhorted and pub-
> licly assisted them to build temples, forums, and houses, praising the zealous and
> upbraiding the slow: rivalry for honour from him took the place of compulsion.

And thus, we learn, the Britons began to study Latin, and affect the
toga.[213] The reality was doubtless much more complicated, but this is
how things were expected to work. And a method expected to work even
in the empire's most new-caught, sullen province was surely ideal for the
proud and sophisticated Greeks of the East. The same Aelius Aristides
addressed the assembly of the province of Asia, citing the 'respect, benefactions, and deference on every matter' which that province had enjoyed
from its governors, thus making it 'seem more than equal in honour with
most of Rome's subject peoples'.[214] 'To the same extent that we are honoured more than others by the emperors and the annual governors . . . to
that extent must we take care not to do anything which might seem ill to
them.' Ruling was altogether easier when governors inspired thoughts
like these in their subjects.[215] And not only ruling: governors used the
fierce rivalry between Nicomedia and Nicaea to cover up their plundering of the province of Bithynia, for by calling one of the two cities 'first'
either in speech or writing, they ensured that it would defend their conduct, no matter how vile that conduct had been.[216]

The esteem of Roman governors was highly honorific. During the
third-century persecutions, a Christian author writes, the life of the faithful was characterized by 'sentences, confiscations of property, proscrip-
tions, seizures of goods, removals from office, disdain for worldly glory,
contempt for praise and blame from governors and city councillors, and
endurance of threats, cries, dangers, persecutions, wanderings, woe, and
various afflictions'.[217] Contempt for governors' praise and blame was the

---

[213] Tac. *Agric.* 21, 'honoris aemulatio'.

[214] Aristid. 23. 11 (Behr), αἰδὼς καὶ φιλανθρωπία καὶ τὸ συγκεχωρηκὸς εἰς ἅπαντα . . .
ὁμοτίμους.

[215] Aristid. 23. 79 (Behr). Cf. D. Chr. 32. 52, 38. 33; Lib. *Ep.* 1351. 3; and Julian, *Ep.* 84a
(Bidez), 430b, for ruling in this way urged upon one of Julian's pagan high priests.

[216] D. Chr. 38. 36–7.   [217] Euseb. *Hist. Eccl.* 7. 11. 18.

close companion of virtuous disdain for worldly glory in the Christians' upside-down universe, and clearly both were unusual: the governor's opinion was a very large part of a provincial gentleman's standing in the world.[218] Predictably, it was boasted of local dignitaries that they had been 'testified to by governors', or proconsuls, or procurators, and a city can be found making the same boast.[219] It might be said of a subordinate official that he 'believed . . . that nothing adds more splendidly to his dignity than the testimony of so great a governor'.[220]

What forms did honour from governors take? Just like the emperor's letters, the letters of officials were honorific, and sometimes inscribed on stone. Officials sent letters in praise of those who had made themselves useful, as here for protecting a governor against prosecution:

Copy of the letter of Aedinius Julianus, praetorian prefect, to Badius Comnianus, procurator and acting governor:
. . . When I was governor of the province of Gallia Lugdunensis, I met many excellent men, among whom was one Sollemnis, a priest from the city of Viducasses. I began to esteem him on account of the seriousness of his principles and his noble character. And to those considerations was added this: when some who felt that they had been injured . . . by my predecessor, Claudius Paulinus, . . . tried to get up a prosecution in the council of the Gauls, as if by agreement of the Gallic provinces, my friend Sollemnis resisted this attempt, pleading that his home city, which had chosen him as a representative to the council, had given him no orders about a prosecution, and, indeed, had praised Paulinus; by this argument he ensured that all abandoned the accusation. Thus I came more and more to esteem and approve him.[221]

The honorific quality of such a letter is easily understood, but even a letter from a governor asking a local notable to assist in official business— the making of preparations for the reception of the emperor—was honorific in itself, and was proudly inscribed along with the honours of cities, of the province, and letters from the emperor:

Caelius Florus to Opramoas son of Apollonius, an extremely honoured man, greetings. I have written publicly to your city, in order that everything necessary may be prepared for the very auspicious arrival of our lord [the emperor]. But not ignorant of the private goodwill you bear towards me, I thus share with you this

---

[218] Cf. Apul. *Flor.* 17; Jos. *AJ* 18. 151.   [219] Robert (1946*b*), 21–3; city, *IGR* iii. 714.
[220] *AE* 1931. 38. 11–12, 'nihil splendidius sibi at dignitatem testimonio tanti praesidis'; see pp. 198–9 above.
[221] Pflaum (1948), col. 2 ll. 1–28. Officials' letters to private men as honorific, Aristid. 50. 75 (Behr); Apul. *Apol.* 94–5; Greg. Naz. *Ep.* 10. 14; Lib. *Or.* 1. 231; *Ep.* 725 (and their wide readership); Liebeschuetz (1972), 196. Also honorific, the fact of correspondence, Basil, *Ep.* 104, 110.

most necessary concern and bring the matter to your attention in order that you may recognize the reverence owed to the matter, both on my account and on that of your city.

Not surprisingly, it is possible to discover Opramoas elsewhere taking care of other little bits of business for the governor.[222] We must imagine governors writing a great many letters of both these types: thankful congratulations and requests for aid, both honorific. And high officials wrote testimonials for lesser officials; the sixth-century John Lydus includes in his treatise the testimonials he received upon retirement from the emperor and the praetorian prefect, the latter 'an honour worth as much as a great deal of money'.[223]

Nor was the governor limited to the writing of letters. As he proceeded through the province on his assizes he lodged at other men's houses. Inconvenient and expensive for them, no doubt, but useful, as guaranteeing access to his ear; and honorific, for to be a governor's 'host and friend' was something recorded on stone.[224] Notable provincials competed to play host to a great Roman official; not so to his base retainers, and a man accustomed to entertain praetors and consuls might protest bitterly at having such low creatures billeted on him.[225]

Once ensconced, the governor held dinners: the householder specified the number his dining-room would hold, and the governor issued invitations.[226] These dinners were exclusive, and it was an honour to be invited. One should not crash the governor's dinners, Plutarch warned, for that will earn one a reputation for unseasonable ambition for honour.[227] Close attention was paid to how the official greeted and seated his guests.[228] The fortunate diners returned home bursting to relate the flattering remarks the governor had made about them—or queasy, if he decided instead to chortle about the tortures he had inflicted that day.[229] 'I defer to them, I praise them in words, I honour them,' said Cicero, describing how he was dealing with the prickly tax-farmers of his

[222] Quoted, *TAM* ii. 905 ch. 13. Opramoas takes care of business for governors, *TAM* ii. 905 chs. 15, 17, 46.

[223] John Lyd. *Mag.* 3. 29–30, ταύτην τὴν τιμὴν ἀντὶ πολλῶν χρημάτων; cf. 3. 20; Amm. Marc. 15. 5. 3; and Pliny, *Ep.* 10. 85, 86a and b.

[224] Quass (1993), 157 n. 443.   [225] Cic. 2 *Verr.* 1. 64–5.

[226] Plut. *Quaest. Conviv.* 707b–708b; cf. Cic. 2 *Verr.* 1. 65.

[227] Exclusive, Musurillo (1954), 7. 1. 49–59; honorific, Lib. *Ep.* 732; Eunap. *VS* 491; do not crash, Plut. *Quaest. Conviv.* 710a, φιλοτιμίας ἀκαίρου δόξαν.

[228] Plut. *Aem. Paul.* 28. 4; Greeks (of the 160s BC) were amazed at Paullus' ability to give each his proper meed of honour.

[229] Praises, Plut. *de se Ips. cit. Inv. Laud.* 546d–e; tortures, [Pelagius], *de Div.* 6. 2 (= *PL* Suppl. 1. 1386).

province of Cilicia, whose profiteering he was attempting to control. 'The Greeks discharge their debts at a reasonable rate of interest, and the affair is delightful to the tax-farmers, since they get my honorific words and frequent invitations paid out in full measure.'[230] A useful passage, for it brings out the self-consciousness, even the cynicism, of this method of ruling.

Governors' embraces and kisses were honorific, as were their presents.[231] When Libanius received a silver cup and ivory writing-tablets from a praetorian prefect, he wrote, 'My intimates rushed in gratulating and congratulating me: I was an object of envy because of the honour.'[232] For a high official to call upon subjects in their own houses was to do them very great honour, as it was for him to emerge from his official residence to hear the rhetorician Libanius deliver a speech in the city council-chamber.[233] Cicero's request to a governor on behalf of a protégé—'show every species of generosity . . . not only in deed, but in words and even in looks; . . . how powerful such things are in a province . . . I have a notion'—would have made perfect sense if written to a governor of the second century AD or the fourth.[234]

Like honours from emperors, governors' honours were esteemed for buttressing the local regimes of honours in their areas of responsibility. Cities and provincial councils reported the honours they had bestowed upon their benefactors, as Sala did above (p. 198), and the governor wrote in congratulation.[235] The actual presence of high officials in the city permitted their honour to be borrowed even more conveniently. Thus the chanting of the assembly of Oxyrhynchus in honour of the president of the city council, upon the visit of the governor and chief financial officer of Egypt:

Lords Augusti! Good fortune, O Governor! Good fortune to the Financial Officer! Hurrah for the President! Hurrah for the glory of the city! Hurrah for Dioscorus, first of the citizens! Under you our blessings increase yet more, O

---

[230] Cic. *ad Att.* 6. 1. 16, 'obsequor, verbis laudo, orno . . . si illa iam habent pleno modio verborum honorem, invitationem crebram'.

[231] Embrace, Aristid. 50. 107 (Behr); kiss, Philostr. *VS* 1. 25 (537).

[232] Lib. *Ep.* 1021. 1–3, χαιρόντων τε καὶ συγχαιρόντων. ἐγὼ δὲ τῆς μὲν τιμῆς ἐζηλούμην; also Pflaum (1948), col. 3; MacMullen (1962), 159 n. 1.

[233] Lib. *Or.* 2. 9, 1. 112. Cf. Lib. *Or.* 54 for a conspectus of other honours from governors.

[234] Cic. *ad Fam.* 13. 6a. 4.

[235] Cities, *TAM* ii. 905 chs. 1–4, 6–10, 16, 36; Quass (1993), 160 n. 473; and there is honorific congratulation as well when an official confirms the terms of a benefaction, Robert (1940c); *IK Eph.* i. 27. 333–413; Wörrle (1988), 16, lines 108–9 (the city can also request privileges for its benefactor). Province, *TAM* ii. 905 chs. 11, 14, 18–19, 24, 28–9, 43, 53. Cf. for an individual soliciting honour for another, Lib. *Ep.* 1051. 9.

source of our blessings! ... Good fortune to the patriot! Good fortune to the lover of justice, O source of our blessings, founder of the city! ... Let the President receive the vote on this great day, he who is worthy of many votes, for we enjoy many blessings through you, O President! We beg of the Financial Officer this for the President! Good fortune to the Financial Officer! We beg it for the city's President, O Financial Officer, benefactor that you are! We beg it for the founder of the city! The Lords Augusti for ever! A request for the Financial Officer on behalf of the President! The honest man's magistrate! ... We beg you, O Financial Officer, concerning the President! Let the President receive the vote! Let him receive it this great day![236]

There is a great deal more in this vein. And while cities borrowed the governor's honour, he expected the honour of cities and provinces to reward those who did things that he asked.[237]

For cities themselves, honours bestowed by the governor included simple praise: 'I saw a city both well-born and ancient,' said the proconsul, describing his visit to Aezani, 'and inferior in recent building to none of the chiefest cities.'[238] 'With honorific words I banished all previous injuries,' wrote governor Cicero, describing his visit to Laodicea.[239] The visit of a governor to a city was also honorific. The ambassador begs him to come to a festival: 'If you be persuaded, I will gain prestige for having persuaded you, the proceedings will gain prestige; the city will gain prestige. The god will be gratified. But if I fail ... the city will have no festival, but a disaster.'[240] By choosing to visit or not, the governor is depicted as having in his power the honour both of the ambassador who had come to ask him, and of the town itself.

The official who could use honour to get his way could use dishonour as well. Lucius, the hero of Apuleius' *Metamorphoses*, was sold fish at an outrageous price in the market-place at Hypata. Departing with his purchases, he met a magistrate in his state with rods and retainers, an old friend from his schooldays at Athens, now the market inspector of the town. Seeing the bad quality of the fish and discovering what they had cost, the official demanded that their seller be pointed out.

When I indicated the little old man—he was sitting in a corner—the official immediately denounced him in the harshest possible tones, as befitted the

---

[236] *Sel. Pap.* 239. 3–16 (trans. adapted from Hunt and Edgar); see also *TAM* ii. 905 chs. 3, 14, 28, 30.

[237] *TAM* ii. 905 chs. 15, 17. [238] *IGR* iv. 572 with Robert (1937), 302.

[239] Cic. *ad Att.* 5. 20. 1, 'honorificisque verbis'.

[240] Men. Rhet. 425. 10–16, ἐνδοξότερος ἐγώ ... ἐνδοξότερα δὲ τὰ δρώμενα, σεμνοτέρα δὲ ἡ πόλις. Cf. ibid. 428. 27–8; Reynolds (1982), no. 48.

authority of his office. 'Now,' cried he, 'you don't even spare my friends, or any other visitors! You mark up worthless fish at high prices, and reduce this flower of the Thessalian region to the semblance of a deserted, barren cliff by the costliness of your comestibles. You'll not get off scot-free! I'll show you how rogues will be punished while I am magistrate!' And he upended *my* basket on the open pavement and ordered his retainer to trample on the fishes and wholly destroy them with his feet. And content with this display of stern morality he advised me to be off, saying, 'It seems to me that such a great insult is punishment enough for the old fellow.'[241]

The joke lies in the obliteration of the hero's supper to punish a grasping fishmonger, whose stock of overpriced fish is undamaged. In the process a rare glimpse is offered of the operation of local authority: the peccant merchant is humiliated. The same method was used on a grander level. When the governor of Cilicia became displeased with the conduct of Tarsus, part of his response was a sulphurous letter.[242] And if an official thought his own standing inadequate to do what he wanted to do—dishonouring ancient Sparta effectively, for example, required very great honour indeed—he might solicit a furious letter from the emperor.[243] Since Caesar was displeased with them, his lieutenant Mark Antony summoned the magistrates of Naples and Cumae—and then bade them return the next day, announcing that rather than seeing them, he proposed to recreate himself with enemas.[244] Strategic humiliations were directed also at other officials. The future emperor Julian, when crown prince in Gaul, endeavoured to bring an official to heel thus: 'With many present, who I knew would report it to him, I said, "Certainly he will correct his reports: they are an absolute disgrace." '[245]

Explicitly honorific or insulting acts aside, much of the administrative business of officials was perceived to have honour consequences. When the council at Antioch failed to appoint a Syriarch to preside over important games, the governor, naturally anxious that the games should go on, appointed one from Beroea. To Libanius, by this action he

has destroyed a city of the first rank, and raises up one not even of the second rank and permits it to insult its better . . . He [the governor] was not sent, O emperor, to confound the proper order of the cities, to outrage the prestige that properly

[241] Apul. *Met.* 1. 25 (trans. adapted from Hanson).
[242] D. Chr. 34. 15 with C. P. Jones (1978), 79. Cf. Lib. *Or.* 15. 74.
[243] Philostr. *VA* 4. 33.
[244] Cic. *ad Att.* 10. 13. 1; cf. 2*Verr.* 3. 61–2, 105 for insult used to corrupt ends.
[245] Julian in Gaul, Julian, *Ep.* 14 (Bidez), 385b; cf. Amm. Marc. 17. 3. 5. See also [Victor], *Vir. Ill.* 72. 6.

belonged to some, and to pile the lesser upon the greater . . . He, having brought in that fellow from Beroea to the end he did, cried out to all that this city must depend upon that other, must yield up the title of Metropolis to it, that our council must yield to theirs, our citizens to theirs, that we must acknowledge them as our betters. You could know the insult from the pleasure it gave our enemies, and the grief our well-wishers. You [O emperor] would not wish that the cities should be insulted. But he would wish to insult them.[246]

A well-disposed governor, by contrast, was able to make a city like Prusa 'more distinguished', in this case by approving the construction of a portico, particularly important for a shabby city 'formerly inferior even to our neighbours'.[247] Governors' wide latitude to supervise civic and provincial affairs gave them control over many of the components of a city's prestige.[248] At the individual level, to protect a man's friend from his creditors, or get a friend an official post, was to honour the intercessor.[249] Productive of honour too was the power that being known to be able to get favours from the governor conveyed.[250] Legal business was an enormous part of what a governor did; a legal judgement in a man's favour was an honour, against him, an insult.[251] The dishonour was redoubled if a flogging was ordered; association of this punishment with slavery guaranteed it top place in the list of humiliations to which a free man could be subjected.[252] Relations between officials were envisaged in the same way. The praetorian prefect fined the governor of Syria. 'This causes him hurt,' wrote Libanius, endeavouring to get this fine overturned; 'for Nicetius, despite the many offices he has held, is a poor man. But the punishment carries with it something sharper than the loss: disgrace.'[253]

That a leavening of honour and disgrace was felt in a great many official acts should not be doubted. But honour was also a way of talking about what governors did that could hide terrible realities. Phileas was a man of high status, rich enough to feed a whole city. Much to the regret of the Prefect of Egypt, he was also a Christian, hurtling willingly towards

[246] Lib. *Or.* 33. 22–3, ἀξίωμα λυμανούμενος; cf. for similar acts, Norman (1983), 156.

[247] D. Chr. 40. 5, τὴν πόλιν . . . σεμνοτέραν ποιεῖν, with C. P. Jones (1978), 112.

[248] Cf. Cic. *Balb.* 43; D. Chr. 45. 6. Latitude, Burton (1987).

[249] Basil, *Ep.* 32, τιμῶν; and Lib. *Ep.* 1426. 4, τιμή. Cf. Cic. *ad Fam.* 13. 26. 2, 13. 31. 1; Lib. *Ep.* 275. 2; Greg. Naz. *Ep.* 106, 208. 5.

[250] Greg. Naz. *Ep.* 154. 3; Lib. *Or.* 1. 211.

[251] Aristid. 50. 79 (Behr), τιμή; and Cic. 2*Verr.* 2. 58, *ignominia, contumelia.* Legal business, Burton (1975).

[252] Saller (1994), 134–42; Brown (1992), 54; and esp. Lib. *Or.* 14. 20.

[253] Lib. *Ep.* 21. 3, ἀδοξία.

martyrdom. 'Remember that I have honoured you,' said the prefect; 'I could have subjected you to outrage in your own city; but I wished to honour you, and thus did not.' He could have continued to have him tortured, that is, but was not going to.[254] Subjects also cloaked the realities of power in the language of honour. Much of our evidence about all relations with officials comes from letters asking them for favours, and in such a context the chattering about honour may conceal something quite different. If we knew only of the letter which Pardalas wrote to Severus on Aristides' behalf, we might conclude that Severus had deferentially yielded to Aristides' honour, honoured him with praise, and moved to grant the immunity. In fact we know (as we do in almost no other case) that a threatening letter from Rufinus really settled the matter. A subject's letter, noting the deference he or another was owed, offering or calling in favours, promising honour or alluding to disgrace, may often have been accompanied by a letter like Rufinus', or by a bag of silver, a persuasive argument indeed. Yet the request, perhaps for favours dubious even by the standards of a Roman official's broad prerogative, still had to be made, whatever the real reasons for granting it. Best, then, to allude vaguely to what had to be done as 'honours', and offer face-saving pretexts for granting the favour.[255] It was most effective to corrupt the governor without making him feel corrupt.

Indeed, sometimes the rhetoric of honour offers only the thinnest cover to other considerations. When a man 'distinguished by his virtues, and also by his fortune, if that has anything to do with it,' is recommended to a governor, we suspect that the money, and not merely the distinction it confers, may indeed have quite a lot to do with it.[256] When the interests of a man 'brilliant in the number of his friends' are urged upon an official, we are certainly justified in concluding that it is primarily the power of those many friends, rather than the renown derived from them, that is being communicated.[257] Yet the language of honour permits one not to say so too abruptly. Honour and power of other types usually lay in the same hands in the Roman world. Thus the language of honour could be used to imply power of other types, to hint at reasons wholly outside the realm of honour for which favours should be granted.

---

[254] Musurillo (1972), 27. b. 5, 'memento quod te honoraverim. in civitate enim tua potuissem te iniuriari. volens autem te honorare non feci'. Phileas' wealth, b. 5. 4; tortures, a. 1.

[255] Cf. Brown (1992: 35–47) for classical *paideia* used in this way.

[256] Cic. *ad Fam.* 13. 13. 1, 'fortuna . . . ornatus'.

[257] Greg. Naz. *Ep.* 29. 4, λαμπρὸς δὲ φίλων περιουσίᾳ, see above, n. 155; cf. Cic. *ad Fam.* 13. 31.

What gracefully hid the subject's strength, moreover, could gracefully hide the ruler's weakness. Was his awe at Aristides' reputation the only emotion Severus felt when contemplating Aristides' letter of recommendation from the Roman emperor? But he could hide his fear or ambition behind a show of deference. Severus hid also behind the honours he bestowed upon Aristides in court. Faced with a situation in which a legal judgement on Aristides' case would offend, whichever way he decided, the governor honoured Aristides to avoid making such an open decision. Smyrna got the point, was honoured with being allowed to appear to decide, and Aristides was granted his immunity. Here honour stands in place of an official act; it cloaks it so completely as to make the official act itself unnecessary. Such polite communication was an important role for honour in all its ramifications, useful to officials and subjects alike. For reasons such as these it is hardly surprising that the realm of honour could expand to comprehend almost everything an official did. When the governor was faced with too much work, some things must be done, other things neglected, or, in Libanius' words, 'some things honoured, others cast aside'.[258] To envision all the governor's acts in honour terms was not at an impossible distance from reality, and it was agreeable and convenient to all.

Officials and Subjects in Late Antiquity

The struggle of Aristides and Severus was a failure of government. A representative of imperial authority wanted a subject to do something, but the subject escaped his grasp. Roman government was at its most effective when official hierarchies recapitulated the social hierarchy, when lawful authority, the ability to coerce, and the preponderance of honour lay in the same hands; where that was not the case, Roman government worked less well. This was true even within government. As governor of Cilicia, Cicero had the legal standing to give orders to his high-born quaestor Coelius Caldus. But when Coelius was coming to Cilicia (none too speedily, naturally), Cicero, prompted by letters of recommendation and by a letter in which Coelius had dilated upon his own high rank, wrote to him toadyingly, 'Whatever distinctions I can confer upon you, I will, in order that everyone may know that I have taken into account your prestige and that of your ancestors.'[259] Obviously Cicero

---

[258] Lib. *Ep.* 1459. 5; cf. 994. 1, 1287. 2; Cic. *ad Fam.* 13. 25, 64; Greg. Naz. *Ep.* 70. 2.

[259] Coelius, Cic. *ad Fam.* 2. 19. 2, 'ut omnes intellegant a me habitam esse rationem tuae maiorumque tuorum dignitatis'.

felt an overwhelming necessity to defer to Coelius; he was hardly going to give him orders.

Men like Coelius and Aristides, men who could pull social rank on their superiors or rulers, were uncommon in their own time. Cicero was a rare *novus homo* who had become consul. He thus operated with a deficit of prestige and was weak when faced with a self-assured *nobilis*. Aristides was one of the premier practitioners of the most revered form of high culture, a rarity himself; there were not a great many people who could treat a distinguished consular like Severus as he did. Yet imagine a world where there were countless Aristides-like subjects who could manœuvre around Cicero-like governors. Such was the world of late antiquity.

Among the many forces hampering the smooth working of government in the late period were two related problems: under-honourable governors and over-honourable subjects. Both of these were the emperors' creations, the results of imperial policy. Under-honourable governors were the emperors' safeguard. It was a cornerstone of fourth-century imperial administration, along with the rigorous separation of military and civil authority, that persons of lower standing should be selected to govern provinces (which were now also smaller, and more numerous) than had been the case under the high empire. We have seen that amidst the alarms of the later third century, persons of senatorial status, those of the highest prestige, came to be excluded from most responsible positions.[260] Although after Diocletian they worked their way back into the upper levels of administration, emperors' suspicion long kept them out of provincial governorships, the crucial juncture at which subject and government met. In the first and second centuries AD the majority of governors of provinces were senators, former praetors or consuls, whether they served as proconsuls or as *legati Augusti pro praetore*.[261] By contrast in the fourth century, at least into the 360s, the majority of provincial governors enjoyed the rank of *praeses*, with the degree of honour of *perfectissimus*.[262] That is, in the principate's terms, they were mere equestrians. By imperial will, late-antique governors never enjoyed the effortless superiority of honour over their subjects that a governor of the second century had taken for granted.

An abundance of over-honourable subjects had its roots in the system of official precedence which was so prominent a feature of late-antique government. In a world where office and honour were so closely linked,

---

[260] Above, p. 189.   [261] E. Birley (1981), 16–32; Eck (1974), 228.
[262] Ensslin (1956), 605–13.

not the least problem presented by any administrative reform was establishing the prestige that was to be enjoyed by any new office that such a
reform created. Best, if possible, to drag up from the past some glittering
old title, or bestow formal approval on a term people had long been using
informally.[263] Where change in the structure of government was slow, as
under the principate, the problem would solve itself: over time aristocratic perception and then tradition would grant the new posts their
proper prestige, and over time a term might grow up to describe it. Thus
holders of the highest equestrian post, the vastly powerful praetorian prefecture created by Augustus, were eventually 'extremely eminent men',
viri eminentissimi. And when the emperors granted their prefects consular ornaments, or later adlected them to the senate *inter consulares*, rendering them *clarissimi*, they were perhaps doing no more than
acknowledging an equivalence of dignity that had long existed in the
minds of the aristocracy.[264]

But the fourth century saw a larger, faster-changing government, and
a vastly greater number of new posts which waxed and waned in importance. The emperor's solution was to yoke new posts to old—for example, 'We deem the Chief of the Office List of the notaries to rank among
the proconsuls'—or to rank them in relation to old—'The two Counts of
the Largesses are to have precedence over the honours of procon-
sulars.'[265] What naturally developed was a system of official precedence
complicated enough to delight any modern protocol officer: its handbook, the *Notitia Dignitatum* or *Distinction of Dignities*, happily survives.
Titles of honour—*perfectissimus, clarissimus, spectabilis*, and *illustris*—
came to define sections of the list, encompassing a number of different
offices, but those offices were ranked among themselves as well. In the
early fifth century, for example, the *spectabiles* ('admirables') in the West
were (in descending order):

Chief (*primicerius*) of the Office List of the Sacred (i.e. imperial)
   Bedchamber
Chief of the Office List of the Notaries
The Comptroller (*castrensis*) of the Sacred Palace

---

[263] Old title revived: e.g. *quaestor sacri palatii*, A. H. M. Jones (1964), 104 (and the real
quaestorship was not even dead); informal usage approved: *praeses*, Ensslin (1956), 599–605;
consularis (for a governor), Arnheim (1972), 56–7.

[264] When the granting of consular ornaments to praetorian prefects yielded to adlection
is a puzzle, Nicols (1988), 206–7; Chastagnol (1992), 220–9.

[265] Yoke, *CTh* 6. 10. 3 (381); cf. 6. 24. 11 (432), 6. 25 (416), 6. 26. 4 (386). Relation, *CTh* 6.
9. 1 (372), 'proconsularium honoribus praeferantur'; cf. 6. 14. 1 (372).

Master of the Memory (dealt with rescripts)
Master of Letters (petitions from towns, enquiries from governors)
Master of Petitions (trials)
Proconsul of Africa
Vicar (super-governor) of the City of Rome
Vicar of Italy
Vicar of Africa
(followed by two more vicars)
Military Count (*comes*) of Italy
Military Count of Africa
(followed by four more counts)
General (*dux*) of the Borders of Mauritania Caesarensis
General of the Borders of Tripolitania
(followed by ten more *duces*)[266]

Late-antique law reveals delicious elaborations. Within a rank, precedence went to him who held the office earlier, but those who held codicils of honorary office ranked after those who had actually held the office.[267]

Precedence was no arbitrary imperial fantasy. Rather, the emperor's legislation endeavoured in the first place to codify and clarify a system of social rank which already existed in the minds of his officials and subjects. It is highly unlikely that the emperor valued the practical services of the Proconsul of Africa higher than those of the mighty Vicar of Africa, who ruled five provinces to the proconsul's one; or, among the higher-ranking *illustres*, those of the Prefect of the City of Rome higher than those of his great marshals, the *magistri militum*; but they rank higher in the *Notitia Dignitatum* because they were traditional posts still held by members of the most magnificent ancient families.[268]

Indeed, the emperor worked to keep the structure of the administration congruent with the socially ascribed status of his officials. John

---

[266] *Not. Dig.* Oc. 1. 15–49. Dating the sections and subsections of the *Notitia* is perplexing: different passages may offer glimpses from the 390s to the 430s, but there is little scholarly agreement: see A. H. M. Jones (1964), 1417–28; Ward (1974); Demougeot (1975).

[267] Elaborations, see esp. *CJ* 12. 8. 2 (440 or 441); date of office, *CTh* 6. 7. 2 (380), 6. 35. 13 (386); actual holders vs. honorary holders, *CTh* 6. 22. 5 (381); Cass. *Var*. 6. 10. 4. Also, honorary rank tended to become disassociated from actual rank and to decline in value: thus by 383 a vicar holding praefectorian codicils only ranked as a proconsul, *CTh* 6. 22. 7. pr. (383). On all this, Delmaire (1984); Löhken (1982; best taken with Drinkwater (1985)).

[268] Prefect vs. *magistri*, *Not. Dig.* Oc. 1. 4–7; or perhaps they were equal, precedence to go by date of office, *CTh* 6. 7. 1 (372), 6. 8 (422). Proconsuls and prefects, Chastagnol (1960), 400–57.

Lydus describes the genesis of a new bureau under the emperor Arcadius: some shorthand-writers in the office of the praetorian prefect were regularly seconded to assist high officials, where they accumulated profits, power, and 'extraordinary prestige'. After such great success they thought it 'unworthy' to return to their former positions, and the emperor agreed, establishing for them a special office, the *Augustales*, thirty strong.[269] The emperor yields to the honour conferred upon his officers from elsewhere.

Yet the emperor did not confine himself merely to smoothing out inconcinnities between the official rank and the perceived honour of his officials. The system of precedence lent itself to use in government, serving as a way for the emperor to reward those whose services he valued most, regardless of their standing in aristocratic eyes. This produced more inconsistencies.[270] Thus Ammianus Marcellinus grumbled when Valentinian raised military *duces* (many of them barbarians) to be *clarissimi*, thereby scorning the laudable precedent of Constantius, who had held them to the rank of *perfectissimi*.[271] Most anomalous was the high precedence of the imperial chamberlains. One of them heads the list of *spectabiles* above, and another, the High Chamberlain, ranks among the lofty *illustres*, just below the *magistri militum*. Yet no precedence, no matter how high, could elevate to respectability such loathsome creatures, triply scorned as eunuchs, freedmen, and barbarians, their great power bitterly resented.[272]

The system of precedence, then, existed in a state of tension between the expectations of the aristocracy (in which, fundamentally, it was rooted) and the ambitions of the emperor to turn it to his own ends. The clash between aristocratic perceptions and imperial desires is illustrated by the sharply declining attractiveness of the praetorship to certain high fourth-century officials. Early in the century, when powerful vicars had languished as mere equestrian *perfectissimi*, a rich vicar might have been delighted to take up a praetorship, despite its expensive games, as an augmentation to his honour. By 340, with a second senate at Constantinople,

[269] The *Augustales* under Arcadius (not related to the earlier priests of the imperial cult), John Lyd. *Mag.* 3. 9–10, τιμῆς ἐξοχωτάτης . . . περιγινομένων, with A. H. M. Jones (1964), 587–9. As Stein (1922: 43–4) noted, John seems to have muddled the date of this reform; but it is John's way of describing it that is interesting. See *CTh* 6. 15 (413) for smoothing out another wrinkle.

[270] See *CTh* 6. 8 (422); 6. 12 (399) and 6. 30. 19 (408) for raising the precedence of offices as a reward to individual holders, or at least alleging so.

[271] Valentinian, Amm. Marc. 27. 9. 4 with A. H. M. Jones (1964), 142–3, 378–9; Constantius, Amm. Marc. 21. 16. 2.

[272] On the *praepositus sacri cubiculi*, eunuchs, and resentment of them, A. H. M. Jones (1964), 567–70; Hopkins (1978), 172–96.

there came to be praetors there too, who gave games just like the praetors in Rome.[273] Yet in 359, by which date vicars were deemed *clarissimi*, the emperor was reduced to a plaintive decree:

Surely you remember, gentlemen of the senate—nor shall the oblivion of any expanse of time destroy your memory—that Facundus, the former proconsul, and Arsenius, the former vicar, were glorified by the insignia of the praetorship, nor did either of them think the praetorship beneath their dignity. What can be more illustrious than these examples? This ought—it really ought—to have reminded others who have held the proconsulship and vicariate, that the praetorship is not beneath their merits. The brilliant *fasces* ought to have been sought; the glory of so great a title ought to have been desired . . . [274]

Of course they were not: the proconsulship had always stood above the praetorship, but the vicariate now conferred no less honour. Try as he might, the emperor could not persuade his great officials to take up an expensive post which offered no meaningful accretion to their honour.[275]

Despite such dangers, the system of precedence became an essential tool of late-imperial government. Not only could the emperor regulate the precedence of given offices, but the precedence of high offices could be granted to those who had not held any office at all, or who had held or were retiring from inferior offices, by codicil.[276] As Eusebius said of Constantine,

He distinguished each of those known to him with various marks of honour . . . some received an abundance of money, others of property; others the rank of prefect, or the honour of a seat in the senate, or consular status; many enjoyed provincial governorships, others countships of the first, second, and third rank. Upon myriads of others he conferred the rank of *perfectissimus*, and many other ranks of distinction; for the emperor thought up new distinctions in order to honour more people.[277]

There's the rub: too many new distinctions. The emperor created an unwieldy mass of over-honourable subjects. His generous distribution of honours to help him rule his empire increasingly came to hamper his officials' efforts to govern their provinces, by gnawing at the roots of rulership by honour at the provincial level.

[273] *CTh* 6. 4. 5 (340); on the praetorship at Constantinople, Dagron (1974), 125–7, 150–1.
[274] *CTh* 6. 4. 15; cf. 6. 4. 28 (396); Lib. *Or.* 12. 12.
[275] For rank of vicars, *PLRE* i, *fasti.*
[276] *CTh* 6. 21 (425), 22 *passim*; Sid. *Ep.* 5. 16; Cass. *Var.* 6. 10–12, 7. 37–8; Hirschfeld (1901), 590.
[277] Eus. *VC* 4. 1, αὐτῷ γνωριζομένων ἕκαστον διαφόροις τιμῶν ἀξιώμασι . . . εἰς γὰρ τὸ πλείονας τιμᾶν διαφόρους ἐπενόει Βασιλεὺς ἀξίας.

The scale of the problem can be estimated. A second-century senatorial governor would have admitted to few social equals in his province. The Roman senate numbered around six hundred, and most senators lived in Italy, whatever their origins.[278] Of course, the honour of being a senator of Rome was not confined to the individual; it encompassed his family, and lingered on in his descendants.[279] As more and more provincials were enrolled in the senate, perhaps approaching half its number by the close of the second century, provincial senators left an increasing number of high-status relatives in the provinces.[280] But however insinuating and clinging senatorial honour was, participants in it outside Italy will have numbered in the hundreds rather than the thousands. There were also cultural heroes like Aristides in the provinces, and plutocrats like Opramoas, perhaps without high Roman rank, but who expected (and could command) exacting deference from governors; but they were not particularly numerous either. There were also some lower-status governors, for equestrians ruled places like Sardinia and the Cottian Alps, but in such places very high-status subjects were rare. To great Egypt, also ruled by an equestrian, Roman senators were explicitly forbidden to go.

Compare the 360s AD. Now the average governor was a mere *perfectissimus*, not a senator. Above him loomed not one, but two senates. By Constantine's time the Roman senate alone had swollen to two thousand members. The senate at Constantinople was small at first, and not as distinguished, but by the late 350s it also had two thousand members.[281] At the same time, the old regulations which held senators near the capital were widely ignored: these innumerable *clarissimi* were scattered all over the empire.[282] And they too had relations, who partook of their honour.[283] An inscription from Timgad from the 360s gives a glimpse of the situation at a single point on the map: the province, Numidia, was governed by a *consularis* (a *vir clarissimus*), and the town's municipal *album* lists ten *viri clarissimi*—roughly his social equals—associated with the town. Of these, Chastagnol thinks that at least six were local men (as

---

[278] Talbert (1984), 134–52; and for the great concentration of high-status persons in Italy, see the *album* of Canusium from AD 223, *CIL* ix. 338 = *ILS* 6121 (only partially reproduced).

[279] Thus *clarissimus puer*, *clarissima femina*, *clarissima puella*, in inscriptions from the second half of the 2nd cent., Chastagnol (1992), 172–4.

[280] Provincial senators, Chastagnol (1992), 160. Provincial relations, Hopkins (1983), 190–3.

[281] Chastagnol (1970), 190; for Constantinople, also (1992), 261–5; Dagron (1974), 130; and on the new senate in general, pp. 119–90.

[282] Chastagnol (1977), 51–4.

[283] The eventual heritability of *clarissimus* rank (A. H. M. Jones (1964), 528–9) is a legal consequence of this attitude.

opposed to great patrons living elsewhere).[284] Now Timgad was a substantial town, but there were other substantial towns in Numidia as well. Even if we limit ourselves to towns well attested by fourth-century epigraphy, there are at least five other appreciable cities. If each had six local *clarissimi*, the governor would have faced thirty-six social equals.[285]

Not only did the provinces throng with *clarissimi*; the more typical *perfectissimus* governor was surrounded by swarms of other *perfectissimi*. Other governors of that rank leaving office may have produced over forty *perfectissimi* per year.[286] But there were also the *perfectissimi* by codicil: myriads according to Eusebius, and laws suggest that even during Constantine's reign the practice of granting codicils of rank, often in exchange for bribes, had got quite out of hand.[287] One ground for receiving codicils from the emperor was retirement from a sufficiently high post in the imperial bureaucracy, and it is not unlikely that the bureaucracy, by the 360s, was producing well over two hundred and seventy *perfectissimi* every year.[288] Most of these will no doubt have had lower

---

[284] *ILS* 6122 with Chastagnol (1978), 100–1; date, pp. 40–8; local *clarissimi*, pp. 23–4.

[285] Lepelley (1979–81), ii. 383–494: the five cities are Cirta (the seat of the governor), Cuicul, Lambaesis, Mascula, and Thibilis. And 36 is very close to the number of senators, 34, we would derive from the crude method of dividing 4,000 senators among the 117 provinces of the *Not. Dig.*

[286] The *Not. Dig.* lists 71 *praesides perfectissimi* (there will have been more earlier in the cent.). Assuming an average term of 1.5 years (A. H. M. Jones (1964), 381), *c.* 47 will lay down their office each year—many, of course, will advance to higher office, see the tables of Kuhoff (1983).

[287] *CTh* 6. 38 (317) with *CJ* 12. 32; *CTh* 12. 1. 5 (317), 6. 22. 1 (321 or 324), and later, 6. 22 and 12. 1 *passim*.

[288] In 362 *numerarii* (on whom Ensslin (1937*b*)), accountants on governors' staffs, were made *perfectissimi* after retirement (*CTh* 8. 1. 6); in 365 their term of office was set at three years (8. 1. 9), their attested term on other staffs too (8. 1. 13 (382), 15 (415), 17 (433)); the term, like the perfectissimate (Ensslin (1937*b*), 1307), will have been general. Counting conservatively I extrapolate at least 240 *numerarii* from the (*c.*AD 390–430) *Not. Dig.* (adding A. H. M. Jones (1964), 449–50, 589, on the praetorian prefectures), following *Not. Dig. Or.* 43–4 for governors' staffs for the whole empire (Oc. 43–5, which show two *tabularii* for governors, is an anachronism for the 360s: accountants were later doubled to discourage corruption (*CTh* 8. 1. 12 (382)); see also 8. 1. 9 (365) with A. H. M. Jones (1949), 47 n. 99, for the name change, which stuck longer in the West). Thus *c.*80 *numerarii* a year become *perfectissimi*. But officers who preceded *numerarii* in the *Not. Dig.* received privileges before them: while retired *numerarii* of the praetorian prefect were permitted to adore the purple (and thus admitted to the honorary status of *protectores et domestici*) first in 382 (*CTh* 8. 1. 13), the higher-ranking *cornicullarii* could do so from 365 (8. 7. 8). The elevation of the *numerarii* to the perfectissimate presupposes the prior elevation of their superiors in precedence: over 580, extrapolating from the *Not. Dig.* (but some of the offices which rank above *numerarii* in precedence on some staffs may not have existed in the 360s). Assuming the same average term as the *numerarii* (a guess, but not unreasonable, cf. *CTh* 6. 30. 3 (379)), *c.*190 become *perfectissimi* each year; 80 + 190 = 270. These are only the *perfectissimi* retirees at whose numbers we can guess: by the 360s there were also some *primipilares*, *CTh* 8. 4. 3

precedence within the perfectissimate than the governor, but the large numbers are suggestive.[289]

Some of this great quantity of new honour in the provinces was old honour now wearing a Roman hat. The distinguished Aristides' fourth-century analogue, Libanius, was an honorary praetorian prefect.[290] But most of it was genuinely new. What were the results of the existence of so many grandees in provinces ruled by men of mediocre status? The power of officials is less in relation to that of many of their subjects. Olympius of Antioch was characteristic of his time. Appointed governor of Macedonia while quite young, he thereafter avoided further offices. He had a seat in the Roman senate but lived in the East. 'The one desire of our governors is to gain his approval,' said Libanius.[291] If so, this was a man more powerful than the governor who was supposed to be governing him. This could be to the good, as distinguished subjects could supervise the conduct of an increasingly corrupt officialdom, an ability alluded to in a letter of appointment to a sixth-century governor: 'Consider how full your province is of nobles! You have both those who are bound to speak well of you, and those who may presume to criticize, because there is no power in the world which will free the judgement of your fame from the mouths of men.'[292] A comparatively humble governor quailed before the opinion of such great men, and their words would be attended to at the centre of affairs. An obstacle to bringing malfeasant governors to justice in Cicero's time, and in Pliny's, was the poor figure the provincial envoys cut before the senate; in the face of such wretches ('almost clad in skins', as Cicero put it), the senate naturally deferred to the accused. But by the fifth century, when a praetorian prefect was accused, the mission from Gaul to Rome was led by a man of prefectorian rank, the grandson of a consul, a man who would be listened to.[293]

Yet at the same time, it was far harder for governors to rule. A law of AD 395 insisted that 'town councillors who have obtained the honorary rank of count ought to respect those to whose rule they are entrusted, and should not think that they have earned this rank of honour so that they

---

(317); *actuarii*, 8. 1. 10 (365); some notaries, clerks in the *scrinia*, *agentes in rebus*, *admissionales*, assistants of the *castrensis*, and functionaries in the offices of the sacred largesses and *res privata*, 6. 35. 7 (367); *rationales* (Delmaire (1989), 182–4, 190), fiscal procurators (ibid. 209–11), and others, Hirschfeld (1901), 589; cf. *CTh* 10. 7. 1 (317), 12. 1. 5 (317).

[289] All we know is that *praesides* outrank retired *principes agentum in rebus* who outrank *rationales* in turn, *CTh* 6. 28. 2 (380).

[290] *PLRE* i, s.v.

[291] Lib. *Ep.* 70; *PLRE* i, s.v. Olympius 3.

[292] Cass. *Var.* 7. 2. 3, *fama*.

[293] Cic. *Scaur.* 45; and cf. *Flac. passim*; Pliny, *Ep.* 4. 9. 14. By contrast, Sid. *Ep.* 1. 7. 4.

can despise the orders of judges.'[294] And compare this with imperial remarks to a praetorian prefect in a law of 439:

You deem it hurtful to the public good that the decurions [who have obtained senatorial rank] are withdrawing themselves from the actions of the judges using the respect due to their rank/honour [*dignitas*]. For there is no compulsion upon debtors if the debt-collector defers to the debtor. Thus, by this law perpetual in its application, We decree that hereafter no decurion shall usurp for himself the insignia of senatorial rank, and no decurion shall be given permission to mingle in the association of *clarissimi* [persons of senatorial rank].[295]

Here habits of social deference working against the purposes of government can be seen hampering justice and the collection of taxes, two of the chief objectives of Roman government. 'I too have had title and dignity,' announced a late-antique grandee, quoting from Virgil and elegantly demanding an official's deference.[296] But a great many could make the same claim. The more subjects of high prestige there were in the provinces, the harder the provinces were to govern.

Slowly, the emperors moved to deal with the problem. Over the course of the fourth century the emperors gradually recruited persons of higher status to be governors: in some provinces the *perfectissimus praeses* was replaced by a *clarissimus consularis*, and by the 360s and 370s, *clarissimi* were increasingly being appointed as *praesides*.[297] But this promotion did no more than keep pace with the general rising tide of inflated status in society. The governors never really caught up, for even when a governor was a *clarissimus*, his difficult subjects could procure for themselves codicils making them even more magnificent *spectabiles* or *illustres*. The rising status of fourth-century governors was a symptom of, not a cure for, the problems the emperors created for provincial government by trying to ensure that their governors were insignificant, undangerous men.

Governing distinguished subjects was difficult enough for the fourth-century governor who at least came to his modest post with personal honour appropriate to it; even harder if, as often, the honour an official brought to his post from his background was inadequate. In the fourth

---

[294] *CTh* 12. 1. 150, 'curiales qui honorariam adepti sunt comitivam, formidare debent eos, quorum sunt moderationi commissi nec se existimare ideo meruisse dignitatem, ut iudicum praecepta despiciant'.

[295] *NTh* 15. 1. 2, 'sed et quod motibus se iudicum reverentia subtrahunt dignitatis, publicis commoditatibus noxium esse perspicitis. Cessat enim debitorum conpulsio, si debitori deferat executor'. Cf. *CTh* 6. 29. 2. 3 (356 or 357); 15. 3. 6 (423); A. H. M. Jones (1964), 545.

[296] Sid. *Ep.* 4. 14. 2 (= *Aen.* 2. 89–90), 'nomenque decusque gessimus'.

[297] *Consulares*, Chastagnol (1966). *Perfectissimi praesides*, Roueché (1989a), 40–1 with *PLRE* i, *fasti*; there were a few earlier, Chastagnol (1966), 216–17.

century a number of factors conspired to ensure that this would often be the case. First, even as responsible offices were thrown open again to men of senatorial birth, their evolving outlook discouraged years of service in the provinces. In this era a year in an official position was regularly followed by a decade of *otium*; and just as had been the case with patricians under the high empire (although patrician status now was a non-hereditary degree of honour granted by the emperor), the highest aristocrats flitted elegantly through a short sequence of highly honorific posts that were often sinecures. The degree to which the emperors were willing to call upon men of the highest honour to help them rule, therefore, was not necessarily matched by those men's willingness to help.[298]

Failing such men, positions—and the *Notitia* lists one hundred and seventeen territorial governorships—often came to be filled with persons of lower status. The Proconsul of Asia during the reign of Julian, for example, was one Dulcitius, according to Libanius a shorthand-writer of repulsively low origin, and representative of a whole class of such men who rose to high rank.[299] Under the principate, when the lower reaches of the imperial service had been filled with slaves and freedmen, there was never much possibility of their systematically advancing to positions of authority; in the fourth century, the clerks and functionaries were freeborn, powerful because of their access to the great, and capable of aggrandizing themselves and their friends. Senior bureaucrats can therefore be seen advancing to governorships and other posts of high responsibility.[300] And while prodigious jumps from the stews of society to high position caused comment and revulsion, the quiet seepage of men of town-councillor stock into governorships and other offices, revealed by the voluminous correspondence of Libanius and confirmed anecdotally, was so usual that it caused remark chiefly because it was emptying the councils; thus the emperor's legislation to prevent it.[301]

When an official without the appropriate background took office, the attitude of his more distinguished subjects towards him made it

[298] *Otium senatoris* and offices, Matthews (1975), 1–31; Kuhoff (1983) for detailed treatment of patterns of office-holding.

[299] Dulcitius, Teitler (1985), s.v. Dulcitius 1, *et passim* for other *notarii* who rose to extremely high rank. No doubt Teitler (pp. 64–8) is right to suppose that Libanius (*Or.* 42. 24–5) exaggerates the low social origins of such men before the mid-4th cent., but they were certainly not the kind of people who would have become proconsuls in the 2nd cent.

[300] *CTh* 6. 10. 2 (381), 6. 28. 2 (380); and see Clauss (1980), 104–5; Delmaire (1989), 105–11, for examples; cf. *PLRE* i, s.v. Ablabius 4. In general on social mobility through office-holding, MacMullen (1964), 50.

[301] Petit (1955), 345, 397–403; (1956), 166 with 194–5; Liebeschuetz (1972), 174–80, and see *CTh* 12. 1 *passim*, for emperors' attempts to stop it.

extremely difficult for him to get things done. Bishop Synesius was at odds with the low-born governor Andronicus, and wrote to his fellow bishops:

Remind yourselves who he is, compared to me, to me—if nothing else— descended from those whose lineage, right from Eurysthenes who led the Dorians into Sparta to my own father, is inscribed on public monuments. He, however, is a man who could not name his grandfather, nor even his father, they say, except that conjecture allows that he leapt from a tunny-fish look-out point into the governor's carriage. Let him be struck dumb by the brilliant honour in the city, and ashamed at his own deficiencies! I myself, until I entered the priesthood, was weighed down with honour, and never tasted dishonour.[302]

A man of Andronicus' status in society, whatever his official post, was expected to defer to Synesius. To fail to do so—to ignore the bishop's views on justice and revenue—was to fail to give Synesius his due, to insult him. Gaining the co-operation of the haughty bishop, was, under these circumstances, next to impossible. Such an environment tended to see a *de facto* division of officialdom into those to whom deference was owed and those to whom it was not (regardless of their official position and its precedence)—a division into those for whom office was a legitimate sign of social status, and those for whom it was adventitious, and whom it could not elevate from the dregs.

Not surprisingly, even other officials were unwilling to pay deference to *honorati*—the class of imperial office-holders and former office-holders, numerous enough, now, to form their own order—of lowly origin. Emperors were forced to reiterate that governors were required to treat former *principes* of the *agentes in rebus* with the respect due to the senatorial rank they were granted upon their retirement.[303] The governors' reluctance is hardly surprising. After all (in the words of an emperor), 'Many men from everywhere are flocking to the department of the *agentes in rebus* as though it were an asylum; men whose lives and birthstatus are culpable and ignoble and show that they have been spat out from servile filth!'[304] Yet the emperor could hardly abandon those he had rewarded with distinctions which aristocratic opinion was unwilling to endorse. So he was compelled to defend, legally, the rights of such persons to 'reverence' from his own officials. We have seen the emperor

---

[302] Synes. *Ep.* 41 (Garzya, pp. 63–4), οὗτος οὖν τὴν ἐν πόλει λαμπρότητα τεθαυμακὼς αἰσχυνέσθω τοῖς ἐλλείμμασιν. ἀλλ' ἔγωγε τὸ μέχρι τῆς ἱερωσύνης καὶ τιμῆς ἐνεφορήθην καὶ ἀτιμίας οὐκ ἐγευσάμην.
[303] *CTh* 6. 27. 5 (386) and 12 (398 or 399; reading 'iudices ordinarios' with Gothofredus).
[304] *CTh* 6. 27. 18 (416).

regulating acts of respect—kissing, admission to the *salutatio*—among his active officials; but he stipulated such rights for his former officials as well.[305] *Honorati* were entitled also to wide access to the governor's person; were even entitled to sit with him on the bench when he dispensed justice.[306]

Yet such regulations had consequences for the day-to-day operation of government in the provinces, for they severely circumscribed the traditional latitude of governors to rule by artfully discriminating honours and dishonours. A mid-fourth century inscription from North Africa carefully lists the order in which persons were to be admitted to the governor's morning *salutatio*. 'First, senators, and counts, and honorary counts, and administrators, second the chief and *cornicularius* of his staff, and palatine officials', and so on.[307] By having the order inscribed the fourth-century governor admits that his freedom of choice is gone. A decurion who procured codicils making him an honorary count had a legal right to a kiss from his governor, no matter how little help to that governor the decurion had been.[308] Some governors naturally found such regulations intolerable, and schemed to win back their prerogatives: the *honorati* have the right to be admitted at the *salutatio*? Then hold as few as possible, only four a month. The *honorati* have the right to sit with the judge on his bench? But the judge can raise himself up on a vast cushion, 'desiring to despoil them of the honour'.[309] Libanius does not approve of this governor: he gets a good rhetorical blasting for his insolence. But Libanius knew perfectly well (and deplored in other speeches) the alarming consequences of legally required 'honours' for provincial administration. Such rights of access were ruthlessly exploited by powerful men, and the governor was not alone even in his bath. Thus the *honorati* enjoyed undue influence upon him.[310]

Well known is the damage to civic prosperity, and eventually even to imperial government, inflicted by immunities from civic burdens and the various purely legal privileges enjoyed by the numerous *honorati* of the late empire.[311] But at the same time as the late-antique emperors rewarded their servants and supporters with financial and legal advantages, they were also trying to bestow upon them social advantages, honours, the spoils of the precedence system. This was by nature more

---

[305] *CTh* 6. 18. 1 (412), 'nullam honorabiles viri in publicis salutationibus patiantur iniuriam'; 6. 28. 8. 2 (435).

[306] *CTh* 6. 26. 16 (410 or 413), as *reverentia*. On these rights, Liebeschuetz (1972), 189–91.

[307] *CIL* viii. 17896 with Chastagnol (1978), 75–88.   [308] *CTh* 12. 1. 109 (385).

[309] Lib. *Or.* 56. 2–4, βουλόμενος ἀφελέσθαι τὴν τιμήν.   [310] Lib. *Or.* 51–2.

[311] Immunities, n. 4 above; legal privileges, A. H. M. Jones (1964), 487–94.

problematic: honour exists in the mind of the observer. Although the emperor's right to grant honour, by virtue of his own honour, was very great, the mind of the observer revolted when honour was granted to the wrong kind of people—when it beheld a freedman given praetorian insignia (in Pliny's day) or, later, contemplated the hated eunuch chamberlains, so highly honoured, yet so utterly honourless. How the emperor's *honorati* were received in the wider world varied. Whatever the reaction, however, provincial government suffered. If the honour of the *honorati* was admitted and deferred to, then low-status governors were weak; if not, the emperor stepped in, degrees of honour increasingly became thorny bundles of legal rights and privileges, and the governor was weakened in that way.

The fourth century saw a debilitating struggle between the interests of the emperor's own power and that of his officials. He bolstered his rulership with methods of granting honour more sophisticated than ever before—elaborate ceremony, precedence, a nuanced system of honorary rank. At the same time, he protected his position by ensuring that his officials were men small enough to be no threat. Yet the dwarf governors of the second policy were expected to rule the giant subjects the emperor had raised up with the first. This was hardly the essential malaise of the time, and it may have been more a symptom than a cause of the fever. But considered alongside the many other deficiencies of fourth-century government, it was part of the reality of a late-antique provincial government which worked far less well than when the house of Caesar or the Antonines ruled.

CONCLUSION

When the future emperor Sulpicius Galba was governor in Spain, he had a Roman citizen crucified for poisoning his ward. When the convict cried the laws and his status from the cross, Galba had him taken down, and then hoisted up again on a cross loftier than the others, and painted white, 'as if intending to lighten the punishment by some solace and honour'.[312] A sick joke, even by rough Roman standards; but funny because it winked at the way a Roman governor ruled. When the first Epistle of Peter describes 'governors sent by the emperor to punish those who do ill and praise those who do well', it nicely encapsulates the ancient view of a governor's methods in his province.[313] Just like the emperor, he seemed

---

[312] Suet. *Galba* 9. 1, 'quasi solacio et honore aliquo poenam levaturus'.
[313] 1 *Pet.* 2: 14.

to rule by terror mixed with honour. No doubt, indeed, many of the techniques he used were copied from the emperor, both by the natural imitation which was so strong a force in a culture of honour, and because they were effective; and no doubt the emperors drew their techniques from the provincial experience of Republican governors like Cicero, already masters of eking out other forms of power with honour. For honour served the governor not only as a form of power in its own right, but as a way to veil power, especially the power of terror, which at the same time expanded terror's threat. Honour made the governor a prickly, explosive, unpredictable creature, but his prickliness was understandable, even laudable, by the standards of those around him.

This useful touchiness was natural to those who lived in a society in which honour and shame were so important. Yet it arose also from the fact that honour was an essential element, perhaps even the most important, in the ancient conception of office. The pallid, impersonal, machine-like images by which the modern imagination grapples with its government were hardly to be inspired by an officialdom so shot through with pride, so violently competitive, so obviously human rather than mechanical. The state and its minions, as we imagine them, would have recalled to a great Roman official the *ergastula*, the slave workhouses, on his estates—nothing he could bear to be involved with himself. Roman government did not imagine itself as a government in our sense. Its members imagined something more akin to a football league, a realm of glory, profit, and competition—and some administration.

This was an outlook of the greatest consequence for the way Roman provincial government worked. It made subjects into an audience to whose wishes the performers had, to a certain extent, to bow. Thus honour also served the subject as a real form of power over his governors; but he too used it to conceal, to sugar the bribes and threats by which he strove to control his rulers. Honour played a vital role in creating what flexibility and responsiveness there was in Roman government, and that, in turn, generated consent in the governed. For the more responsive Roman government was to the needs of its greater subjects, the happier those subjects would be with Roman rule. But if the influence of subjects over their immediate rulers became too strong, the delicate balance might tip too far in the direction of haughty, powerful subjects. Under those circumstances government might be weakened, not strengthened. Such weakness was part of the fourth- and fifth-century twilight of empire.

5

The Roman Army

ANCIENT observers describe the Roman army as the third essential constituency of the imperial system, with the aristocracy and the Roman *plebs*.[1] Perhaps, indeed, the army could somehow be imagined as the *plebs* of Rome in arms, conferring ideological legitimacy on the emperor at the senate's side. But the army's fundamental role in empire is perfectly clear: the Roman empire depended, in the last resort, upon violent force, and so, in the last resort, it depended upon the discipline and loyalty of the soldiers who exerted that force. Thus, finally, we turn to examine the role honour played in their lives.

That honour played a role is hardly surprising. The marriage of honour and soldiering has endured even to the present day. A new duelling handbook was prepared for the Argentine army in 1954, and reissued in 1961.[2] Even in phlegmatic Anglo-Saxon lands, Victorian and Edwardian soldiers constantly reflected on honour, on glory, in their memoirs; and despite the battering their code suffered on the Western Front, officers can still be heard musing—sometimes with the soft irony that signals something passing but not quite passed—over the honour of man and of regiment. Modernity's assault on the cult of honour has been turned back most frequently at camp gates. Much about Roman military honour is familiar, or can be reasoned from the familiar; this is an easier subject to understand.

Yet it is a harder subject as well, because of the nature of the evidence. It is not possible to rely on Roman soldiers' own writings to study their attitudes in detail; at best, their limited leavings—inscriptions and papyri—allow us to confirm the opinions of the aristocratic historians, but often not even that. Frequently, élite sources must be called upon untested for insight into the outlooks of their inferiors. This presents a problem: while aristocrats' speculations into the motives of their equals, whatever their value as facts, do allow us to make deductions about

---

[1] See above, Ch. 3 n. 69.   [2] Stewart (1994), 69.

patterns of expectations among that lofty set, their speculations about their inferiors' motives may reveal nothing more than aristocrats' social contempt, ignorance, or guile.

Suspicion of contempt would arise if aristocratic authors consistently portrayed soldiers as base and honourless creatures, identifying them with the slaves and the infamous whom they saw when they looked down from their high seats. If soldiers' honour seemed instead to be identical to aristocrats', appeared to be assimilated to the authors' own values, suspicion of ignorance might be justified. Suspicion of guile might develop if the outlooks assigned to soldiers seemed to carry a great deal of polemical weight—if, like Tacitus' clean-living Germans and rebelliously speechifying Britons, they seemed to serve as ciphers, intended chiefly to tell aristocratic Romans about themselves and their empire. None of these is the case. While aristocratic authors do often bristle with contempt, with fear, or with hatred at soldiers, they recognize in soldiers a sense of honour and shame, if sometimes regrettably in abeyance. They see a stern code different from their own, one that touches theirs only at points, but for which they sometimes show a more than sneaking admiration.

The picture that the historians offer of soldiers' values is, in fact, remarkably consistent, and probably accurate. Caesar, Velleius Paterculus, and Ammianus Marcellinus were fighting soldiers themselves. Others had commanded Roman soldiers in camp if not in battle, or watched wars from close up, or were related to officers.[3] Tacitus refers in passing to 'those who best understand the military mind', and because of the importance of that mind to imperial politics it was hardly an abstruse study, even for civilians.[4] The accuracy of historians' speculations about soldiers' motives in individual cases may be no better than their speculations about men of their own order, but broader realities can still be drawn from what they expected to happen.

THE COMMUNITY OF THE ARMY

Even now the ethos of soldiers is strikingly different from that of the world beyond the wire, even in short-service armies constantly bom-

---

[3] Cassius Dio ruled Upper Pannonia, a province with legions, 80. 1. 3. Josephus fought in and was a keen spectator of the war he described. Suetonius' father was an officer, *Otho* 10. 1.

[4] Tac. *Ann.* 1. 32, 'militaris animos altius coniectantibus'. On Tacitus and his military knowledge, Syme (1958), 157–75; for speculations as to his military career, p. 68.

barded by civilian allurements. This was much more the case in the Roman imperial army: soldiers served for decades in isolated border camps, in contact with only such civilians as camped with them to serve their needs, surrounded perhaps by savages (so a soldier from Italy would have thought), perhaps by enemies, whose camp-fires they dimly glimpsed in the mists, whose javelins they feared at night. 'Soldiers' special pride is in their camp; that is their city, that their *penates*.'[5] Long years in such conditions made soldiers uncomfortable when they returned home (if they had a home to go to), so they continued to live around the camps when they retired, or were settled in groups with other veterans.[6] The army was a starkly separate community, a separate community of opinion with its own standards of conduct, a community in which the esteem and disapproval of fellow members was a tremendously powerful force. In battle, soldiers fight harder where their comrades can see them, where 'nothing done well or shamefully could be concealed, and lust for praise and fear of disgrace drove both sides on to bravery'.[7] But order can break down at night, when the anonymity of darkness saps soldiers' sense of shame.[8]

Soldiers' membership in the community of the army, in the smaller community of the unit, or in the group of units that shared a campaign, was of tremendous psychological importance to them. On the humble tombstones of soldiers, the number of years served in the army and the units they served with were very often recorded. Of Dazas the Maezian, son of Scenus, posterity was to learn only that he lived twenty-seven years, and served for ten as a cavalryman in Licco's squadron of the sixth Dalmatian auxiliary cohort.[9] After Vitellius' defeat, the soldiers of his German army, expecting to be massacred by Vespasian's troops, 'clasped the breasts of the fellow members of their maniples, hung upon their necks, begged a last kiss, begging them not to desert them'.[10] For a commander of soldiers to imply that their bad conduct had set them outside the boundaries of the army was crushing, as, famously, when Julius Caesar brought his mutinous tenth legion to heel simply by addressing them as 'citizens' (*Quirites*) rather than soldiers.[11] A prefect of the camp

---

[5] Tac. *Hist.* 3. 84, 'proprium esse militis decus in castris: illam patriam, illos penatis'.

[6] Soldierly separateness and solidarity, MacMullen (1984*b*), on retirement, pp. 441–2. And see Juv. 16. 20–2 on soldiers' common cause when one is sued.

[7] Caes. *BG* 7. 80, 'neque recte ac turpiter factum celari poterat, utrosque et laudis cupiditas et timor ignominiae ad virtutem excitabant'; cf. Hirt. *BG* 8. 42; Tac. *Hist.* 2. 42.

[8] Caes. *BC* 1. 67, 2. 31; Tac. *Hist.* 4. 36.   [9] *ILS* 2576.

[10] Tac. *Hist.* 4. 46; cf. *Ann.* 1. 21.

[11] Suet. *Jul.* 70; long remembered, Tac. *Ann.* 1. 42; *HA Sev. Alex.* 52. 3, 53. 10–54. 4 (fiction). Cf. Tac. *Hist.* 3. 24, 'pagani'; Dio 72(73L). 9. 2a.

under Vitellius gained the same end by ordering the centurions not to make the rounds of a mutinous encampment, and forbade the usual trumpet calls: this secession of the officers brought the soldiers to their senses.[12]

Yet the fundamental weakness of the community of the army was not common soldiers falling away from it, but the awkwardness of aristocratic officers' membership in it. It is a topos in the historians that the good officer in the Roman army shares the menial labours of his troops. He eats camp food, sleeps on the ground, bandies vulgar jests with the rankers, mucks in, and ostentatiously roughs it in a way that would have got an Edwardian subaltern cashiered for conduct unbecoming an officer.[13] This is puzzling, for among the aristocracy, not only did a stigma attach to manual labour, but without the softening influence of some relationship of dependency like patronage, even returning the greetings of far social inferiors was by no means expected.[14] Certainly the base did not warrant the least consideration: a remark made by Tiberius during his sulk on Rhodes—that he wanted to visit the sick—was misinterpreted by his retainers, who rousted the ill out of bed and arranged them, infirmity by infirmity, in a public portico for their master's inspection. Tiberius was appalled when he arrived—no doubt he had expected to visit a few liverish notables at home—and 'was for a long time uncertain as to what he should do, but finally he went around to each one individually, apologizing for what had happened, even to the obscure and poorest'. Imagine! Most men of his rank, clearly, would have thought it beneath themselves to apologize to the obscure and poor, no matter how much pain and inconvenience they had inflicted on their inferiors.[15] Supercilious hauteur was the norm: 'The greatest honour the multitude can enjoy from their betters is not to be scorned by them.'[16]

In civilian life, the poor repaid the contempt of the rich with hatred.[17] Similarly, hostility between social classes was always waiting to break out in the army: it could manifest itself horribly in mutinies, and in time of

---

[12] Tac. *Hist.* 2. 29.

[13] Plut. *Mar.* 7. 3; cf. *Cato Min.* 9. 4; *Ant.* 4. 2; Tac. *Hist.* 2. 5; Suet. *Tib.* 18. 2; Dio 72(73L). 8. 3; *HA Pesc. Nig.* 11. 1–3; Amm. Marc. 17. 1. 2.

[14] Libanius is remarkable because he returns greetings, *Or.* 2. 6; cf. D. Chr. 66. 3. And certainly don't trade insults with inferiors, Aul. Gel. 7. 11. 1.

[15] Suet. *Tib.* 11. 2. Cf. Amm. Marc. 27. 3. 4, the 4th-cent. *plebs* were prepared to believe that the Prefect of the City had said that he would rather use the wine from his estates to quench lime-kilns than sell it to the people cheaply.

[16] Plut. *Nic.* 2. 4, an editorial comment.

[17] MacMullen (1974: 119), picking out Plut. *Praec. Ger. Reip.* 822a.

civil war.[18] So it was exactly the civilian background that made conde-
scending (to use the word in its old sense) conduct essential for officers
in the army. The military opinion-community was by its nature fragile,
for its embrace of men of widely different social origins placed a great
vertical strain upon it. The officer carried burdens, slept beneath the
stars, and belched loudly precisely to show that he did *not* scorn his baseborn troops, as a man from his rank in society would naturally be
expected to do; he acted this way to show that he was a member of their
community, and was willing to live by their standards.[19] Thus the soldiers' rioting against Verginius Rufus, who was acclaimed emperor by his
troops, but refused to assume the purple. The soldiers' 'admiration for
the man, and his reputation, remained, but they hated him as having
scorned them.'[20]

Aristocratic officers had to work at being part of the army. The qualities scorned in the camps were different from those which brought scorn
in the salons of Rome. Tacitus, for example, noted that the army of Upper
Germany in AD 68 'scorned the legate Hordeonius Flaccus: he was unwell
on account of old age and lameness, lacking constancy and *auctoritas*.'[21]
Old age, revered among the aristocracy, could inspire contempt in the
great locker-room of the army, a fact which proved troublesome for
Galba and Nerva.[22] But far more offensive was the taint of effeminacy,
still scorned in armies today.[23] To punish a unit of cavalry that fled in battle, Julian had them marched through the camp and expelled dressed in
women's clothes, 'deeming this punishment worse than death for manly
soldiers; and this turned out well both for him and them, for in the second German War they recalled the disgrace inflicted upon them and were
almost the only troops who fought well.'[24] If this was the most extreme
disgrace that the ingenuity of Julian could concoct, one can imagine what
the soldiers thought of an emperor who seemed to them to dress in
women's clothes voluntarily: Macrinus, or Elagabalus.[25] And then there
was Severus Alexander, notoriously under the thumb of female relations,
and jeered in time of revolt as the 'mean girly-man', as 'the cowardly
child, his mother's slave'.[26] Accused of involvement in the rebellion of

---

[18] MacMullen (1984*b*), 451–5.   [19] Belching, Suet. *Vit.* 7. 3.
[20] Tac. *Hist.* 2. 68, 'manebat admiratio viri et fama, set oderant ut fastiditi'.
[21] Ibid. 1. 9, 'spernebat'.
[22] Galba, Tac. *Hist.* 1. 5; Plut. *Galba* 19. 1. Nerva, Dio 68. 3. 3–4. But not always, Herod. 2.
5. 8. Extreme youth perceived to create contempt as well, *HA Maxim.* 7. 3.
[23] Cf. the contemporary British army, Hockey (1986), 33–6.   [24] Zos. 3. 3. 5.
[25] Macrinus, Herod. 5. 2. 4–5. Elagabalus, Dio 79(80L). 13–19; Herod. 5. 6. 10–7. 1, 5. 8; *HA
Elag.* 5, 14–15, and some of the stories may even be true. Cf. Tac. *Hist.* 1. 30.
[26] Herod. 6. 9. 5; cf. 6. 8. 3.

Antonius Saturninus, a military tribune and a centurion cleared themselves before Domitian by confessing that they were the rebel's lovers, 'and on that account could have been of no influence with the commander or the soldiers'.[27] Such a role, clearly, destroyed the possibility of respect among the soldiers. Many years before, Marius had decorated a soldier who killed his own officer when the latter attempted to force his lust upon him.[28]

For an aristocrat to become part of the community of the army was difficult. He might go too far even in sharing the soldiers' drudgery, and so sacrifice their respect.[29] Soldiers wanted their officers to act like them, but not be like them. Tacitus imagined Germanicus wandering around his army's camp in disguise, to hear what his soldiers said about him, and hearing 'one praising the high birth of the general, another his good looks, many his endurance and affability, some in jests and some seriously, but all agreed'. Perhaps, at first, the soldiers' concern with their officer's high birth looks suspiciously patrician—suspiciously Tacitean— and the alleged circumstances, a general creeping around his camp to taste of his fame like Henry V, do not lend credence. But most aristocratic authors are certainly in agreement in thinking that *nobilitas* was important to soldiers.[30] In his advice for emperors, Cassius Dio insisted that the army needed to be commanded by real aristocrats, for 'if you entrust affairs to trivial and chance men [as opposed to aristocrats] . . . you will soon fail in great matters. For what good could an ill-educated or low-born person ever do? . . . Who of the soldiers themselves would not scorn to be commanded by such a man?'[31] And Roman soldiers themselves endorse such advice: when Claudius' freedman Narcissus ascended the tribunal to urge a reluctant army to take ship for Britain, he was shouted down with jeers of 'Io Saturnalia!' The troops were not about to take orders from a freedman.[32] The senatorial generals under whom a soldier had campaigned might be listed on his tombstone, with the addition of '*c.v.*' (*clarissimus vir*) so that there could be no mistake.[33] In fact, there is nothing surprising in this: even now the preference of British other ranks

---

[27] Suet. *Dom.* 10. 5 with Dio 67. 11. 4.

[28] Plut. *Mar.* 14. 3–5; cf. Polyb. 6. 37. 9. Cf. also incest as unacceptable, Tac. *Ann.* 14. 2.

[29] Zos. 1. 29. 1; but Titus manages to do it 'incorrupto ducis honore', Tac. *Hist.* 5. 1. Caracalla neglects the duties of commanding in favour of soldiers' labours, Dio 77(78L). 13. 1–2.

[30] Tac. *Ann.* 2. 13, 'cum hic nobilitatem ducis, decorem alius, plurimi patientiam, comitatem, per seria per iocos eundem animum laudibus ferrent'. Cf. Vitellius, Tac. *Hist.* 1. 9; Plut. *Galba* 22. 5; Dio 64(63L). 4. 2. *Contra*, Herod. 8. 8. 1 for resentment of high birth.

[31] Dio 52. 8. 6–7; cf. 51. 3. 5; Onasander, *Strat.* 1. 17–18; HA *Macr.* 5. 5 for the fear.

[32] Dio 60. 19. 3.   [33] *ILS* 2311.

for polo-playing, ex-public-schoolboy officers over officers drawn from backgrounds similar to their own can be pointed out, even if it has much weakened since Queen Victoria's day. Certainly Roman soldiers did not find it impossible to follow men like Diocletian and Maximinus Thrax, bold soldiers but hardly drawn from the pinnacles of society. But all things being equal they too preferred the military hierarchy to echo the social hierarchy: it was especially flattering to the common soldiers to see those of high status outside the army emphasize their community with fighting men by sharing their labours and way of life.

HONOUR AND SHAME IN THE ARMY

The extraordinary discipline of the classical Roman army—the ability of its highly trained soldiers to hold their ground and perform complicated close-order manœuvres under the most trying circumstances—attracted envying notice in antiquity, and has continued to do so into modern times.[34] Yet this proper emphasis on Roman soldiers' automaton-like virtues must not be allowed to conceal the fiercely competitive, Homeric, quality of Roman fighting. After the fall of Jerusalem, Titus paraded his men.

> Those who competed in a more distinguished manner by virtue of their great strength, and had thus cast lustre not only upon their own lives by their acts of courage, but also rendered his campaign more glorious by virtue of their successes, to them he said he would give prizes and honours immediately, in order that no one who had set his mind to surpassing another should fail to gain his just requital.[35]

The army was a society characterized by vehement competition for honour, and by an equally strong sense of shame. Honour and shame among soldiers were grounded in success in war: in contrasting Alpine tribesmen with Roman regulars, Tacitus noted that 'they were unused to camps and command, and for them there was no distinction in victory, and no shame in flight'.[36] It was characteristic of Roman soldiers, on the other hand, to brood over the question, 'What shall we answer to anyone who asks us about our victories and defeats?'[37] In the speeches historians

---

[34] Jos. *BJ* 3. 102–8, and remembered wistfully in late antiquity, Veg. *Mil. passim.*

[35] Jos. *BJ* 7. 11, τὸν μὲν αὐτῶν βίον ἀριστείαις κεκοσμηκόσι, τὴν δ᾽ αὐτοῦ στρατείαν ἐπιφανεστέραν.

[36] Tac. *Hist.* 2. 12, 'neque in victoria decus esset neque in fuga flagitium'; cf. *Ann.* 2. 14; Jos. *BJ* 6. 42.

[37] Tac. *Hist.* 3. 13. Soldiers tell tall tales to remove the stigma from defeat, ibid. 3. 61; Herod. 8. 3. 9 with *HA Maxim.* 22. 3.

give to generals before battles, the glory of victory and the disgrace of defeat are constant themes; the speeches are hardly history, but the sentiments are likely to be conventional.[38] In battle or campaign, shame at a setback drives soldiers on to greater efforts.[39] Their leaders might rely on this dread of disgrace. Thus the emperor Severus, it was reported, charged alone against the army of his rival Albinus to shame his fleeing men into fighting on, and Herodian believed that Maximinus plunged into a German mire to shame his troops into pursuing fleeing Germans.[40]

In the army it was the qualities and deeds that conduced to victory which were honoured: in the first place, physical courage.[41] Thus soldiers' inscriptions vaunt decorations 'for bravery', or even boast heroic deeds, like cornering King Decebalus in Trajan's Dacian War, and carrying away his head.[42] Soldiers were fiercely competitive for a reputation for courage, and Roman battles could take on a Homeric cast with a single soldier rushing out from his formation and distinguishing himself with extraordinary heroism, inspiring others to emulate him. 'Why do you hesitate, Vorenus? What occasion for proving your bravery are you waiting for? This day will settle our rivalry!' shouted one of Caesar's centurions at another, and charged alone at the thickest ranks of the enemy. The man he had goaded leapt from the ramparts and followed, 'terrified for his reputation among all'. In fact, the rivalry was not settled. Each saved the other's life in the ensuing fighting, they withdrew within the fortifications 'with the greatest glory', and 'it was impossible to decide which was the better man in bravery'.[43]

Cowardice inspired contempt, and a soldier accused of cowardice might commit suicide on the spot to liberate himself from the imputation.[44] Surrender, needless to say, always carried with it the taint of cowardice, and might therefore involve manœuvres to free it from that stigma. Thus the odd ritual which Vitellius' army insisted on for its sur-

---

[38] e.g. Jos. *BJ* 3. 480–3; Tac. *Ann.* 15. 12; Dio 62. 9. 1; Herod. 4. 14. 8.

[39] Caes. *BC* 3. 74; Tac. *Hist.* 5. 15; Jos. *BJ* 3. 153–6, 5. 488; cf. Caes. *BG* 7. 17.

[40] Severus, Dio 75(76L). 6. 7; Maximinus, Herod. 7. 2. 6–7; both with Jos. *BJ* 5. 94: abandoning one's general more disgraceful even than flight. Cf. Jos. *BJ* 4. 39; Zos. 3. 19. 4.

[41] Conspectus of honourable qualities, Jos. *BJ* 6. 81. Bravery, Caes. *BG* 6. 40; Jos. *BJ* 6. 90; Tac. *Hist.* 3. 84, 4. 2; Herod. 6. 3. 6.

[42] 'Ob virtutem', *ILS* 2337, 2658. Cf. EJ 247, legion honours a *primuspilaris* 'honoris et virtutis caussa [sic]'. Decebalus, *AE* 1970. 583 with Speidel (1970), who notes that while the inscription claims the soldier captured him, the king probably committed suicide, Dio 68. 14. 3.

[43] Caes. *BG* 5. 44, 'omnium veritus existimationem'; 'summa cum laude'. Cf. Jos. *BJ* 5. 312–14, 6. 82–90.

[44] Contempt, Tac. *Hist.* 2. 30. Suicide, Suet. *Otho* 10. 1 and Dio 64(63L). 11. 2.

render to Vespasian's: marching down with their standards, they were received by their erstwhile enemies arrayed for battle and surrounded by them, so that, having been placed in an impossible tactical position, they could then surrender 'not without distinction'.[45] This was the same impulse that drove the surrendering German commander of the Cherbourg arsenal in 1944 to insist that an Allied tank fire upon the gate, to offer him an honourable pretext.

Not only bravery, but all the qualities that produced success in war were honourable. For a soldier of enormous strength, battle was an opportunity to gain distinction. Thus a Roman cavalryman, reaching down from his horse to seize a fleeing Jew by the ankle, hoisted his armoured captive in the air and carried him off to be admired by Titus, commander at the siege of Jerusalem.[46] A soldier's epitaph reads:

> Once I was most renowned on the Pannonian shore;
> amidst a thousand Batavians the strongest.
> With Hadrian watching I swam the huge waters
> of Danube's deep in arms.
> While a bolt from my bow hung in the air—
> while it fell—I hit and shattered it with another arrow.
> Neither Roman nor Barbarian, no soldier with his spear,
> no Parthian with his bow, could defeat me.
> Here I lie. My deeds I have entrusted to the memory of this stone.
> Whether another after me will emulate my deeds has yet to be seen.
> I am the first who did such things: my own exemplar.[47]

This sense of rivalry was characteristic. Tacitus imagines Agricola's soldiers and sailors in a boasting contest, 'talking up their deeds and dangers, the depths of forests and mountains on one side, of tempests and waves on the other: soldierly bragging compared the conquest of Ocean to the conquest of land and foeman.'[48] The ability to go without sleep was also highly esteemed in military circles, and in this Commodus' general Ulpius Marcellus excelled. As a regimen he fasted, or ate only bread so stale it made his gums bleed, 'in order to have the greatest reputation possible in wakefulness'. He persecuted his subordinates with messages through the night so they would think he never slept.[49] The construction

---

[45] Tac. *Hist.* 3. 63, 'non sine decore'. On surrender, cf. Herod. 2. 13. 11, 5. 4. 9.

[46] Jos. *BJ* 6. 161–3.

[47] Small. *Nerva* 336, 'notissimus', discussed by Speidel (1991). Cf. *ILS* 2528, 'viro sagittandi peritissimo'.

[48] Tac. *Agric.* 25. 1; cf. 33. 5 for the honour of passing over difficult terrain.

[49] Dio 72(73L). 8. 4–5, ἵν' ὡς μάλιστα διαγρυπνεῖν δοκῇ.

of an earthwork around Jerusalem naturally became a gigantic contest in which 'the soldier strove to please the decurion, the decurion to please the centurion, he in turn the tribune, and the tribunes' rivalry for glory reached the legionary legates; of their rivalry Titus Caesar himself was the referee.'[50] There is more than a passing similarity between the psychology of the building of these entrenchments and that of the erection of public works in an ancient town. Everything soldiers did, in short, could become a competition; naturally, in such an emulous environment, leading by example was of the greatest importance.[51]

Military rank not only established its holder's position in the hierarchy of obedience, it also conferred honour within the community of the army. The 'honour of rank' was as meaningful in military as in civilian life.[52] Soldiers were fiercely jealous of their rivals' advancement. The law depicts them as 'gnawed upon by another's honour' if they were demoted.[53] The honorific or funerary inscriptions of an aristocrat often catalogue the offices he has held in the greatest detail; this makes sense because each office was an ornament to him, each conferred a quantum of honour. Significantly, soldiers—even quite humble soldiers—sometimes displayed the same loquacity in describing each rank and posting they had held.

C. Luccius . . . Sabinus, decurion of Beneventum, while still living made [this tomb] for himself, his wife Ofillia Parata, and his brother Luccius Verecundus, and his posterity. He served in the First Urban Cohort at the side of the tribunes, was an attendant (*secutor*), orderly (*optio*) of the hospital, orderly of the prison, aide (*singularis*), clerk (*beneficiarius*) of a tribune, put in charge of the examination of witnesses by Annius Verus, Prefect of the City; he was also officer in charge of the watchword, orderly, standard-bearer, clerk of the treasury, orderly in charge of records, senior clerk of a tribune, clerk of Valerius Asiaticus, Prefect of the City. He was discharged by the emperor Hadrian when Servianus . . . and Vibius Verus were consuls [AD 134].[54]

Here was a man who became a civic decurion after retirement, but during his service never reached the rank of centurion. Yet he was proud

---

[50] Jos. *BJ* 5. 503, φιλοτιμία.

[51] Fronto, *Princ. Hist.* 14 (van den Hout); *HA Hadr.* 10. 4; Dio 69. 9. 3–4; Herod. 3. 6. 10, a topos about the good officer, closely related to his sharing soldiers' fatigues. Officers imitate the commander, the soldiers the officers, Tac. *Hist.* 2. 68; Dio 65(64L). 4. 4.

[52] Eus. *Hist. Eccl.* 10. 8. 10, τιμὴ ἀξιώματος; cf. 7. 15, 8. 4. 3.

[53] *CTh* 7. 1. 10 (367), 'morsu honoris alieni'. Cf. Caes. *BG* 5. 44.

[54] *ILS* 2117. A uniquely full *cursus*; trans. adapted from J. B. Campbell, but the English equivalents of many of the functions are approximate. It is especially tombstones that soldiers erect for themselves while still alive that list their ranks in detail, Forni (1979), 227.

enough of his military career to describe it in detail. By contrast, men who had advanced from the ranks to careers as centurions tended not to list their sub-centurion ranks, or might reduce some of them to a formula, 'all positions in the hobnailed ranks performed', adapting the common formula of the high-aiming civic dignitary, 'all offices performed'.[55] There were zones of honour in the army; a centurion competed more with centurions, some of whom were directly commissioned from the equestrian order, and less with rankers.[56]

The fact that, as in all armies, rank was a social distinction as well as a purely functional indicator of relative duty, makes sense of the fact that morning in a Roman camp was very much like morning in a Roman city. Soldiers attended the centurions' *salutatio*, centurions the military tribunes', all the officers the legionary commander's.[57] Higher military ranks enjoyed not only authority but precedence over lower: 'It is disgraceful, Caesar, that you should be chatting with a centurion when the prefects stand without,' said the centurion—a stickler—himself.[58] At the same time, soldiers' respect for civil offices, offices outside their own hierarchy, was notoriously unreliable. By the fourth century for soldiers to be 'harsh and savage towards civil dignitaries' was an 'established custom'.[59]

The make-up of military honour did not include the emphasis on gravity, on self-restraint, that characterized civilian aristocrats. When insulted, soldiers killed people. An innocent jape, cutting soldiers' sword-belts and then asking whether they had their swords, sparked a massacre of the civilian jokers.[60] If a centurion asked a civilian a question, and the latter was so disrespectful as not to answer, the soldier might knock him off his donkey with his vine stick.[61] Tacitus emphasized soldiers' thin skins, their bloody taste for vengeance, and the awful consequences of this even for cities in turbulent times.[62] But how was this undisciplined lashing-out, this violent self-wilfulness, reconciled with the minutely regulated, precise army that observers so admired? Stern discipline is part of

---

[55] Not listing, E. Birley (1988 (1941)), 199–200. *ILS* 2085, 'omnibus officiis in caliga functo' (earlier in his career those ranks had been listed more fully, 2084). Cf. 6717, 'omnibus honoribus functo'.

[56] On the solidarity of the centurionate despite its diversity of social background, Dobson (1970), 100–2.

[57] Jos. *BJ* 3. 87; cf. Tac. *Hist.* 2. 80.

[58] Dio 69. 19. 1.

[59] Amm. Marc. 14. 10. 4. Cf. Tac. *Hist.* 3. 80; Dio 65(64L). 10. 4.

[60] Tac. *Hist.* 2. 88 (loss of sword was a great disgrace, Apul. *Met.* 9. 41); and they cut down those who jostle them too. Cf. *HA Tyr. Trig.* 8. 6, 22. 3, 32. 3.

[61] Apul. *Met.* 9. 39.   [62] Tac. *Hist.* 1. 51, 3. 32; cf. Caes. *BC* 2. 13; Suet. *Vesp.* 8. 2.

the answer, discipline which controlled the unruly manifestations of soldiers' pride. The centurion's rod was always at the ready, and should he break it during a vigorous thrashing, he might call out 'bring another', giving rise to a wry nickname, *Cedo-Alteram*.[63] Roman soldiers quailed before the terrible authority of their generals; it could seem that those entitled to beat and execute them were beyond number.[64] But discipline was also something that lived in the hearts of soldiers. Tacitus alludes to their 'love of obedience'.[65] And although a rabble-rousing mutineer could be imagined comparing soldiers' obedience to that of slaves, who obey unwillingly, from fear, a clear distinction of kind in obedience could also be conceived: 'Let one obey another as a soldier, not as a slave.'[66] In fact, obedience itself was an honourable quality. 'Where is the glory of the old discipline?' Tacitus imagined Germanicus asking mutineers. The mutiny begins to come apart when a sense of 'shame and glory enters into the soldiers', and then they want to wash out the stain on their honour by making war upon the barbarians.[67] The contemplation of disobedience, mutiny, and defection to the enemy not only inspired fear of punishment in soldiers; it also inspired shame. A great many Roman soldiers caught up in the Batavian revolt in AD 70 were guilty on all those counts, and when they fell back into Roman hands, 'they stood, dejected by a consciousness of their own disgrace, their eyes fixed upon the ground ... they remained hidden in their tents, avoiding even the light. It was not so much fear and danger as shame and disgrace which stunned them.' When they were forgiven, the general explicitly ordered their comrades not to insult them for their conduct.[68]

Naturally, then, faced with mutiny, commanders strove not only to mollify and terrify the mutineers, but to inspire shame in them. 'Deeds of this kind are restrained by shame or fear.'[69] The speeches Tacitus supplies for leaders at such junctures, or reports on briefly, dwell upon disgrace.[70] Even if soldiers had disobeyed orders, some point of honour could still be appealed to. Pompey lay on the ground in the camp gate, daring the troops to trample him, and Germanicus brought two legions to their

---

[63] Tac. *Ann.* 1. 23.

[64] Jos. *BJ* 3. 102–3; Tac. *Ann.* 1. 26, 'verbera et necem cunctis permitti'. Cf. J. B. Campbell (1984), 303–14.

[65] Tac. *Ann.* 1. 28, 'amor obsequii'; *Hist.* 2. 19, 'parendi amor'; cf. *Ann.* 1. 19.

[66] Tac. *Ann.* 1. 17 vs. *HA Aur.* 7. 8, 'alter alteri quasi miles, nemo quasi servus obsequatur' (fiction).

[67] Tac. *Ann.* 1. 35, 'ubi veteris disciplinae decus'; 1. 43, 'pudor et gloria intrat'.

[68] Tac. *Hist.* 4. 72, 'conscientia flagitii ... pudor ac dedecus obstupefecerat'. Cf. 4. 62.

[69] Caes. *BC* 2. 31, 'pudore aut metu'; cf. Sall. *Jug.* 100. 5.

[70] Tac. *Ann.* 1. 39, *dedecor*; 1. 48, *infamia*; *Hist.* 1. 30, *fama*; 4. 58, inspires *pudor*, 59.

senses by sending his wife and child out of their camp, and into the care of Gauls.[71] Also to be understood as attempts to shame are the acts of officers who call upon their soldiers to kill them, or threaten to commit suicide standing before their assembled troops.[72] Even troops who had mutinied might shy from the disgrace of their commander's killing himself before them.

Similarly, Roman soldiers' famous steadiness in battle was a result both of the ferocious punishments that unsteadiness elicited and of their profound emotional investment in the standards of conduct that those punishments enforced. At a bad moment in the siege of Jerusalem, with Romans fleeing to their camps, the Jews came upon the camp sentries. 'There is a unit ... stationed in front of the camp, and it is the terrible law of the Romans that whoever of that unit should withdraw for any reason dies. They stood fast, preferring a brave death to one from punishment. And many of those fleeing, ashamed at their plight, turned back.'[73] After a disastrous incident of insubordination by his troops, Josephus has Titus call 'fighting without commanders the greatest shame of all'. After all, 'Among the Romans, even victory—without the word of command—is a disgrace.'[74] Soldiers are ashamed to act without proper commanders. After its defection to the Gauls in AD 70, the Sixteenth Legion was ordered on the road by its new masters. Contemplating this, 'the better part were struck by shame and disgrace. What kind of march would this be? Who would be the leader on the road?' In fact the leader was 'Claudius Sanctus, horrible to look upon with an eye gouged out, and even more feeble in spirit'. For that reason and others 'open country and daylight uncovered their ignominy'.[75] Just as with the exquisite cadences, the spit and polish, of the British Guards Division, so the discipline of the Roman army was only in part imposed on the soldiers from without. It was also something they believed in, and enforced upon themselves and each other, with the honour and shame characteristic of Graeco-Roman society as a whole.

The Guards regiments' pride in their turnout (of old they even washed their coal, men said) is redoubled by their sense of rivalry with the other Guards regiments, and a horror of being compared unfavourably to the

---

[71] Pompey, Plut. *Pomp.* 3. 3, effective from αἰδώς. Germanicus, Tac. *Ann.* 1. 40–4, *pudor* (41).

[72] Demand killing, Tac. *Ann.* 1. 18; Dio 68. 3. 3. Threaten suicide, Tac. *Ann.* 1. 35; *Hist.* 3. 10.

[73] Jos. *BJ* 5. 483, αἰδούμενοι; holding ground from shame, cf. 3. 207, 6. 20, 6. 160.

[74] Ibid. 122, τὸ πάντων αἴσχιστον; 5. 125, δίχα παραγγέλματος ἀδοξεῖται.

[75] Tac. *Hist.* 4. 62, 'melior pars rubore et infamia'; 'detexit ignominiam campus et dies'; cf. 4. 58 for Vocula's attempt to inspire shame on this ground.

lesser regiments of the British army. This sense of rivalry between formations was also extremely strong in the Roman imperial army. While
brawls between privates sparked by regimental rivalry and abetted by
beer are by no means unknown in the contemporary British army (and
often winked at by their superiors, for both aggressiveness and regimental pride are held essential to their fighting quality), such quarrels in the
Roman army could break into pitched battles, and play a role in civil war.

In AD 69 a friendly wrestling match between a Gallic auxiliary and a
trooper of the Fifth Legion turned into a massacre when the victorious
Gaul mocked his fallen foe, and the enraged legionaries slew two cohorts
of Gauls.[76] Bad blood continued thereafter, and there was more fighting.[77] At the same time, Vitellius, whose army this was, dismissed his élite
Batavian auxiliary cohorts to Germany because they vaunted themselves
to such an extent over the legionaries that fighting had to be quelled
repeatedly.[78] These picked troops arrived home in time to participate in
their countrymen's great revolt against the Romans. During a riot under
Commodus the Urban Cohorts were delighted to take the side of the people against the guard cavalry, whom they hated.[79] Rivalry was especially
intense between legions. During a mutiny, three legions agreed in principle to combine, but pride prevented the soldiers of any of them from sub-
merging their unit in another, so they planted all their standards in a
mass.[80] One of the reasons why his Eastern troops were so eager to follow
Vespasian into revolt was that visiting soldiers from units in Vitellius'
army, despite their wild appearance and savage accents, ridiculed them as
their inferiors.[81]

Of the British ranker of his day, Garnet Wolseley (1833–1913), the very
model for the Modern Major-General, wrote breathlessly, 'What can be
finer than his love of regiment, his devotion to its reputation, and his
determination to protect its honour! To him the "The Regiment" is
mother, sister, and mistress. That its fame may live and flourish he is prepared to risk all and to die without a murmur.'[82] No doubt Kipling's
ironic soldiers would have had a thing or two to say about that; but the
regiment was, and remains, a strong focus of loyalty, and Wolseley's definition of that loyalty in terms of honour would have struck a chord in a
Roman camp. To Roman eyes too the rivalry between units was a rivalry
over honour.[83] Military units, like soldiers or cities, were entities with

---

[76] Tac. *Hist.* 2. 68.   [77] Ibid. 2. 88.
[78] Ibid. 1. 64, 2. 27, 66, 69.   [79] Herod. 1. 12. 9.
[80] Tac. *Ann.* 1. 18; cf. 1. 23, 28.   [81] Tac. *Hist.* 2. 74.
[82] Wolseley (1903), ii. 375–6.
[83] Cf. Amm. Marc. 29. 6. 13, 'de honore certabant et dignitate'.

honour. Thus the 'honour of the praetorian cohorts' might be cried up in a shouting match between the soldiers of Otho and Vitellius.[84] But with Vitellius' victory, that honour was impugned, for he allowed any soldier who desired—not just picked men—to enrol in the cohorts at Rome, thus 'convulsing the honour of the camp'.[85] At a vital moment in the siege of Jerusalem the Roman engines were saved from the flames by the stout resistance of an auxiliary unit from Alexandria, 'acting more bravely than their reputation, for they surpassed more distinguished units in that battle'.[86] Naturally, glorious success in war contributed to unit honour.[87] Just as for men, so battle was an arena for rivalry for honour among units.[88] The glorious deeds of another army inspired envy, and a lust to emulate.[89]

Leaders relied upon the pride soldiers had in the honour of their units. As dawn broke over the terrible night battle between the Flavian and Vitellian armies outside Cremona, Vespasian's general Antonius Primus, as Tacitus tells it, addressed his soldiers.

When Antonius could recognize and be recognized by his troops, he stirred them up, some by shame and insults, many by praise and exhortation, all by hope and promises. Why had they taken up arms again? He asked the Pannonian legions: it was on this field that they might cleanse the mark of their previous disgrace; where they could regain their glory. . . . He said much to the soldiers of the Third Legion, calling to mind their deeds old and new, their defeats of the Parthians under Mark Antony's command, the Armenians under Corbulo, and recently the Sarmatians. Then, angrily, to the praetorians, 'If you are defeated now, peasants, what other commander, what other camp will accept you? There are your standards and arms, and death to the defeated! For disgrace you have already drained to the lees!'[90]

And when the same general came to attack the enemy camp outside Cremona, he distributed the gates and walls among the legions to assail, 'that the division of labour might distinguish the brave from the craven, and that the troops might be set afire by a rivalry for glory'.[91]

---

[84] Tac. *Hist.* 2. 21, *decus.*   [85] Ibid. 2. 94, 'convulsum castrorum decus'.

[86] Jos. *BJ* 5. 287, παρὰ τὴν σφετέραν ὑπόληψιν ἀνδρισάμενοι· καὶ γὰρ τῶν ἐνδοξοτέρων διήνεγκαν; cf. 3. 65; Tac. *Hist.* 2. 32, 43, 3. 1.

[87] Tac. *Hist.* 2. 11; Jos. *BJ* 5. 41, ἐπίσημον δι' ἀνδρείαν.

[88] Tac. *Agric.* 26. 2, 'de gloria certabant'; Hirt. *BG* 8. 19.

[89] Tac. *Hist.* 2. 4; cf. Dio 62. 10. 2.

[90] Tac. *Hist.* 3. 24, 'alios pudore et probris, multos laude et hortatu . . . accendens . . . illos esse campos, in quibus abolere labem prioris ignominiae, ubi reciperare gloriam possent. . . . nam ignominiam consumpsistis'. Cf. 5. 16.

[91] Ibid. 3. 27, 'contentione decoris accenderentur'. Cf. Jos. *BJ* 5. 502; *ILS* 5795.

Just as with regiments of the British army, so the pride of units was invested particularly in their standards. Battle honours were arranged upon their shafts like the figures on a totem-pole.[92] When the Twenty-first Legion, 'distinguished with an ancient glory', lost its eagle to the parvenu First *Adiutrix* at Bedriacum, fired by 'shame and anger', it counter-attacked with great bravery and drove back its enemies.[93] Again, officers relied upon this. When an army turned to flight, if its general could get the standard-bearers to turn and face the enemy, the rest of the soldiers, ashamed by his reproaches, might turn as well.[94] A panicked standard-bearer was cut down by his general, who seized the standard and charged the foe; his cavalry, struck by shame, followed him, and the engagement was won.[95] In short, as Wolseley wrote, 'It is this intense feeling of regimental rivalry that is the life-blood of our old, historic army, and makes it what it is in action.'[96]

HONOUR AND THE POLITICAL LOYALTY OF SOLDIERS

Had the Roman army merely attended to its military business— protected the borders, trounced barbarians, guarded the emperor, kept the peace, assisted the governors—it would be enough to point out the role of honour and shame in military ferocity and discipline. But the role the Roman army played in imperial politics draws attention to the question of soldiers' political loyalty as well. Bonds of loyalty and discipline might well cross: soldiers supported different emperors from their officers, and imprisoned or killed their officers accordingly.[97] It was not enough, therefore, for emperors, or would-be emperors, to rely solely upon the allegiance of aristocratic officers, and their soldiers' obedience to them. So far as the circumstances of emperors and usurpers allowed, they were concerned with the personal loyalty of each and every soldier in the army. That personal loyalty could be extreme, as the popular Otho found after the defeat of his army at Bedriacum. His soldiers begged him to fight on. When he chose instead to halt the ravages of civil war by suicide, many of them committed suicide as well, 'not from fear, but out of competition for honour and love of the emperor'.[98]

---

[92] Maxfield (1981), 219.

[93] Tac. *Hist.* 2. 43, 'vetere gloria insignis', with Plut. *Otho* 12. 4, ὑπὸ αἰσχύνης καὶ ὀργῆς ἐμπεσόντες.

[94] Dio 74(75L). 6. 6, αἰσχυνθέντες; cf. Caes. *BG* 4. 25.

[95] Tac. *Hist.* 3. 17, *pudor.*   [96] Wolseley (1903), i. 309.

[97] Tac. *Hist.* 3. 13–14, 4. 27; Dio 78(79L). 32. 4.

[98] Tac. *Hist.* 2. 49, 'neque ob metum, sed aemulatione decoris et caritate principis'.

A first basis of the soldiers' loyalty was the religious strength of the military oath: upon joining the army, a soldier swore an oath to obey and protect the emperor. Once a year, on the anniversary of the emperor's accession, that oath was renewed. During a rebellion, a usurper likewise administered an oath to his soldiers. Modern cynicism easily discounts the oath as a basis of fidelity—certainly it was broken frequently enough—but to do so is wrong.[99] Herodian, in a speech that he puts in the mouth of Pupienus, referred to this oath as the awful secret of the Roman empire, while Cassius Dio argued that Tiberius was worried about the loyalty of the German and Pannonian legions, but not that of the troops in Italy, having bound the latter with oaths.[100] Tacitus referred to the city soldiery as 'imbued of old by the oath to the Caesars, and led to desert Nero more by a clever manœuvre than by their own nature'.[101] The oath was used into the Byzantine period, its longevity excellent proof of a belief in its efficacy. Nor, in fact, is the strength of a religious scruple surprising. The Roman army was a highly sacralized community. The standards, already touched upon as the focus of unit pride, were held to be sacred.[102] There was a cult of discipline to which dedications were made.[103] Military units, camps, clubs, buildings, even the oath itself had a *genius* which was worshipped by soldiers.[104]

Next there was the loyalty that the strong military sense of community inspired. Emperors worked assiduously to cultivate this allegiance. They appeared in uniform, shared the soldiers' toils with them when they went on campaign (like other good officers), and addressed their troops as *commilitones*, 'my fellow soldiers'.[105] 'What are you doing, my fellow soldiers? I am yours and you are mine,' some reported Galba to have cried before his murder, grasping for what was expected to be a strong claim to fealty.[106] To the troops of the late Marcus Aurelius, Commodus said that

he loved us all equally; he used to greet me as 'fellow-soldier' rather than son. . . . When I was a small child he entrusted me to your loyalty; and on this account I

---

[99] J. B. Campbell (1984: 19–32) on the oath, its religious strength, and arguing its greater historical significance than civilian loyalty oaths.

[100] Herod. 8. 7. 4 and Dio 57. 3. 2.

[101] Tac. *Hist.* 1. 5, 'longo Caesarum sacramento imbutus'.

[102] Helgeland (1978), 1473–8.   [103] E. Birley (1978), 1513–15.

[104] Speidel (1978*b*), *genius sacramenti*, 1547–8.

[105] J. B. Campbell (1984), 32–59. But Augustus avoids *commilitones* as *ambitiosius*, and thus damaging to his *maiestas*, Suet. *Aug.* 25. 1. Uniform, Alföldi (1970 (1934–5)), 161–86, and esp. Dio 60. 17. 9; 78(79L). 3. 2, Caracalla had clothes that looked like armour for the Eastern heat, which discouraged assassination as well.

[106] Suet. *Galba* 20. 1; cf. Dio 77(78L). 3. 1–2.

trust I may easily gain your goodwill, owed me as a foster-child by the elder of you, by my contemporaries as your schoolfellows in arms.[107]

Soldiers had special loyalty to cadets of the imperial family who had been brought up in the camps, and to men who had been their own, successful, officers.[108] If there was fighting to be done, as so often in the third century, they wanted a good soldier as emperor, thus their choice of Maximinus, 'a brave and austere fellow soldier, a man who lived his life among weapons and warlike deeds', to replace the timid and cowardly Severus Alexander.[109] But when he failed in war, he was discarded in his turn.[110]

Soldiers also felt a strong dynastic loyalty, which might be appealed to in time of crisis. Tacitus has Germanicus allude to Julius Caesar and Augustus in a speech to mutinous soldiers. 'I am not yet like them,' he says, 'but I rise from their line.' After Germanicus' death, Piso (much suspected) is advised that he can expect little loyalty from the troops, in the face of 'their deep-seated love of the Caesars'.[111] That love was enough to elevate Claudius to the purple at the praetorians' hands.[112] Perhaps the most striking illustration of this dynastic sentiment was emperors' invention of blood relationships to previous emperors who had been popular with the army. Septimius Severus solemnly proclaimed himself the son of Marcus Aurelius; Elagabalus was claimed to be the son of Caracalla, in order to appeal to the soldiers.[113] These two stood at the beginning of a long tradition.

Finally, of course, there was pay to keep the soldiers loyal.[114] Tacitus, in his brief description of the ingredients of the Augustan peace, pointed to material benefits as essential to control of the army.[115] Certainly soldiers were greedy, and that greed could be converted into obedience.[116] One simply promised them money if they did what one wanted: Otho, for example, promised some praetorians fifty thousand sesterces apiece for their help against Galba.[117] Herodian describes how soldiers backing

---

[107] Herod. 1. 5. 3–4.

[108] Cadets, cf. Herod. 6. 9. 3; Suet. *Gaius* 9. Officers, Tac. *Hist.* 3. 44; Herod. 2. 9. 9.

[109] Herod. 6. 9. 5; cf. 6. 8. 4; in contrast to Alexander, Herod. 6. 6–8.

[110] Herod. 8. 5. 2–3, 8–9.

[111] Tac. *Ann.* 1. 42 and 2. 76. Cf. *Hist.* 3. 38; Amm. Marc. 26. 7. 10, 16.

[112] Dio 60. 1. 3 and Jos. *AJ* 19. 217–23.

[113] Severus, A. Birley (1972), 184; Elagabalus, Herod. 5. 3. 10, 5. 4. 2–3; *HA Macr.* 9. 4; cf. 3. 9 (with much nonsense).

[114] J. B. Campbell (1984), 157–98.   [115] Tac. *Ann.* 1. 2.

[116] Greed, a topos, Tac. *Ann.* 1. 16; Herod. 2. 6. 14, 5. 8. 3; *HA Carac.* 2. 8.

[117] Suet. *Otho* 5. 2; cf. Plut. *Galba* 24. 1.

Elagabalus waved their purses—bulging with Julia Maesa's money—at the ramparts of a camp loyal to Macrinus, to demonstrate the advantages of defection.[118] Suetonius thought that he knew the first time an emperor had stooped to such tactics: when Claudius was raised to the purple by the praetorians, he promised them each fifteen thousand sesterces.[119] Legionaries' yearly pay was modest, but they received an enormous bonus—by the end of Augustus' reign worth thirteen years' salary—upon retirement.[120] Politically, this was wise, because this bonus was hostage to soldiers' continued good conduct and loyalty. During the mutiny of AD 14, Tacitus has a centurion point this out to the rebellious troops. 'Will Percennius and Vibulenus give their wages to the soldiers, and give lands to those who have retired?' he asked, naming two influential soldiers among the mutineers.[121]

Discipline, religion, personal and dynastic loyalty, and greed are more than ample to explain soldiers' allegiance. But there is more to their loyalty as well: a martyr act offers a series of glimpses into less familiar territory. Dasius, the soldier, was a Christian. In the account of his martyrdom his commander strives to persuade him to sacrifice: 'Venerate the images of our lords the emperors, who give us peace, our supplies, and each day lay plans for our every advantage.' To this the soldier replies, 'I have the gift of the Heavenly emperor; it is by *his* favour that I am supported; I am wealthy from his ineffable generosity.'[122] The commander adduces reciprocal obligations. Since the soldier receives so much from the emperors, he must honour them in return. Dasius neatly parries by adducing his reciprocal obligations to God. Even by the standards of martyr acts this one is bad testimony, but the existence of a strong sense of reciprocal obligation within the army, and between soldiers and the emperor in particular, is easily paralleled.

Debts of favours extended horizontally among approximate equals in rank, a phenomenon observable when one centurion writes to another to get a tenant out of a bothersome civic burden, and acknowledges the favour-debt he thereby owes for the service; or when a soldier whose life was saved in battle confers the civic crown upon his saviour, revering him as a parent for the rest of his days for having performed a parent's

---

[118] Herod. 5. 4. 2–3 with 5. 3. 11. Cf. p. 256 below for Cassius Dio's (different) account of this incident.

[119] Suet. *Claud.* 10. 4. [120] J. B. Campbell (1984), 161–2.

[121] Tac. *Ann.* 1. 28. Such punishments, Suet. *Aug.* 24. 2; Herod. 2. 13 with Dio 74(75L). 1. 1–2; in the law, J. B. Campbell (1984), 310–11.

[122] Musurillo (1972), 21. 7, χάριτι διαιτῶμαι.

benefaction—giving life.[123] Debts of favours also extended vertically over the huge social gulfs that separated commanders from soldiers. A veteran of Augustus', the story goes, called upon the emperor to represent him in court. Pleading business, the emperor sent a friend in his place, to which the old soldier replied, 'Whenever you needed help, I didn't send someone else in my place, but personally faced dangers everywhere for you.' This brought the emperor clattering to the soldier's defence—he was obligated.[124] Inscriptions put up by soldiers expressed their indebtedness to the officer or governor who promoted them or granted them some other boon, and relations of patronage within the army were openly boasted about.[125]

The significance of this is that the historians often ground soldiers' political loyalty—both to emperors and usurpers—in their sense of gratitude. 'Why do you do this, fellow soldiers? Why do you fight against your benefactor's son?' cried military partisans, displaying Elagabalus, Caracalla's alleged son, to soldiers on the other side during an early third-century civil war—and successfully too, for the opposition dissolved.[126] How convenient for Macrinus, planning the murder of Caracalla, that he had laid a humbly born but stout centurion under an obligation to him. The centurion wielded the knife.[127] Gratitude was bound up with soldiers' financial emoluments as well. Herodian reports that Didius Julianus, hearing of the approach of Severus' army, made a distribution of money to his soldiers; but since he had earlier promised money that he had not paid, 'they took the large sum, but felt no feeling of obligation. They thought he was paying a debt, rather than giving a present.'[128] Didius found himself on the wrong side of reciprocity, his donative of no use. But his purpose, in Herodian's eyes, reveals part of the purpose of donatives—the sums of money given to the troops on imperial accessions, adoptions, their anniversaries, imperial birthdays, and the like.[129]

[123] Centurions, *P.Oxy.* 1424; cf. Bowman and Thomas (1983), no. 22. *Corona civica*, Maxfield (1981: 70–4), still awarded in the traditional manner in the 1st cent. AD; and see esp. Cic. *Planc.* 72 for the obligation. Cf. Caes. *BC* 1. 74.

[124] Dio 55. 4. 2. Cf. Tac. *Ann.* 1. 28, 2. 13; *Hist.* 2. 37; Jos. *BJ* 7. 6; Dio 77(78L). 13. 6.

[125] *AE* 1917–18. 74–5; 76, 'patrono inconparabili promotus ab eo'; *ILS* 2609, 'gratias agimus omnes commilitones'; EJ 270. Cf. p. 159 above for the obligation promotion imposes. Significant also is the military posting of *beneficiarius*, 'he who has received a *beneficium*', see Breeze (1974).

[126] Dio 78(79L). 32. 3 (but Herodian's version is different, above, n. 118). Cf. Caes. *BC* 3. 90; Tac. *Ann.* 1. 42; Suet. *Galba* 20. 1.

[127] Herod. 4. 13. 2–5. Cf. Suet. *Otho* 4. 2.

[128] Herod. 2. 11. 8, χάριν οὐκ ᾔδεσαν; cf. Plut. *Galba* 8. 1.

[129] Donatives and their occasions, J. B. Campbell (1984), 186–98; late empire, Bastien (1988).

They were not only bribes—although Julianus had recently bought the empire at auction—or rewards; they were also intended to inspire gratitude. Constantius chose for a mission of the greatest possible sensitivity—the arrest of the Caesar Gallus, who was thought to be on the verge of rebellion—soldiers 'obligated to him by his favours to them . . . and who he was certain could not be turned aside by bribes or any feeling of pity'.[130] Old rewards, in other words, were expected to be a solid defence against new rewards: soldiers would feel under an obligation, and thus obey, just as aristocrats did. It was not just a question of acquiring as much money as possible; it was a matter of honour.

The appeal to Dasius' reciprocal obligations having failed, his commander changed tack. 'Supplicate, O Dasius, the sacred images of our emperors: even the barbarian tribes revere and are subject to them.' 'I attend to no one but the undefiled and eternal God.' 'You forget, Dasius, that every man is subject to the emperor's decree and the imperial laws.' And the future saint replies, 'Do you whatever is enjoined upon you by the impious and defiled emperors.'[131] Thus the conventional double duty to the emperor, to obey and to revere, arises and is dismissed. The double duty appears elsewhere in a military context as well, and not only towards emperors. 'The generals had no prestige, the soldiers no respect; there was neither command nor obedience'—thus Pliny the Younger on the decayed state of military discipline under Domitian.[132] Just as in a civilian context, the sense of shame enforced this respect. 'Shame before and reverence for their commander stayed them,' wrote Tacitus of a small force under Vitellius' general Fabius Valens, 'but these chains do not last long among men terrified of danger and mindless of disgrace.'[133]

Herodian at least thought that this reverence had political significance. In the speech he has Septimius Severus give to his soldiers on the occasion of his revolt, reverence keeps company with the military oath as a part of loyalty. 'Your faithfulness, and your worshipful disposition towards the gods to whom you swore, and your honour for the emperors, whom you revere, you have already shown.'[134] Tacitus might well

---

[130] Quoted, Amm. Marc. 14. 11. 19, 'milites . . . quos beneficiis suis oppigneratos elegerat imperator'. Cf. Cic. *ad Fam.* 10. 24. 2.

[131] Musurillo (1972), 21. 8–9, καὶ αὐτὰ τὰ βάρβαρα ἔθνη σέβονται καὶ δουλεύουσιν.

[132] Pliny, *Ep.* 8. 14. 7, 'ducibus auctoritas nulla, nulla militibus verecundia, nusquam imperium nusquam obsequium'. Cf. Herod. 3. 8. 5 and 8. 7. 5 for the pairing of εὐταξία, 'discipline', and αἰδώς, 'reverence'; also Jos. *BJ* 6. 263.

[133] Tac. *Hist.* 3. 41, 'pudor . . . et praesentis ducis reverentia morabatur, haud diuturna vincla apud pavidos periculorum et dedecoris securos'.

[134] Herod. 2. 10. 2, τὸ πιστὸν ὑμῶν καὶ πρός τε θεοὺς σεβάσμιον, οὓς ὤμνυτε, πρός τε βασιλέας τίμιον, οὓς αἰδεῖσθε, δεδηλώκατε.

have agreed with Herodian. In a celebrated passage, he imagines the difference of opinion that existed in Rome over how to deal with the great legionary mutinies of AD 14. Tiberius had sent Germanicus and Drusus to deal with the situation. Critics complained that

the soldiers could not be put down by the not yet full-grown *auctoritas* of two youths. Tiberius should have gone himself and applied the imperial *maiestas*. They would have yielded when they saw an emperor, great in experience, and master of punishments and rewards. . . . [But Tiberius considered that] the German army was stronger, the Pannonian closer, the one supported by the resources of the Gauls, the other threatening Italy. Which first, then? And suppose those postponed took fire at the insult? But through his sons he could approach both at once, while keeping his *maiestas* safe, reverence for which was always greater at a distance. . . . Those resisting Germanicus or Drusus he could mollify or break himself, but what other recourse would there be if the emperor was scorned?[135]

How exactly Tacitus expected the imperial *maiestas* to work, beyond rewards and punishments, is not clear. But evidently soldiers' reverence for it, greater at a distance and however fragile, plays a role in their loyalty.

Finally Dasius' commander played his trump. 'You have some time, if you would like to consider how you might be able to live among us—with distinction.' 'I spit on and detest those emperors of yours and their honours.'[136] The legate extends the lure of honour, it is refused, and Dasius goes to his martyrdom, glorious in Christian eyes. Again, parallels are numerous. Soldiers were not only concerned about each others' good opinion, they were devoted to earning that of their superiors, and especially that of the emperor. The hero of the Batavian shore, whose epitaph was offered above, wanted eternity to know and admire the fact that he swam the Danube under Hadrian's eye; the mighty cavalryman before Jerusalem did not dangle his captive before his comrades, but before Titus, his general, who praised him. An engineer of the Third Legion set down in stone for posterity the correspondence of his superiors about his

---

[135] Tac. *Ann.* 1. 46–7, 'dissideat interim miles neque duorum adulescentium nondum adulta auctoritate comprimi queat. ire ipsum et opponere maiestatem imperatoriam debuisse cessuris ubi principem longa experientia eundemque severitatis et munificentiae summum vidissent. . . . ac ne postpositi contumelia incenderentur. at per filios pariter adiri maiestate salva, cui maior e longinquo reverentia. . . . resistentisque Germanico aut Druso posse a se mitigari vel infringi: quod aliud subsidium si imperatorem sprevissent?' Cf. 1. 42; *Hist.* 1. 19; and for holding imperial *auctoritas* in reserve, *Hist.* 1. 29.

[136] Musurillo (1972), 21. 10, ὅπως δυνηθείης ζῆν μεθ' ἡμῶν ἐν δόξῃ. . . . τῶν βασιλέων σου καὶ τῆς δόξης αὐτῶν καταπτύω καὶ βδελύσσομαι.

excellent work.[137] On 1 July AD 128, Hadrian watched manœuvres of that same legion in its camp at Lambaesis in North Africa. There, under the blazing sun, he addressed to each unit of the legion and their attached auxiliaries a commentary on how they had done:

To the cavalry of the Sixth Cohort of Commagenians: it is difficult for the cohorts' cavalry to give satisfaction by themselves; it is even more difficult for them not to give dissatisfaction after the manœuvres of the auxiliary cavalry: they [the auxiliaries] cover more ground, have more javelin-throwers, they wheel to the right in close array, they perform the Cantabrian manœuvre in tight formation . . . None the less, you made us feel less oppressed by the heat by doing what needed to be done energetically.[138]

This speech survives because this passage and others (rather more effusive) about the performance of units and their officers, along with further remarks later in the month about other units, were proudly inscribed on a column-base at the legionary camp. Such commentary was referred to by Cassius Dio in his narrative as 'honouring' the soldiers, and it is clear that the soldiers and their officers wanted everyone to know that they had been thus honoured.[139] As Wolseley wrote of one of the men who commanded him when he was a young officer, 'I was pleased beyond measure with the kind expressions he used towards me—what children we all are, and how easily tickled by a great man's praise! What a lever it is for him to work with who knows how to use it deftly!'[140]

In battle, soldiers fought better under the eyes of their generals and emperors.[141] At a crucial juncture in the siege of Jerusalem, Titus' staff forbade him to descend from his vantage point and join the fighting: it was too important to the morale of the men that he be seen watching them, that he serve as agonothete, president of the games.[142] The general's eye inspired the troops with *philotimia*, competition for honour.[143] The general's eye also inspired hope of decorations for bravery, financial rewards, and promotion. After a battle, the general paraded his army, and these were awarded.[144] Thus it was a wise innovation of one of Domitian's generals to have the names of soldiers and their centurions written on their shields, so that the identities of those fighting well or ill could be known; a much safer method than that of Constantius' soldiers

---

[137] *ILS* 5795. Cf. Caes. *BG* 1. 40–1; Pliny, *Paneg.* 15. 5.   [138] Small. *Nerva* 328.
[139] Dio 69. 9. 3, ἐτίμα, with *HA Hadr.* 10. 2. Cf. Suet. *Galba* 6. 3.
[140] Wolseley (1903), i. 308.   [141] MacMullen (1984b), 451.
[142] Jos. *BJ* 6. 132–5, 142, 146.   [143] Plut. *Otho* 10. 1; cf. Jos. *BJ* 5. 310–11.
[144] Jos. *BJ* 7. 5–15 with Maxfield (1981), 116.

later, who fought without their helmets so that their faces could be seen.[145]

It is striking how soldiers' concern for the praise of their superiors shines through all military awards. Soldiers' gravestones regularly name the emperor who gave a decoration. Thus, for example, the gravestone of M. Blossius Pudens, centurion of the Fifth Legion, notes that he was 'decorated with military decorations by the emperor Vespasian Augustus'.[146] The Roman military decorations of the empire were not merely impersonal testimonies to bravery, a claim to the esteem of one's comrades; rather, they signalled also that the emperor had himself honoured the hero.[147] When it is recorded of another soldier that he was 'honoured by the divine . . . Antoninus with seventy-five thousand sesterces and a grade of promotion on account of the ardour of his courage against the enemies', it seems that promotion and cash grants could be viewed in the same personal, honorific light.[148] Indeed, the emperor who granted a soldier his promotion is sometimes mentioned on the soldier's tombstone just as was the emperor conferring a decoration.[149] And if a soldier was chosen by a high official to assist him, his gravestone might proudly name the officer in question. Luccius Sabinus, whom we met above, especially wanted the reader of his gravestone to learn that Valerius Asiaticus, twice consul in the early second century, chose, out of all the soldiers in the Urban Cohorts, Luccius as his *beneficiarius*.[150] Similarly, the 'honourable' aspect of an honourable discharge comes to life when we consider that the emperor who discharged the soldier was sometimes named, and that a soldier could be celebrated as a 'veteran honoured with retirement benefits'.[151] The civilian aristocracy's fastidiousness at being seen to serve for pay comes at once to mind as an explanation for such phrases, but it was hardly decisive. This was a paid, professional army. There was no shame in obedience, no shame in taking money.

Over some honours to soldiers the emperors exercised that jealous monopoly which signals that they were protecting something they deemed an important part of their power. When Junius Gallio proposed

---

[145] Names, Dio 67. 10. 1; cf. Veg. *Mil.* 2. 18. Without helmets, Amm. Marc. 20. 11. 12.

[146] *ILS* 2641.

[147] The usual Latin formula *donatus donis* is translated into Greek with forms of τιμάω: *IGR* i. 824, iii. 230, 551; and in Latin *honoratus* (*ILS* 2696) is sometimes seen. For the personal quality of decorations, cf. J. B. Campbell (1984), 200.

[148] *ILS* 7178, *honoratus*. Cf. Dio 58. 18. 2; Zos. 4. 40. 2.

[149] Honorific quality of promotions, *AE* 1970. 583 = Speidel (1970); *ILS* 2080, 2213, 2666.

[150] Above, n. 54. Cf. *ILS* 2118, 2404, 9089.

[151] *Honesta missio*, emperor named, e.g. *ILS* 2180–1, 2313. *Veteranus commodis honoratus*, *AE* 1910. 155, with Speidel (1983*b*).

that the veterans of the praetorian guard be permitted to sit among the *equites* at the theatre, he was savagely rebuked by Tiberius, and consequently ejected from the senate, exiled, and imprisoned.[152] Under the empire the emperor and his relations came to monopolize the giving of military decorations, which were most generously awarded in campaigns in which the emperor himself participated.[153] They created a personal bond, as between Tiberius and his veterans: 'Is that you we see, *imperator*?' 'I served with you in Armenia, *imperator*.' 'I in Raetia.' 'I was decorated by you in Vindelicia.' 'I in Pannonia.' 'I in Germany.'[154] It was wholly appropriate to cast decorations onto the funeral pyre of the emperor who granted them, an honour in return.[155] The bond had political significance; it could not be allowed to develop between the soldiers and anyone else.

This imperial anxiety leads us to look for occasions when the conferment of honour on soldiers played its role in politics. It is striking that when Otho was rushed to the praetorian camp during Galba's last hours he 'stretched out a hand in affection to the common soldier, threw kisses, and [in Tacitus' opinion] acted the slave in every respect to become the master'. Kisses, of course, are an honour: this is how Otho spent those crucial moments—not, for example, handing out the million sesterces with which he had equipped himself a few days before.[156] And if Otho's conduct is kept in mind, then that of the high-born fourth-century usurper Procopius, a relation of the late emperor Julian's, makes sense as well. Faced with some units of his rival Valens' army, he approached the enemy's bristling spears alone and picked out a soldier he recognized (or pretended to), one Vitalianus. He greeted him in a friendly way, took him by the hand, and kissed him. Both armies were stunned. Then a few observations on the loyalty oath and a comparison of Valens' base antecedents with his own quickly brought Valens' force over to his side.[157] Perhaps Procopius took a leaf out of Julian's book. When Constantius sent for some of his Western troops for an Eastern war, Julian met the unwilling soldiers outside Paris—an honour—praised those he knew, and, 'in order to treat with greater honour those about to

---

[152] Tac. *Ann.* 6. 3; Dio 58. 18. 3–4. Cf. *HA Hadr.* 23. 8.

[153] Maxfield (1981), 113, 116–17 (with exceptions); J. B. Campbell (1984), 199–202. Suet. *Aug.* 25. 3 notes that Augustus granted them 'sine ambitione ac saepe etiam caligatis', implying that political advantage often played a role in their granting to officers.

[154] Vel. Pat. 2. 104. 4.   [155] Dio 56. 42. 2.

[156] Tac. *Hist.* 1. 36, 'nec deerat Otho protendens manus adorare vulgum, iacere oscula et omnia serviliter pro dominatione'. Cf. Suet. *Vit.* 7. 3. HS 1,000,000, Suet. *Otho* 5. 2.

[157] Amm. Marc. 26. 7. 15–17.

go far away', had their officers to dinner. Before dawn Julian awoke to the cries of the soldiers acclaiming him emperor—to his amazement and alarm, at least according to the official version.[158] In an earlier day even addressing soldiers by name—part of the textbook condescension of the 'good officer' archetype—could take on a dark political significance, as a sinister play for allegiance.[159] It was best, in troubled times, to announce the adoption of an imperial heir to the praetorian guard rather than the senate, for the honour might confirm their loyalty.[160] One builds up a faction among soldiers, in short, 'with gifts and all kinds of honours'.[161]

Emperors also built loyalty and encouraged excellence by honouring soldiers as units. The Fourteenth Legion 'had particular fame, from having suppressed the rebellion of Britain; and Nero added to its prestige by singling its men out as his best.' Thus it was especially loyal to Nero, and that loyalty was inherited by Otho.[162] Just as emperors profited cheaply from the rivalries of cities by granting and confiscating civic titles, so the emperor granted part of his own name to units that had done well, in the same way as a British regiment might be invited to add 'The King's Own' to its name.[163] In the first and second centuries such grants were made to legions especially for political loyalty; that is, for loyalty in contests against usurpers rather than barbarians. Thus, after the suppression of the rebellion of Camillus Scribonianus, Claudius named the Seventh and Eleventh legions *Claudia Pia Fidelis* ('Claudian, loyal and true').[164] Legions and auxiliary formations in Lower Germany which did not join those in Upper Germany in Saturninus' revolt, but remained loyal to Domitian, became *Pia Fidelis Domitiana*.[165]

Besides imperial names, units could be granted decorations just like soldiers. Thus the heroic *Ala Siliana*, a cavalry unit, *bis torquata bis armil-*

[158] Amm. Marc. 20. 4. 12–14, 'utque honoratius . . . tractaret'. A conspiracy seems highly likely, Bowersock (1978), 46–54; but see also Matthews (1989), 98–9. Cf. Zos. 2. 47. 2 for dining officers; and for the custom of honorific reception of military units, 5. 7. 5.

[159] Archetype, Pliny, *Paneg.* 15. 5; *HA Sev. Alex.* 21. 7. As politics, Tac. *Ann.* 4. 2; *Hist.* 1. 23.

[160] Tac. *Hist.* 1. 17, 'honorificum id militibus fore'.

[161] Herod. 6. 8. 3, παντοδαπαῖς τιμαῖς ᾠκειώσατο.

[162] Tac. *Hist.* 2. 11, 'et praecipui fama quartadecumani, rebellione Britanniae compressa. addiderat gloriam Nero eligendo ut potissimos, unde longa illis erga Neronem fides et erecta in Othonem studia'. Cf. *Ann.* 1. 25.

[163] Maxfield (1981), 233–4; J. B. Campbell (1984), 90–3; cf. esp. 'Ala Aug(usta) o[b] virtut(em) appel(lata)', *RIB* 893. But sometimes such names signify no more than when the unit was raised, Holder (1980), 14–18.

[164] Dio 55. 23. 4, 60. 15. 4.

[165] Saturninus, Ritterling (1893); Holder (1980), 37–8. Also, for speculations about *cognomina* given for Batavian revolt, Holder (1980), 17, 33, 36, 39, 45; for a revolt between AD 185 and 187, Fitz (1983), 31; J. B. Campbell (1984), 90.

lata, was decorated with torques and arm-rings twice.[166] Units could also be given titles other than imperial names: 'strong', 'lucky', 'Mars' ', 'victor', 'immovable', 'unconquered', and 'swift', recapitulating many of the qualities honourable in the military context, all granted, no doubt, for heroism in war.[167] But other titles were granted for political loyalty: 'loyal and true', seen above, was widespread, also granted (for example) by Septimius Severus for support against Clodius Albinus; or 'sure and steadfast', granted for supporting Marcus Aurelius against Avidius Cassius; or 'loyal avenger', granted by Severus against Niger.[168]

By the early third century, in a process parallel to the inflation of city titles, the granting of imperial names to military units had run out of control. After a few years of an emperor's reign, the great majority of units possessed them. Severus Alexander elaborated the system by granting two different imperial epithets to units: a formation might be *Severiana*, or *Alexandriana*, or both.[169] Imperial names were becoming so common they were no longer a distinction. So it is hardly surprising that the army of the fourth century had an explicit system of precedence for military units, just as it had one for dignitaries: it shares the *Notitia Dignitatum*. The Western *Notitia* helpfully lists units of the field army under their regional commanders. As a consequence it is known that, in the Italian army, the Ferocious Moorish Horse outranked the Steadfast Junior Valentinian Horse, but were outranked by the Alan Companions. But what if the Ferocious should be transferred to Gaul? Then, another table informs us, among the cavalry they will outrank the Lucky Constantinian Horse, but be outranked by the Senior Honorian Horse.[170] No doubt

---

[166] *Ala Siliana*, *AE* 1930. 92. For these decorations, Holder (1980), 35–7; Maxfield (1981), 218–26. One-time block grants of citizenship were also given as a reward to auxiliary units, signified by the addition of *C(ivium) R(omanorum)* to the unit's titles, Holder (1980), 30–5; Maxfield (1981), 227–32; and the title might last a long time, although the citizenship was only conferred on members of the unit at granting.

[167] *Fortis*, *ILS* iii, p. 449; *felix*, pp. 449, 451, 454; *Martia*, p. 458; *victrix*, pp. 453, 458–60; *firma*, pp. 458, 463. For *invicta* and *velox*, Holder (1980), 39–40. In general, Maxfield (1981), 233.

[168] *Pia fidelis*, Ritterling (1924–5), 1314, cf. 1660, 1755; for auxiliary units, Holder (1980), 37–9 (perhaps not always given for political loyalty, *CIL* xvi. 160). Also, plain *fidelis*, Holder (1980), 40; *ILS* 1076; *fida*, *CIL* xvi. 43; plain *pia*, *ILS* iii, p. 452. *Certa constans*, Ritterling (1924–5), 1708; *pia vindex*, Ritterling (1924–5), 1312; *ILS* iii, pp. 443, 450.

[169] Fitz (1983), 11–26; for rate of granting, p. 12; for speculations on circumstances of granting, pp. 278–81; Severus Alexander, pp. 124–40. Commodus may have intended the same policy, Dio 72(73L). 15. 2.

[170] Comparing *Not. Dig.* Oc. 7. 163–5 (the *distributio numerorum*, or precedence list by location) with Oc. 6. 60–2 (precedence list of cavalry units in the West under the *magister equitum praesentalis*; there is a similar list for infantry). For this aspect of the *Notitia*, see esp. A. H. M. Jones (1964), 1418–19, 1421–3. Precedence surely existed in earlier centuries too. How else to organize a parade?

there were delightful anomalies and curiosities: in the British army regimental precedence is based on seniority of entrance onto the English establishment (seniority seems to have been important in the Roman system too), and thus the Life Guards come first, followed by the Blues and Royals. But as the result of some nineteenth-century sleight of hand, the Royal Horse Artillery rides first on parade when they are parading with their guns; otherwise they come third. As a reward for its heroism at Waterloo the Rifle Brigade (then the 95th Foot, with low rank, as its high number indicates) was taken off the order of precedence entirely, placed 'to the left of the line'. Thus while it might seem to a crass observer that the Royal Green Jackets (into which the Rifle Brigade has been amalgamated) always march last of the cavalry and infantry, they would insist that they are marching parallel to the other regiments, in a line all their own.[171]

We must imagine the emperor or his marshals similarly using the precedence system to honour units for bravery and political loyalty; or to punish them, humiliating them by demotion, for displaying the opposite qualities—just as a legion fighting the natives in Spain under Agrippa was once dishonoured for defeat by being deprived of its title 'Augustan'.[172] As Julian's dressing cowardly troops as women hints, in the army, just as in civilian life, punishing individuals and units had a large element of shame to it. Humiliating inadequate soldiers by feeding them on barley rather than wheat was an old custom, and Suetonius describes Augustus punishing negligent centurions 'with various ignominies', ordering them, for example, to stand all day before his tent holding clods of earth.[173] Building up a military faction might involve removing marks of disgrace from one's soldiers: such marks, whatever their nature, must have been very numerous.[174] But such humiliations were best administered carefully. Perceived insults to units could have tremendous political consequences. An army's honour encompassed its commander: Galba's insult to Verginius Rufus could be imagined as one of the reasons why Verginius' legions supported Vitellius.[175] Tacitus, as we have seen, expected Tiberius to brood about the mutinous legions of Germany and

---

[171] Ascoli (1983), 68–92: the continuing process of regimental amalgamation may alter some of the details.

[172] Diocletian and Maximian's making the Ioviani and Herculiani first in precedence 'pro merito virtutis' (Veg. *Mil.* 1. 17) is still reflected in *Not. Dig. Oc.* 5. 145–6, 7. 3–4. For demotion, Amm. Marc. 29. 5. 20. Cf. Elton (1996), 94–5. Agrippa, Dio 54. 11. 5, ἀτιμώσας.

[173] Suet. *Aug.* 24. 2, 'variis ignominiis' (cf. Veg. *Mil.* 1. 13 for barley).

[174] Tac. *Hist.* 1. 52; Suet. *Vit.* 8. 1; Herod. 6. 8. 8.   [175] Plut. *Galba* 22. 1.

Pannonia: the mutiny might worsen if he insulted one by going first to the other.[176]

CONCLUSION

A modern soldier transported to a Roman camp would find much familiar in the ethos of the men there: their fierce pride in person and unit, the subtle mingling of discipline as enforced and discipline as felt. But the paralysing shame that sometimes gripped soldiers, and their ferocious competitiveness, might strike him as odd, and he would not feel compelled to join in, say, the mass suicide of Otho's soldiers, undertaken at once out of affection for their emperor and at the same time as a bizarre contest for honour.[177]

A Roman aristocrat, by contrast, transported to a Roman camp—a usual event, since such men commanded the army—would have found those qualities familiar and would naturally rely upon them in commanding troops in peace and war. Other things too would have reminded him of honour at home: the round of *salutationes* in the morning, the statues and honours for officers and governors raised by soldiers, units, and veterans; honours for the emperor and the imperial cult (probably a larger part of military life than civilian); the tendency of soldiers to break into acclamations just as if they were the *plebs* of a town.[178] Familiar also was the appeal to soldiers' political loyalty through honour and shame: that was a conventional way Roman imperial politics worked. Striking, by contrast, how open other, probably more important, spurs to loyalty were: bribes, pay, and punishments, which were so often decently hidden beneath the rhetoric of honour among civilian aristocrats. For the make-up of soldiers' honour—what was honourable, what shameful—was strange, and strange too were the degrading things an officer had to do to gain the respect and honour of his troops. The tenor of military honour was also strange: hard-edged, uncompromising, cruel. Most striking of all was soldiers' pride in obedience to orders, an obedience which slavery placed under a stigma among the civilian aristocracy, and which had thus wrapped about itself a stifling cocoon of euphemism, *politesse*, and evasion in civilian life. The army was a different world of honour—one of countless different worlds in the empire, where standards of honour could vary so much between social classes, votaries of religions, even

---

[176] Above, n. 135.   [177] Above, n. 98.

[178] Honours, *ILS* 1070, 2733, 2738; imperial cult, Fishwick (1987–92), 593–608; acclamation, Plut. *Galba* 18. 4; *CTh* 7. 20. 2 (320 or 326); *HA Diad.* 1. 6–8 (fictional).

professional groups—and one where the values of the common soldiers were uneasily dominant over those of the aristocracy. Soldiers had to be met on their terms; if an officer was to win the devotion of his troops, he had to show some of the quality of a Maximinus Thrax, the soldiers' emperor.

At the same time, the honour of army and aristocracy touched at many points. The soldiers liked a 'proper officer', one of suitably lofty extraction. The Graeco-Roman aristocracy was a fighting nobility in origin, the heirs of Diomedes and Camillus, and martial achievement, however much they might shudder at its rigours, never lost its glory among them. A major source of information about the Roman army is the inscribed civic honours of former officers, where their purely military accomplishments, their postings, their decorations, even the fact that an equestrian officer 'slew Valao, chief of the Naristi, with his own hand' are lovingly recorded.[179] Such deeds brought honour in the empire's senate houses as well as in the camps. Indeed, the army was a broad avenue of social mobility into the civic aristocracy: retired chief centurions, *primipilares*, took up in municipalities positions appropriate to their equestrian status and the six hundred thousand sesterces they received on retirement. Little disgrace seems to have attached to the fact that many such men started as common soldiers, recruits from the depths of society. Some of their sons even became Roman senators; others had equestrian careers (as indeed had some of their fathers after becoming *primipilares*). But a great many sons chose to spend their own lives in the army.[180] Thus the Roman army was not just a road into the civilian ruling class: it was its own world, with its own intense satisfactions, its own singular code, its own honour.

[179] Valao, *AE* 1956. 124.
[180] Dobson (1970), (1978); but Cassius Dio (52. 25. 6–7) did not want former rankers themselves in the senate.

6

Agamemnon's Empire

ACCORDING to Synesius, the peasants of North Africa thought that Agamemnon ruled the Roman empire. This was a strangely wise mistake. For just as the values of Greeks and Romans of the empire recalled in many ways the values of the warlike aristocracies from which they arose, so too did rulership always have a Homeric strain to it. Honour defined the Homeric king's position: a king might say, 'Be king equally with me, take half my honour.'[1] The king was distinguished by his right to receive the greatest honour.[2] And of mortal men he had the greatest power over the distribution of honours and disgraces. When Achilles withdraws from the fighting, he cries out to the High King Agamemnon, 'You will tear apart your heart in self-reproach, that you did no honour to the best of the Achaeans.'[3] In Caesar Augustus there was a great deal of Mussolini, but there was something of Agamemnon as well.

The eye of honour is not like the jeweller's eye, which sees what others do not only when it looks into the depths of a diamond. It is more like the general's eye, forever rendering the natural world into terrain, restlessly sweeping the landscape for cover and enfilade even in retirement. In the Roman world the eye of honour saw honour wherever it looked—in men, in institutions, in things; it saw a world where all human affairs and interactions breathed with glory and disgrace. Honour was an all-embracing outlook by which, incidentally, the whole business of government—of ruling, being ruled, and ruling the rulers—could be conceived, a way of talking and thinking as compelling, ample, and inclusive as our familiar modern rhetoric of power.

The significance of honour in government extends from the most ruthless form of psychological coercion to the most trivial form of politeness. A great deal could be done directly with honour by relying on and exploiting the norms of a society which felt its call strongly. We have

---

[1] Hom. *Il.* 9. 616, τιμή, with 6. 193; cf. 20. 180–1.
[2] *Il.* 1. 278–9, 12. 310–21; *Od.* 1. 393.
[3] *Il.* 1. 243–4; cf. 1. 412, 9. 62, 13. 461; and see McGlew (1989).

emphasized three mechanisms, conjuring engines out of the silent, unspoken rhythms of ancient life: the selling of praise or extortion by the threat of blame; deference, reverence or respect; and gratitude, the reciprocity of favours. Powerful in civil society, in the context of government these methods buttressed other forms of power wielded by persons in authority. Emperors, officials, and officers used the lure of honour and the threat of disgrace to control those they ruled over or commanded. They took advantage also of the fact that spirited parochial loyalty—civic loyalty in the civilian world, unit loyalty in the army—manifested itself as vigorous concern for the honour which the ancient mind invested in cities and legions. Thus cities and legions too could be honoured and dishonoured by their rulers, and since their citizens and soldiers felt an intense anxiety about their honour, about their place in relation to their hated rivals, a wise government could use their particularistic devotion as a basis of political power.

The rulers profited also from the fact that Greeks and Romans were brought up to revere and obey high honour, to view favours as objects of strict reciprocity, and to feel shame at departure from these unwritten laws. To stress the significance of gratitude—the basis of patronage—to Roman government is hardly unusual: its importance has been widely accepted for half a century. In these pages the goal has been to set relations of gratitude in their proper context—in a wider world of honour-based forms of influence. For rulers benefited from the fact that by virtue of their honour and power they were well placed to subvert the rules that all had learned as children. By virtue of honour all men were not equally vulnerable to disgrace; in inflicting dishonour not all men were equally strong. By virtue of strength some could compel others to honour them and not dishonour them.

Emperors and governors participated in the same culture of honour as their subjects. It was natural, therefore, that rulers should seek honour, fear disgrace, and punish those who insulted them. It was natural too that they should revere honourable men and cities, and that they too should automatically do favours for those who did favours for them. Those, moreover, whose rule relied in part on the norms of the honour culture were in no position to secede from it. The loyalty of the rulers to the laws of honour allowed an increasing number of subjects to get the better of their governors; it helped great cities to a degree of control even over the emperor. Honour spoke to what otherwise might have been a deaf despotism, softened an austere and inflexible autocracy, and provided subjects with a way—however imperfect—of ruling those who were set to rule them. Thus it played its role in creating consent to Roman authority, especially in those honourable men who governed the cities of the empire, and upon whom the emperor and his officials relied.

While honour was one of but a few strands of Homeric rulership, it was one of many under the empire. Yet it gained wider significance because it was a venerable and exceedingly respectable strand. For much of the power in the empire was not respectable: a tyranny ruled by, and ruling over, men who felt that a stigma attached to obedience and pay was a tyranny in which the *arcana imperii* were likely to remain arcane. Honour played its role in hiding the terrible realities of power, greed, slavish obedience, and fear, crafting 'the pleasing illusions which made power gentle and obedience liberal, which harmonized the different shades of life, and which, by a bland assimilation, incorporated into politics the sentiments which beautify and soften private society'.[4] Sometimes this concealment was conscious: the letter to a threatened governor alluding to a subject's distinction in rhetoric as grounds for granting a favour is sent to offer a pretext, not a reason. The banner of honour which covered Caracalla's exile of his political enemies to unhealthy provinces as governors was a *ruse de guerre* as well. But such concealment was also unconscious, almost instinctive. For although only one form of power among many, honour was a fundamental way of thinking and talking about all forms of power. In his Roman oration, Aelius Aristides offers a rather modern vision of how the Roman army was organized.

You begin with one man, who presides over and supervises everything, provinces, cities, camps, and the generals themselves, and you end up with one man who commands four, or two—I've left out all the ranks in between—and just as the spinning of yarn always proceeds from more to fewer strands, thus, the ranking of soldiers one over another proceeds to its end.

In this wool-spinning metaphor we see the lines of a modern table of military organization, a structure we recognize. Aristides is trying to describe a hierarchy of strict obedience to constituted authority. Yet in the same description, he casually describes the military superior as ἐντιμότερος, 'the more honourable one'.[5] Given the point Aristides is trying to make, this seems strikingly inappropriate to us, but it will never have seemed so to a Greek or a Roman. They naturally drew on honour's lexicon to describe all relations of authority.

---

[4] Burke (1955 (1790)), 87.   [5] Aristid. 26. 87–8 (Behr; trans. adapted from Behr).

Josephus too reveals the process of scabbing over other, wounding, power relations with the rhetoric of honour. Caligula commanded Petronius, the governor of Syria, to install the emperor's statue in the temple at Jerusalem, by force if necessary. Extravagant demonstrations by the Jews, to whom this was the most atrocious sacrilege, persuaded Petronius to disobey the emperor. Yet, as Josephus tells it, before the governor was persuaded to disobey he explained his grim duty to the Jews (who had protested that the plan violated their Law): 'It is necessary for me to cleave to the law of my master; if I contravene it, and spare you, I will be executed—and justly. And then he who sent me, rather than I, will make war upon you, for like you I am under orders.'[6] A rare, honest description of a governor's relationship with the emperor, we think, and echoed in Josephus' description of the same events in a later work.[7] But on another occasion in that later work, Josephus had Petronius describe his motives differently. 'It is right', said the governor, 'that he who has obtained so great an honour [from the emperor] by appointment [as governor] should do nothing against him.'[8] Here the magnitude of the honour granted defines the degree of obedience owed: obedience from fear and respect for authority in the first passage is converted into obedience as a function of reciprocity for honour. There is no artifice here: without noticing, Petronius, Josephus, or his informant, has quietly made the insensible change of category that countless thousands of the empire's inhabitants made every day.

Honour as a way of thinking and talking overwhelmed what seems to us distant, and unrelated, conceptual territories like an intellectual kudzu, masking but not changing the reality of harsh power relations. Honour, whether used consciously or unconsciously, served to muffle the shouting of orders, the jingle of coins, and the screams of the tortured. Viewing the world in honour terms made ruling the empire easier and made living in it, and obeying it, more tolerable. An iron tyranny seemed to give way to a golden commonwealth of honourable persons and cities. Gilt, we think; but the mirage was connived in by rulers and ruled alike. It was one of the conspiracies of the imagination without which rulership, any rulership, cannot long endure. We can hardly guess what profound needs are served by our own conspiracy to imagine those who rule us as 'the state', or 'the government'. To make them seem impartial, just, or merely distant? To absolve ourselves from

---

[6] Jos. *BJ* 2. 195.   [7] Jos. *AJ* 18. 265; cf. 304.
[8] Ibid. 18. 279, τιμῆς τοσαύτης ἐπιτετευχότα.

responsibility for our elected rulers' actions? It was alien to the Roman mind to imagine those who ruled them as 'the state'. They preferred to live instead in a glittering imagined empire all their own, an empire of honour.

Appendix

The Latin and Greek Lexicon of Honour

BOTH Latin and Greek articulated the cognitive realm we call honour with a rich and allusive vocabulary. Where honour terms are translated in the text of this book, the originals are usually given in the notes. Here the purpose is to describe how the meanings of some of the more common Latin and Greek honour words relate to each other, differ from one another, and, especially, to show that, whatever their connotations, they aim at a common concept. They are a family of words as similar in their relationship to each other as are evil, wickedness, badness, villainy, vice, and all the other words by which English articulates its broad realm of moral depravity. The Latin and Greek terms are none of them full synonyms, identical in denotation and connotation; moreover, many of them are used—some more commonly—in environments (neglected here) wholly outside that of honour. δόξα can mean no more than an opinion, *claritas* can refer to brightness of colour; but there is a milieu—very roughly that of honour, in English—where the fields of the words' significance overlap. Instances of the words being used interchangeably are offered to establish commonality of sense, as are definitions in the scholastic and lexicographical traditions (which mix ancient and medieval scholarship). Modern authors are adduced, some of whom make cases from repeated pleonastic usage and from context. The treatment here is summary and impressionistic, although literature is cited for those who wish more detail. But the reader should be warned against the corporate vice of scholarship in this area, that of drawing over-nice distinctions. The meaning of words is a sloppy business. A project like this is much easier with languages still spoken: see Bourdieu (1966: 209), for an analysis of the vocabulary of honour in modern Algeria.

LATIN

Latin honour words show two roughly parallel axes of differentiation: the social standing of those to whom they are ascribed, that is, the size of the accumulation of honour they signify, and their place in what we might call the process of honour. Honour words appropriate to all classes of Romans tend to be marked by the source of the honour; words describing the honour of great Romans frequently connote not only the fact of honour but its effects, the power honour exerts in society. For the words discussed see generally *TLL* s.vv., especially the rubric *adposita et synonyma* for similarities of meaning between words, and particularly Knoche's entry for *gloria*, essential for the whole topic; also Hellegouarc'h (1963), valuable but fond of distinctions finer than the evidence warrants.

Latin words which are regularly used to describe honour across the social spectrum are marked, to a greater or lesser degree, by the origin of the honour they describe. First, there are words which imply the thing or deed which will be perceived as honourable, words whose meaning stretches from a specific quantum of honour conveyed to honour as a quality that invests an individual. Thus *gloria* (*OLD* 'praise or honour accorded to persons . . . by general consent, glory'; see Knoche (1934); Philipp (1955); and esp. Drexler (1962)), with its lingering martial flavour, refers to the quality of honour as it invests an individual, but it is also possible to speak of a *gloria*, that is 'an action, etc. that brings glory, distinction', a victory in battle, for example, or 'a person or object that brings glory, ornament' (*OLD*). The possession or accomplishment of a *gloria*, in the one sense, confers *gloria*, in the other. Working in the same way, but weighting the source more and the resulting quality less, is *decus* (*OLD* 'high esteem, honour, glory, a particular source of honour, an ornament') which can be used interchangeably with *gloria*, Cic. *ad Fam*. 10. 12. 5; *ad Att*. 13. 28. 2; *CGL* iv. 225. 14 (and see Piscitelli Carpino (1979), 261 n. 52). In the sense of a claim to honour a *decus* can create *gloria* (Tac. *Hist*. 2. 24, 3. 60). *Decus* can be glossed (*CGL* iv. 437. 15) as 'ornamentum dignitatis'.

Next, there are words which go a step further towards the origin of honour, stressing its publicly attributed quality. Both *laus* (*OLD* 'praise, esteem, renown, reputation') and *fama* (*OLD* 'news, public opinion, good name, glory, renown') signify the way honour comes to exist, by praise and public reputation (indeed, in this sense, *fama* can mean 'ill-repute'). Thus *gloria* can come into being from *laus* and *fama*: 'gloria est frequens de aliquo fama cum laude' (Cic. *Inv*. 2. 166; cf. 1*Phil*. 29). Like *decus*, they also signify a claim to such praise (*laus*, 'a cause of praise, praiseworthy thing, act, or quality' *OLD*; ≈ *decus*, *CGL* v. 285. 22; *fama* (more rarely) 'a source or object of fame' *OLD*), and finally the quality of being praised or well spoken of that results. In this context *laus* and *fama* are close to *gloria* in meaning, and, as Hellegouarc'h (1963: 375) observes, often used as synonyms: *fama* ≈ *gloria*, Pliny, *NH* 14. 48-9 (both applied to freedmen); Juv. 7. 79–81; Tac. *Ann*. 12. 28; *Hist*. 4. 6. *Laus* ≈ *gloria*, Cic. *Off*. 1. 116; Livy 38. 58. 7, and see Harris (1979: 17–18). Extremely similar to *fama* is *existimatio* (*OLD* 'opinion, public opinion, reputation', and see Hellegouarc'h (1963), 364), which can be used interchangeably with it, *Rhet. Her*. 4. 14, Cic. *ad Fam*. 13. 73. 2; Yavetz (1974), 48–9; and with other honour terms, Cic. *Div. Caec*. 71; Yavetz (1974), 51.

Broadest of all is *honos* or *honor* (*OLD* 'high esteem, honour, an honour, public office'; see Klose (1933) and the superior Drexler (1988 (1961))). *Honor* is glossed as *gloria, decus,* or *laus, CGL* iv. 412. 29. It can be used interchangeably with *gloria* (Hellegouarc'h (1963), 386) to refer generally to the quality of honour a man has (≈ *gloria,* Cic. *Sul.* 83; Tac. *Dial.* 12. 5-6), and, like *decus* (*CGL* iv. 52. 21), to refer to any claim to honour ('a thing which confers honour or distinction' *OLD;* ≈ *gloria* in this sense, Cic. *Mur.* 12). But it often points at a specific thing that gives one a claim to honour: public office. Like *fama* and *laus,* it extends further to encompass a way in which honour comes to be, but it alludes not to generalized reputation, but to a specific act of honouring, that is, 'a particular mark of esteem, *an* honour' (*OLD;* thus the common verbal form *honoro*). In this sense it, too, can create *gloria,* Hellegouarc'h (1963: 387). Finally, it describes a man's attitude towards another, his honorific disposition which inspires acts of honouring (below, p. 276).

The Latin honour words which can be applied to men of all conditions thus stretch from the quality which invests the individual who has honour to the state of mind of the other individual who initiates the process that creates that quality.

To the Roman mind *gloria* shines (Philipp (1955), 56). As we direct our eyes up the social order to where there is much of it, it shines very brightly indeed. Thus there are words describing large quantities of honour—the honour of great men—which rely upon the shining metaphor. Common are *claritas/claritudo* (*OLD* 'brightness, distinction, fame') with *clarus* and *praeclarus.* As Seneca (*Ep.* 102. 17, adapting a Greek truism, see p. 277 below) suggests, its difference from *gloria* is social: 'gloria multorum iudiciis constat, claritas bonorum'. Sharing in the metaphor are *splendor* (*OLD* 'brightness, glory') with *splendidus,* and *illustris* (*OLD* 'bright, shining, distinguished, famous'). These words can extend as far as *decus* does into the sources of honour: *claritas* can be 'a particular distinction' (*OLD*), and *splendor* is used in this sense, but not usually further: as honour waxes it leaves its origins behind. Borrowed from the physical realm, these words are used very commonly outside the realm of honour. But as honour words they express a quality that can be created by *gloria* (Cic. *Sen.* 8) and *laus* (Sen. *Ep.* 102. 9) and things which are *clarus* and *illustris* create *gloria* and *fama* in turn (Pliny, *Ep.* 6. 29. 3). They are used synonymously with honour words discussed above: *claritas/claritudo* ≈ *gloria,* Sall. *Cat.* 3. 1–2; *Jug.* 1. 3-2. 4; Pliny, *NH* 34. 5; *splendor* ≈ *decus,* Val. Max. 6. 9. 13; Tac. *Hist.* 1. 84; and appearing pleonastically with *gloria,* Hellegouarc'h (1963: 459). *Illustris* ≈ *laus,* Cic. *Rep.* 3. 5–6; Tac. *Ann.* 4. 26; ≈ *inclutus, nobilis, gloriosus, CGL* iv. 350. 49. Also appropriate to those with a great deal of honour are the abstract noun and adjective made from *honor: honestas* (*OLD* 'title to respect, honourableness, honour, moral rectitude, integrity') and *honestus* (*OLD* 'regarded with honour or respect, of high rank, morally worthy of respect'). Both have a moral flavour, hinting at moral excellence as a source of honour.

Finally, there are abstract nouns, appropriate to high personages, which imply not merely the possession of honour, but its effectiveness in society. In the first sense *dignitas* (*OLD* 'worthiness, excellence, rank, office, esteem, honour'; see

Wegehaupt (1932); Drexler (1966 (1944)); Garnsey (1970), 224–5; Piscitelli Carpino (1979); and Veyne (1990), 205–6) is used synonymously with other honour words. Hellegouarc'h (1963: 400) notices a kinship in meaning to *existimatio*, *fama*, *laus*, and *gloria* (cf. Piscitelli Carpino (1979), 256; and see esp. Cic. *ad Fam.* 11. 5. 3). Piscitelli Carpino (1979: 257) links *dignitas* with *honos*, cf. *CGL* iv. 525. 4; also ≈ *decus*, *CGL* iv. 52. 21. *Dignitas* extends back into the sources of honour to signify a claim to honour, and, like *honos*, can refer specifically to office as the source of that claim. But in its sense of 'worthiness' it extends in the opposite direction to imply the attraction for favours, honours, and all good things that honour confers (Hellegouarc'h (1963), 397–8). Men can thus be moved into action by the *dignitas* of others, Cic. *Sex. Rosc.* 4.

A very great quantity of honour can also be described as *auctoritas* (*OLD* 'influence, authority, prestige, esteem, repute'), upon which there is a large literature as a consequence of its appearance in Augustus' *Res Gestae*, 34: see especially Heinze (1960 (1925)); Grant (1946), 443–5, for literature; and Magdelain (1947). *Gloria* can create it, Cic. *ad Fam.* 12. 14. 7; and it can be used synonymously with other honour terms: ≈ *gloria*, Cic. *Deiot.* 12; ≈ *honor*, Aul. Gel. 7. 14. 3. Piscitelli Carpino (1979: 259–60) stresses the similarity of *auctoritas* to *dignitas* in Cicero's usage; cf. Balsdon (1960), 44–5; Caes. *BG* 7. 30; *CGL* iv. 312. 3. It has an even stronger positive force than *dignitas*, stressing not merely the right to receive by virtue of honour, but the right to command (Hellegouarc'h (1963), 300–1). Thus Cicero (*ad Fam.* 16. 9. 4) urges his freedman amanuensis to take ship with Mescinius; or 'si minus, cum honesto aliquo homine, cuius auctoritate navicularius moveatur'. That is, he should travel with a man who possesses honour in the passive sense, a *vir honestus*, who will be able to use his honour in the active sense, *auctoritas*, on the ship owner. This sense of a right to command can harden to such a degree as to take *auctoritas* right out of the realm of honour (by our lights), and into that of legal authority or undifferentiated power: *OLD* 'right or power to authorize or sanction', '(of laws, etc.) force, authority', '(of magistrates, etc.) authority, command', and further, 'right of ownership, title', or even 'an informal decree of the senate'. Or perhaps these non-honour meanings were prior and *auctoritas* came to be naturalized into the vocabulary of honour.

The acme of honour is *maiestas* (*OLD* 'the dignity of a god or exalted personage, majesty, grandeur'; see Kübler (1928), 542–4; Drexler (1956); Gundel (1963); Hellegouarc'h (1963), 314, who notes its relationship to *maior*; one might render it 'greaterness'). So vast is the honour it conveys that it is regularly used to refer to the prestige of gods and political entities: 'maiestas est amplitudo ac dignitas civitatis', as Cicero defines it (*de Orat.* 2. 164). Thus, to offend against the *maiestas* of the Roman people is to commit treason, and the word has a long life in that context (Bauman (1967), (1974)). To Ovid's mind, *Maiestas* arose from the union of *Honor* and *Reverentia*, *Fasti* 23-6. *Maiestas* is closely related to honour words: ≈ *honor*, Val. Max. 2. 10. pr; ≈ *gloria*, *CGL* iv. 605. 3, v. 298. 44; ≈ *claritas*, Livy 5. 14. 2-5; Val. Max. 2. 10. 6. Its similarity to *dignitas* is noticed by Drexler (1956), 196;

Hellegouarc'h (1963), 317 n. 7; and Piscitelli Carpino (1979), 259 n. 35; to *auctoritas*, by Hellegouarc'h (1963), 315. The power of an individual's *maiestas* is even greater than that of *auctoritas*: one obeys *auctoritas*, but *maiestas* can be imagined to exert almost physical force (Drexler (1956), 197; and e.g. Livy 9. 10. 7); it seizes people, or stuns them, into or out of action. Thus like *auctoritas* the meaning of *maiestas* shades out of our realm of honour, here into our realms of undifferentiated power, greatness, and holiness (see Bauman (1967), 1–15).

Dignitas, auctoritas, and *maiestas* all demand a response: 'dignitas est alicuius honesta et cultu et honore et verecundia digna auctoritas', Cic. *Inv.* 2. 166. *Reverentia, veneratio* (Drexler (1956: 197)) and *verecundia* (see also Livy 24. 44. 10) are all appropriate emotions, and so is *honor* (see also Val. Max. 2. 1. 6). We have come full circle. A view directed upwards through the social ranks follows the process of honour from honour's sources to honour's results, one of which is to inspire *honor* in the sense of a disposition to honour, the meaning of *honor* which extends furthest back into the origins of honour. We should note also that the differentiation of Latin honour words by social standing is relative to the position of the observer: while we almost always see the words used in aristocratic authors, and thus according to aristocratic standards, in the context of a humble burial society a rich freedman, a very grand person to the members, could have *maiestas* (*ILS* 7889). But certainly Cicero and his friends would never describe the honour of a freedman in such terms.

Greek

The entire circuit of the process of honour is encompassed in a single Greek word, the overwhelmingly common τιμή (LSJ 'worship, esteem, honour, dignity, present of honour'; and see esp. Greindl (1938), 56–82; Alexiou (1995), 40–7). Not marked for the status of its possessor, τιμή extends all the way from the feeling that an individual has that inspires him to honour another, to honour conveyed (thus τιμάω), to a claim to honour, especially a political or religious office, to honour as a quality investing an individual, to the worthiness for honours and favours that honour bestows upon its possessor and which inspires τιμή in the first sense. And in its sense as 'worthiness', τιμή elicits from those around it other appropriate emotions, αἰδώς (LSJ 'reverence, awe, respect, shame, sense of honour') and its cognates, and σέβας (LSJ 'reverential awe, reverence, worship, honour') and its cognates, on which see Cairns (1993: esp. 13, 95-103, 137, 207–14, 432). This sense of τιμή also allows it to be used as the Greek word for 'price'. Common related words are τίμιος (LSJ 'held in honour, worthy, conferring honour, honourable') and ἔντιμος (LSJ 'in honour, honoured').

Τιμή has the widest meaning of all ancient honour words; it describes honour in nearly all its aspects and at all social levels. Like Latin words, other Greek honour words are differentiated by status and their place in the process of honour, occupying only a portion of τιμή's range; but unlike in Latin the axes of process and social status are not approximately parallel. Greek words which imply the results of honour will be considered first, then those that imply its causes.

Some of the range of τιμή is shared by ἀξίωμα (LSJ 'that of which one is thought worthy, an honour, honour and reputation, rank, position'; and esp. Steinkopf (1937), 94-5), with a meaning extending from a claim to honour (≈ τιμή, Dio 52. 20. 3; and, like τιμή, being a usual word for an office) to honour as it invests an individual, to the right to deference by virtue of honour. It is appropriate to high personages. Also for great persons and implying results is σεμνότης (LSJ 'solemnity, dignity') with σεμνός (LSJ 'august, stately, majestic'). Thus Photius s.v. σεμνόν ≈ μέγα ἔνδοξον, ἀξιωματικόν, ὑπερήφανον. Cognate to σέβας (see above), σεμνός has a strong religious flavour, but used as an honour word on the human level (e.g. D. Chr. 31. 138; Plut. *de Frat. Amore* 491b) it fades off into physical description of a dignified carriage, and in a bad sense can describe a pompous and haughty aspect.

No less grand, although extending in the opposite direction towards the sources of honour, is κλέος (LSJ 'rumour, report, fame, glory'; see esp. Greindl (1938), 5–30; and see Venske (1938: 3–4) for its aristocratic connotations), extending from the origins of honour in report and discussion, to a claim to honour, to the quality that invests an individual. In the latter two cases its sense is frequently close to that of τιμή, Greindl (1938: 96–7). Of the Homeric honour words which survived in classical prose (κῦδος, LSJ 'glory, renown' remained poetic), κλέος maintained the strongest links to its past, and has a distinct heroic savour. Related are εὔκλεια (LSJ 'good repute, glory') and εὐκλεής (LSJ 'of good report, famous').

The second-century AD lexicographer Pollux (and his later interpolators) offers a storm of approximate synonyms for κλέος.

ΚΛΕΟΣ, δόξα, φήμη, ὄνομα, λαμπρότης, εὐδοκίμησις, καὶ ἀκμὴ δόξης, ἔνδοξος, ὀνομαστός, λαμπρός, ζηλωτός, ἐπιφανής, περίβλεπτος (5. 158, excluding the B and C MSS readings; on many of these words see Schmidt (1889), 89–96).

These words' commonality with κλέος lies in their coverage of honour as a quality that invests an individual, and in some cases their extension back towards the sources of honour. Like κλέος they tend not to connote honour's results. δόξα (LSJ 'opinion, repute, honour, glory'; and esp. Greindl (1938) 87–93; Alexiou (1995), 24–33) and φήμη (LSJ 'report, good report, fame'; and esp. Greindl (1938), 82–6) have much the same range of meaning as κλέος (≈ φήμη, Schmidt (1889), 85–9; ≈ δόξα, Greindl (1938), 102; Alexiou (1995), 30–3; ≈ both, Hesychius s.v. κλέα; εὔκλεια ≈ δόξα, Suda s.v. εὔκλεια; δόξα ≈ φήμη, Hesychius s.v. δόξα) but without the heroic implication in classical times, for anyone can have them: δόξα μέν ἐστιν ὁ παρὰ τῶν πολλῶν ἔπαινος· κλέος δὲ, ὁ παρὰ τῶν σπουδαίων (Ammon. *Diff.* s.v. δόξα). These words signify the public perception in which honour is rooted, δόξα in thoughts and opinions, φήμη, like κλέος, in speech, and in this sense one can have bad κλέος, δόξα, or φήμη. They extend to signify a claim to honour and the honour that invests an individual (φήμη less commonly) and in those contexts are used synonymously with τιμή (≈ δόξα, Hesychius s.v.; Cramer (1835–7), ii. 432. 18; Greindl (1938), 102; Steinkopf (1937), 94; ἀξίωμα ≈ δόξα, Plut. *Ages.* 6. 3 and 7. 1).

Related to δόξα are the common ἔνδοξος (LSJ 'held in esteem or honour, of high repute'; ≈ τίμιος, Hesychius s.v.; ≈ ἐπίσημος (LSJ 'notable, remarkable'), Ammon. *Diff.* s.v. ἔνδοξος; ≈ εὐκλεής, *Suda* s.v.), and εὔδοξος (LSJ 'of good repute, honoured'; εὔκλεια ≈ εὐδοξία, Hesychius s.v. εὔκλεια). Like the remaining words in Pollux' list, they imply standing in society, a great deal of honour. From a chosen or tested metaphor comes εὐδόκιμος (LSJ 'in good repute, honoured, favoured, glorious'; see Alexiou (1995), 34–40; Pollux's abstract quality of εὐδοκίμησις (LSJ 'good repute, reputation, credit') is rare). Also appropriate for high-status persons are ὄνομα (LSJ 'name, fame'; see de Romilly (1973), 49) with ὀνομαστός (LSJ 'of name or note, famous'; ὀνομαστοί ≈ ἔνδοξοι, περιβόητοι, Hesychius s.v. ὀνομαστοί; cf. Plut. *Ages.* 24. 3); and, arising from the shining metaphor so powerful in Latin, λαμπρότης (LSJ 'brilliancy, splendour'; see de Romilly (1973), 50; Alexiou (1995), 22–4) with the very common λαμπρός (LSJ 'bright, well-known, illustrious') which, in the superlative, becomes the Greek translation for *clarissimus*, the imperial senator's rank of honour. Visual metaphors also give rise to ἐπιφανής (LSJ 'coming to light, manifest, conspicuous, famous, renowned'; ≈ ἐπίσημος, Hesychius s.v.) with περιφανής (LSJ 'conspicuous', 'famous'). περιφάνεια ≈ λαμπρότης, δόξα, Hesychius s.v. περιφάνεια. Finally, περίβλεπτος (LSJ 'looked at from all sides, admired of all observers').

Greek and Latin

Where occasionally Latin is translated into Greek, or vice versa, the relationship of one word to another is illuminated. Famously, *auctoritas* was rendered by ἀξίωμα in Augustus' *Res Gestae* (34. 3). Plutarch glossed the Latin *honor* with τιμή and δόξα (*Quaest. Rom.* 266f); and in an imperial decree (*IK Eph.* i. 43. 2) 'honorem Asiae ac totius provinci[a]e dignitatem' is translated as τειμὴν τῆς Ἀσίας καὶ ὅλης τῆς ἐπαρχίας τὸ ἀξίωμα (line 15). In the school texts for teaching the other language to schoolboys the following equivalences can be found (listed in the order in which they are discussed above):

gloria ≈ δόξα, καύχημα (*CGL* ii. 34. 26)
gloriosus ≈ εὐκλεής (*CGL* iii. 372. 76)
decus ≈ δόξα, κόσμος, εὐπρέπεια (*CGL* ii. 39. 11)
fama ≈ φήμη (*CGL* ii. 70. 23)
honus, honor ≈ τιμὴ θεῶν, τιμὴ ἀνθρώπων (*CGL* ii. 69. 16)
honestus ≈ ἔντιμος, ἀξιόλογος (*CGL* ii. 69. 11)
honoratus ≈ τετιμημένος, ἔνδοξος, ἐπίσημος (*GCL* ii. 69. 15)
claritas ≈ λαμπρότης (*CGL* ii. 101. 57)
clarus ≈ ἔνδοξος, ἐπιφανής (*CGL* ii. 101. 55)
splendor ≈ λαμπρότης (*CGL* 2. 187. 18)

inlustris ≈ ἐπιφανής, ὑψηλοπέτης, μετέωρος, ἔνδοξος (*CGL* ii. 83. 52–3)

insignis ≈ ἐπίσημος, ἔξοχος (*CGL* ii. 87. 14)

dignitas ≈ ἀξίωμα (*CGL* ii. 49. 41)

τιμή ἐπὶ ἀξίας ≈ *hic honor, honestas, hic honus* (*CGL* ii. 455. 38)

ἀξίωμα ≈ *hec* [sic] *dignitatio, haec dignitas, honos, meritum* (*CGL* ii. 232. 3)

μεγαλειότης, δόξα ≈ *maiestas* (*CGL* iii. 278. 48)

ἔνδοξος ≈ *gloriosus, inclytus* [sic] (*CGL* ii. 298. 16)

εὔδοξος ≈ *gloriosus* (*CGL* iii. 249. 49)

λαμπρός ≈ *clarus, splendidus* (*CGL* ii. 358. 30)

λαμπρότης ≈ *claritas, claritudo, hic splendor, hic candor* (*CGL* ii. 258. 32-3)

περιφανής ≈ *inlustris, nobilis* (*CGL* ii. 405. 30)

References

Achard, G. (1973), 'L'Emploi de *boni, boni viri, boni cives* et leurs formes superlatives dans l'action politique de Cicéron', *Études classiques*, 41: 207–21.

Adkins, A. H. W. (1960), ' "Honour" and "Punishment" in the Homeric Poems', *BICS* 7: 23–32.

Alexiou, E. (1995), *Ruhm und Ehre: Studien zu Begriffen, Werten und Motivierungen bei Isokrates* (Heidelberg).

Alföldi, A. (1970 (1934–5)), *Die monarchische Repräsentation im römischen Kaiserreiche* (Darmstadt, 1970) (reprinting 'Die Ausgestaltung des monarchischen Zeremoniells am römischen Kaiserhofe', *Mitteilungen des Deutschen Archäologischen Instituts (Röm. Abt.)*, 49 (1934), 3–118, and 'Insignien und Tracht der römischen Kaiser', *Mitteilungen des Deutschen Archäologischen Instituts (Röm. Abt.)*, 50 (1935), 2–158).

Alföldy, G. (1973), *Flamines Provinciae Hispaniae Citerioris* (Anejos de Archivo Español de arqueologia, 6; Madrid).

—— (1977), *Konsulat und Senatorenstand unter den Antoninen: Prosopographische Untersuchungen zur senatorischen Führungsschicht* (Bonn).

—— (1981), 'Die Stellung der Ritter in der Führungsschicht des *Imperium Romanum*', *Chiron*, 11: 169–215.

Alston, R. (1995), *Soldier and Society in Roman Egypt* (London).

Amelang, J. S. (1986), *Honored Citizens of Barcelona: Patrician Culture and Class Relations, 1490–1714* (Princeton).

Ameling, W. (1983), 'Eine neue Inschrift aus Prusias ad Hypium', *Epigraphica Anatolica*, 1: 63–74.

Arjava, A. (1991), 'Zum Gebrauch der griechischen Rangprädikate des Senatorenstandes in den Papyri und Inschriften', *Tyche*, 6: 17–35.

Arnheim, M. T. W. (1972), *The Senatorial Aristocracy in the Later Roman Empire* (Oxford).

Ascoli, D. (1983), *A Companion to the British Army, 1660–1983* (London).

Austin, N. J. E., and Rankov, N. B. (1995), Exploratio: *Military and Political Intelligence in the Roman World from the Second Punic War to the Battle of Adrianople* (London).

Avery, W. T. (1940), 'The *Adoratio Purpurae* and the Importance of the Imperial Purple in the Fourth Century of the Christian Era', *MAAR* 17: 66–80.

Badian, E. (1958), *Foreign Clientelae (264–70 BC)* (Oxford).

Bagnall, R. S., Cameron, A., Schwartz, S. R., and Worp, K. A. (1987), *Consuls of the Later Roman Empire* (American Philological Association Monograph 36; Atlanta).

BALSDON, J. P. V. D. (1960), '*Auctoritas, Dignitas, Otium*', *Classical Quarterly*, NS 10: 43–50.

BARLOW, F. (1980), 'The King's Evil', *English Historical Review*, 95: 3–27.

BARNES, T. D. (1971), *Tertullian: A Historical and Literary Study* (Oxford).

—— (1981), *Constantine and Eusebius* (Cambridge, Mass.).

—— (1982), *The New Empire of Diocletian and Constantine* (Cambridge, Mass.).

BARNISH, S. (1988), 'Transformation and Survival in the Western Senatorial Aristocracy, *c.* AD 400–700', *PBSR* 56: 120–55.

BARTSCH, S. (1994), *Actors in the Audience: Theatricality and Doublespeak from Nero to Hadrian* (Cambridge, Mass.).

BASTIEN, P. (1988), *Monnaie et* donativa *au bas-empire* (Wetteren).

BAUMAN, R. A. (1967), *The* Crimen Maiestatis *in the Roman Republic and Augustan Principate* (Johannesburg).

—— (1974), *Impietas in Principem* (Munich).

BEHR, C. A. (1968), *Aelius Aristides and the Sacred Tales* (Amsterdam).

BERGER, A. (1914), '*Illustris*', *RE* ix/1: 1070–85.

BESCHAOUCH, A. (1966), 'La Mosaïque de chasse à l'amphithéâtre découverte à Smirat en Tunisie', *Comptes rendus de l'Académie des inscriptions et belles-lettres*: 134–57.

BIRLEY, A. (1972), *Septimius Severus: The African Emperor* (New York).

—— (1981), *The* Fasti *of Roman Britain* (Oxford).

BIRLEY, E. (1978), 'The Religion of the Roman Army: 1895–1977', *ANRW* ii. 16. 2: 1506–41.

—— (1988 (1941)), 'The Origins of Legionary Centurions', *The Roman Army Papers, 1929–1986* (Amsterdam, 1988), 189–205 (repr. from *Laureae Aquincenses*, 2 (1941), 47–62).

BLACK-MICHAUD, J. (1975), *Cohesive Force: Feud in the Mediterranean and the Middle East* (Oxford).

BLOCH, M. (1924), *Les Rois thaumaturges: Étude sur le caractère surnaturel attribué à le puissance royale, particulièrement en France et en Angleterre* (Paris and Strasburg).

BLOCKLEY, R. C. (1983), *The Fragmentary Classicising Historians of the Later Roman Empire: Eunapius, Olympiodorus, Priscus and Malchus*, ii (Liverpool).

BLUM, W. (1969), Curiosi *und* Regendarii*: Untersuchungen zur geheimen Staatspolizei der Spätantike* (Munich).

BOATWRIGHT, M. T. (1991), 'Plancia Magna of Perge: Women's Roles and Status in Roman Asia Minor', in S. B. Pomeroy (ed.), *Women's History and Ancient History* (Chapel Hill, NC), 249–72.

BÖCHER, O. (1980), *Die Johannesapokalypse* (Erträge der Forschung, 41; Darmstadt).

BOLLINGER, T. (1969), Theatralis licentia*: Die Publikumsdemonstrationen an den* *öffentlichen Spielen im Rom der früheren Kaiserzeit und ihre Bedeutung im politischen Leben* (Winterthur).

BORZSÁK, S. (1939), 'Ornamenta', *RE* xviii/1: 1110–22.

BOULVERT, G. (1974), *Domestique et fonctionnaire sous le haut-empire romain* (Paris).

BOURDIEU, P. (1966), 'The Sentiment of Honour in Kabyle Society', in Peristiany (1966), 193–241.

BOWERSOCK, G. W. (1969), *Greek Sophists in the Roman Empire* (Oxford).

—— (1978), *Julian the Apostate* (London).

—— (1983), 'The Imperial Cult: Perceptions and Persistence', in B. F. Meyer and E. P. Sanders (eds.), *Jewish and Christian Self-Definition*, 3 (Philadelphia), 171–82.

—— (1985), 'Hadrian and Metropolis', *Bonner Historia-Augusta-Colloquium 1982–83* (Bonn), 75–88.

—— (1987), 'The Mechanics of Subversion in the Roman Provinces', in K. Raaflaub (ed.), *Opposition et résistances à l'empire d'Auguste à Trajan* (Entretiens sur l'Antiquité classique, 33; Geneva), 291–317.

BOWMAN, A. K. (1971), *The Town Councils of Roman Egypt* (Toronto).

—— and RATHBONE, D. (1992), 'Cities and Administration in Roman Egypt', *JRS* 82: 107–27.

—— and THOMAS, J. D. (1983), *Vindolanda: The Latin Writing-Tablets* (*Britannia* Monograph 4; London).

BREEZE, D. J. (1974), 'The Organization of the Career Structure of the *Immunes* and *Principales* of the Roman Army', *Bonner Jahrbücher*, 174: 245–92.

BREMEN, R. VAN (1996), *The Limits of Participation* (Amsterdam).

BROWN, P. (1982 (1971)), 'The Rise and Function of the Holy Man in Late Antiquity', in id., *Society and the Holy in Late Antiquity* (London, 1982), 103–152 (repr. from *JRS* 61 (1971), 80–101).

—— (1988), *The Body and Society* (New York).

—— (1992), *Power and Persuasion in Late Antiquity: Towards a Christian Empire* (Madison).

BRUNT, P. A. (1961), 'Charges of Provincial Maladministration under the Early Principate', *Historia*, 10: 189–227 (repr. in id., *Roman Imperial Themes* (Oxford, 1990), 53–95).

—— (1974a), 'Conscription and Volunteering in the Roman Imperial Army', *Scripta Classica Israelica*, 1: 90–115 (repr. in id., *Roman Imperial Themes* (Oxford, 1990), 188–214).

—— (1974b), 'Marcus Aurelius in his *Meditations*', *JRS* 64: 1–20.

—— (1975a), 'Did Imperial Rome Disarm her Subjects?' *Phoenix*, 29: 260–70 (repr. in id., *Roman Imperial Themes* (Oxford, 1990), 255–81).

—— (1975b), 'The Administrators of Roman Egypt', *JRS* 65: 124–47 (repr. in id., *Roman Imperial Themes* (Oxford, 1990), 215–54).

—— (1981), 'The Revenues of Rome', *JRS* 71: 161–72 (repr. in id., *Roman Imperial Themes* (Oxford, 1990), 324–46).

—— (1988*a*), *The Fall of the Roman Republic and Related Essays* (Oxford).

—— (1988*b*), 'The Emperor's Choice of *Amici*', in P. Kneissl and V. Losemann (eds.), *Alte Geschichte und Wissenschaftsgeschichte: Festschrift für Karl Christ zum 65. Geburtstag* (Darmstadt), 39–56.

BRUUN, C. (1990), 'Some Comments on the Status of Imperial Freedmen', *ZPE* 82: 271–85.

BUCKLER, W. H. (1937), 'A Charitable Foundation of AD 237', *JHS* 57: 1–10.

—— and ROBINSON, D. M. (1932), *Sardis*, vii: *Greek and Latin Inscriptions* (Leiden).

BUDER, L. (1989), 'Dealer Guilty of Ordering Officer Killed', *The New York Times*, vol. 139 no. 48082 (12 Dec. 1989) p. B1.

BURKE, E. (1955 (1790)), *Reflections on the Revolution in France*, ed. T. H. D. Mahoney (Indianapolis, 1955; orig. pub. 1790).

BURKERT, W. (1985), *Greek Religion*, trans. J. Raffan (Cambridge, Mass.).

BURTON, G. P. (1975), 'Proconsuls, Assizes, and the Administration of Justice under the Empire', *JRS* 65: 92–106.

—— (1977), 'Slaves, Freedmen and Monarchy', review of Boulvert (1974), *JRS* 67: 162–6.

—— (1987), 'Government and the Provinces', in J. Wacher (ed.), *The Roman World* (London), i. 423–39.

CAIRNS, D. L. (1993), *Aidōs: The Psychology and Ethics of Honour and Shame in Ancient Greek Literature* (Oxford).

CAMERON, A. (1976), *Circus Factions: Blues and Greens at Rome and Byzantium* (Oxford).

CAMPBELL, J. (1964), *Honour, Family and Patronage: A Study of Institutions and Moral Values in a Greek Mountain Community* (Oxford).

CAMPBELL, J. B. (1975), 'Who Were the "*Viri Militares*"?' *JRS* 65: 11–31.

—— (1984), *The Emperor and the Roman Army, 31 BC–AD 235* (Oxford).

CANTARELLA, E. (1991), 'Homicides of Honor: The Development of Italian Adultery Law over Two Millennia', in D. I. Kertzer and R. P. Saller (eds.), *The Family in Italy from Antiquity to the Present* (New Haven), 229–44.

CARCOPINO, J., and GSELL, S. (1931), 'Le Base de M. Sulpicius Felix et le décret des décurions de Sala', *Mélanges d'archéologie et d'histoire*, 48: 1–39.

CARO BAROJA, J. (1966), 'Honour and Shame: A Historical Account of Several Conflicts', in Peristiany (1966), 81–137.

CHAMPLIN, E. (1991), *Final Judgments: Duty and Emotion in Roman Wills, 200 BC–AD 250* (Berkeley and Los Angeles).

CHARLESWORTH, M. P. (1937), 'The Virtues of the Roman Emperor: Propaganda and the Creation of Belief', *Proceedings of the British Academy*, 23: 105–34.

CHASTAGNOL, A. (1960), *La Préfecture urbaine à Rome sous le bas-empire* (Paris).

—— (1966), 'Les Consulaires de Numidie', in J. Heurgon, G. Picard, and W. Seston (eds.), *Mélanges d'archéologie, d'épigraphie et d'histoire en l'honneur de J. Carcopino* (Paris), 215–28.

CHASTAGNOL, A. (1970), 'Les Modes de recrutement du sénat au IVᵉ siècle après J.-C.', in C. Nicolet (ed.), *Recherches sur les structures sociales dans l'antiquité classique* (Paris), 187–211.

—— (1977), 'Le Problème du domicile légal des sénateurs romains à l'époque impériale', in *Mélanges offerts à Léopold Sédar Senghor* (Dakar), 43–54.

—— (1978), *L'Album municipal de Timgad* (Bonn).

—— (1992), *Le Sénat romain à l'époque impériale* (Paris).

CHRISTOL, M. (1986), *Essai sur l'évolution des carrières sénatoriales dans la seconde moitié du IIIᵉ siècle ap. J.-C.* (Paris).

CLARK, G. (1991), 'Let Every Soul be Subject: The Fathers and the Empire', in L. Alexander (ed.), *Images of Empire* (*Journal for the Study of the Old Testament*, Suppl. 122; Sheffield), 251–75.

CLAUSS, M. (1973), *Untersuchungen zu den* principales *des römischen Heeres von Augustus bis Diokletian:* Cornicularii, speculatores, frumentarii (Bochum).

—— (1980), *Der* Magister Officiorum *in der Spätantike (4.–6. Jahrhundert): Das Amt und sein Einfluss auf die kaiserliche Politik* (Munich).

CLEMENTE, G. (1972), 'Il Patronato nei collegia dell'impero Romano', *Studi classici e orientali*, 21: 142–229.

COHEN, D. (1991), *Law, Sexuality, and Society: The Enforcement of Morals in Classical Athens* (Cambridge).

—— (1995), *Law, Violence, and Community in Classical Athens* (Cambridge).

COLIN, J. (1965), *Les Villes libres de l'Orient gréco-romain et l'envoi au supplice par acclamations populaires* (Brussels).

COLLINS, A. Y. (1976), *The Combat Myth in the Book of Revelation* (Missoula).

CORBIER, M. (1977), 'Le Discours du prince, d'après une inscription de Banasa', *Ktèma*, 2: 211–32.

COTTON, H. (1981), 'Military Tribunates and the Exercise of Patronage', *Chiron*, 11: 229–38.

COUSIN, G., and DIEHL, CH. (1886), 'Inscriptions de Cadyanda en Lycie', *BCH* 10: 39–65.

CRAMER, J. A. (1835–7), *Anecdota graeca e codd. manuscriptis bibliothecarum Oxoniensium*, 4 vols. (Oxford).

CROOK, J. (1976), '*Sponsione Provocare*: Its Place in Roman Litigation', *JRS* 66: 132–8.

DAGRON, G. (1974), *Naissance d'une capitale: Constantinople et ses institutions de 300 à 451* (Paris).

D'ARMS, J. H. (1981), *Commerce and Social Standing in Ancient Rome* (Cambridge, Mass.).

—— (1984), 'Control, Companionship and *Clientela*: Some Social Functions of the Roman Communal Meal', *Échos du Monde Classique/Classical Views*, 28: 327–48.

DEININGER, J. (1965), *Die Provinziallandtage der römischen Kaiserzeit von Augustus bis zum Ende des dritten Jahrhunderts n. Chr.* (Munich).

DELATTE, L. (1942), *Les Traités de le royauté d'Ecphante, Diotogène et Sthénidas* (Liège).

DELMAIRE, R. (1984), 'Les Dignitaires laïcs au Concile de Chalcédoine: Notes sur la hiérarchie et les préséances au milieu du Vᵉ siècle', *Byzantion*, 54: 141–75.

—— (1989), *Largesses sacrées et* res privata: *l'*aerarium *impérial et son administration du IVᵉ au VIᵉ siècle* (Rome).

DEMOUGEOT, E. (1975), 'La *Notitia dignitatum* et l'histoire de l'Empire d'Occident au début du Vᵉ siècle', *Latomus*, 34: 1079–1134.

DENIAUX, É. (1993), *Clientèles et pouvoir à l'époque de Cicéron* (Paris and Rome).

DILKE, O. A. W. (1957), 'The Literary Output of the Roman Emperors', *Greece and Rome*, 4: 78–97.

DIONISOTTI, A. C. (1982), 'From Ausonius' Schooldays? A Schoolbook and its Relatives', *JRS* 72: 83–125.

DOBSON, B. (1970), 'The Centurionate and Social Mobility During the Principate', in C. Nicolet (ed.), *Recherches sur les structures sociales dans l'antiquité classique* (Paris), 100–16.

—— (1978), *Die* Primipilares: *Entwicklung und Bedeutung, Laufbahn und Persönlichkeiten eines römischen Offiziersranges* (Cologne).

DREXLER, H. (1956), '*Maiestas*', *Aevum*, 30: 195–212 (repr. in id., *Politische Grundbegriffe der Römer* (Darmstadt, 1988), 31–48).

—— (1962), '*Gloria*', *Helikon*, 2: 3–36.

—— (1966 (1944)), '*Dignitas*', in R. Klein (ed.), *Das Staatsdenken der Römer* (Darmstadt, 1966), 231–54 (repr. from *Göttinger Universitätsreden*, 15 (Göttingen, 1944)).

—— (1988 (1961)), '*Honos*', in id., *Politische Grundbegriffe der Römer* (Darmstadt, 1988), 55–72 (repr. from *Romanitas*, 3 (1961), 135–57).

DRINKWATER, J. F. (1985), review of Löhken (1982), *Latomus*, 44: 421–7.

DUCOS, M. (1990), 'La Condition des acteurs à Rome: Données juridiques et sociales', in J. Blänsdorf (ed.), *Theater und Gesellschaft im Imperium Romanum* (Tübingen), 19–33.

DUNCAN-JONES, R. (1982), *The Economy of the Roman Empire: Quantitative Studies*, 2nd edn. (Cambridge).

—— (1990), *Structure and Scale in the Roman Economy* (Cambridge).

—— (1994), *Money and Government in the Roman Empire* (Cambridge).

DUPONT, F. (1992), *Daily Life in Ancient Rome*, trans. C. Woodall (Oxford).

DUTHOY, R. (1976), 'Recherches sur la répartition géographique et chronologique des termes *sevir Augustalis, Augustalis* et *sevir* dans l'Empire romain', *Epigraphische Studien*, 11: 143–214.

—— (1978), 'Les *Augustales*', *ANRW* ii. 16. 2: 1254–1309.

—— (1984), 'Sens et fonction du patronat municipal durant le Principat', *L'Antiquité classique*, 53: 145–56.

DYCK, A. W. (1980), 'Cicero, de Officiis 2. 21–22', *Philologus*, 124: 200–11.

EASTON D., and DENNIS, J. (1969), *Children in the Political System: Origins of Political Legitimacy* (New York).

ECK, W. (1974), 'Beförderungskriterien innerhalb der senatorischen Laufbahn, dargestellt an der Zeit von 69 bis 138 n. Chr.', *ANRW* ii. 1: 158–228.

—— (1980), 'Rom, sein Reich und seine Untertanen: Zur administrativen Umsetzung von Herrschaft in der hohen Kaiserzeit', *Geschichte in Köln*, 7: 5–31.

—— (1982), 'Einfluss korrupter Praktiken auf das senatorisch-ritterliche Beförderungswesen in der hohen Kaiserzeit?' in W. Schuller (ed.), *Korruption in Altertum: Konstanzer Symposium, Oktober 1979* (Munich), 135–51.

—— (1984a), 'Senatorial Self-Representation: Developments in the Augustan Period', in F. Millar and E. Segal (eds.), *Caesar Augustus: Seven Aspects* (Oxford), 129–67.

—— (1984b), '*CIL* VI 1508 (MORETTI, *IGUR* 71) und die Gestaltung senatorischer Ehrenmonumente', *Chiron*, 14: 201–17.

ELLIS, S. P. (1991), 'Power, Architecture and Decor: How the Late Roman Aristocrat Appeared to his Guests', in E. K. Gazda (ed.), *Roman Art in the Private Sphere: New Perspectives on the Architecture and Decor of the Domus, Villa, and* Insula (Ann Arbor), 117–34.

ELTON, H. (1996), *Warfare in Roman Europe, AD 350–425* (Oxford).

ENSSLIN, W. (1929), '*Spectabilis*', *RE* iiiA/2. 1552–68.

—— (1937a), '*Perfectissimus*', *RE* xix/1. 664–83.

—— (1937b), '*Numerarius*', *RE* xvii/2. 1297–1323.

—— (1956), '*Praeses*', *RE* Suppl. viii. 598–614.

EPSTEIN, D. (1987), *Personal Enmity in Roman Politics, 218–43 BC* (Beckenham, Kent).

ÉTIENNE, R. (1958), *Le Culte impériale dans la péninsule ibérique d'Auguste à Dioclétien* (Paris).

FEARS, J. R. (1977), Princeps a Diis Electus: *The Divine Election of the Emperor as a Political Concept at Rome* (Papers and Monographs of the American Academy at Rome, 26; Rome).

FISHER, N. R. E. (1992), Hybris: *A Study in the Values of Honour and Shame in Ancient Greece* (Warminster, Wilts.).

FISHWICK, D. (1987–92), *The Imperial Cult in the Latin West*, 2 vols. (Leiden).

—— (1990a), 'Votive Offerings to the Emperor?' *ZPE* 80: 121–30.

—— (1990b), 'Dio and Maecenas: The Emperor and the Ruler Cult', *Phoenix*, 44: 267–75.

FITZ, J. (1983), *Honorific Titles of Roman Military Units in the 3rd Century* (Budapest).

FORBIS, E. (1988), 'The Language of Praise in Roman Honorary Inscriptions for Italian Municipals, AD 1–300' (Diss. University of North Carolina at Chapel Hill).

FORNI, G. (1979), 'L'anagraphia del soldato e del veterano', in D. M. Pippidi (ed.),

Actes du VIIe congrès international d'épigraphie grecque et latine (Bucharest and Paris), 205–28.

FOWDEN, G. (1982), 'The Pagan Holy Man in Late Antique Society', *JHS* 102: 33–59.

FOXHALL, L. (1990), 'The Dependent Tenant: Land Leasing and Labour in Italy and Greece', *JRS* 80: 97–114.

FRANK, T. (1937), 'Curatius Maternus and his Tragedies', *AJP* 58: 225–9.

FRIEDLÄNDER, L. (1907–13), *Roman Life and Manners under the Early Empire*, trans. L. A. Magnus, 4 vols. (London).

GAGÉ, J. (1933), 'La Théologie de la victoire impériale', *Revue historique*, 171: 1–43.

GALSTERER-KRÖLL, B. (1972), 'Untersuchungen zu den Beinamen der Städte des *Imperium Romanum*', *Epigraphische Studien*, 9: 44–145.

GARNSEY, P. (1968), 'The Criminal Jurisdiction of Governors', *JRS* 58: 51–9.

—— (1970), *Social Status and Legal Privilege in the Roman Empire* (Oxford).

—— and SALLER, R. (1987), *The Roman Empire* (Berkeley and Los Angeles).

GAUTHIER, P. (1985), *Les Cités grecques et leurs bienfaiteurs* (*BCH* Suppl. 12; Paris).

GEAGAN, D. J. (1967), *The Athenian Constitution after Sulla* (*Hesperia* Suppl. 12; Princeton).

GIARDINA, A. (1977), *Aspetti della burocrazia nel basso impero* (Rome).

—— (1988), '*Amor civicus*: Formule e immagini dell'evergetismo romano nella tradizione epigraphica', in A. Donati (ed.), *La Terza età dell'epigrafia* (Faenza), 67–85.

GILLIARD, F. D. (1966), 'The Social Origins of Bishops in the Fourth Century' (Diss. University of California at Berkeley).

GILMORE, D. D. (1987*a*) (ed.), *Honor and Shame and the Unity of the Mediterranean* (A Special Publication of the American Anthropological Association, 22; Washington, DC).

—— (1987*b*), 'Honor, Honesty, Shame: Male Status in Contemporary Andalusia', in Gilmore (1987), 90–103.

GLEASON, M. W. (1995), *Making Men: Sophists and Self-presentation in Ancient Rome* (Princeton).

GOODMAN, M. (1983), *State and Society in Roman Galilee, AD 132–212* (Totowa, NJ).

—— (1987), *The Ruling Class of Judaea* (Cambridge).

GRANT, M. (1946), *From Imperium to Auctoritas: A Historical Study of the Aes Coinage in the Roman Empire, 49 BC–AD 14* (Cambridge).

GREINDL, M. (1938), *ΚΛΕΟΣ ΚΥΔΟΣ ΕΥΧΟΣ ΤΙΜΗ ΦΑΤΙΣ ΔΟΞΑ: Eine bedeutungsgeschichtliche Untersuchung des epischen und lyrischen Sprachgebrauches* (Munich).

GRIFFIN, M. (1991), '*Urbs Roma, Plebs* and *Princeps*', in L. Alexander (ed.), *Images of Empire* (*Journal for the Study of the Old Testament*, Suppl. 122; Sheffield), 19–46.

GUNDEL, H. G. (1963), 'Der Begriff *Maiestas* im politischen Denken der römischen Republik', *Historia*, 12: 283–320.

HABICHT, C. (1956), *Gottmenschentum und griechische Städte* (Munich).

HAEHLING, R. VON (1978), *Die Religionszugehörigkeit der hohen Amtsträger des römischen Reiches seit Constantins I Alleinherrschaft bis zum Ende der Theodosianischen Dynastie* (Bonn).

HAHN, J. (1989), *Der Philosoph und die Gesellschaft* (Wiesbaden).

HALFMANN, H. (1986), Itinera principum: *Geschichte und Typologie der Kaiserreisen im römischen Reich* (Stuttgart).

HALL, M. D. (1992), 'The Reluctant Rhetor: A Recently Published Inscription from Late Imperial Ephesos', *ZPE* 91: 121–8.

HANDS, A. R. (1968), *Charities and Social Aid in Greece and Rome* (Ithaca, NY).

HANELL, K. (1935), 'Neokoroi', *RE* xvi/2. 2422–8.

HARL, K. W. (1987), *Civic Coins and Civic Politics in the Roman East AD 180–275* (Berkeley and Los Angeles).

HARMAND, L. (1957), *Un aspect social et politique de monde romain: Le Patronat sur les collectivités publiques des origines au bas-empire* (Paris).

HARNACK, A. (1981 (1905)), Militia Christi: *The Christian Religion and the Military in the First Three Centuries* (Philadelphia, 1981) (trans. D. G. Gracie from the 1905 Tübingen edn.).

HARRIS, W. V. (1979), *War and Imperialism in Republican Rome, 327–70 BC* (Oxford).

HATCH, E. (1989), 'Theories of Social Honor', *American Anthropologist*, 91: 341–53.

HEINZE, R. (1960 (1925)) 'Auctoritas', in id., *Vom Geist des Römertums* (Stuttgart, 1960), 43–58 (repr. from *Hermes*, 60 (1925), 348–66).

HEINZELMANN, M. (1976), *Bischofsherrschaft in Gallien* (Munich).

HELGELAND, J. (1978), 'Roman Army Religion', *ANRW* ii. 16. 2: 1470–1505.

HELLEGOUARC'H, J. (1963), *Le Vocabulaire latin des relations et des partis politiques sous la République* (Paris).

HENGEL, M. (1989), *The 'Hellenization' of Judaea in the First Century after Christ*, trans. J. Bowden (London).

HENRICHS, A. (1968), 'Vespasian's Visit to Alexandria', *ZPE* 3: 51–80.

HERRMANN, P. (1968), *Der römische Kaisereid: Untersuchungen zu seiner Herkunft und Entwicklung* (Göttingen).

HERZ, P. (1978), 'Kaiserfeste der Prinzipatszeit', *ANRW* ii. 16. 2: 1135–1200.

—— (1990), 'Die musische Agonistik und der Kunstbetrieb der Kaiserzeit', in J. Blänsdorf (ed.), *Theater und Gesellschaft im Imperium Romanum* (Tübingen), 175–96.

HIRSCHFELD, O. VON (1891), 'Die Sicherheitspolizei im römischen Kaiserreich', *Sitz. Akad. Wiss. Berlin* (1891), 845–77 (repr. in id., *Kleine Schriften* (Berlin, 1913), 576–612).

—— (1901), 'Die Rangtitel der römischen Kaiserzeit', *Sitz. Akad. Wiss. Berlin* (1901), 579–610 (repr. in id., *Kleine Schriften* (Berlin, 1913), 646–81).

HOCKEY, J. (1986), *Squaddies: Portrait of the Subculture* (Exeter, 1986).

HÖGHAMMAR, K. (1993), *Sculpture and Society: A Study of the Connection between*

Free-Standing Sculpture and Society on Kos in the Hellenistic and Augustan Periods (Uppsala).

HOLDER, P. (1980), *Studies in the* Auxilia *of the Roman Army from Augustus to Trajan* (BAR Int. Ser. 70; Oxford).

HOLFORD-STREVENS, L. (1989), *Aulus Gellius* (Chapel Hill, NC).

HONORÉ, T. (1978), *Tribonian* (London).

HOPKINS, K. (1978), *Conquerors and Slaves: Sociological Studies in Roman History*, i (Cambridge).

—— (1980), 'Taxes and Trade in the Roman Empire (200 BC–AD 400)', *JRS* 70: 101–25.

—— (1983), *Death and Renewal: Sociological Studies in Roman History*, ii (Cambridge).

—— (1991), 'Conquest by Book', in *Literacy in the Roman World* (*Journal of Roman Archaeology*, Suppl. 3; Ann Arbor), 133–58.

HOPWOOD, K. (1983), 'Policing the Hinterland: Rough Cilicia and Isauria', in S. Mitchell (ed.), *Armies and Frontiers in Roman and Byzantine Anatolia* (BAR Int. Ser. 156; Oxford), 173–87.

—— (1986), 'Towers, Territory and Terror: How the East was Held', in P. Freeman and D. Kennedy (eds.), *The Defence of the Roman and Byzantine East*, i (BAR Int. Ser. 297(i); Oxford), 343–56.

—— (1989), 'Bandits, Elites, and Rural Order', in A. Wallace-Hadrill (ed.), *Patronage in Ancient Society* (London), 171–87.

ISAAC, B. (1990), *The Limits of Empire: The Roman Army in the East* (Oxford).

JACQUES, F. (1981), 'Volontariat et compétition dans les carrières municipales durant le Haut-Empire', *Ktèma*, 6: 261–70.

—— (1984), *Le Privilège de liberté: Politique impériale et autonomie municipale dans les cités de l'occident romain (161–244)* (Rome).

JOBST, W. (1978), *11. Juni 172 n. Chr.: Der Tag des Blitz- und Regenwunders im Quadenlande* (*Sitz. Öst. Akad. Wiss.*, phil.-hist. Klasse, 335; Vienna).

JOHNSON T., and DANDEKER, C. (1989), 'Patronage: Relation and System', in A. Wallace-Hadrill (ed.), *Patronage in Ancient Society* (London), 219–42.

JONES, A. H. M. (1949), 'The Roman Civil Service (Clerical and Sub-Clerical Grades)', *JRS* 39: 38–55.

—— (1964), *The Later Roman Empire, 284–602*, 2 vols. (Oxford).

—— (1974), 'Taxation in Antiquity', in id., *The Roman Economy* (Oxford), 151–86.

JONES, C. P. (1978), *The Roman World of Dio Chrysostom* (Cambridge, Mass.).

—— (1986), *Culture and Society in Lucian* (Cambridge, Mass.).

JORY, E. J. (1984), 'The Early Pantomime Riots', in A. Moffatt (ed.), *Maistor: Classical, Byzantine, and Renaissance Studies for Robert Browning* (Canberra), 57–66.

—— (1988), 'Publilius Syrus and the Element of Competition in the Theatre of the Republic', in N. Horsfall (ed.), *Vir Bonus Discendi Peritus: Studies in Celebration of Otto Skutsch's Eightieth Birthday* (*BICS* Suppl. 51), 73–81.

KASTER, R. A. (1988), *Guardians of Language: The Grammarian and Society in Late Antiquity* (Berkeley and Los Angeles).

KEIL, B. (1913), 'Ein *ΛΟΓΟΣ ΣΥΣΤΑΤΙΚΟΣ*', Nachrichten von der königlichen Gesellschaft der Wissenschaften zu Göttingen, phil.-hist. Klasse (1913), 1–41.

KEIL, J. (1932), 'Vorläufiger Bericht über die Ausgrabungen in Ephesos', *Jahreshefte des Österreichischen Archäologischen Instituts*, 27: 5–72.

KENNEDY, D., and RILEY, D. (1990), *Rome's Desert Frontier from the Air* (London).

KIM, C.-H. (1972), *Form and Structure of the Familiar Greek Letter of Recommendation* (Society of Biblical Literature, Diss. Series 4).

KLAUSER, T. (1974), 'Der Ursprung der bischöflichen Insignien und Ehrenrechte', in E. Dassmann (ed.), *Gesammelte Arbeiten zur Liturgiegeschichte, Kirchengeschichte und Christlichen Archäologie* (Munich), 195–211.

KLOSE, F. (1933), *Die Bedeutung von* honos *und* honestus (Breslau).

KNEPPE, A. (1994), Metus Temporum: *Zur Bedeutung von Angst in Politik und Gesellschaft der römischen Kaiserzeit des 1. und 2. Jhdts. n. Chr.* (Stuttgart).

KNOCHE, U. (1934), 'Der römische Ruhmesgedanke', *Philologus*, 89: 102–24.

KOTULA, T. (1974), 'Snobisme municipal ou prospérité relative? Recherches sur le statut des villes Nord-Africaines sous le bas-empire Romain', *Antiquités Africaines*, 8: 111–31.

KRAMER, J. (1992), 'Letter from Europe', *The New Yorker*, vol. 68 no. 14 (25 May 1992), 40–64.

KRAUSE, J.-U. (1987), 'Das spätantike Städtepatronat', *Chiron*, 17: 1–80.

KÜBLER, B. (1928), '*Maiestas*', *RE* xiv/1. 542–59.

KUHOFF, W. (1983), *Studien zur zivilen senatorischen Laufbahn im 4. Jahrhundert n. Chr.: Ämter und Amtsinhaber in Clarissimat und Spektabilität* (Frankfurt).

KUNKEL, W. (1973), *An Introduction to Roman Legal and Constitutional History*, 2nd edn., trans. J. M. Kelly (Oxford).

LAHUSEN, G. (1983), *Untersuchungen zur Ehrenstatue in Rom* (Rome).

LE BOHEC, Y. (1989), *Les Unités auxiliares de l'armée romaine en Afrique proconsulaire et Numidie sous le haut empire* (Paris).

LENDON, J. E. (1990), 'The Face on the Coins and Inflation in Roman Egypt', *Klio*, 72: 106–34.

LEPELLEY, C. (1979–81), *Les Cités de l'Afrique romain au bas-empire*, 2 vols. (Paris).

LEPPIN, H. (1992), *Histrionen: Untersuchungen zur sozialen Stellung von Bühnenkünstlern im Westen des römischen Reiches zur Zeit der Republik und des Principats* (Bonn).

LESQUIER, J. (1918), *L'Armée romaine d'Égypte d'Auguste à Dioclétien* (Cairo).

LEUNISSEN, P. M. M. (1989), *Konsuln und Konsulare in der Zeit von Commodus bis Severus Alexander (180–235 n. Chr.)* (Amsterdam).

LEVICK, B. (1983), 'The Senatus Consultum from Larinum', *JRS* 73: 88–115.

LEWIS, N. (1970), ' "Graeco-Roman Egypt": Fact or Fiction', *Proceedings of the Twelfth International Congress of Papyrology* (American Studies in Papyrology, 7; Toronto), 3–14.

—— (1984), 'The Romanity of Roman Egypt: A Growing Consensus', *Atti del XVII Congresso internazionale di papirologia,* iii (Naples), 1077–84.

LIEBENAM, W. (1900), *Städteverwaltung im römischen Kaiserreiche* (Leipzig).

LIEBERMAN, S. (1944–5), 'Roman Legal Institutions in Early Rabbinics and in the *Acta Martyrum*', *Jewish Quarterly Review,* 35: 1–57.

LIEBESCHUETZ, J. H. W. G. (1970), review of Blum (1969), *JRS* 60: 229–30.

—— (1972), *Antioch: City and Imperial Administration in the Later Roman Empire* (Oxford).

—— (1990), *Barbarians and Bishops: Army, Church, and State in the Age of Arcadius and Chrysostom* (Oxford).

LIEBS, D. (1978), 'Ämterkauf und Ämterpatronage in der Spätantike', *Zeitschrift der Savigny-Stiftung für Rechtsgeschichte,* RA 95: 158–86.

LIFSHITZ, B. (1973), 'L'Ancienne Synagogue de Tibériade, sa mosaïque et ses inscriptions', *Journal for the Study of Judaism,* 4: 43–55.

LLOYD-JONES, H. (1990 (1987)), 'Honour and Shame in Ancient Greek Culture', in *Greek Comedy, Hellenistic Literature, Greek Religion and Miscellanea: The Academic Papers of Sir Hugh Lloyd-Jones* (Oxford, 1990), 253–80 (repr. from *Antike und Abendland,* 33 (1987), 1–28 (in German)).

LÖHKEN, H. (1982), Ordines Dignitatum: *Untersuchungen zur formalen Konstituierung der spätantiken Führungsschicht* (Cologne).

LOPUSZANSKI, G. (1951), 'La Police romaine et les chrétiens', *L'Antiquité classique,* 20: 5–46.

MACCORMACK, S. G. (1975), 'Latin Prose Panegyrics', in T. A. Dorey (ed.), *Empire and Aftermath: Silver Latin,* ii (London), 143–205.

—— (1981), *Art and Ceremony in Late Antiquity* (Berkeley and Los Angeles).

McCORMICK, M. (1986), *Eternal Victory: Triumphal Rulership in Late Antiquity, Byzantium, and the Early Medieval West* (Cambridge).

McGLEW, J. F. (1989), 'Royal Power and the Achaean Assembly at *Iliad* 2.84–393', *Classical Antiquity,* 8: 283–95.

MACMULLEN, R. (1962), 'The Emperor's Largesses', *Latomus,* 21: 159–66.

—— (1963), *Soldier and Civilian in the Later Roman Empire* (Cambridge, Mass.).

—— (1964), 'Social Mobility and the Theodosian Code', *JRS* 54: 49–53.

—— (1966), *Enemies of the Roman Order* (Cambridge, Mass.).

—— (1968), 'Constantine and the Miraculous', *GRBS* 9: 81–96 (repr. in id., *Changes in the Roman Empire: Essays in the Ordinary* (Princeton, 1990), 107–16).

—— (1974), *Roman Social Relations* (New Haven).

—— (1976), *Roman Government's Response to Crisis, AD 235–337* (New Haven).

—— (1980), 'How Big was the Roman Imperial Army?' *Klio,* 62: 451–60.

—— (1981), *Paganism in the Roman Empire* (New Haven).

—— (1984*a*), 'The Roman Emperors' Army Costs', *Latomus,* 43: 571–80.

—— (1984*b*), 'The Legion as a Society', *Historia,* 33: 440–56 (repr. in id., *Changes in the Roman Empire: Essays in the Ordinary* (Princeton, 1990), 225–35).

MacMullen, R. (1985), 'How to Revolt in the Roman Empire', *Rivista storica dell'antichità*, 15: 67–76 (repr. in id., *Changes in the Roman Empire: Essays in the Ordinary* (Princeton, 1990), 198–203).

—— (1986a), 'Judicial Savagery in the Roman Empire', *Chiron*, 16: 147–66 (repr. in id., *Changes in the Roman Empire: Essays in the Ordinary* (Princeton, 1990), 204–17).

—— (1986b), 'Personal Power in the Roman Empire', *AJP* 107: 512–24 (repr. in id., *Changes in the Roman Empire: Essays in the Ordinary* (Princeton, 1990), 190–7).

—— (1988), *Corruption and the Decline of Rome* (New Haven).

—— (1990), 'The Historical Role of the Masses in Late Antiquity', in id., *Changes in the Roman Empire: Essays in the Ordinary* (Princeton), 250–76.

Magdelain, A. (1947), Auctoritas Principis (Paris).

Magie, D. (1950), *Roman Rule in Asia Minor, to the End of the Third Century after Christ*, 2 vols. (Princeton).

Malcolm, N. (1990), 'The Vacuum Left by the Ascent to the Higher Priggery', *The Spectator*, vol. 265 no. 8463 (22 Sept. 1990), 6.

Marrou, H. I. (1982 (1948)), *A History of Education in Antiquity* (Madison, 1982) (trans. G. Lamb from the 1948 Paris edn.).

Marshall, A. J. (1972), 'The *Lex Pompeia de Provinciis* (52 BC) and Cicero's *Imperium* in 51–50 BC: Constitutional Aspects', *ANRW* i. 1: 887–921.

Mathisen, R. W. (1993), *Roman Aristocrats in Barbarian Gaul: Strategies for Survival in an Age of Transition* (Austin, Tex.).

Matthews, J. (1975), *Western Aristocracies and Imperial Court* (Oxford).

—— (1989), *The Roman Empire of Ammianus* (Baltimore).

Maxfield, V. A. (1981), *The Military Decorations of the Roman Army* (Berkeley and Los Angeles).

Mayhew, H. (1987 (1882)), *Mayhew's London Underworld*, ed. P. Quennell (London, 1987) (selections from H. Mayhew, *London Labour and the London Poor*, iv: *Those That Will Not Work* (London, 1882)).

Meeks, W. A. (1993), *The Origins of Christian Morality: The First Two Centuries* (New Haven).

Merkelbach, R. (1978), 'Der Rangstreit der Städte Asiens und die Rede des Aelius Aristides über die Eintracht', *ZPE* 32: 287–96.

Meyer, E. A. (1990), 'Explaining the Epigraphic Habit in the Roman Empire: The Evidence of Epitaphs', *JRS* 80: 74–96.

Millar, F. (1964), *A Study of Cassius Dio* (Oxford).

—— (1977), *The Emperor in the Roman World* (London).

—— (1983), 'Empire and City, Augustus to Julian: Obligations, Excuses and Status', *JRS* 73: 76–96.

—— (1984), 'Condemnation to Hard Labour in the Roman Empire, from the Julio-Claudians to Constantine', *PBSR* 52: 124–47.

—— (1990), 'The Roman *Coloniae* of the Near East: A Study of Cultural

Relations', in H. Solin and M. Kajava (eds.), *Roman Eastern Policy and Other Studies in Roman History* (Helsinki), 7–58.

MITCHELL, S. (1976), 'Requisitioned Transport in the Roman Empire: A New Inscription from Pisidia', *JRS* 66: 106–31.

—— (1983), 'The Balkans, Anatolia, and Roman Armies across Asia Minor', in S. Mitchell (ed.), *Armies and Frontiers in Roman and Byzantine Anatolia* (BAR Int. Ser. 156; Oxford), 131–50.

—— (1987), 'Imperial Building in the Eastern Roman Provinces', *HSCP* 91: 333–65.

—— (1993), *Anatolia: Land, Men, and Gods in Asia Minor*, 2 vols. (Oxford).

MOMMSEN, T. (1887–8), *Römisches Staatsrecht*, 3 vols., 3rd edn. (Leipzig).

MOUSSY, C. (1966), *Gratia et sa famille* (Paris).

MROZEK, S. (1978), '*Munificentia privata* in den Städten Italiens der spätrömischen Zeit', *Historia*, 27: 355–68.

—— (1987), *Les Distributions d'argent et de nourriture dans les villes italiennes du haut-empire romain* (Brussels).

MUIR, E. (1993), *Mad Blood Stirring: Vendetta and Factions in Friuli during the Renaissance* (Baltimore).

MÜLLER, A. VON (1977), Gloria Bona Fama Bonorum: *Studien zur sittlichen Bedeutung des Ruhmes in der frühchristlichen und mittelalterlichen Welt* (Historische Studien, 428; Husum).

MUSURILLO, H. A. (1954), *The Acts of the Pagan Martyrs: Acta Alexandrinorum* (Oxford).

—— (1972), *The Acts of the Christian Martyrs* (Oxford).

NEESEN, L. (1980), *Untersuchungen zu den direkten Staatsabgaben der römischen Kaiserzeit (27 v. Chr.–284 n. Chr.)* (Bonn).

—— (1981), 'Die Entwicklung der Leistungen und Ämter (*Munera et Honores*) im römischen Kaiserreich des zweiten bis vierten Jahrhunderts', *Historia*, 30: 203–35.

NERI, V. (1981), 'L'elogio della cultura e l'elogio delle virtù politiche nell'epigraphia latina del IV secolo d.C.', *Epigraphica*, 43: 175–201.

NEUSCHEL, K. (1989), *Word of Honor: Interpreting Noble Culture in Sixteenth-Century France* (Ithaca, NY).

NEWHOUSE, J. (1993), 'Profile: Tweaking the Dragon's Tail', *The New Yorker*, vol. 69 no. 4 (15 March 1993), 89–101.

New York Times (1993), 'Guess Who Came to Dinner' (no byline), vol. 143 no. 49510 (9 Nov. 1993), p. A14.

NICOLS, J. (1979), 'Zur Verleihung öffentlicher Ehrungen in der römischen Welt', *Chiron*, 9: 243–60.

—— (1980a), '*Tabulae patronatus*: A Study of the Agreement between Patron and Client–Community', *ANRW* ii. 13: 535–61.

—— (1980b), 'Pliny and the Patronage of Communities', *Hermes*, 108: 365–85.

—— (1988), 'Prefects, Patronage and the Administration of Justice', *ZPE* 72: 201–17.

NICOLS, J. (1990*a*), 'Patrons of Greek Cities in the Early Principate', *ZPE* 80: 81–100.

—— (1990*b*), 'Patrons of Provinces in the Early Principate: The Case of Bithynia', *ZPE* 80: 101–8.

NIPPEL, W. (1995), *Public Order in Ancient Rome* (Cambridge).

NIXON, C. E. V. (1983), 'Latin Panegyric in the Tetrarchic and Constantinian Period', in B. Croke and A. M. Emmet (eds.), *History and Historians in Late Antiquity* (Sydney), 88–99.

NOCK, A. D. (1930), '*ΣΥΝΝΑΟΣ ΘΕΟΣ*', *HSCP* 41: 1–62.

—— (1932), review of L. R. Taylor, *The Divinity of the Roman Emperor*, *Gnomon*, 8: 513–18.

NORMAN, A. F. (1983), 'Libanius: The Teacher in an Age of Violence', in G. Fatouros and T. Krischer (eds.), *Libanios* (Darmstadt), 150–69.

NÖRR, D. (1966), Imperium *und* Polis *in der hohen Prinzipatzeit* (Munich).

NORTH, H. (1966), Sophrosyne: *Self-Knowledge and Self-Restraint in Greek Literature* (Ithaca, NY)

OLIVER, J. H. (1953), 'The Ruling Power: A Study of the Roman Empire in the Second Century after Christ through the Roman Oration of Aelius Aristides', *Transactions of the American Philosophical Society*, NS 43: 871–1003.

—— (1979), 'Antoninus Pius to Ptolemais Barca about the Capitolia', *GRBS* 20: 157–9.

PALLAS, D., CHARITONIDIS, S., and VENENCIE, J. (1959), 'Inscriptions Lyciennes trouvées à Solômos près de Corinthe', *BCH* 83: 496–508.

PASCHOUD, F. (1967), *Roma Aeterna: Études sur le patriotisme romain dans l'Occident latin à l'époque des grandes invasions* (Rome).

PATTERSON, O. (1982), *Slavery and Social Death* (Cambridge, Mass.).

PERISTIANY, J. G. (1966) (ed.), *Honour and Shame: The Values of Mediterranean Society* (Chicago).

PERNOT, L. (1993), *La Rhétorique de l'éloge dans le monde gréco-romain*, 2 vols. (Paris).

PETIT, P. (1955), *Libanius et la vie municipale à Antioche au IVe siècle après J.-C.* (Paris).

—— (1956), *Les Étudiants de Libanius* (Paris).

PFLAUM, H. G. (1948), *Le Marbre de Thorigny* (Paris).

—— (1950), *Les Procurateurs équestres sous le haut empire romain* (Paris).

—— (1970), 'Titulature et rang social durant le haut-empire', in C. Nicolet (ed.), *Recherches sur les structures sociales dans l'antiquité classique* (Paris), 159–85.

—— (1971), 'Une lettre de promotion de l'empereur Marc Aurèle pour un procurateur ducénaire de Gaule Narbonnaise', *Bonner Jährbucher*, 171: 349–66.

—— (1978), 'Les Salaires des magistrats et fonctionnaires du haut-empire', *Les 'Dévaluations' à Rome, époque républicaine et impériale*, i (Rome), 311–13.

PHILIPP, G. B. (1955), 'Zur Problematik des römischen Ruhmesgedankens', *Gymnasium*, 62 (1955), 51–82.

Piscitelli Carpino, T. (1979), '*Dignitas* in Cicerone: Tra semantica e semiologia', *Bollettino di Studi Latini*, 9: 253–67.

Pitt-Rivers, J. A. (1966), 'Honour and Social Status', in Peristiany (1966), 21–77.

—— (1971), *The People of the Sierra*, 2nd edn. (Chicago).

Pleket, H. W. (1974), 'Zur Soziologie des antiken Sports', *Mededelingen van het Nederlands Instituut te Rome*, 36: 57–87.

Potter, D. S. (1990), *Prophecy and History in the Crisis of the Roman Empire: A Historical Commentary on the Thirteenth Sibylline Oracle* (Oxford).

—— (1994), *Prophets and Emperors: Human and Divine Authority from Augustus to Theodosius* (Cambridge, Mass.).

Premerstein, A. von (1912), 'Griechisch-Römisches aus Arkadien', *Jahreshefte des Österreichischen Archäologischen Instituts*, 15: 197–218.

—— (1937), *Vom Werden und Wesen des Prinzipats* (Munich).

Price, S. R. F. (1984*a*), *Rituals and Power: The Roman Imperial Cult in Asia Minor* (Cambridge).

—— (1984*b*), 'Gods and Emperors: The Greek Language of the Roman Imperial Cult', *JHS* 104: 79–95.

Quass, F. (1993), *Die Honoratiorenschicht in den Städten des griechischen Ostens* (Stuttgart).

Raaflaub, K. (1974), Dignitatis Contentio: *Studien zur Motivation und politischen Taktik im Bürgerkrieg zwischen Caesar und Pompeius* (Munich).

Raepsaet-Charlier, M.-T. (1975), 'La Datation des inscriptions latins dans les provinces occidentales de l'Empire Romain d'après les formules "IN H(ONOREM) D(OMUS) D(IVINAE)" et "DEO, DEAE" ', *ANRW* ii. 3: 232–82.

Rathbone, D. (1993), 'Egypt, Augustus and Roman Taxation', *Cahiers du centre G. Glotz*, 4: 81–112.

Rawson, E. (1991 (1990)), 'The Antiquarian Tradition: Spoils and Representations of Foreign Armour', in *Roman Culture and Society: the Collected Papers of Elizabeth Rawson* (Oxford, 1991), 582–98 (repr. from W. Eder (ed.), *Staat und Staatlichkeit in der frühen römischen Republik* (Stuttgart, 1990), 157–73).

Reinhold, M. (1988), *From Republic to Principate: An Historical Commentary on Cassius Dio's Roman History, Books 49–52 (36–29 BC)*, (American Philological Association, Monograph 34; Atlanta).

Reynolds, J. (1978), 'Hadrian, Antoninus Pius and the Cyrenaican Cities', *JRS* 68: 111–21.

—— (1982), *Aphrodisias and Rome* (*JRS* Monograph 1; London).

Ritterling, E. (1893), 'Zur römischen Legionsgeschichte am Rhein. II. Der Aufstand des Antonius Saturninus', *Westdeutsche Zeitschrift*, 12: 203–42.

—— (1924–5), 'Legio', *RE* xii/1–2. 1186–1837.

Rives, J. B. (1995), *Religion and Authority in Roman Carthage from Augustus to Constantine* (Oxford).

Robert, L. (1934), 'Notes de numismatique et d'épigraphie grecques', *Revue Archéologique*, 35: 48–61 (repr. in *Opera Minora Selecta*, ii (Amsterdam, 1969), 1012–25).

—— (1937), *Études anatoliennes: Recherches sur les inscriptions grecques de l'Asie Mineure* (Paris).

—— (1938), *Études épigraphiques et philologiques* (Paris).

—— (1940a), *Les Gladiateurs dans l'orient grec* (Paris).

—— (1940b), 'La Titulature de la ville de Sardes', *Hellenica*, 1: 56–9.

—— (1940c), 'Un édifice du sanctuaire de l'Isthme dans une inscription de Corinthe', *Hellenica*, 1: 43–53.

—— (1946a), 'Divinités éponymes', *Hellenica*, 2: 51–64.

—— (1946b), 'Ulpia Heraclea', *Hellenica*, 3: 5–31.

—— (1948a), 'Épigrammes d'Aphrodisias', *Hellenica*, 4: 127–35.

—— (1948b), 'Un juriste romaine dans une inscription de Beroia', *Hellenica*, 5: 29–34.

—— (1948c), 'Épigrammes relatives à des gouverneurs', *Hellenica*, 4: 35–114.

—— (1948d), 'Épigramme d'Égine', *Hellenica*, 4: 5–34.

—— (1949a), 'Sur une monnaie de Synnada: *ΤΡΟΦΕΥΣ*', *Hellenica*, 7: 74–81.

—— (1949b), 'Le Culte de Caligula à Milet et la province d'Asie', *Hellenica*, 7: 206–38.

—— (1955), 'Dédicaces et reliefs votifs', *Hellenica*, 10: 5–166.

—— (1960a), 'Addenda aux tomes I-X', *Hellenica*, 11–12: 542–95.

—— (1960b), 'Recherches épigraphiques', *Revue des études anciennes*, 62: 276–361 (repr. in *Opera Minora Selecta*, ii (Amsterdam, 1969), 792–877).

—— (1960c), '*ΑΙΤΗΣΑΜΕΝΟΣ* sur les monnaies', *Hellenica*, 11–12: 53–62.

—— (1960d), 'Épitaphes et acclamations byzantines à Corinthe', *Hellenica*, 11–12: 21–52.

—— (1965), *D'Aphrodisias à la Lycaonie* (Paris; published as *Hellenica*, 13).

—— (1967), 'Sur des inscriptions d'Éphèse: Fêtes, athlètes, empereurs, épigrammes', *Revue de philologie*, 41: 7–84.

—— (1969), 'Les Inscriptions', in J. des Gagniers *et al.*, *Laodicée du Lycos: Le Nymphée. Campagnes 1961–1963* (Quebec and Paris), 247–389.

—— (1977a), 'La Titulature de Nicée et de Nicomédie: La Gloire et la haine', *HSCP* 81: 1–39.

—— (1977b), 'Documents d'Asie Mineure', *BCH* 101: 43–132.

—— (1980), *À travers l'Asia Mineure: poètes et prosateurs, monnaies grecques, voyageurs et géographie* (Athens).

—— (1981), 'Une épigramme satirique d'Automédon et Athènes au début l'empire', *Revue des études grecques*, 94: 338–61.

—— and Robert, J. (1989), *Claros* i: *Décrets hellénistiques*, fasc. 1 (Paris).

Rogers, G. M. (1991a), *The Sacred Identity of Ephesos: Foundation Myths of a Roman City* (London).

—— (1991*b*), 'Demosthenes of Oenoanda and Models of Euergetism', *JRS* 81: 91–100.

ROGERS, R. S. (1933), 'Ignorance of the Law in Tacitus and Dio: Two Instances from the History of Tiberius', *TAPA* 64: 18–27.

—— (1947), 'Roman Emperors as Heirs and Legatees', *TAPA* 78: 140–58.

—— (1959), 'The Emperor's Displeasure—*amicitiam renuntiare*', *TAPA* 90: 224–37.

—— (1960), 'A Group of Domitianic Treason-Trials', *Classical Philology*, 55: 19–23.

ROMILLY, J. DE (1958), '*Eunoia* in Isocrates or the Political Importance of Creating Good Will', *JHS* 78: 92–101.

—— (1973), 'Le Thème de prestige dans l'œuvre de Thucydide', *Ancient Society*, 4: 39–58.

—— (1977), *The Rise and Fall of States According to Greek Authors* (Ann Arbor).

ROUECHÉ, C. (1984), 'Acclamations in the Later Roman Empire: New Evidence from Aphrodisias', *JRS* 74: 181–99.

—— (1989*a*), *Aphrodisias in Late Antiquity* (*JRS* Monograph 5; London).

—— (1989*b*), 'Floreat Perge', in M. M. Mackenzie and C. Roueché (eds.), *Images of Authority: Papers Presented to Joyce Reynolds on the Occasion of her Seventieth Birthday* (*PCPS* Suppl. 16; Cambridge), 206–28.

—— (1993), *Performers and Partisans at Aphrodisias in the Roman and Late Roman Periods* (*JRS* Monograph 6; London).

ROULAND, N. (1979), *Pouvoir politique et dépendance personelle dans l'antiquité romain: Genèse et rôle des rapports de clientèle* (Brussels).

ROYDEN, H. L. (1988), *The Magistrates of the Roman Professional Collegia in Italy from the First to the Third Century AD* (Pisa).

RUBIN, Z. (1980), *Civil-War Propaganda and Historiography* (Brussels).

RUDHARDT, J. (1958), *Notions fondamentales de la pensée religieuse et actes constitutifs du culte dans la Grèce classique* (Geneva).

RUDICH, V. (1993), *Political Dissidence under Nero: The Price of Dissimulation* (London).

RUGGIERO, E. DE (1895), '*AFRICAE (caput)*', *Dizionario epigraphico di antichità romane*, i (Rome), 350.

SADDINGTON, D. B. (1985), '*Praefecti Fabrum* of the Julio-Claudian Period', in E. Weber and G. Dobesch (eds.), *Römische Geschichte, Altertumskunde und Epigraphik: Festschrift für Artur Betz zur Vollendung seines 80. Lebensjahres* (Vienna), 529–46.

STE CROIX, G. E. M. DE (1954), '*Suffragium*: From Vote to Patronage', *British Journal of Sociology*, 5: 33–48.

—— (1981), *The Class Struggle in the Ancient Greek World* (Ithaca, NY).

SAINT-SIMON, L. DE (1983–8), *Mémoires*, ed. Y. Coirault, 8 vols. (Paris).

SALLER, R. P. (1982), *Personal Patronage Under the Early Empire* (Cambridge).

—— (1989), 'Patronage and Friendship in Early Imperial Rome: Drawing the

Distinction', in A. Wallace-Hadrill (ed.), *Patronage in Ancient Society* (London), 49–62.

SALLER, R. P. (1994), *Patriarchy, Property and Death in the Roman Family* (Cambridge).

SANTERO, J. M. (1983), 'The "*CULTORES AUGUSTI*" and the Private Worship of the Roman Emperor', *Athenaeum*, 61: 111–25.

SCHINDLER, F. (1972), *Die Inschriften von Bubon (Nordlykien)* (*Sitz. der Öst. Akad. Wiss.*, phil.-hist. Klasse, 278; Vienna).

SCHMIDT, J. H. H. (1889), *Handbuch der lateinischen und griechischen Synonymik* (Leipzig).

SCHÜRER, E. (1973–87), *The History of the Jewish People in the Age of Jesus Christ (175 BC–AD 135)*, rev. and ed. G. Vermes, F. Millar, and M. Goodman, 3 vols. (Edinburgh).

SCOTT, K. (1931), 'Greek and Roman Honorific Months', *Yale Classical Studies*, 2: 201–78.

—— (1933), 'The Political Propaganda of 44–30 BC', *MAAR* 11: 7–49.

SHAW, B. D. (1984*a*), 'Bandits in the Roman Empire', *Past and Present*, 105: 3–52.

—— (1984*b*), 'Among the Believers', *Échos du Monde Classique/Classical Views*, 28: 453–79.

—— (1987), 'The Family in Late Antiquity: The Experience of Augustine', *Past and Present*, 115: 3–51.

SHERWIN-WHITE, A. N. (1966), *The Letters of Pliny: A Historical and Social Commentary* (Oxford).

—— (1973), 'The *Tabula* of Banasa and the *Constitutio Antoniniana*', *JRS* 63: 86–98.

SINGER, K. (1973), *Mirror, Sword and Jewel: The Geometry of Japanese Life* (London).

SINNIGEN, W. G. (1961), 'The Roman Secret Service', *Classical Journal*, 57: 65–72.

SMITH, R. R. R. (1987), 'The Imperial Reliefs from the Sebasteion at Aphrodisias', *JRS* 77: 88–138.

SPAWFORTH, A. J. (1994), 'Corinth, Argos, and the Imperial Cult: Pseudo-Julian, *Letters* 198', *Hesperia*, 63: 211–32.

—— and WALKER, S. (1985), 'The World of the Panhellenion: I. Athens and Eleusis', *JRS* 75: 78–104.

—— —— (1986), 'The World of the Panhellenion: II. Three Dorian Cities', *JRS* 76: 88–105.

SPEIDEL, M. P. (1970), 'The Captor of Decebalus: A New Inscription from Philippi', *JRS* 60: 142–53.

—— (1978*a*), *Guards of the Roman Armies: An Essay on the* Singulares *of the Provinces* (Bonn).

—— (1978*b*), 'The Cult of the *Genii* in the Roman Army and a New Military Deity', *ANRW* ii. 16. 2: 1542–55.

—— (1983*a*), 'The Roman Army in Asia Minor: Recent Epigraphical Discoveries and Researches', in S. Mitchell (ed.), *Armies and Frontiers in Roman and Byzantine Anatolia* (BAR Int. Ser. 156; Oxford), 7–34.

—— (1983*b*), 'Cash from the Emperor', *AJP* 104: 282–6.

—— (1991), 'Swimming the Danube under Hadrian's Eyes', *Ancient Society*, 22: 277–82.

SPERBER, D. (1978), *Roman Palestine 200–400: The Land* (Ramat-Gan).

STEIN, A. (1912), 'Griechische Rangtitel in der römischen Kaiserzeit', *Wiener Studien*, 34: 160–70.

—— (1922) *Untersuchungen über das* Officium *der Prätorianerpräfektur seit Diokletian* (Vienna).

—— (1927), 'Zur sozialen Stellung der provinzialen Oberpriester', in *Epitymbion Heinrich Swoboda Dargebracht* (Reichenberg), 300–11.

STEINKOPF, G. (1937), *Untersuchungen zur Geschichte des Ruhmes bei den Griechen* (Halle).

STEWART, F. H. (1994), *Honor* (Chicago).

STRUBBE, J. H. M. (1984–6), 'Gründer kleinasiatischer Städte: Fiktion und Realität', *Ancient Society*, 15–17: 253–304.

SWIFT, L. J., and OLIVER, J. H. (1962), 'Constantius II on Flavius Philippus', *AJP* 83: 247–64.

SYME, R. (1939), *The Roman Revolution* (Oxford).

—— (1958), *Tacitus*, 2 vols. (Oxford).

—— (1971), *Emperors and Biography: Studies in the* Historia Augusta (Oxford).

—— (1988 (1981)), 'Rival Cities, Notably Tarraco and Barcino', in *Roman Papers*, iv (Oxford, 1988), 74–93 (repr. from *Ktèma*, 6 (1981), 271–85).

TALBERT, R. J. A. (1984), *The Senate of Imperial Rome* (Princeton).

TCHERIKOVER, V. A. (1964), 'Was Jerusalem a *"Polis"*?' *Israel Exploration Journal*, 14: 61–78.

TEITLER, H. C. (1985), Notarii *and* Exceptores (Amsterdam).

THOMAS, K. (1971), *Religion and the Decline of Magic* (New York).

THOMPSON, E. A. (1980), 'Barbarian Invaders and Roman Collaborators', *Florilegium*, 2: 71–88.

THOMPSON, L. A. (1965), 'Cicero's Succession-Problem in Cilicia', *AJP* 86: 375–86.

THOMPSON, S. (1985), *The Apocalypse and Semitic Syntax* (Cambridge).

TREGGIARI, S. (1969), *Roman Freedmen During the Late Republic* (Oxford).

—— (1973), 'Domestic Staff at Rome in the Julio-Claudian Period, 27 BC to AD 68', *Histoire Sociale/Social History*, 6: 241–55.

USENER, H. (1913 (1900)), 'Italische Volksjustiz', in id., *Kleine Schriften*, iv (Leipzig, 1913), 356–82 (repr. from *Rheinisches Museum*, 56 (1900), 1–28).

VAN DAM, R. (1986), 'Emperor, Bishops, and Friends in Late Antique Cappadocia', *Journal of Theological Studies*, NS 37: 53–76.

VENSKE, W. (1938), *Plato und der Ruhm* (Würzburg).

VEYNE, P. (1990), *Bread and Circuses: Historical Sociology and Political Pluralism*, trans. and abridged by B. Pearce (London).

VILLE, G. (1981), *La Gladiature en Occident des origines à la mort de Domitien* (Paris and Rome).

WALCOT, P. (1970), *Greek Peasants, Ancient and Modern* (New York).

WALLACE-HADRILL, A. (1981*a*), 'The Emperor and his Virtues', *Historia*, 30: 298–323.

—— (1981*b*), 'Family and Inheritance in the Augustan Marriage Laws', *PCPS* 27: 58–80.

—— (1982), '*Civilis Princeps*: Between Citizen and King', *JRS* 72: 32–48.

—— (1983), *Suetonius* (London).

—— (1989), 'Patronage in Roman Society: From Republic to Empire', in A. Wallace-Hadrill (ed.), *Patronage in Ancient Society* (London), 63–87.

—— (1990), 'Roman Arches and Greek Honours: The Language of Power at Rome', *PCPS* 36: 143–81.

—— (1994), *Houses and Society in Pompeii and Herculaneum* (Princeton).

WALLACE-HADRILL, J. M. (1971), *Early Germanic Kingship in England and on the Continent* (Oxford).

WALTZING, J.-P. (1895–1900), *Étude historique sur les corporations professionnelles chez les romains depuis les origines jusqu'à la chute de l'Empire d'Occident*, 4 vols. (Louvain).

WARD, J. H. (1974), 'The *Notitia Dignitatum*', *Latomus*, 33: 397–434.

WARD-PERKINS, B. (1984), *From Classical Antiquity to the Middle Ages: Public Building in Northern and Central Italy AD 300–850* (Oxford).

WARMINGTON, B. (1954), 'The Municipal Patrons of Roman North Africa', *PBSR* 9: 39–55.

WEAVER, P. R. C. (1972), *Familia Caesaris* (Cambridge).

WEES, H. VAN (1992), *Status Warriors: War, Violence and Society in Homer and History* (Amsterdam).

WEGEHAUPT, H. (1932), *Die Bedeutung und Anwendung von* dignitas *in den Schriften der republikanischen Zeit* (Breslau).

WEISMANN, W. (1972), *Kirche und Schauspiele* (Würzburg).

WEISS, P. (1991), '*Auxe Perge*: Beobachtungen zu einem bemerkenswerten städtischen Dokument des späten 3. Jahrhunderts n. Chr.', *Chiron*, 21: 353–92.

WESCH-KLEIN, G. (1990), Liberalitas in Rem Publicam: *Private Aufwendungen zugunsten von Gemeinden im römischen Afrika bis 284 n. Chr.* (Bonn).

WHITTAKER, C. R. (1964), 'The Revolt of Papirius Dionysius, AD 190', *Historia*, 13: 348–69.

WICKERT, L. (1954), '*Princeps (civitatis)*', *RE* xxii/2. 1998–2296.

WIEDEMANN, T. (1992), *Emperors and Gladiators* (London).

WINKLER, J. J. (1990), *The Constraints of Desire: The Anthropology of Sex and Gender in Ancient Greece* (New York).

WISEMAN, T. P. (1985), 'Competition and Co-operation', in T. P. Wiseman (ed.), *Roman Political Life, 90 BC–AD 69* (Exeter), 3–19.

—— (1987), '*Conspicui postes tectaque digna deo*: The Public Image of Aristocratic and Imperial Houses in the late Republic and Early Empire', in *L'Urbs: Éspace urbain et histoire* (*Ier siècle av. J.-C.–IIIe siècle ap. J.-C.*) (Rome), 393–413.

WISTRAND, E. (1976), *The So-called* Laudatio Turiae (Göteborg).

—— (1978), *Caesar and Contemporary Roman Society* (Göteborg).

WOLSELEY, G. J. (1903), *The Story of a Soldier's Life*, 2 vols. (London).

WÖRRLE, M. (1988), *Stadt und Fest im kaiserzeitlichen Kleinasien: Studien zu einer agonistischen Stiftung aus Oinoanda* (Munich).

YAVETZ, Z. (1974), '*Existimatio, Fama*, and the Ides of March', *HSCP* 78: 35–65.

ZANKER, P. (1983), *Provinzielle Kaiserporträts: Zur Rezeption der Selbstdarstellung des Princeps* (Munich).

—— (1988), *The Power of Images in the Age of Augustus*, trans. A. Shapiro (Ann Arbor).

ZIEGLER, R. (1978), 'Antiochia, Laodicea und Sidon in der Politik der Severer', *Chiron*, 8: 493–514.

—— (1985), *Städtisches Prestige und kaiserliche Politik: Studien zum Festwesen in Ostkilikien im 2. u. 3. Jh. n. Chr.* (Düsseldorf).

ZIMMER, G. (1989), Locus datus decreto decurionum: *Zur Statuenaufstellung zweier Forumsanlagen im römischen Afrika* (Munich).

INDEX

CPSIA information can be obtained at www.ICGtesting.com
Printed in the USA
236130LV00001B/25/A